The Service Systems Toolbox

Integrating

Lean Thinking, Systems Thinking, and Design Thinking

By
John Bicheno

**Lean Enterprise Research Centre,
Cardiff Business School
and
Service Management,
University of Buckingham**

Production and Inventory Control, Systems and Industrial Engineering Books
PICSIE Books
Buckingham, England
2012

Published by

PICSIE Books
Telephone and FAX: +44 (0) 1280 815023
www.picsie.co.uk
email: picsiebook@btinternet.com

Copyright © John Bicheno 2008, 2012

ISBN 978-0-9568307-0-8

British Library Cataloguing-in-Publication Data
A catalogue record for this book is available from the British Library.

Printed in the United Kingdom by Lightning Source UK Ltd

For My Grandchildren

Acknowledgements

Many have contributed to my journey into Lean and Lean Service.

Eric Hall and Val Bolitho started me off. My eternal thanks. Peter Checkland introduced me to Systems – an unexpected delight. George Davidson of Toyota inspired. Roy Marcus added entrepreneurial flair, and changed my direction. VS Mahesh continues to influence and inspire all those he teaches, including me. Simon Elias and Sarah Lethbridge moved us cheerfully forward. Claire Gardner supported. John Seddon and Richard Davis continue to share their groundbreaking material most generously. Christian Hansen was patient as we learned and re-learned together. He once again commented helpfully on this new edition. John Darlington keeps me on the ground by reminding about the bottom line. Steve Spear, Mike Rother and Wally Hopp inspired during visits to Cardiff.

Through years at Buckingham and Cardiff I have worked with and visited numerous service organisations from both the private and public sectors in UK, Denmark, South Africa, and USA. My thanks to all of them.

A whole generation of Buckingham Service Management students, and all MSc Lean Service classes in Cardiff thought that I was teaching them, but the reverse was true. Others who deserve special mention include Viktor Peters, Alex Speciale, Deba Correia, Ido Rieger, Kate Mackle, Neil Dewfield, James Carr, Bjarne Olsen, Joakim Hillberg, Linus Larsson, Jacob Austad, René Pedersen, Glynis Caulfield, Tomas Baek, Nick Downham, Justin Watts, Andy Brophy, Steve Langan, Robin Howlett, Steve Beasley, and Danny Platt. And last but not least, Sally – my patient and gentle critic and counsel.

Errors, of course, are mine. I still have lots to learn.

JB

Buckingham, September 2011

"'I know' seems to describe a state of affairs which guarantees what is known, guarantees it as a fact. One always forgets the expression, 'I thought I knew.'"

Ludwig Wittgenstein, *On Certainty*.

Foreword to this Edition

Abraham Maslow is credited with the statement, "To a man with a hammer, everything looks like a nail". For as long as the subject of management has been in existence, the world has been presented at regular intervals with a new *master* tool. PERT, CPM, OR, MBO, TQM, ISO, BS series BPR, Six Sigma, CRM: these and countless other tools, techniques and approaches have each been marketed to unsuspecting managers by unscrupulous academics and management consultants as the new panacea of all evil.

While they were bad enough when applied like Maslow's hammer in factories, the use of such approaches in design, delivery and management of services has been nothing short of a disaster.

Many of us have been at the receiving end of it for most of our lives, helplessly witnessing a new 'flavour of the month' sweeping the corporate world, swallowing billions of dollars on yet another useless attempt to solve all the problems with just one new "hammer".

What John Bicheno has done in his new book is to help everyone involved with **design, delivery or management of services** deal with these periodic avalanches, or to use the currently popular term, tsunamis. He combines erudite scholarship, direct *gemba* experience in mining, manufacturing and service, academia and factories, research, teaching and consulting across several countries and continents to present us with a superb collection of relevant approaches, systems, tools and techniques which, in his own words (see P 61) we can use *"as a prompt or as a source of some suitable ideas"*.

There are very few academics who have straddled the world of manufacturing and service as effectively as John Bicheno. Having been his colleague in designing and teaching the unique MSc (Service Management) programme at the University of Buckingham for two decades, and for a shorter period at Cardiff, I make that statement with a great deal of confidence.

John Bicheno has, in this book, made a special effort to warn the reader against the common failing of using a 'cut and paste' approach for transferring what is appropriate for manufacturing to the service context. Unlike Mao's little Red book or any other doctrinaire rulebook, John's book ought to be used as a constant source for learning **'and deciding'** what is most appropriate for whatever context one finds oneself in.

In today's age, when one mistakes data and information for knowledge, and worse still, wisdom, it would be all too tempting to use this book as a mere source of data and information. That would be quite inappropriate. The essence of "service management" requires that a student/academic/practitioner should first develop a holistic view of the inter-connected nature of this subject and then only seek to choose the appropriate portion of the book to use in solving any problem. This book must be read rapidly to get a holistic view before digging deep for the diamonds that are to be found in every page.

John's style of writing is a reflection of the man himself: simplicity, humility, creating Value and lean thinking. I read the entire book in less than two days and was left gasping with admiration that this stupendous task has been accomplished in such a seemingly effortless manner. Only a true expert in the field, with a strong intrinsic motivation for sharing his years of wisdom and knowledge can achieve that effect through a book.

My guess is that any executive who uses this book properly should generate an ROI of over 1000% on his investment in buying the book. That is good EVA! I will not be surprised if that proves to be an understatement. To use a Service Management *mantra*, I have used the principle of UPOD (Under promise, over deliver).

Happy and profitable reading.

V S Mahesh
Managing Director – VSM Consulting Services & Visiting Professor, University of Buckingham
Ex- Director of Centre for Service Management, University of Buckingham, former VP (HR) of Taj Group of Hotels and Wipro Group of companies

Foreword to the First Edition

Note: The First Edition was called *The Lean Toolbox for Service Systems*, 2008

John Bicheno has a well-deserved reputation for an encyclopaedic knowledge of tools and techniques for performance improvement. In this compendium he extends his repertoire to service organisations. There are more tools here than you may use in a lifetime; it is a jamboree of things to do that will appeal to managers.

But what to do? It is not a question of which tool do I use but what problems do I have, and do I understand my problems? Taiichi Ohno's favourite word was 'understanding'. To understand problems and thus realise opportunities we have to learn how to study the work and learn how to avoid being misled by many of management's current assumptions about problems and their causes.

Ohno also insisted we should never codify method. Had his warning been heeded we might have avoided the misguided attempts to apply the tools developed in manufacturing to service organisations. The well-publicised failures have damaged the reputation of 'lean' and put back the opportunity for significant improvement. This compendium is a timely contribution, steering service organisations away from misguided advice. We should remember that Ohno did not call his innovation 'lean' – he didn't want it called anything. He could, perhaps, foresee the folly of a label.

Ohno's contribution was a profound challenge to management's paradigm. He found counter-intuitive truths. I hope this book helps you to find them too.

John Seddon
Managing Director, Vanguard Consulting
Visiting Professor, LERC, Cardiff University

CONTENTS

How to Read this Book

This book is aimed at a wide spectrum of service operations: from repetitive office tasks, through classic customer-facing operations such as hotels and health, to field service and to consulting and design.

The book also covers some conventional Lean theory.

The book is not intended to be read from cover to cover.

Part 1 covers the inter-related concepts of Lean, Systems, and Design as they apply to service. I believe this is relevant to all service practitioners. Don't miss reading about Seddon's 'Check' methodology and about 'Muda, Muri, Mura'.

Part 2 covers the major concepts and models in Lean, Systems, and Design Thinking.

Part 3 covers a classification for Lean Service and gives approaches to mapping in various types of service situation. There is no one single mapping tool that is applicable to all service. Mapping is a way of understanding the end-to-end system and of keeping the big picture in mind. Mapping as presented here is a three-level approach. The top level is applicable to all service, the second level is situation specific, and the third level is only required where micro detail is necessary.

Part 4 covers the essential service tools from the areas of Lean, Systems, and Design; some, for example Total Productive Administration, may be considered approaches in themselves.

Keep in mind that there is quite a bit of overlap and interaction between the sections.

I hope you find the book useful.

Best wishes

John Bicheno

An Illustrative Case Study

Southwest Airlines is probably the most successful airline in history. It does not use the phrases Lean Thinking, Systems Thinking, or Design Thinking. Yet it embodies all of them. To illustrate the links between Southwest's success and some concepts described in this book, consider:

- Lean Thinking and System Thinking: Southwest seems to understand that profits are made end-to-end: on value adding time, including flight time, turnaround time, and length of working day. All three need attention. So an efficient flight with an inefficient turnaround won't do.
- Muda, Muri, Mara: Kingman's equation shows the exponential relationship between waiting time and utilisation. As utilisation or load tends towards 100%, delays increase exponentially. Many Southwest flights have some vacant seats – they are not fully loaded. The time taken for that last 10% of load factor may simply not be worth the time lost when looked at from the point of view of total value adding (flying) time.
- Airport Usage: don't use airports with very high runway utilisation, like Heathrow. Kingman's equation predicts long and uncertain delays in such situations.
- Changeover: time parked at a stand is waste, it should be minimised. Classic Lean principles on reducing changeover time are most relevant. Further, to reduce non value adding changeover time, Southwest uses open seating.
- Understand customer needs: most airline customers would like to travel directly, not via a hub. A hub may help with load factor, so using hubs may make sense from the airline's point of view, but not from the customer's point of view. Southwest has avoided the hub and spoke system and prefers point-to-point.
- Bottlenecks and Teamworking: the whole team pitches in during non-value adding changeover time. Co-ordination between the different functions (pilots, agents, fuelers, etc.) reduces the time, much like Goldratt's sequence of identify the bottleneck, exploit it, subordinate, elevate. All pitching in is referred to as 'creating boundary spanners'. Blame is avoided – a parallel with Lean style 'drive out fear' and 'create thinking people'.
- Standardisation and people: there are of course specific roles, each with standard work, but this is not rigid. People are encouraged to 'be themselves'. See the section on Fun with Moments of Truth.
- Standardisation and equipment: Southwest uses only one type of airplane.
- Surfacing and problem solving: the whole team looks at problems, especially delays, straight away. In Lean, surface the problem and improve the process rather than blame the person.
- Partnering and Building Relationships: this standard Lean practice is applied to unions, airports, aircraft suppliers, and all other suppliers.

About Lean Service and The Toolbox

Introduction and Positioning

Why Lean Thinking, Design Thinking, Systems Thinking?

Lean, Design, and Systems Thinking form a trilogy.

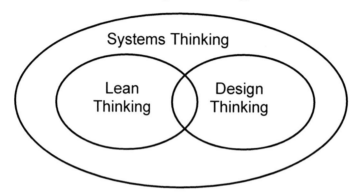

Lean Thinking is a well established philosophy relating to flow, value and waste. Its power has been demonstrated in countless manufacturing organisations, and increasingly in service organisations. But despite these virtues, to some, 'Lean' has become overly associated with the denominator of the value ratio (benefit / cost). Lean thinking is about best practice, and learning from the best. Lean is about reliability, or as Ackoff says, 'doing things right'. It is about optimising current value streams. But Lean should not neglect the numerator: it should also be about benefits to customers – better, right first time, more helpful, more friendly – and not just less expensive.

Design thinking is very much focused on the numerator of the equation, on the creative side of a business. Design thinking observes, questions and probes user needs. It relates to future operations. While you may be busily focused on best practice, there is the danger of not seeing disruptive changes that come from unexpected directions. Design is about validity, or as Ackoff, quoting Drucker, said, "There is a big difference between doing things right and doing the right thing – there is a distinction between efficiency and effectiveness …..The righter you do the wrong thing – the wronger you become – if you make a mistake doing the wrong thing and correct it – you become wronger. If you make a mistake doing the right thing and correct it – you become righter…. Therefore it's better to do the right thing wrong then the wrong thing right".

Lean Thinking overlaps with Design Thinking. As Ohno said about the Toyota Production System, "To tackle the variety problem we saw the need for the worker to design and control the line steps so that he or she would be able to perform different operations according to what is needed."

Systems thinking incorporates both Lean Thinking and System Thinking. It is holistic. It 'seeks not to be reductionist' (to quote Peter Checkland). Systems thinking is about thinking. The whole is more than the sum of the parts; it is synergistic. A Systems Thinker embraces complexity. Systems thinking integrates Lean Thinking and Design Thinking, thereby revealing new opportunities.

Russell Ackoff talks about resolving, solving, and dissolving problems. Traditional service managers resolve problems by discussion. Lean-oriented service managers solve problems by the scientific method. Design- and Systems-thinkers 'dissolve' problems by creativity. However, problems are never 'solved' in service systems. Rather, as Ackoff said with his usual wit, we move from 'mess to improved mess'.

Traditional managers talk about 'my' department and quickly resort to 'my' qualifications. Lean-, Design-, and Systems-thinkers talk about 'our' problems and 'our' processes. Tim Brown, co-founder of the design consultancy IDEO, asks people not 'what do you do?', but 'what are you working on or learning about?'

Today, service organisations both public and private sector face many 'wicked' problems. A wicked problem is one 'that is difficult or impossible to solve because of incomplete, contradictory, and changing requirements that are often difficult to recognise. Moreover, because of complex interdependencies, the effort to solve one aspect of a wicked problem may reveal or create other problems,' (Wikipedia). Only by combining Lean, Design, and Systems Thinking can the service manager of today hope to deliver satisfactory solutions to their customers or clients.

Both Lean-thinkers and Design-thinkers need to be Systems-thinkers to remain effective. But a Systems-thinker without Lean and Design skills will not be effective because many valuable lessons and insights have accumulated from these fields.

Hence, the Trilogy of this book – Lean Thinking, Design Thinking, Systems Thinking. All three should exist in an effective service organisation.

This book presents a set of core tools for Lean service operations. Particular attention is given to mapping tools in service. A prime theme throughout the book is the emphasis on System. Tools without system can only be piecemeal and incremental, and will ultimately yield disappointing results. Design Thinking, the newest of the trilogy, represents an exciting departure for many service managers.

The book does not present core Quality and Six Sigma tools or philosophy, except where they integrate with mapping tools. Quality and Six Sigma tools are described in the companion book *Six Sigma and the Quality Toolbox*.

This book does touch on the 'people aspects' of Lean service, but is not comprehensive in this area. The reader should certainly also consult texts such as Mann's *Creating a Lean Culture*, Mahesh's *Thresholds of Motivation*, and Pink's *Drive.* Nor is the book comprehensive about IT in service.

The Lean Toolbox, Fourth edition (2009) mainly presents the Lean manufacturing tools and philosophy. Although *The Service Systems Toolbox* aims to be self-contained with respect to Lean, there is nevertheless a continuum of manufacturing and service. It may be that concepts of scheduling, for example, which are fully described in *The Lean Toolbox,* are only cursorily described in this book, and some readers may wish to refer to *The Lean Toolbox* for a fuller explanation.

We are all in Service!

The creativity methodology TRIZ (see Mann) teaches is that there is an evolution, applicable to many if not all organisations, where profits or customers are relevant. The stages are:

- Commodity - the raw material or goods are offered to customers;
- Product - materials are combined into a product that is designed;
- Service - it is the service that is purchased rather than the product;
- Experience - the service is combined with other features to give the customer an integrated experience;
- Transformation - a series of experiences transforms the customer.

Every service can be located somewhere on this spectrum. And the trend is clear. In that respect, all business is evolving towards service, experience, and transformation. Lean Thinking, Design Thinking, and Systems Thinking are increasingly relevant as the progression takes place.

So 'service' in this book is not just 'the office' or 'administration', which have been the focus of several publications, but is service in wider situations, which are not necessarily repetitive, where 'takt' time is not applicable, and where task times may be both long and variable. Service in this context could mean anything from a hospital to a university, from an administrative process to a consultancy, from a warehouse to field service maintenance, following the customer experience or transformation.

Moreover, we should not confuse 'service' with the service industry sector classification found in government publications and used by economists. For these people, there is a distinction between 'manufacturing sector' and 'service sector'. Today this classification seems of limited use. All businesses are evolving.

'Service' in this publication will be taken to mean the 'service concept', 'product service bundle' or 'service experience'. These are all the activities both 'hard' and 'soft' that provide value to the customer along a value stream. We will not be concerned with the making of 'hard' products – that is the focus of the many books on Lean manufacturing. However, the book will certainly be relevant to service activities within manufacturing companies.

The focus of the book is also on 'Lean'. The book is not about, but does overlap with

- general service operations management (for example by Johnston and Clark or Metters and Metters);
- services marketing (for example by Zeithaml, Bitner and Gremler);
- 'process management' (for example the many texts on Six Sigma).

The book is about practical tools that can be applied immediately for real gains in service quality, customer satisfaction, and productivity. It attempts to provide a set of tools, particularly mapping tools, which have wider applicability, but to embed them in a wider philosophy of system understanding.

We are all Beginners at Lean Service

Two of the most powerful aspects of the Toyota system are Humility and Reflection. Humility means the possibility that we are wrong – we still have a long way to go along the path to Lean. Even Watanabe, Toyota Chairman, says that after 40 years with Toyota he still has much to learn. If that is true in manufacturing, it is even truer in service. Reflection is the ability – and time – to contemplate where we could have done better. Without these two the manager or consultant is a danger to himself and to his customers.

Nassim Taleb writes that the human mind suffers three ailments as it comes into contact with history. I feel that the same three ailments apply, or should apply, to Lean. Taleb's points are:

1 **The illusion of understanding** – when the true system is far more complex.
2 **The retrospective distortion**, or how we can assess matters only after the fact. We are all very wise when explaining failure after the event, much less so before the event. And we think we know the characteristics of success but are often proved wrong in the longer term – a point made by Rosenzweig. So we need to set out to learn and reflect, and have humility.
3 **The overvaluation of factual information, and the handicap of authoritative and learned people, particularly when they create categories**. We love facts on Lean achievement, like reduction in lead time and improvements in quality. While it is good and reasonable practice to collect these facts, beware. Deming said, 'The true facts you'll never know'. I can hear him now saying that. In systems there is often the 'push down, pop up principle'. Solve one problem and another raises its head. Have you ever noticed how the 'push down' is always reported, but less frequently the 'pop up'? And in this book I categorise quite a bit – I would be wise to take heed of Taleb, and I recommend you should do so too!

Further Reading

Russell Ackoff, *The Art of Problem Solving*, Wiley, 1978
Tim Brown, *Change by Design*, Harper, 2009
Darrell Mann, *Hands-on Systematic Innovation*, IFR, 2004
Nassim Nicholas Taleb, *The Black Swan*, Penguin Allen Lane, 2007
Jeffrey Liker, *The Toyota Way,* McGraw Hill, 2004. Liker devotes one of his Toyota principles to *Hansei* (relentless reflection).

Value and Value Stream Focus

The concepts of Value, the Value Stream and Flow are the first three Lean Principles. These are the starting points of this book. The book is ultimately about improving customer value through focusing on value streams - the cross-functional sequence of activities that should be capable of giving the customer an experience that is required, when and where it is required, without hassle. This requires the sequence of activities to flow without waste.

The concept of the Value Stream, or end-to-end process, so well described for a manufacturing context in Womack and Jones' *Lean Thinking*, is fundamental to Lean. It has application in many service contexts. It is highly relevant to this book. But Value in service requires far more consideration, so there is an extended section on this and related concepts.

Of course, giving the customer a hassle-free experience is the first priority. Although this is still unfortunately relatively rare, customers expect it. It is a 'basic' (Kano) or 'qualifier'. Yet in administration, and particularly service, it is frequently no longer good enough to give basic service. 'Performance' must aim to delight. This book will attempt to give pointers.

Russell Ackoff says that Effectiveness is the Efficiency with which Value is attained. We could summarise with Effectiveness = Efficiency x Value.

In other words you have to do the right things right. Doing the wrong things right will not be effective. In turn, this means we have to understand Value. What do you have to do for the next customer, and for the final customer?

Don't manage cost; manage value. When value increases, the cost will decrease. This message is from Deming, from Toyota, from Feigenbaum, from Seddon, and from many others.

John Kay in his book *Obliquity* spoke about improvement by 'oblique' methods. Go for lead time reduction and service improves. Go for decreasing errors and customer satisfaction improves. Go for flow and costs decrease. But, ironically, go for cost reduction and costs are very likely to increase! Why? Because a cost focus often brings worse service that backfires through increased failure demand. The Toyota brake failure debacle was a classic instance. Toyota apparently instructed its chief designers to reduce costs. They did. As reported in *Fortune* magazine, they shared components between models and outsourced supply. Worse, as reported in *The Times*, Toyota USA compounded its problems by failing to notify customers and delaying recalls. This resulted in Toyota agreeing to pay the maximum possible fine.

Reference: Dearbail Jordan, 'Fined for not being speedy enough', *The Times*, 22 December 2010, page 47.

Part 1: Lean in Service

1.1 Basic Concepts in Service

Lean Thinking, Systems Thinking, Design Thinking, People, and IT

The Lean System

In manufacturing, Toyota has long had the idea that Lean, or TPS (Toyota Production System), is really about system. Unfortunately many would-be followers of Toyota ignored the system aspect and went piecemeal into tools and techniques – often with disappointing results. This is now slowly being corrected as managers realise the system dimension.

Then came service. There are now potentially two problems. The first is to avoid the manufacturing mistake of leaping into tools and ignoring the system aspect. The second is to avoid using manufacturing tools in a service context. As with the manufacturing experience, there will be some limited success despite these problems.

As Richard Davis of Vanguard has pointed out, much of what goes under the heading of Lean Service is merely trying to adapt the manufacturing tools derived from Toyota, instead of deriving what to do from the more fundamental, profound systems ideas that Ohno and Toyota used to develop TPS. Kate Mackle, famous Lean consultant, warns about the many activities that are done 'in the name of Lean' without understanding the fundamental principles and interconnections.

The Lean Systems Thinker does not think in terms of 'optimising' functions or departments, but in terms of end-to-end value streams made up of the integration of marketing, sales, design, engineering, manufacture, distribution, and service. Note that the office is only a small part. These value streams are tied together by information.

And, while cost reduction is a natural consequence of 'Lean', it is not its purpose. It is said that any fool can reduce cost. And you can reduce your weight by cutting off your leg! But no. The purpose of Lean is to increase capacity by designing a system that responds optimally to customer demand'. See 'Watch out for the toolheads', Vanguard Education, 2006, www.lean-service.com/6-23.asp.

In Lean Systems we are concerned with absorbing variety and limiting unnecessary variation, both arrival variation and process variation.

There still remains a misunderstanding about the term 'system'. Lean is NOT a technical system, it is a LEARNING SYSTEM. The tools are best regarded as tools with which to learn more about the system. So, taking a manufacturing example, kanban is not a tool or technical system for inventory reduction but a way of learning more about improvement. TPS can also stand for Thinking People System. This is even more appropriate in Lean Service operations.

Systems Thinking is at least as significant, powerful and useful as Lean Thinking. The two overlap. Systems thinking attempts to remain holistic, to see the customer experience as a totality, not divided by vertical silos or organisational boundaries. And Design Thinking integrates and extends Lean Thinking and Systems Thinking.

1.2 Lean Thinking

Lean Service is not Lean Tools!

There is a danger that Lean is thought of as a box of tools to be cherry-picked. But it is an end-to-end value stream that delivers service to customers. Tools are 'cause and effect' – actions not interactions. No doubt some tools used individually give good results. A wonderfully designed office cell serving a morass of poorly controlled inventory is a waste. A 5S programme without follow-through into flow is largely a waste. Office kanban working in a situation of unlevelled demand can be waste. And so on. Even if all these were sorted out through good value stream mapping and a well-directed kaizen programme, Lean may still fail to deliver its true potential. Ohno did not have a Lean toolbox. He had in mind a vision of where he wanted to be. The system first, THEN the necessary tools.

Five Lean Principles and Service

Womack and Jones in *Lean Thinking* (1996) set out five Lean Principles: Value, value stream, flow, pull, and perfection. These have served all who would seek to implement Lean, especially Lean manufacturing, very well. In the intervening period, Lean has expanded massively into service and administration. Perhaps, therefore, it is appropriate to re-cast the five principles, even though this is probably presumptuous. The proposal for the revised 5 is:

1 **Purpose:** stand back and ask about what the service system is there to do. Are we in the 'drills' business or the 'holes' business? Are we selling cosmetics or are we selling 'hope'? In the public sector, it may be useful to think about the 'function-service' bundle – a passive or active fire service, police, or health care? In the private sector it is the 'product-service bundle'. Here, purpose is closely aligned with the business model. The mix between product-service and function-service gives the opportunity for competitive advantage. Hence, is Rolls Royce aerospace in the engine business or in the 'power by the hour' business? Zara competes on speed, bringing fashion to customers quickly but for a short sales window. Uniqlo, by contrast, has a business model that sells a limited range of core clothing items that remains available for much longer periods. From a Lean perspective, Zara emphasises time reduction but Uniqlo emphasises cost reduction.

   Womack and Jones' first Lean Principle was 'Value'. This remains a good starting point. Value is more than 'defect free' or 'satisfaction', but extends these to include the full product service bundle experience. It asks why a customer would select one bundle offering from another, and why they would 'defect' from one provider to another. Note that this is a dynamic concept – a

Zara customer might defect to Uniqlo in different economic conditions or new internet purchasing options.

An earlier section discussed the importance of considering purpose, value, root definition, function and ideal final result. Select those that are most appropriate, but spend enough time on this or opportunities will be missed.

2 **A System** is more than the sum of its parts. Like a human, or an airplane. It is the holistic concept that is more important than the parts. An airplane comprises parts that have no aspirations to fly – just the opposite, in fact! And it is the system in dynamic interaction with its environment that enables it to survive and prosper. An airplane without sufficient forward movement crashes. A system has feedback, both positive and negative, that enables it to adjust. A flying airplane continually makes adjustments to changing conditions, or it falls. Redesign will need to relate to these and other characteristics – total system improvement, not sub-system improvement; interactions between parts; adjustment to a changing environment; end-to-end; dynamic not static; and feedback. In any system there are likely to be several stakeholders each with different, valid aspirations. Example: a prison: rehabilitation or punishment? The concept of "value stream" used in Lean manufacturing remains a powerful concept, but sometimes does not capture the essential interactive features found in service. Hence a system diagram is richer than a value stream process map.

Please refer also to the later section on Systems Thinking.

3 **Flow** is at the heart of Lean. Flow is concerned with lead time reduction, end-to-end. As Ohno once said, "All we are trying to do is to reduce the time from order to cash". Note this clever statement – it is not just about physical operations, but includes information flows before, during, and after the physical flows. So, keep it moving. "It" is the focus of the purpose - the product, the patient, the customer, but not the machine or the worker. Never delay the customer by an activity that has relevance to the organisation but not the customer. Don't waste his or her time (Womack and Jones, 2005). Mackle talks about "creating flow, maintaining flow, organising for flow, and measuring for flow". To this can be added Design for flow, Supply for flow, Distribute for flow (Mackle in Bicheno, 2006). Note that we are not talking tools here – like a "House of Lean". We are saying that there should be focus on identifying and eliminating all the barriers to flow. This would include understanding demand and bottlenecks. Demand is of two types – value demand and failure demand. The latter results from errors or omissions in your own system, and should be eliminated. See separate section. Organising for flow means redesign of the value streams end-to-end, probably using what Womack calls a "value stream architect" who has the cross-functional vision. Maintaining flow includes all activities for sustaining and improving flow. Measuring flow should also relate to end-to-end measures, particularly the cumulative time to respond to customer requirements.

Of particular relevance for ideas and improvement is an appreciation of process time, utilisation, and variation. This was discussed in the last section.

4 **Perfection** is an aspirational goal, which everyone should strive for. It has internal and external dimensions. Internally it is about better quality, and ever-higher process capability. It is about variation, mistakes and complexity (Hinckley, 2000). Reduce all three by attention to all 6 'M's of the fishbone diagram: Manpower, Machines, Materials, Methods, Mother Nature effects, and appropriate Measures. This gives 6 x 3 = 18 cells for ideas. But note that reducing variation is not an absolute; if this is taken too far, failure results – the opposite of perfection. This is Ashby's 'Law of Requisite Variety'. Externally, perfection is about zero defections (of those customers you value), and about enhancing the total customer experience. Thus, internally we can use a process map, and externally we can use a "service blueprint" to track a customer's "moments of truth". Perfection is an end-to-end concept – it will need to cover the entire product-service bundle experience.

5 **People,** last but by no means least, are the true engine of Lean. Lean continues to be a revolution and a revelation with respect to the use of people. No longer are "bring your brain to work", and "people are our most important assets" meaningless, hollow clichés. An organisation where everyone contributes ideas will be both more effective and efficient than an organisation that relies on the select few. And people can make direct observations that can transform an organisation. Take IKEA, an organisation founded on the observation that it is difficult to move furniture in your car. Hence the idea of flat packs.

Mahesh and others have spoken of the "Pygmalion Effect". This effect is now beyond doubt: if one group of schoolchildren is continually told that mathematics is difficult and useless, and another group is continually told and shown that mathematics can be fun, is widely used and, like a computer game, is challenging and rewarding – the difference in eventual mathematical ability will be marked. This study has been replicated many times. Another study showed marked differences with Israeli recruits. Instructors were told that one group had special ability and the other had none when in fact there was no difference. The instructors reported vastly different outcomes. In industrial and service settings, several studies have shown similar results. See Ariely, 2008, Mahesh, 1993.

Liker says, *"Lean systems will degrade without on-going improvement from every single employee through a myriad of simple, quick changes. What brings Lean structures to life is people – people engaged in continual improvement".*

System degradation is the natural system state. It is called Entropy and is the Second Law of Thermodynamics. It applies to Lean as much as it does to all natural systems.

Muda, Muri, and Mura

What do the following questions have in common?

- Why are some banks moving their call centres back to the UK?
- Why is there a high likelihood of delay when arriving at Heathrow airport?
- Why does SouthWest Airlines frequently fly less than full?
- Why are some Six Sigma projects pure waste?
- Who is right in the acrimonious debate about standard work on Mark Graban's Lean blog?
- Why is job release from the resource immediately upstream of the bottleneck important?
- Why decrease, not increase, the speed limit when traffic volume increases on the highway?
- Why does Toyota prefer a 10:2 / 10:2 shift pattern rather than 24/7?

The answer is that all these questions are related through one fundamental equation: Kingman's equation.

The quantitative aspects of the equation are explored in Part 4. Here we examine the essential inter-relationships.

Queuing is probably the most universal characteristic in service. It occurs everywhere from call centres, to air traffic control, to every clerical operation. Queuing involves both people and information. Nobody likes queuing. And a focus on queues in Lean service helps to get to root issues. Why?

Queuing is closely linked to flow – queues slow down flow. Cost, Quality, Delivery (the fundamental three relating to competitiveness) are directly related to Queuing. Queuing directly influences delivery. Longer queues lead indirectly to increased cost and poorer quality. These are Muda (or waste).

Do you have a situation where customers arrive exactly evenly? Or where all service times are exactly the same? If you answer is 'No' - and it is never 'Yes' - then you need to understand the wisdom of Muri and Mura.

The study of queues began in call centres in Sweden with Erlang in 1909, was developed by Oxbridge Professors Kendall and then Kingman in the late 1950s, and has now transferred into manufacturing via for, example 'Factory Physics' (Hopp and Spearman, 2008).

Toyota talks about three 'M's' – Muda (waste), Muri (overburden), and Mura (unevenness). Knowing about all three gives a more complete understanding of Lean. The three are interlinked, and are fundamental to an understanding of Lean service.

The relationship can be demonstrated very simply by playing a dice game in pairs, with one player the customers and the other the process capacity. The game is fully described in the book "The Lean Games Book', but the resulting graph has the shape shown in the figure. This is the classic queuing theory relationship.

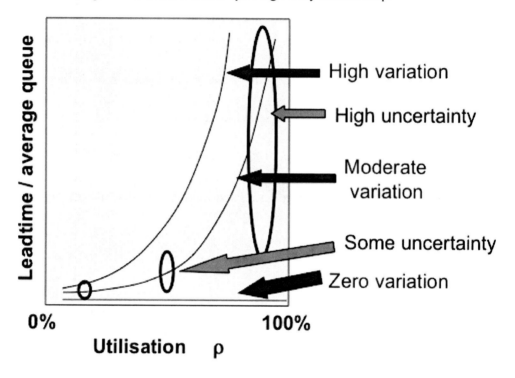

The vertical axis of the graph is the average queue length. Of course, this is directly related to the time a customer must wait for service. The horizontal axis is capacity utilisation defined as the ratio of the average arrival rate divided by the average service rate. This is known by the symbol ρ in queuing theory. At the right hand side, or 100% utilisation, or ρ, the average customer arrival rate (for example the customers arriving per hour) is exactly matched by the average service rate (for example the average number of customers that can be served per hour).

Notice, from the graph:
- Customer queues are near zero where there is quite a bit of extra capacity.
- Work queues start to accumulate severely when the arrival rate of customers nears the capacity. The curve is exponential, not linear.
- The 'turn up' of the graph begins before 100% - typically between 70% and 90% of capacity in service situations. Working at higher rates of utilisation will risk dissatisfied customers.

- If there were no variation, the average queue time would be zero. There would always be more capacity than customers at any level of utilisation below 100%.
- The range or uncertainty in the queue length (shown by the vertical distance between the zero variation case or X axis and the variation curves) is also highly dependent on the utilisation. At low utilisation, the range is small – there is never a bad hour. But at high utilisation customer wait time in the queue is highly unpredictable. Customers may be lucky and have a short wait, or very unlucky.

Relating back to Toyota, variation in the customer arrival rate and variation in the service capacity is unevenness (Mura). Utilisation (or ρ) is directly linked with overburden (Muri).

So the lesson is that unevenness and being overburdened are enemies of service. They are a major source of waste. If either customer arrival variation or customer service time variation can be reduced, this will reduce customer wait times. You need to reduce the process variation and be very careful of order variations like promotional activity. And you need to run at less than 100% of capacity – because if you don't your queue times will be both long and unpredictable. Mura and Muri lead to Muda.

Some might say that quantification is not necessary – that the system can find its own level. But in all service there is a question of resource trade-off. You can provide huge capacity, reduce response times, and hence improve the 'quality' of service – but at a cost. And the reverse. The point is that the curve is non linear, and is affected by variation. To know where you are on the curve, even approximately, is valuable insight for decision makers in setting resource levels. Without knowing this, you cannot claim to understand the system.

The dilemma of course is that providing extra capacity (or reducing the utilisation) costs money. Ideally you would like to work at both high capacity and to have short queues. Let us explore this dilemma. Take a look at the graph. There are two strategies to reduce queue or wait time – reducing utilisation (or moving from right to left along the horizontal axis), or reducing variation (moving from high variation to low variation at the same level of utilisation). We will explore both.

Utilisation, Load and Capacity

As we have seen, utilisation relates directly to queues or customer delay. Queues annoy customers, reduce the efficiency of a process, and take up space. Now…

   Utilisation = Load / Capacity

The arrival rate of work can be termed 'Load'. This is the amount of work coming into the system. But Load has two components: Value Demand and Failure Demand.

$$\text{Load} = \text{Value Demand} + \text{Failure Demand}$$

Value demand is true, first time, customer demand. Failure demand results from not doing something correctly or from not doing something at all, from the customers' point of view. It is repeat demand. So in order to reduce Load, the first thing to do, as John Seddon says, is to tackle failure demand. Or try to 'do it right the first time' – DIRFIT as John Goodman says.

The service rate is the Capacity of the system. And Capacity also has two components, as identified by Ohno of Toyota: Work and Waste. Ohno spoke about activity = work + waste; Wally Hopp says 'capacity = base capacity – detractors'.

$$\text{Capacity} = \text{Work} + \text{Waste}$$

Waste is any activity that does not add value. It is all the extra things that get in the way of real work. Waste is discussed in a separate section, but we can summarise wastes as being TIM WOOD (Transport, Inventory, Motion, Waiting, Overproduction, Overprocessing, and Defects) or DOWNTIME (Defects, Overproduction, Waiting, Non value adding processes, Transport, Inventory, Motion, and Employees not using their brains to full potential). If we can replace waste with work we will add to usable capacity. Of course, defects can also cause failure demand.

Note that this is not about working harder or faster. So,

$$\text{Utilisation} = (\text{Value Demand} + \text{Failure Demand}) / (\text{Work} + \text{Waste})$$

Approaching the service nirvana of high capacity but low queue time therefore means tackling both failure demand and waste. These are two parallel but related activities. Their reduction must be the first priority. Seek to eliminate both. 'Elimination' is a strong word, an ideal, that may take forever as new opportunities are uncovered.

Then there remains the second strategy of reducing variation. Variation needs to be reduced in both arrivals rate and service rate. Unevenness causes cost in service by requiring more resources or inventory to be provided. How to reduce variation?

Arrival variation can be tackled or smoothed by a range of approaches including
- Informing customers about busy periods
- Pricing
- Booking, appointments, and timetables (or, in general, scheduling customers)
- Working with customers (and suppliers) to encourage a more even flow of orders or deliveries.

- Prioritising by moving some types of less urgent work to lower demand periods.
- Policies relating to internal customers – such as smoothing reporting work over the month.
- Not encouraging unevenness by, for example, inappropriately times promotional activities or quantity discounting.
- If demand can be predicted, then arrival variation can be handled more effectively. In John Seddon's opinion 'all transactional service organisations have largely predictable demand'. That is a good comment, but it depends on time horizon: predictable next minute? no; predictable next hour? maybe; predictable next week? yes; predictable next year? probably; predictable in 5 years? no.
- Of course, sometimes, deliberate policies that encourage customer arrival lumpiness can be advantageous – such as the launch of iPhone or iPad.

Service process variation can be tackled by approaches such as

- Flexibility of workforce, moving into overload situations at short notice. (It may be argued that this is about capacity rather than variation.)
- Training to handle high frequency occurrence jobs very well.
- Six Sigma or Lean tools, aimed at reducing variation particularly.
- 5S.
- Standard work – but take care not to over-standardise, which may cause failure demand. In this respect variation and failure demand are related. Standardise only the repeatable.
- These last two carry the risk of making other parts of the system worse, and need to be treated with caution. They are discussed in later sections.

Please note: see the section on Variation and Queues in Section 3 of this book, for further exploration of the interactions of arrival variation, process variation, and utilisation.

1.3 Systems Thinking

Service is System

The essence of Lean is the Systems Approach. Systems thinking is holistic. Peter
Checkland, UK Systems guru, more widely recognised in Japan than in his home UK,
says 'the systems approach seeks not to be reductionist'. 'Seeks' because it is quite
hard to keep the end-to-end system in view when almost the whole business world, and
the whole academic world, is organised by function.

Hence, anyone who claims to be a 'systems thinker' is misguided or arrogant. This is
similar to West Churchman's comment on John Saxe's poem about blind men
describing an elephant, which he said was often told as a piece of arrogance – claiming
that only the story teller had the big picture. No-one has the big picture. But we should
all SEEK to be systems thinkers.

Ohno said, 'All we are trying to do is to reduce the time from order to cash'. Note the
systemic nature of this statement. Lean is not about manufacturing or service but about
the system that brings both of these together. Toyota is a 'systems' company rather
than a manufacturing company. Toyota learned their systems craft from, among
others, Deming. Ohno saw economies of flow rather than economies of scale.

The late, great, and hugely entertaining, systems thinker Russell Ackoff, who was
Emeritus Professor at Wharton, talks about resolving problems by discussion, solving
problems by fact-based tools approach, which is better, and dissolving problems by
understanding the purpose of the system and using innovative thinking, which is best
of all. Non-Lean practitioners resolve 'inefficiencies', beginner Lean practitioners
solve problems by removing waste, but the experienced Lean practitioner improves the
whole system. Ackoff also says that a system is more about INTERACTIONS than
ACTIONS. In healthcare, for example, it is the interactions between many
professionals that count towards the success of a patient's recovery. In office systems
it is the handoffs and rework loops that make the difference.

The systems approach means the focus should be on the organisation or entity as a
whole before paying attention to the parts. This is a very hard thing to do for most
managers and other workers who have been brought up and educated in 'vertical silos'.
That is why, in this book, the first port of call is to try to understand the system as a
whole. What is its purpose? A related focus is on the customer. Again, this is
different from Lean manufacturing where the focus is on the object being made. This,
in turn, was an important move forward from traditional mass production where the
prime focus was on the efficiency of individual departments, people or machines. If
we don't remain systemic we quickly get into the 'push down, pop up principle' where
we solve one problem and then another emerges because we have sub-optimised. That
has also been the problem in many service operations: in call centres call productivity
improved but complaints rose; in hospitals imposing targets on A&E often increased

wait time – in at least one instance, ambulance drivers drove around the car park until the measured queue decreased; in offices the implementation of ERP has often meant a slowdown in reaction time, and so on. In healthcare it is sometimes pointed out that increasing the human lifespan is good overall, but increases the load on hospitals that must cater for more ever-older patients. Another way of saying this is 'Systems bite back'.

Water is a liquid at normal temperatures. Its constituents, oxygen and hydrogen, are gases. You can never understand the properties of water by studying oxygen and hydrogen. Likewise Lean and Lean tools. Lean is a system – it is more than the sum of its components. Systems are in constant interplay with their environment – it is not obvious where the boundary is, what should be outsourced, or the extent to which customers and suppliers should be involved in improvement or design. Systems adapt continuously but at a faster rate when threatened. Ant colonies are examples. Systems evolve. Bugs develop immunity to insecticides. Is this true 'kaizen culture'? It is a question of how to recognise and kill off inappropriate tools while developing new and stronger ones.

Lack of system appreciation is often counterproductive (or amusing, depending on your viewpoint). Thus a patient entering a hospital for one problem, but catching a bug is considered to be two patients each with their own recovery time. Worse, the hospital is rewarded twice. The patient, of course, sees only the end-to-end time – if he doesn't die en route.

Another analogy is the human body. Layout, supermarkets and buffers provide the skeleton; pull systems and information flows are the circulation system; vision and strategy are the eyes and brain; control, deployment and measurement come from the nervous system; quality and improvement come from the muscular system; and energy and getting rid of waste come from the digestive system. The body needs them all for 'simple, slim and speedy' Lean (to quote Katsuaki Watanabe, Toyota President). So it is not surprising that TPS stands not only for Toyota Production System but also for Thinking People System. Stafford Beer made the human body into a powerful analysis aid with his Viable System Model, described later in this book.

Pfeffer's book *What Were They Thinking?* gives numerous examples of top management from major corporations adopting practices that could be termed 'non-systems thinking'. (Pfeffer does not use the term 'systems thinking'.) Examples are top-down announcements of cutting staff or wages when a company gets into financial trouble, or driving staff with threats and rewards. These practices ignore the impact on the system in favour of short-term 'solutions'. Such non-systems thinking will prove ineffective for any organisation, even disastrous, sometimes immediately and almost invariably in the medium term. The executive, however, may be rewarded for his short-term results while his successor is blamed. During the period of writing this book, the UK parliament is debating how to reduce public service pensions while at the same time 'ring fencing' their own pensions. Systems bite back. It is a system boundary issue.

1.4 Service Design Thinking

In manufacturing the realisation has grown that being truly Lean requires beginning at the design stage. It is often too late when products arrive at the shop-floor manufacturing stage – too many wastes are already built in. So it is with service. A poorly designed service, and the facilities that go with it, can never fully be compensated for by excellent service delivery.

Design Thinking is different from operations thinking. Roger Martin explains this well by citing James March (of 'The Behavioural Theory of the Firm' fame) who stated that a firm might engage primarily in *exploration* (seeking new knowledge) or *exploitation* (seeking payoff from existing knowledge or refinement of the knowledge). The former is the realm of Design Thinking, the latter operations thinking. Operations have been the traditional area of Lean Thinking. Systems Thinking encompasses both areas. Today, most Western organisations cannot compete, in either manufacturing or service, unless they embrace exploration or design thinking.

The British Design Council has for years used the 'Double Diamond' approach to design. This is a two-stage approach. The top diamond is about Discover and Define, the bottom Diamond is about Develop and Deliver. This is roughly equivalent to exploration and exploitation, or to open thinking and closed thinking, to design thinking and operations thinking. Yet another view is that the top diamond is concerned with heuristics and the lower diamond with algorithms.

In the value engineering methodology the expanding half of each diamond is supposed to indicate 'right brain' non-linear thinking, while the contracting half indicates 'left brain' linear thinking.

In the figure we prefer to show two overlapping diamonds to break the notion that there is some sort of 'stage gate' between exploration and exploitation. Indeed the stages are contiguous.

Design Thinking and Lean Thinking both harness the creative skills of employees, but do so in different ways – or, using systems language, with different system boundaries. Design thinking is much more open. There is a blank sheet of paper to begin. Lean Thinking is about creativity within given parameters – developing ways in which a given product or service can be better delivered.

Design Thinking includes Co-creation (a phrase from Prahalad and Ramaswamy) that extends to including not only employees but also customers. It also includes co-makership (a phrase from Giorgio Merli (1991) or Bevan (1989)) that emphasises creative co-development with suppliers.

Design thinking cuts through the traditional barriers that frequently exist between industrial design and operations, between R&D and product and service design, between service designers and customers, and between those that design the service and those that deliver the service. Design thinking is therefore a natural extension of Lean Thinking.

Design Thinking is about moving towards 'Experiment First, Then Design' rather than Design then trial. Design authority Ron Mascitelli tells about making a wooden table, varnishing it, and then discovering problems with the varnish. Far better to test the varnish on a sample of the wood first. Likewise in software or service design, just do enough to test and get feedback. In other words, learning.

The figure below is derived from the Design Council model, and has similarities to the problem solving funnel used within Lean, the knowledge funnel used by Roger Martin, and the Value Engineering representation.

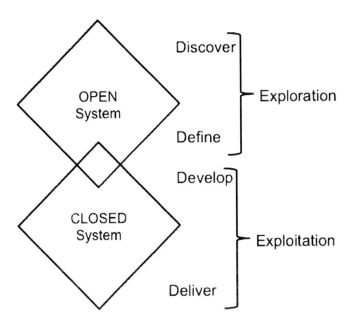

The figure shows stages of evolution, perhaps of a new service or product, perhaps an improvement, moving through four stages. The stages are frequently not uni-directional. Many recursions take place. The figure can be related to several concepts discussed throughout this book.

- The problem area is 'Discovered'. This may involve several of the following:
    o Visiting the gemba for direct observation;
    o Understanding customer needs;
    o Defining value for the clients (there may be several);
    o Questioning the system boundary;
    o Developing a rich picture of the problem situation;

- o A 'Painstorm' – identifying customer's greatest pain points (used by Intuit).
- The Define stage may involve
  - o The 'Check' stage as discussed later in this book;
  - o Defining the Purpose;
  - o Developing a 'Root Definition' or definitions.

- The top diamond is explored, by for instance:
  - o Generating alternatives via creative thinking techniques;
  - o Drawing conceptual models;
  - o Using the Viable System Model;
  - o Expanding the system boundary;
  - o End to end thinking;
  - o Benchmarking;
  - o Examining occurrences in the 'long tail' of the distribution;
  - o Examining the process, not the person;
  - o Keeping options open rather than closing them down too early;
  - o ….

- Develop: here the defined area is explored, by for instance
  - o Lean analysis tools, including mapping;
  - o Muri and Mura;
  - o Kaizen events;
  - o Idea management;
  - o A3 analysis;
  - o Pareto analysis;
  - o Root cause analysis;
  - o 5 why thinking;
  - o SIPOC;
  - o Six Sigma tools for variation reduction;
  - o Modelling and simulation;
  - o Cost benefit tools;
  - o …

- Deliver: Methods and tools include
  - o Leader standard work;
  - o Visual management;
  - o 5S;
  - o Standard work;
  - o Detail waste reduction;
  - o …

We may note that

- Not all problems or situations progress through all four stages, nor should they. Rather, there is evolution from top to bottom as understanding develops and experience is gained. Take planning an overseas journey: once there was considerable uncertainty. Now you book your flight on-line from home. Now the top stages can be progressed through very rapidly. For effective design, there is therefore a need to understand current customers, current technology, and current service delivery practice.

- Systems Thinking is highly relevant in the top three areas of discover, define, and develop
- Design thinking is most relevant in the top diamond, but Lean Thinking also plays a role.
- Both Daniel Pink and Roger Martin discuss 'heuristics' and 'algorithms'. Both make the point that competing on heuristics rather than algorithms is already a necessity for work, especially in the West. A heuristic sets the general course, but allows adaptation. For instance 'keep going up' is a heuristic that will get you to the top of a mountain – if not to the summit, at least to a localised peak. An algorithm is more specific. It provides much more detailed instruction: 'walk 100m, turn right'. An extreme case of an algorithm is computer code. Heuristics are found in the explore stage, algorithms in the develop and deliver stage. They overlap in the refine stage. Heuristics are more applicable in professional services and interactive services. Algorithms are more applicable in transactional service. Pink makes the point that extrinsic motivators MAY be applicable with algorithmic work, but that intrinsic motivators are the only successful type in heuristic work.
- You should only attempt 'algorithms' when the system is routine. Parts of some service jobs are like this, but virtually no service job is completely algorithmic
- Lean thinking is most relevant in the lower diamond. Much of lean thinking has been too narrowly defined, being limited to the 'deliver' stage only. This is Fake Lean leading to 'Lean is Mean' accusations, and to a disrespectful use of employees whose opinions are not sought despite being on the front line.
- Industrialised working and traditional Lean thinking (emphasising a high degree of standard work) is NOT appropriate in open ended, exploratory situations. Design thinking allows variety to be designed into processes.
- There will be more standard work as one progresses from top to bottom. In the top diamond, standard work may only be appropriate in outlining the main stages. At the bottom of the lower diamond many tasks (but not all) will have standard work. Note: Standard work is NEVER fixed in stone. See the later section on this topic.
- There may be different starting and end points. Some situations are clear and can start at the develop stage. But beware, defining a problem too narrowly may be what Ackoff calls 'resolving' the problem rather than 'dissolving' it, by systems or design thinking. Other situations may carry the 'solution' too far – reducing the 'solution' to algorithm status (too closely specified standard work?) when a heuristic solution would be more appropriate.
- Chris Anderson, Nassim Taleb and Clayton Christensen are authors who discuss opportunities beyond the usual Pareto 'top problems'. Anderson discusses the huge opportunities that lie unseen in 'the long tail' of the sales or inventory distribution. Taleb discusses the opportunity and threats that lie in the 'power distribution' of very infrequent but potentially hugely significant

events. Christensen discusses 'disruptive technology' that is rejected for all the right business reasons but turns out to be the winner. All these are examples where conventional analysis, beginning with the develop stage, fails. Design Thinking helps to break this mindset.

This is summarised in the figure below.

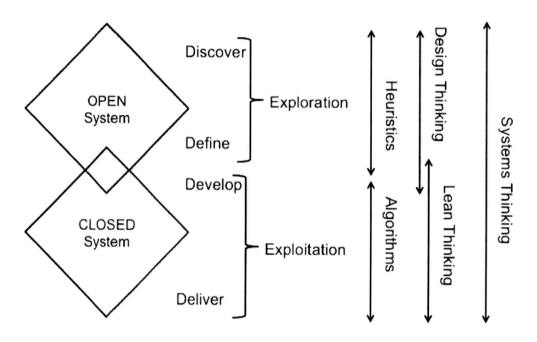

References

J Bevan, *Co-makership*, Management Decision, V27, n3, 1989
Giorgio Merli, *Co-makership*, Productivity Press, 1991
C.K. Prahalad and v. Ramaswamy, 'Co-opting Customer Competence', *Harvard Business Review*, January 2000
Marc Strickdorn et al, *This is Service Design Thinking*, BIS Publishers, 2010
Roger Martin, *The Design of Business*, Harvard, 2009
Rob Austin and Lee Devin, *Artful Making*, FT Prentice Hall, 2003
Note: Dick Stringer of the South African Value Management Foundation in the early 1980' s used a similar Design figure.
Roger Martin, 'The Innovation Catalysts', *Harvard Business Review*, June 2011.
Ronald Mascitelli, *Mastering Lean Product Development*, Technology Perspectives, 2011

1.5 Value and Purpose

Value, Purpose, Root Definition, Ideal Final Result, and Basic Function are useful overlapping concepts applicable to Lean, Systems and Design.

Value is Womack and Jones' first Lean Principle. However, this first principle was written with manufacturing in mind. Value for a product is to do with its worth, what customers are prepared to pay for. But for service, particularly public service, 'value' is more complex. Hence, other words are sometimes more apt. Improvement should start with a clarification of what it is that customers or clients require from a service system. Here, we examine some of these words, beginning with 'value'.

- A starting point for Value is what customers are prepared to pay for. It is linked with need. A 'need' is more stable than a 'want'. For example, does a customer want a hole (a 'need') or a drill (a 'want')?

- But, who are the 'customers'? In the public sector this is not an easy question. 'Customers' may not be able to 'defect'. Some may take actions that lead to 'the tragedy of the commons', and the 'NIMBY' effect. So collective interests of need to be balanced against the sometimes conflicting interests of individuals. There is danger of 'we know best' arrogance here. Whilst this book is not concerned with the political process, the systems thinking viewpoint is (as C West Churchman said) 'that the systems approach begins when you first see the world through the eyes of another.' No-one can see the whole picture. The appropriate system boundary should always be a consideration. This leads onto the 'Root Definition' concept (see below).

- Mark Moore, of Harvard adds, 'In the public sector, the arbiter of public value is not an individual, but a collective, acting through the instrumentality of representative government.' In contrast with private value that accrues to an individual who purchases a private good, public value is created when a service benefits society as a whole. 'But one has to ask the question whether "customer satisfaction" is the ultimate goal of all or even most government activities. Often, that seems doubtful – even for those government activities that deliver benefits and confer privileges on individual clients, let alone those such as law enforcement, regulation, and tax collection that inflict costs and impose obligations rather than deliver benefits. The reason is at least in part that most often in government we are interested in achieving social outcomes, and that goal may or may not include or require customer satisfaction. Indeed, in an important way, once we say that our interest is in achieving social results rather than customer satisfaction, the customer or client of the government becomes a means to an end (the achievement of the desired social outcome) rather than an end in itself (unless the desired social outcome is to make the client happy)'….'Government managers typically have much less discretion to define the purposes of their organizations, and the ways they intend to pursue those purposes. Government managers are both surrounded and thickly engaged by what we came to call their "authorizing environment."…. They demand and get significantly more information. Moreover, because they cannot sell their shares if they are disappointed, they use the "voice" option much more than the "exit" option.'

- Porter, of Harvard Business School, says: 'In competitive terms, value is the amount buyers are willing to pay for what a firm provides them. Value is measured by total revenue, a reflection of the price a firm's product commands and the units it can sell.'

- From a Lean perspective, this is a little too simple. First, there is present value – what present customers are willing to pay for. This is the usual way of identifying waste. Then there is future value – what tomorrow's customers are willing to pay for, but today's customers may not be. This is relevant in research and development and design. These represent different value streams – so you should not judge a current manufacturing stream in the same way as an R&D stream.

- Similarly, there are today's customers and tomorrow's customers. And today's customers come in different categories – those that are very valuable, an intermediate set, and a third set that are just not worth having. Perhaps your products or services are inappropriately focused. So waste may be different depending on the customer group: for a lonely pensioner chatting is value-adding activity; for anyone in a hurry speed of service is value adding.

- Russell Ackoff says that Effectiveness is the Efficiency with which Value is attained. We could summarise with Effectiveness = Efficiency x Value.

In other words you have to do the right things right. Doing the wrong things right will not be effective. In turn, this means we have to understand Value. Value enhancement is arguably more important than waste reduction, especially in service. Thus, for example in car servicing, it may prove highly effective to get the technician to 'waste his time' by talking to customers directly rather than indirectly via a service agent. And it may improve value to give a discount to those owners who do not avail themselves of a courtesy car.

- A very useful, straightforward, exercise is to get the customers of each function in the organisation to define what Value means to them. For example:

  o IT:
    To provide meaningful, fast information to support decision-making
    To facilitate the flow of information to IT users
    …..

  o HR:
    To identify suitable candidates for posts that need to be filled
    To provide advice to managers concerning training and development

...
o Marketing:
To understand customer needs
To provide information and brand awareness to customers
To identify market segments

....
o Field Service:
To solve customer problems
...
...others....

Having stated these definitions of value, it is then much easier to identify waste, being anything that is not covered by these requirements.

In service, value is a Moment of Truth experience, the totality of all the experiences. So value is getting the exact product or service you require, in the right quantity, at the right time, with perfect quality of course, and at the right price. Moments of Truth are multiplicative. An example is the cumulative effect of getting a car on which you compromise for colour, which is delivered a week late, with minor faults, and including extras which you don't want but for which you are asked to pay. The basic product is fine, but the total experience is poor. It is sobering to think that customers are continually tallying up their score of your business at each successive Moment of Truth.

- Kano, speaking about quality, talks about 'Basics', 'Performance Factors', and 'Delighters' (see separate section). Much the same can be said about value. There are some activities that are basic to value – defect-free has become a basic in some industries. There is 'performance' value – lead time for example in some businesses – and 'delighter' value. Moreover, as in the Kano model, value is dynamic.

- Zeithaml and Bitner talk about four meanings for value. First, 'value is low price'. For these customers, lowest price is best. This is seen as the ultimate Lean, interpreted narrowly – cut out all activities that do not directly contribute to the product or service in the short term. No frills. Second, 'value is whatever I want in a product or service'. This focuses on benefits, not price. This is the classic marketing approach – selling the experience of owning a top-brand pair of trainers rather than the shoes themselves. Or a power tool company selling holes not drills. Here, the Lean company needs to understand its customers' requirements deeply. Here, the classic marketing statement – 'We know half of our promotional activities are waste, but we don't know which half' – comes to mind. Third, 'value is the quality I get for what I pay'. Here expectations are directly linked to price – pay more, expect more. Having standby services or extra inventory may be expected because the price is so high. Fourthly, 'value is what I get for what I give' – all benefits against all sacrifices, not just money. A luxury car may be worth the price and the wait, but of course customer satisfaction may increase if the wait decreases.

- Ideal Final Result (IFR) is a concept from TRIZ thinking. Darrell Mann explains that an IFR delivers 'all the good stuff with none of the bad stuff'. The ideal may be 'Free, Perfect, Now' for all. Impossible? But over time, many trends are steadily in this direction ... travel, communication, food, health, education ... so take the trend to the limit. Thus the function of a lawnmower may be to 'cut grass' but the IFR would be pleasing grass that does not need cutting. The solution therefore switches from engineering a machine to biology. The IFR extends the Value Analysis concept of function, but in common with VA/VE (and Six Sigma) spends much time on the 'Define' phase. TRIZ and VA/VE share the concept that 'solutions change but functions stay the same'. IFR has similarities to Russell Ackoff's 'Idealised Design' which is a methodology that begins with the notion 'the system burned down yesterday, so what should we do now?' Then work back from the ideal state, rather than the more common (in Lean) working forward from the current state.

  The IFR should consider many attributes of the service, including perhaps cost, quality, speed, reliability, assurance, tangibles, empathy, responsiveness, and many more. For each, the IFR is sought for the customer, the provider, and the supplier. This will reveal several contradictions. For example, the customer wants low cost, the provider wants profit. The customer wants instant response, the provider would like more time. The customer wants 'open all hours', the provider needs to consider staffing. These contradictions are where opportunity for innovation lies. Design Thinking is required, not optimising the present system.

- Root Definition is a phrase associated with Peter Checkland who says that a root definition is 'a concise, tightly structured description of a human activity system which states what the system is; what it does is then elaborated in a conceptual model which is built on the basis of the definition.' (Checkland, 1978.) A system may have several direct clients. Checkland further explains that there are invariably several root definitions, each depending on the observer's 'weltanschauung' or world view, and each of which may be valid. Thus a prison may be a system for rehabilitation or a system for punishment on behalf of society.

- Mike Jackson, of Hull University, advocates what he calls 'creative holism', attempting to join creativity and holistic thinking. Jackson discusses five System Goals, all of which should be sought:

  - Efficiency;
  - Efficacy – the ability to produce a desired result, or 'implementability';

- o Effectiveness: Ackoff says, simply, Effectiveness is the Efficiency with which Value is attained;
- o Elegance;
- o Empowerment.

To this end, there would seem to be considerable congruence with Design Thinking.

- **Purpose** is the reason you are doing the task. 'Why are you in business?' Womack asks. Ask 'what is the purpose of the system from the customer's viewpoint?' Purpose is a word associated with the Vanguard methodology, and is further discussed under 'Seddon's Six Stages of Check'. It is an 'outside in' view, not an 'inside out' view. Purpose is also associated with Deming and Toyota. What Deming says about an aim, could also be applied to Purpose: 'It is important that an aim never be defined in terms of activity or methods. It must always relate to how life is made better for everyone.' Are you performing a task or performing to a purpose? For instance, is a NASA janitor cleaning a toilet or helping to send a man to the moon? Is a bricklayer building a wall or a cathedral?

- Steve Blank of Stanford University says that 'build it and they will come' is true only for life and death products and services such as cancer treatment or the fire service. For all other products and services you need to ask:
  - o What are your customers' top problems?
  - o Does your service concept solve those problems?
  - o Do your customers agree that their problem will be solved or improved?
  - o How much are they willing to pay for the solution?

- **Function.** Value Analysis or Value Engineering (VA/VE) uses the concept of the 'basic function'. 'Function' is invariably expressed as a verb plus a noun. For example, the function of a health care system may be 'to recover health' or more widely 'to ensure health'. There are invariably higher level functions that can be redefined by changing the system boundary – an important concept of systems thinking, discussed later. The powerful creative idea of value analysis is that a function describes what is to be accomplished without stating how it is to be accomplished. This, we believe, is not in conflict with Deming's statement about aim in the previous paragraph, but adds to it. The skill in value analysis is to remain general for the basic function. Supporting functions can then be written. Start with the basic function on the left hand side. This can be further broken down to form a tree diagram, moving from left to right, called a FAST (Function Analysis System Technique) diagram. Reading from left to right answers successive stages of 'how' and reading from right to left gives successive stages of 'why'. For example, for a university you may settle after some debate on 'obtain advanced knowledge' as the basic function. From the left this may break down into supporting functions of 'study full time' and 'study part time'. Successive stages might be 'identify study and work time split' and 'identify necessary finances'. This leads to 'save money' and 'obtain part-time work'. Read from right to left would give the sequence of 'why'. These sequences can then be used to communicate necessity, identify barriers, identify problem causes, and prioritise actions.

It may be argued that these related concepts have not received the attention they deserve in Lean, or other fields for that matter. But if we desire to make effective change such concepts must be seriously considered up front for all but very well pre-defined service systems. That is why this section is presented up-front in the book.

Further reading

Darrell Mann, *Hands-on Systematic Innovation for Business and Management*, IFR Press, 2004
Charles Bytheway, *FAST Creativity and Innovation*, J Ross Publishing, 2007
Mark Moore, *On Creating Public Value*, Working Paper, Kennedy School of Government, 2004
Peter Checkland, *Systems Thinking, Systems Practice*, Wiley, 1978
Mike Jackson, *Review of Systems Thinking*, UK Systems Society Conference, Oxford, 2010
Valerie Zeithaml, Mary Jo Bitner and Dwayne Gremler, *Services Marketing*, 4th edition, McGraw Hill, 2006

1.6 People and Service Operations

This book is not specifically about people in service operations. Yet, of course, people are what service is all about. In Lean manufacturing it is said that it is possible to achieve brilliant results with a brilliant process but average people. In a service context this is not only wrong, but it is also disrespectful. Your people are the key. Yet without good process design peoples' best efforts will be ineffective.

Certainly good processes are needed and that is what much of this book is about. But the front-line staff need to do whatever it takes to deliver a great, customer experience. It's that simple.

'The soft stuff will give you the hard stuff' said Colleen Addullah of WOW! – a multiple J.D. Powers service award winner at the 2010 AME Conference. Having said that, John Shook, author and chairman of Lean Enterprise Institute has made the point that, more recently, the 'technical side' of Lean has come to be seen as simpler than the social side. But simple does not mean easy. Too many organisations, according to Shook, have claimed that they have 'moved on' beyond the tools, when in fact the tools have been bypassed. So a balance is necessary.

With this requirement in mind, the following people-and-service principles should be kept in mind throughout this book. Many overlap with the techniques and tools in the book, and none are in conflict.

- Leadership: 'Gemba' style leadership is required. This means leaders should familiarise themselves first-hand with current customer concerns. Very senior service managers need to spend time on front line employee concerns and problems. This practice is adopted by virtually every famous service organisation. Managing by 'remote control' KPIs is a recipe for disaster. Hopper and Hopper give numerous examples of once-successful companies that have failed after the appointment of 'professional managers' whose prime motivation is profit or shareholder value rather than customer satisfaction.

- Deming spoke about what he called the '94/6' rule: 94% of problems are due to the process and only 6% are due to the people in the process. And only management can fundamentally change the process. If we believe this, then our first response to a problem should not be to seek out a person to blame, but to apologise that the process is deficient in some way. This is a hard thing to do, particularly for Western managers. Sheena Iyengar describes how Americans are basically 'I' oriented, Japanese are 'we' oriented.

- Deming also gave the four elements of what he described as "profound Knowledge'. They are System, Variation, Learning, and Psychology. He said that many managers have a misunderstanding of these elements and that they are the roots of the majority of problems. 'System' means an appreciation of the interactive nature of entities, and that whole is more than the sum of the parts. Focusing on a part (or a person) may make things worse. 'Variation' means an appreciation of common causes and special causes. A reward or punishment for common cause outcomes is counterproductive – like a bonus for a manager where success is a matter of chance. 'Learning' is the ability to use the Plan Do Study Act cycle in a scientific way to build understanding and knowledge: building 20 years of experience rather than repeating the same mistakes for 20 years. Finally, 'Psychology' refers to the use of extrinsic rather than intrinsic motivation. This is discussed briefly below.

- Vision: do your people have a clear vision of themselves and their role in service? Do Ritz-Carlton employees see themselves as 'we are ladies and gentlemen serving ladies and gentlemen', or do they see themselves as just doing a job? Do employees at the telecoms service WOW!' try to 'to deliver a customer experience that lives up to our name', or do they see themselves simply as call centre operators or field technicians? Of course, policies and procedures need to support these words.

- Employee satisfaction: this is the first priority. Satisfied employees deliver customer satisfaction; dissatisfied employees will not do so, irrespective of a Lean or any other process.

- The 'Inverted Triangle' follows from the earlier concepts. Command and control organisations see the CEO or shareholders at the pinnacle with employees reporting upwards to meet targets and to satisfy rules and procedures. Middle managers supervise, report and control. A good Lean service organisation inverts the pyramid. Everyone is seen as ultimately supporting front-line service operations. Managers facilitate improvements and work conscientiously to remove all barriers (including 'red tape', rules, and form filling) that get in the way of front line staff delivering great service. The priority is the customer's experience, not financial or other targets.

- Employee attitude: almost everyone feels good when dealt with by a happy employee, and is 'turned-off' by grumpy officialdom. This chalk and cheese difference costs nothing. It is easier to train for skills and methods than to train for disposition, friendliness and optimism. Humour is a great winner. Managers can certainly set in place systems and procedures that destroy friendliness and disposition, but it is far harder to create these attitudes with people who are inherently negative and critical. In Zulu, the greeting is 'I see you'. Everyone likes to be treated as a person, not an object. From this follows.....

- Respect and Humility – words frequently used with the Toyota system. Respect comes with believing that the true expert in dealing with the operation is the person who works at it all the time. So ask and observe. A lack of respect is not doing so, not caring about conditions that prevent the worker from doing a job correctly, not listening to the workers ideas and concerns. A lack of Humility is about managers thinking they are always right, not listening, rewarding themselves before others, and thinking the order is managers, customers, and employees when in fact it is the reverse.

- Focus on first time right. No customer likes to have to make a second phone call or a return visit as a result of something that the organisation did not get right first time. A customer leaving with any degree of frustration will feedback negatively on the organisation either though lost custom or repeat work. Any system or procedure that prevents this simple requirement from happening is a poor one. 'Empowerment' is a word that is sometimes banded about with little meaning, but front-line service staff must be empowered to eliminate any customer frustration, or to hand over quickly to the person who can take immediate action.

- End-to-End: right first time is closely linked with end-to-end solutions. However efficient a particular step may be, it is the end-to-end experience that counts for a customer. A customer's clock is not re-set every time the customer re-enters for a problem, nor is it re-set at every step in the journey from enquiry to completion. Employees or managers who see their role as dealing with one stage risk alienating customers. Management has an important facilitating role here. Service is teamwork: a great team, not a team of greats.

- Culture: does culture drive performance or does performance drive culture? Both! Often the former is assumed. But in Phil Rosenzsweig's excellent book, *The Halo Effect*, several examples of the latter are given. One story, confirmed by personal experience, is to give groups A and B the same case study. They present back in separate rooms. Irrespective of the presentation, group A is praised and group B is criticised. This is relatively easy with a complex case. Then, almost as an afterthought as far as the groups are concerned, ask the groups about their team dynamics. Guess what? Team A reports a supportive spirit of co-operation. Great 'culture'. Team B reports the opposite. The lesson for Lean service is stark: Culture change is strongly influenced by bringing in a system that allows, encourages and recognises good performance.

- Time and Targets: to achieve high customer satisfaction may require unplanned time and unscripted actions. So any imposed 'standard time' or 'target' that works against this happening is a false economy. Customers remember service at the extremes. Very poor service or extraordinary service on the part of employees results in word-of-mouth dissemination for years to come.

- Intrinsic Motivation: most of the earlier principles relate to employee motivation. It is now becoming widely understood by psychologists, but unfortunately not so widely by managers, that extrinsic motivation (reward and punishment) works only in the short term, if at all. Intrinsic motivation occurs through the work itself. Daniel Pink has shown that extrinsic motivators may destroy creativity, and Alfie Kohn has discussed how 'carrots' destroy effective performance. The first time you pay your son to clean your car may be the last time he will do it for fun. Pay someone specifically to complete a job and the focus may fall on completion time rather than on customer satisfaction. There may, however, be opportunities for personal or company contracts where the person or company promises to pay a forfeit (or money to a disliked charity) where a target is not met.

- Zappo's Shoe store reportedly offers new employees $2000 to leave after their initial training. If they accept it indicates that they lack the intrinsic motivation or commitment that is required to achieve the store's legendary customer service.

- Expected Improvement: 'The way we do things around here'. Like Ritz-Carlton where, every day, stories are shared and celebrated and any problem is dissected to prevent its recurrence or to make improvements. This is not one-off, or done sometimes, but every day. Less frequently will be far less effective. And regular success stories reinforce very effectively. This relates to...

- The Brain: the more you do something, the more likely it is that you will do it again, says Alvaro Pascual-Leone, of the Center for Non-Invasive Brain Stimulation and Professor of Neurology at Harvard Medical School. Regularity establishes the pathways and makes good service the natural way. Repetition of good practice embeds good practice.

- Women and Men: women are the new men, at least in service. While men still outnumber women in manufacturing, construction, logistics, defence, and sport, the reverse is increasingly the case at all levels in service. There are now more women graduating from university than men and the ratio of women to men graduates going into service is approaching 2 to 1 in the West. The 'glass ceiling' is disappearing. The relative buying power of women as customers is growing. A broad generalisation is that women tend to have a less aggressive, more participative, management style than men, and to value service differently. The implications are profound.

References

Scott Berninato, 'Success Gets into Your Head—and Changes It', *Harvard Business Review*, January February, 2010

Joseph Michelli, *The New Gold Standard*, McGraw Hill, 2008 (about Ritz-Carlton)

John Izzo, Keynote address at 2010 AME Conference, Baltimore

Sheena Iyengar, *The Art of Choosing*, Little Brown, 2010

Gary Fellers, *Why Things Go Wrong: Deming Philosophy in a Dozen Ten-minute Sessions*, Pelican, 1999

Alfie Kohn, *Punished by Rewards*, Houghton Mifflin, 1999

Daniel Pink, *Drive: The Surprising Truth about what Motivates Us*, Canongate, 2010

Phil Rosenzweig, *The Halo Effect*, McGraw Hill, 2007

John Shook, *A Fundamental Question*, LEI Newsletter, December 2011

Kenneth Hopper and William Hopper, *The Puritan Gift*, I.B.Tauris, 2010.

1.7   IT in Service Operations

This book is not specifically about IT in service. However, in 2011, we stand on the verge of significant IT developments that are likely to have a great impact on service and administrative operations.

'Web 2.0', 'Cloud computing', imbedded chips, video and data conferencing from your own desk, widespread RFID, and the widespread use of powerful mobile capability such as iPhone and iPad already offer huge opportunity for improvement in service and reduction in waste. Already Twitter and Facebook are leading to a decline in e-mail volume whilst opening up many faster communication channels.

Gonzalez-Rivas and Larsson make the useful point that 'IT' needs to shift emphasis from T (technology) to I (information). Merely providing the data or enabling faster data processing is not good enough. Data needs to be interpreted. The following is increasingly needed:

- Simulation ('what if') capability: this requires models, but with ERP (and the older MRPII) the capability already exists. It is strange how few operations managers make use of tools such as linear programming (LP) optimisation that can, for example, provide powerful insights into the ranges of demands and resource costs that would trigger a change in product or service offerings. Or to the sensitivity of call centre waits to capacity. A simple example of this is given in the section on muda, muri, mura.
- Experimentation capability: Ian Ayers gives several service examples in his book '*Supercrunchers*'. For example the casino group Harrah's Entertainment continually experiments with new layouts, offers, methods, and staffing arrangements. IT has an important role.
- Visualisation capability: linked to simulation (via 3-D graphics) or real time display of operating information.
- Scenario capability: in his book '*The Power to Predict*' Vivek Ranadive gives examples from health, energy, retail, banking, among others on understanding if not reducing, uncertainty.
- Automatic Process Discovery (APD): where data is gathered from customers and processes in real-time automatically, and is summarised and manipulated to reveal multi-faceted views of customer trends, including what the 'outliers' are doing. The importance of monitoring outliers is discussed in Malcolm Gladwell's book '*Outliers*', and in Nassim Taleb's book '*The Black Swan*'.

But, back to operations....

It turns out that the widespread use of distributed computing via PC and the Internet has had both positive and negative impacts on service and office productivity. On the one hand, many job categories have disappeared – clerks, typing, secretarial, filing - and have been converted to 'D.I.Y'. Speed and ease of communication has increased dramatically, but this has sometimes brought chaos because multiple versions of files are kept and lost, inordinate time is spent on unnecessary e-mail, and 'solutions' proliferate as several parties design their own solutions. System incompatibility issues arise. Faster and faster computers are demanded as data volumes and communication expand and applications are extended – the majority of which are simply not required by many users. Complexity then detracts.

Blackberry (and now Twitter) is common during meetings, and after work. Ashby's Law of Requisite Variety would imply that attempting to monitor such activity is doomed to failure.

For service, the implications of a 'new generation' of IT represent significant opportunity. To name a few:

- Continual, widespread monitoring of products and services – started on web sites but massively expanded via personal data devices and Twitter – makes unsatisfactory products and services identifiable much sooner. Word-of-mouth, already highly influential for service, becomes much more important and mass advertising becomes less important. Blogging is a much faster 'grapevine' than face-to-face.
- iPad and similar devices become a mobile medium for transport and display of images – news, games, TV, mail, e ticketing, books, education, and reduce the need to meet face-to-face – better and easier than laptops and phones.
- Mobile RFID: Radio Frequency Identification is, after some delay, beginning to have real impact on inventory status and movement monitoring. But other applications are already well established in security, hospital patient monitoring, childcare, vehicles, recycling and disposal, to name a few. The implications for fresher, more reliable, safer, service are large.
- Imbedded chips: like RFID, imbedded chips are able to monitor the status of your appliances, your food, your car, or your safety and then, through your home network, to order replacements or service.

A customer with a personal data assistant is a different proposition from a traditional customer. Real-time communication on transport delays, service calls and deliveries, appointments with the doctor and dentist, instant check-in, updated price adjustments, will all shortly become expected – a Kano 'basic', not a 'delighter'.

It is interesting to speculate on the role of managers and consultants who may go to the virtual 'gemba'. Going to the real gemba will always be necessary, though perhaps not as frequently, if look, hear, talk, sense, monitor are all possible remotely. Can a Lean Service 'Sensei' work remotely even more effectively than at the Gemba, bearing in mind the wasted time lost for travel?

The evolution from sequential, manual operations through networked operations, and now on to shared, collective operations is surely one of the great challenges for service management. The table below has been developed from a concept by Gonzalez-Rivas and Larsson.

	Sequential	Networked	Shared or Cloud
Type	A linear sequence of stages with some backtracking	A network of stages often with various paths; backtracking.	Principal players working around a common data base or Cloud
Technology	Manual	PC network / internet; possibly workflow	Cloud computing / web 2.0
Files	Single (paper?) transferred between stages	Multiple copies made; unsure who has the latest	Single e file, accessed by all
Own data stores	Little	Much	Little
People working on a project	Sequentially	Simultaneous	Simultaneous
Projects	One at a time	Sequentially	One at a time
Problem resolution	Referred to supervisor	E mail or help desk requests may slow response	Collaborative.
Information	Manual or Visual: Slow	Moderately fast but requiring PC	Instant via PDA
Wastes	Time delay through stages	Rework dangers because of multiple file versions; package redundancy; push	Much less; package use pulled
Analysis	Value stream map; focus on manual ops and layout; 5S? Cell layout a big opportunity	Physical layout irrelevant but 'information spaghetti'; 5S file design; Rework & Failure demand	Physical and info spaghettis not relevant; purpose and 'system conditions' clarification req'd
Dangers	The office factory. Command and control	E-mail is highly disruptive; data security issues; excess data.	
Capacity	Individuals	IT Servers	IT Servers?
Help desk	Unknown?	Essential	Reduced demand

Further Reading

The reader will find a host of useful and relevant material in these two references.

George Gonzales-Rivas and Linus Larsson, *Far from the Factory*, CRC Productivity Press, 2010
Steven Bell and Michael Orzen, *Lean IT*, CRC Productivity Press, 2011

1.8 Integrating Customers, Lean, System, Design, People, and IT

Some integrating thoughts relating to the earlier sections follow.

- Deming taught that approximately equal time should be spent on each of the Plan Do Study Act (or Adjust) stages. But very often very little time is spent on Plan, most time on Do, and minor time on Study and Adjust. How often does management go back and check their assumptions, really reflect on the difference between what was planned and what was achieved, and try to explain the difference? And how much time do they spend on 'holding the gains' by adjusting to the new standards? So, Value is a cumulative process, using the scientific method.

- Similarly with the five Lean Principles: although Womack and Jones did not say as much, there should be the assumption that approximately equal time is spent on each principle. Sometimes it is just a few minutes on Value, and the rest of the time on value stream mapping and preparing for flow – but not actually achieving flow.

- Ask how the savings and improvements made in a Lean implementation can be passed on to the customer. Cost, quality, delivery certainly - but that is only the start. What about new markets and new products that can be created? Remember Ansoff? He discussed growing existing markets by being better or faster, re-segmenting markets (finding unserved niches), and new markets (innovative services and new customers).

- And what about the Customer's Customer? Help the customer to delight his customer. This is thinking about the system boundary. Thinking one stage ahead helps to encourage end-to-end thinking and to limit short-term thinking. Helping the customer to look good with his customers is a path to sustainable relationships. It encourages true partnership.

- Disruptive Technology can help to break through to new customer insight. Clayton Christensen's theory of Disruptive Technology teaches that many companies, booksellers to sailing ship owners, have been caught out by making all the right decisions with current technology but ignoring 'non-viable' startup technologies.

- Likewise TRIZ trends: a powerful TRIZ notion is 'Free, Perfect, and Now'. Many products and services are heading this way, so what is the logical end state? The ultimate is free, perfect and now. Is this possible? Surely not – but think of Google, of Skype, of the near eradication of measles – they are getting close. All good service should be challenged with this idea.

- Why does Apple do so little market research? Because they are focused on customer ideal requirements. The TRIZ concept is the Ideal Final Result (IFR). This takes the 'value' concept into specific detail. It extends 'Free Perfect Now'. List the service or product functions: cost, quality, delivery time, reliability, assurance, appearance, empathy, responsiveness, sound, space, size, other specific features and functions. Make a table with at least three columns – the functions, the customer, the organisation. Perhaps add more columns for other stakeholders. Then, for each function, and in each column, write the ideal – perhaps free, perfect, now, zero, unlimited life. For instance, for a lawnmower, functions could include weight and width. Ideal weight for customer is zero, for manufacturer it is unrestricted. Solution? Hovercraft mower.   Width: Ideal for customer is both wide (for speed) and narrow (for corners); for manufacturer it is one width. Solution? Easy to adjust blades (?). This provocative exercise will reveal interesting ideas and 'contradictions'. The contradictions are where great opportunities lie. Use creativity tools to address these.

- Yet another TRIZ concept is SELF. A very provocative service concept! Can the service be made self-service, self-help, self-correcting, self-ordering, self-answering, self-paying, self-cleaning, self-adjusting, self-packed, self-cooked, self-cooled, and so on. There is a strong trend towards 'self' in service because it places control in the hands of the customer, and reduces waste, cost, and delay.

- Sometimes 'customers' cannot talk – where the 'root' customer is a computer, a car, a house, or an object in general. What would that customer say to you if it could talk? Can you imagine yourself as a patient's heart, as an aircraft engine, as a house that has just been flooded, or an item of clothing? If it is assumed that it would like to keep working well, what are its needs? If you are a pothole, how many times are you visited before being fixed, and are you properly fixed in terms of what you know about demand?

- As Deming warned, be very cautious about bonus incentives. Does it really benefit the customer or the short-term aspirations of senior managers? ('Are you really telling me that even with your generous salary, you will not be able to deliver to the best of your ability without a large bonus? If so, perhaps we hired the wrong person!')

- Finally, don't ever be complacent. Customers' values change. If you are top of the world (like Toyota), be in a panic because then there is only one way to go. Keep in mind the fate of all but two of the Fortune 100 biggest companies in the USA 80 years ago: now they don't exist.

Throw out command-and-control targets that derive fundamentally from management interests and rewards, and replace them with customer-driven, preferably end-to-end measures, which are work-related. Targets are often bad news for service because they so often drive deviant employee responses rather than help the customer. Employees will sometimes cheat and take short cuts to achieve the manager's targets even though it may make things worse for the customer. Example: those (few?) universities that reward only research, but have many dissatisfied students who never see their professors because the professors are researching.

However measures (not targets) can be good news where they are set up to identify problems in the system, not with the employee. 'Work-related' means measures that help the flow of work. Remember that measures motivate. Subjective measures are generally valuable only if they come from a customer – not from a manager. Objective measures are much more useful. Let the customer, not the manager, 'keep the score'.

A measures (and standards) story from *The Telegraph*, 20 September 2010:

It was reported that under the NHS so-called Quality and Outcomes Framework (QOF), a doctor's (GP) practice is rewarded when patients are diagnosed with certain disorders, but not others. Descriptions of disorders that were more helpful to GPs, such as 'stress at work' or 'wheeze', are now upgraded to the less useful but more rewarding 'depression' and 'asthma'. These labels are not only less helpful to GPs but also may affect the insurance status of the patient! Of course, the procedure was well intentioned to identify and compare the prevalence of certain disorders across the country. But linking it with standard descriptions and with rewards produces unintended consequences. Hence the old phrase 'take care of what you measure; you may get what you want!'

Further reading

On Deming: try Gary Fellers, *Why Things Go Wrong: Deming Philosophy in a Dozen Ten-minute Sessions*, Pelican, 1999

On Disruptive Technology: Clayton Christensen at al., *Seeing What's Next*, Harvard, 2004

On TRIZ: Darrell Mann, *Hands-on Systematic Innovation*, IFR, 2004

Note: The phrase 'Command and Control' is frequently (as above) used in a negative sense. But, as pointed out in the wonderful book by Hopper and Hopper, *The Puritan Gift*, Tauris 2010, this is just the opposite of what was originally intended. Thus Lord Nelson's version was that it was essential to decentralise command to the lowest appropriate level, allowing Navy Captains to act on their own initiative within the overall plan. No interim targets or KPIs. Just use your initiative as the battle develops so as to defeat the enemy.

Three Mini Cases integrating Lean, Systems, and Design

5S and the Pharmacy

'Lean is everywhere……

Lean has been a big fad in the health service. An Internet blog crowed over a 'lean' initiative in a pharmacy. The tool heads had worked out which drugs were supplied most often and moved those nearer the counter. It is something you see in manufacturing, it cuts down the time it takes to pick items in warehouses.

A systems thinker joined the blog to say that he had just been studying a pharmacy and found the biggest problem to be incorrect prescriptions. Doctor's handwriting, incorrect dosage and wrong drugs being some of the problems. The pharmacists knew they had to work up-stream to create real improvements. It makes the point you could make with just about any lean intervention. The toolheads do the wrong thing righter, the systems thinkers get knowledge to determine the right thing to do.'

From John Seddon's Vanguard Newsletter 7 June 2010

Comment:

The case is essentially not one of lean vs. systems thinking (or vs. six sigma), it is a question of system boundary (or 'up stream' as it is called here).

- Expanding the boundary nearly always gives benefit.
- You should ALWAYS question the boundary – whether a lean thinker, a systems thinker, or just a thinker.
- But what boundaries? For example: why not expand the boundary to looking at the drug diagnosis problem. Why not also extend to the very choice of drugs that doctors are allowed to prescribe? Why not to the whole drug pricing and contract business that provides drugs to the NHS? Well, all these may yield very significant benefits but are increasingly more challenging. So where the project begins and ends should always be the subject of discussion.
- But what if the client does not agree to the boundary being extended? If the client refuses to let you expand the boundary, should you decline the project? Maybe the project, so expanded, would bog down and result in nothing.
- Kaizen takes very small, non-threatening steps. Again and again. Slow but steady implementation, almost unnoticed. What Toyota has been doing for 60 years. Good psychology! So maybe 5S IS worth doing. At least it sends out a positive signal. Of course, don't be silly about this – like taping up the standard location of your computer on the desk. There are

situations where the 5S methodology (tool?) will get you off to a good start. But don't believe 5S = Lean.
- There are other boundaries to question. Why not look at the drug stocking (inventory) levels in the pharmacy? With the price of some drugs doing so could yield very large savings. That is 'looking downstream'.
- As Checkland said, 'the systems approach SEEKS not to be reductionist' (my emphasis). 'Seeks' because it is arrogant to assume that a wider, holistic solution is always possible.
- The priority should also be DIRFIT (do it right the first time) as John Goodman says. And, if it is not DIRFIT, why not?
- So, most important, is to explore or at least ask, why the situation at the pharmacy arose in the first place. Why did it get into such a mess? The lean phrase for this is 'root cause'; maybe the systems phrase is 'system conditions'. Who cares what it is called as long as it is done.
- Lean thinking and systems thinking? Is value not purpose? Is value stream not system boundary? Is Lean flow not system flow? Do not both seek improvement by working smarter, not harder?

The Box

The story of 'the box' (containerisation) is perhaps the supreme story of expanding the boundary – working up-stream and down-stream, that saved not millions, not billions, but hundreds of billions. This was probably the greatest cost saving innovation in history. Everyone, but everyone, has benefitted from the 95% reduction in transport cost of every item that is moved overseas. This was truly a 'machine that changed the world'. Here was a person, Malcolm McLean, who never spoke of Lean or systems – he just chipped away at his vision. For over 20 years, he pestered Unions, shipping lines, governments, railroads, the US Defence Force, until it was achieved. He suffered many reversals along the route, making and losing two or three fortunes.

Malcolm McLean did not use a value stream map. He had a vision of end-to-end flow. But he also had to be concerned with detailed standards. Container sizes, strength, lifting lugs, doors, trucks, and ships all required standards not just for one country, but worldwide.

At the time of his funeral, every container ship in the world sounded its foghorn.

The lesson? Insistence and persistence with a system vision, maintained over an extended period, at last brought results that changed the world. There were numerous setbacks along the road but McLean never gave up.

The Pothole Story

What applies to potholes may in many respects be applied to other considerations – from the ambulance service to transport. The 'solution' to the pothole problem has been put forward an as example of systems thinking in the public service.

Why Potholes? Potholes have become a big story in the public sector. It is estimated that there are 3.5million holes in English and Welsh roads, and £53 million was spent on damage claims resulting from potholes, to say nothing of the administrative costs and legal costs involved! In common with other services such as health, delaying pothole repair leads to non-linear cost escalation. Possible causes are almost endless, from trapped water turning into ice to uneven wear, with remedies ranging from 'cold mix to hot mix' (with endless formulations), temporary to permanent.

For many public organisations, 'pothole repair' is a combination of a reactive and a proactive process. Reactive in as far as the public makes calls to their local authority or County Council (typically to a call centre) that then eventually sends out a repair gang, normally after at least one visit to the site by a technician to see the nature of the repair that is needed. Proactive in as far as many (every?) road authority periodically sends out assessors to examine the state of repair of roads, and hence plan road resurfacing.

Wiltshire County Council reported the case of the application of systems thinking to potholes. Previously it took 45 days on average from call to repair. Now it takes 12 days. Productivity (measured by the amount of road surfacing material applied) has increased five fold, and pothole teams now actually repair roads for '7, 8 or 9 hours' per day as opposed to '2 or 3 hours' previously. This 'systems thinking' approach involves, apparently:
- The use of 'parish stewards', with local knowledge to feed jobs into the system
- 'Trying to fix all the things' when the gang is there
- Different methods used to fix different types of potholes.

It is pointed out by Seddon that all calls to a call centre about potholes are in fact failure demand. 'Predictable failure demand is preventable.' At this point is worth quoting from a recent Vanguard newsletter (2009), written by John Seddon:

'Imagine the typical design: if you were a pothole, how many people turn up to see you, what do they do, who does the 'value work' (fills you in)? When you study potholes as a system, much of the crazy behaviour you discover is driven by measuring, recording and sorting potholes into their relevant target category, and management's perceived need to control the people who do the work. Systems thinkers design the pothole service against predictable demand, organising workers into geographies, capturing data on potholes when the work is *done* (thus once only and accurately) and ensuring that the workers use their own data on potholes to manage their own work. The result is as much as a five-fold increase in productivity and, most importantly, massive reductions in failure demand.

The systems design for potholes also reveals that much of the reporting of potholes by citizens, while thought of as value demand, is actually failure demand in as much as potholes in certain geographies are entirely predictable.'

Systems Thinking?

Clearly, this approach to potholes is effective. Of course there is 'systems thinking' here, but is it also limited?

If you send out a road or pothole gang - what do they in fact do? Do they do a quick fix, a longer fix, or a really substantial fix? Considerations include road usage and flood water. A parish steward may have an idea of this – certainly a better idea than a gang visiting for the first time. But what about projected usage? Another consideration is the general condition of the road, and how long is it before resurfacing, and should scheduled resurfacing be reviewed? Moreover, the public *really* objects when a pothole is fixed and then the road is resurfaced soon after. Or where a pothole is fixed, and then gas or electricity come along and dig a trench. Thus, fixing a pothole can generate more failure demand.

This is similar in some ways to the classic, OR (operations research) problem of 'light bulb replacement' where the optimal trade-off between replacing a failed bulb, with a call-out cost, and replacing all bulbs, irrespective, at a determined interval, is explored. There is an optimal solution for the simple case.

Does the pothole gang learn, by feedback, on the effectiveness of their solutions?

But first, what is a 'pothole'? There is no clear definition. It is a matter of perception. In our experience the notification of a pothole from the public can range from a small shallow depression (from a notorious 'Mrs. Bucket' figure of BBC TV fame) being immediately notified, to a major series of holes in a rural road that remained unreported for several weeks. And the area over which potholes appear is also relevant – from a single depression to a road looking as though it had been the target of a cluster bomb exercise. There is also a question of public safety. This may be an overriding factor, especially in a time of a litigious public.

Yet another issue is revenue and capital spending – both of which have limits or budgets. Repair is revenue. Resurface is capital. So if a road has a few potholes but is scheduled for resurfacing in (say) a year, what do you do? And, of course, what about the road one mile along, that may fall outside the parish stewards' area, but where there are sufficient funds only to do one or other? How do you decide?

It is certainly a good thing to design the system against predictable demand. But, you have to ask what demand – short-term pothole repair demand, or medium term road usage, or both? In practice, there is another demand – that by city councillors for 'service' to their constituency. This certainly varies according to how close an election is. Similar issues are, of course, found in many public services – health, transport and housing being examples.

So the little pothole problem is actually a complex system problem. Who should decide on the action? Moreover, there are hundreds even thousands of potholes in the average Council area. Who has the time, ability and authority to prioritise and decide?

It can probably be concluded from this that ANY decision will be a sub-optimisation. The 'solution' is quite complex. Certainly not optimal, but moving from what Ackoff calls 'a mess to an improved mess'. In fact, it is a typical complex system problem to which there are better answers, but no best. 'Satisficing' not optimising, as Herbert Simon would say. Then follows a need to put a Deming style 'check' in place, in order to learn more about the problem and the effectiveness of its 'solution'.

To get to a good systems solution involves multi-discipline systems thinking. This includes what Checkland calls building a 'rich picture'. Checkland, amongst other systems thinkers, has a number of useful concepts. One is 'system boundary'. This needs careful, and explicit consideration. Drawing the system boundary too narrowly leads to severe sub-optimisation, maybe even the wrong response. A good solution to the wrong problem - what Ackoff calls doing the wrong thing right – and the righter you do the wrong thing, the wronger you become! Too wide, and the system becomes unworkable. Getting the system boundary right, leads to what Ackoff calls 'Doing the right thing wrong' – in the realisation that you will never get it quite right, but may get it righter. A guideline is first to consider the appropriate decision maker, then to look at his or her decision boundary. This is a concept also used by Senge. Should you be fixing potholes or should you be ensuring safe flow? This is the value of asking what is the system purpose – a concept used by Seddon in the systems context and by Womack in the Lean context. A clear purpose was also a point emphasised by Deming, as articulated by Scholtes (see his Chapters 2 and 5).

Asking about system purpose leads to a good Lean Thinking (but also a good System) question – what is the appropriate value stream to do the work in as flow-like a method as possible?

Standards

Pothole and road repair could also take a leaf out of Toyota maintenance standards. Here, a comprehensive list of 'inspection items' is built up through experience as well as brainstorming. An inspection item would, in the pothole and road case, be something that all who are concerned with identifying problems and monitoring conditions, would look out for – with the idea of anticipating and predicting rather than reacting to failure demand. Each 'inspection item' would have an associated 'judgement standard' which would be a clear description of what to look out for, how to identify the problem. Also, each 'judgement standard', as in TWI (Training Within Industry) would have an associated reason that must be understood. This builds into a learning system with the frequency of monitoring or inspection being derived by experience for different classes of roads and who is best placed to do the monitoring.

The well-established tool of FMEA (failure mode and effect analysis) can also be most useful here. FMEA, of course, attempts to identify the failure modes and to prioritise the risks. Thus a road (and a pothole) having a medium probability death risk, is far more important to address than a high probability situation where the main risk is damage to a car suspension.

It is difficult to see why such thinking could not be applicable right across the pothole end-to-end value stream. However, the degree of standards and standard work would vary along the steam. In customer-facing activities, guideline standards need to be derived from the customer or client. Soft standards may dominate. At the non-customer facing activities, standards are derived from employees. Hard standards may dominate. But throughout, standards should not come to mean targets – especially reward-based targets.

Problem Solving

Lean puts emphasis on 'root cause' problem solving. When the road gang reaches the area requiring repair, a good lean thinker would ask why the pothole(s) have appeared in the first place. They should learn to look around and question. For instance, are the potholes due to flash flood (a special cause), or to simple wear out (common cause), or to increased road usage (could this have been predicted?)? It is a wasted opportunity simply to go out and repair, and not to learn. Good lean thinkers treat every problem as an opportunity to learn.

SAB Miller calls this activity 'when the bobby on the beat meets the body on the beach'. First, look around and see if the murderer is running away. If so, go after him. But if not, collect the evidence before the tide comes in and destroys the evidence. This would mean recording relevant data for later examination.

Is the standard correct? Check the road surface construction standard for that type of road and situation. Check that standard work has been carried out correctly. Are notification procedures in place? If not, why not? If yes, are the standards still appropriate? What can we learn?

Where appropriate, problem solving needs to be both single loop and double loop learning (Argyris, 2008). In singe loop problems (also known as type 1 problems or Apollo 13) the problem is just fixed. But double loop problem solving asks why the problem has arisen in the first place and tries to prevent it occurring again. Maybe the standards need to be revised. Lean practitioners will be familiar with this type of double loop learning. A good Lean system attempts to 'surface' problems. Anything that is unexpected is a problem that needs addressing. In road potholes, this may involve making a prediction on the life of a road, and then, whether the life turns out to be shorter OR LONGER than predicted, a problem is indicated. Then 'crowd' the 'problem' by a multi-discipline team and revise the standard or 'exchange curve'.

References

Marc Levinson, *The Box*, Princeton, 2006
Cost of Potholes: See for instance: www.lga.gov.uk/lga/core and
www.warwickshire.gov.uk/web/corporate/pages
Seddon, John and O'Donovan, Brendon 'Rethinking Lean Service', *Proceedings LERC Annual Conference*, Celtic Manor Resort, 7 July 2007

1.9 The Service Junction

The Service Junction is where two streams or supply chains converge and then proceed together. The streams are those of the service supplier and the service customer. After the junction the supplier and customer streams may merge into a longer term relationship where, for instance, the supplier continues to provide maintenance or insurance over an extended period.

The concept presented here is a means to view the complete customer-supplier system in context. This may reveal present and future opportunities and problems. From a system perspective, this analysis should ask 'what is the appropriate boundary of involvement?' How much do we need to prepare for the customer, should we involve the customer earlier, and how long should we aim to keep in touch with the customer after the transaction.

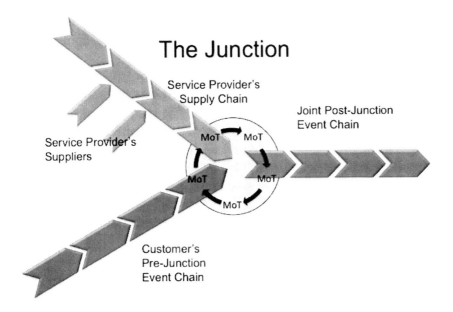

The Supplier stream is about preparation or anticipation. It contains all the steps that the service provider takes prior to meeting the customer. For example, forms may be prepared, restaurant tables laid, hotel rooms made up, or course notes prepared. These steps can be mapped to improve efficiency or effectiveness.

The Customer stream is about need, exploration, and encouragement. It contains all the steps that the customer takes prior to the actual transaction with the service provider. Before the junction, along this stream, it is primarily information provision – there is no commitment. The service provider may assist the customer in recognizing a need or encourage the customer to make use of a service. Many of these activities would be called 'service marketing'. Well known examples include web sites, unsolicited promotions, and loyalty cards. More subtle activities include amazon's 'customers also bought' notices, aircraft engine automatic monitoring, and the Apple computer screen that first comes up when you log onto the Safari web browser. These activities can be mapped or at least listed to improve effectiveness.

At the junction there is interaction between customer and service supplier often leading to commitment on both sides. The commitment may be to take a flight, eat at a restaurant, book for a cinema, consult with a solicitor, or go through an on-line purchase. Here the detailed activities will be of the transactional, interactive, custom, or idealized type as explained at length in Part 3 of this book.

In addition, capacity, queuing and utilization considerations are relevant at the junction. Here, Kingman's equation as explained in Part 1 will be insightful.

The meeting at the junction will be either an encounter or a relationship. An encounter is usually between strangers or systems that may never meet again. It is essentially for the exchange of goods or services. Efficiency is a prime concern. Standardization will often be used. Here there will often not be a continuing linkage between customer and service provider. Although warranties and maintenance contracts will have to be honored there will be no continuing link beyond the life of the product. Here, activities downstream of the junction will be concerned primarily with meeting obligations. However, encounters can lead to word-of-mouth recommendations that initiate activities along the customer stream by other customers.

By contrast, a relationship continues beyond the current activity. There may, for instance, be multiple visits to the same hotel, supermarket, computer store, bookstore, solicitor, alumni group or whatever. Efficiency is of concern, but it is the longer term value or satisfaction that a customer gets from multiple interactions that is of prime concern. Wealth is generated over the long term. Here, activities downstream of the junction will be particularly important.

Upstream Opportunities: Suppliers

Since preparation for the meeting with the customer is what this segment is about, the principles of changeover reduction are useful. (Changeover reduction is discussed in Part 4.) The analogy is with a Formula 1 pit stop change. Here the maximum amount of preparation is done before the car stops. Preparation is called 'external time', when the car is in the pits it is 'internal' time. Internal time is waste to the car or customer and should be minimized. List or map all the activities that are involved at the junction – when the supplier meets the customer. Then shift as many of these 'internal' activities to 'external' as possible without compromising the encounter or relationship.

But beware of 'over standardization' – for example excessive automated voice response or scripting. This can only cause failure demand.

There may be other preparation opportunities. For instance:
- Painting your airplane for fun such as Kalula airways does.
- Exclusive 'pink taxis' for women only, driven by women.
- Asking hotel or restaurant bookers about special occasions and then delivering appropriate 'delighters'.
- For repeat customers, making check-in fast or preparing a hotel room for specific customer requirements, like remembering the type of pillow.
- Making checklists, as is standard practice for airline pilots and, increasingly doctors. (Atul Gawande in his wonderful book on Checklists explains that it is not a question of training or competence, but simply forgetting to do a myriad of things when there is complexity and or pressure.) Gawande makes a powerful case for checklists to be used in many situations.

Strangely, providing less for less may also be attractive. Ryanair and Easyjet have gained many customers this way. Minimalist hotels and car hire are also examples.

Upstream Opportunities: Suppliers of Suppliers

There may be opportunity for suppliers suppliers to give an improved service. For instance, a laundry service could supply towels directly to gym users, or a laundry a direct service to hotel guests bypassing the hotel. Cleaning can be subcontracted, breakdown capacity can be subcontracted to local garages. Of course all these require quality checks.

Upstream Opportunities: Customers:

Of course, many upstream devices have been aound 'forever' – for instance a fuel gauge in a car. But IT has opened up many upstream customer opportunities. Some, for example with Apple computer and Amazon.com have been mentioned above. Loyalty cards are a 'big one' allowing Tesco to not only encourage repeat buying but also analyse individual customer needs. Cars, airplanes, even some appliances, warn their users about needed maintenance.

Inventory systems can warn customers 'you did not place your regular order' burglar alarm can inform the police directly, and 'sat nav' can warn about speed traps.

TRIZ is a fruitful source of upstream opportunity. The concept of 'self' is powerful – self serving, self adjusting, self booking, self ordering, self checking, self repair, self tuning, and more. Some TRIZ principles are also potent to many types of service. (These may also be applicable to the Supplier stream.)

- 'Take out' – remove a part or function
- 'Merge' – two or more systems
- 'Other Way Around' – reverse a sequence
- 'Change a Parameter' – change shape, size, format, speed.

Downstream Opportunities.

After the junction, there are many ways to maintain relationships or even to change the nature of the service. (Professor Scott Sampson of BYU refers to this as 'Serviceization'). Examples:

- Rolls Royce has moved towards 'power by the hour' whereby RR jet engine users pay by usage rather than up-front. The engines may remain the property of Rolls. This introduces a whole new tranche of responsibilities.
- Train the users of a product in its use.
- End-to-end package holidays. Pay up front and 'everything is free' – all you do is sit, eat, sleep and be taken (!!!)
- Alumni Groups. Yes, you get a degree, but you also get into networking and exclusive refresher activities.

To summarise: Much of this book is taken up by analysis and improvement at the junction between customer and service provider. This section asks about expanding the scope to include many more opportunities to enhance customer experience.

Further reading

A related concept is discussed by Scott Sampson of Brigham Young University. It is called PCN or Process Chain Network diagrams. See Scott Sampson, *Understanding Service Businesses*, Wiley, 2005

Further Reading on Part One

Russell Ackoff has written several relevant texts including: *Management in Small Doses; Ackoff's Fables; Beating the System; Management Flaws, Creating the Corporate Future* (to name a few!)

Russell Ackoff, *The Art of Problem Solving*, Wiley, 1978

Chris Argyris, *Teaching Smart People How to Learn*. Harvard Business Review Classics, Boston, 2008

Clayton Christensen, *The Innovator's Solution*, Harvard Business School Press, 2003

Manuel Fernandes, 'The Importance of Value for Business Strategic Management', *Value World*, Vol 30, No 3, Fall 2007

Atul Gawande, *The Checklist Manifesto*, Profile Books, 2010

George Gonzales-Rivas and Linus Larsson, *Far from the Factory*, CRC Productivity Press, 2010

Paul Hawken, Amory Lovins and L Hunter Lovins, *Natural Capitalism*, Little, Brown 1999

H Thomas Johnson and Anders Bröms, *Profit Beyond Measure*, Nicholas Brealey, London, 2000

Darrell Mann, *Hands-on Systematic Innovation*, IFR Press, 2004

Mark Moore and Sanjeev Khagram, *On Creating Public Value*, Working Paper, Harvard University, Kennedy School Of Government, 2004

Jinichiro Nakane and Robert Hall, 'Ohno's Method', *Target*, First Quarter, 2002

Jeffrey Pfeffer, *What Were They Thinking?*, Harvard Business School Press, 2007

Phil Rosenzweig, *The Halo Effect*, Free Press, 2007

Michael Saliba and Caroline Fisher, 'Managing Customer Value', *Quality Progress*, June 2000, pp. 63-69

Louis Savary and Clare Crawford-Mason, *The Nun and The Bureaucrat*, CC-M Productions, 2006 (an excellent book on systems!)

Peter Scholtes, *The Leader's Handbook*, McGraw Hill, New York, 1998

Richard Schonberger, *World Class Manufacturing: The Next Decade*, Free Press, 1996

John Seddon, *Freedom from Command and Control*, Vanguard, 2003

Dean Spitzer, *Transforming Performance Measurement*, AmaCom, 2007

Thomas Stewart and Anand Raman, 'Lessons from Toyota's Long Drive: HBR Interview with Katsuaki Watanabe', *Harvard Business Review*, July August 2007.

James Womack and Daniel Jones, *Lean Thinking*, revised edition, Free Press, 2003

Jim Womack, *The Perfect Process*, Presentation, AME Conference, Chicago, 2002

Valerie Zeithaml, Mary Jo Bitner and Dwayne Gremler, *Services Marketing*, 4th edition, McGraw Hill, 2006

See www.steveblank.com

Part 2   Major Concepts and Models

2.1   Lean Concepts relevant to Service

Value, Purpose, Root Definition, Function, and IFR were introduced in an earlier section. Here we home in on other key Lean concepts.

2.1.1 Gemba and Learning to See

'Gemba' is the place of action – where value is created – often but not necessarily the workplace. But this Japanese word has taken on significance far beyond its literal translation. Taiichi Ohno, legendary Toyota engineer and father of TPS, said, 'Management begins at the workplace'. This whole philosophy can best be captured by the single word: Gemba.

Contrast the Gemba way with the traditional (Western?) way. The Gemba way is to go to the place of action and collect the FACTS. The traditional way is to remain in the office and to discuss OPINIONS. Or worse, review financial KPIs. Gemba can be thought of in terms of the 'four actuals': go to the actual workplace, look at the actual process and observe what is actually happening (gembutsu) and collect the actual data (genjitsu).

Gemba is also a learning-to-see approach to daily work. As you walk around, question what you see. For instance:

- Is it really necessary to have work so spread out, to be done by several people, from several sections?
- Is it really necessary to fill in all those forms? Can they be pre-prepared? Why is it that at check-in or checkout there are so many keyboard strokes?
- Why are customers asked to sign next to the 'X' agreeing that they know all the conditions, when reading them through would take half an hour?
- Can customers (or patients) wait in more comfortable conditions? Why do they have to wait in line anyway? Can they not be called when needed?
- Why are there interruptions in the middle of the process, leading to start-up losses?
- If there was a 'near miss' don't just sigh with relief, try to put in place preventive measures.
- Is a one-stop procedure, or a cell, possible?
- What is the root cause of the problem? Don't just do a patch-up job, but ask if the cause can be eliminated.

None of these questions can be effectively asked or answered by managers sitting at their desks. A questioning culture is only possible if you are at Gemba. So Gemba breaks away from the 'it's not my problem' and 'I only work here' attitude. It is the managers' fault if workers have such attitudes. What can be done to empower employees to make immediate improvements?

Under Gemba, if your organisation has a problem or a decision, go to Gemba first. Do not attempt to resolve problems away from the place of action. Do not let operators come to the manager, let the manager go to the workplace. Spend time at the service counter. This is the basis of so much Japanese management practice: new Honda management recruits spend time working in assembly and in stores; marketers from Nikon spend time working in camera shops, Toyota sends its Lexus design team to live in California for three months, and so on.

Ohno was famous for his 'chalk circle' approach - drawing a circle in chalk on the factory floor and requiring a manager to spend several hours inside it while observing operations, noticing variation, and taking note of wastes. The West too has its devotees. John Sainsbury, who ran the supermarket chain in its heyday, could pass a shelf and see at a glance if prices were wrong. His retirement may account for the decline of a once-great chain. An open plan office, with senior management sitting right there with 'the troops', is Gemba.

Gemba is, or should be, part of implementation. How often is the Western way based on 'change agents', on simulation, on computers or information systems, on classroom-based education? These have a place, of course, but Gemba emphasises implementation by everyone, at the workplace, face-to-face, based on in-depth knowledge. And low cost, no cost solutions rather than big-scale expensive information or technology solutions.

Gemba is often combined with other elements: the Five Whys, Muda (or waste), Policy Deployment, Kaizen, 5S, Seven Tools, and it is a central part of Total Quality. Gemba is a common theme in all of these. So today we hear of 'Gemba Kanri', 'Gemba Kaizen', and 'Gemba TPM'. The word has already appeared in English and American dictionaries.

Finally, let us remind ourselves that Gemba is not a 'Japanese thing'. The Japanese learned it from the Americans – specifically the famous Hawthorne experiments at General Electric in the 1930s. One study concerned the effects of lighting on productivity. Turn up the lights, productivity improves. Turn up the lights further, productivity improves further. Now turn down the lights. What happens? Productivity improves! What was happening was that workers were responding not to lighting levels but to the interest being taken in them by heavyweight researchers. This became known as the Hawthorne Effect. The West promptly forgot the lesson. The Japanese took it on. So, don't sit in your office looking at your Excel spreadsheet and imagine that you are improving productivity – that is management by looking in the rear view mirror. Instead, 'get your butt to the Gemba', and learn to anticipate problems. Actually, the Hawthorne story is an over simplification. In fact, workers were changed during the course of the studies, and Elton Mayo was accused of fudging the results. Nevertheless, the 'gemba' lesson remains.

Further Reading: Masaaki Imai, *Gemba Kaizen*, McGraw-Hill, New York, 1997

2.1.2 Service, Kaizen, and Kata

Many companies find that the biggest test during their Lean transformation is engaging employees in the daily habit of continuous improvement. 40 years ago at Toyota Ohno recognised how vital this is – he stated that "the heart of TPS is management's commitment to empowering employees with the daily practice of continuous improvement".

The concept of bringing about change and improvement by establishing a regular pattern of activity finds strong support both in Lean literature and in other writing. Repetition, learning, small steps, often bottom-up, are recurring themes.

For this to happen service managers are required to help to put it in place:

- Procedures or systems that allow problems (deviations from expected outcomes, or not getting it right the first time) to be identified or 'surfaced' quickly. This may be by visual management boards, complaints, or quick feedback from front line staff.
- Giving front-line staff the authority to resolve or at least mollify customer issues in a one-stop procedure. This would almost certainly involve an apology, which defuses many situations. Beyond this, to define the boundaries within which staff can put in place a temporary fix. Such actions win customer loyalty. Note: this is not 'empowerment' that suggests giving up some authority in a command and control hierarchy, but working together for improvement.
- Addressing accumulations of such problems by identifying routinely, as far as possible, root causes and putting in place countermeasures. Doing this reduces failure demand and thereby frees up capacity to give even better service.

So: Surface > Mollify > Root Cause > Improve

- **David Mann** speaks about the importance of 'Leader Standard Work' whereby change and improvement is process – rather than person-dependent. The process involves a regular, layered sequence, leading to continuous improvement through learning:

  o Team leaders check on possible problems more than once an hour. Note: this is not checking against targets but helping to identify and resolve problems.
  o Supervisors check with team leaders three or four times a day, and hold daily review meetings with all their team leaders gathered around a performance board showing problems and misses. Note, once again, not focused on adherence to targets but on the surfacing of issues.
  o Supervisors talk regularly with value stream managers for any necessary follow-up actions.

In other words, leader standard work is a way to 'surface' issues continually and resolve them quickly. See the section on Leader Standard Work below.

- **Mike Rother**, in his groundbreaking book *Toyota Kata,* and at presentations in Cardiff, speaks about how Toyota creates an improvement mindset by a regular routine. The analogy is with a Karate Kata exercise whereby reflexes or mental models become automatic and embedded in the brain by doing the process over and over again. Research shows that the brain's synapses take time to build paths but these become the dominant, natural way. The key is repetition. This is also discipline. The improvement kata relates to 'how people should go about understanding a situation and developing solutions'. This is not the usual 'Western' way of jumping to answers and solutions, but is about learning. It is encapsulated in the statement, 'The original condition was x. We set a target condition of y. We achieved z, and learned the following in the process.' (Toyota Kata, page 163.) Note that 'target condition' is not a target measure (often sucked out of the air) but a forecast of a future condition based on current knowledge.

Kata is not a method to solve problems but learning and practising a methodology that can be used to move forward. The methodology becomes ingrained. This is very much in line with Steve Spear.

- **Steve Spear**, in his book *Chasing the Rabbit*, (now renamed *The High Velocity Edge*) discusses a relentless method of closing the knowledge gap. There is much we don't know about systems. If you have 'no problem' that is the problem! Forecast expected outcomes or conditions, and then seek to explain any difference between what we expect and what we get. This is 'proper' SDSA as put forward by Deming. Once again, it is a mindset thing. Don't just 'solve problems' but seek to learn what you did not understand. So, it is not good enough to just improve – even if you did better than expected. The point is, why did you do better or worse; what was it that you did not fully understand or anticipate? Once again, real improvement takes place by questioning, not by giving answers. This procedure chimes in well with David Mann and with Mike Rother both of whom advocate relentless daily incremental improvement, whether by leader standard work or 'kata'.
  In fact, all three advocate Deming.

- **Deming**, of course, spoke about the Plan Do Study Act cycle. This is often misunderstood. To Plan you will need first to understand. (Hence, John Seddon's methodology starts with 'Check'.) But a plan is an expectation. Then you 'do'. Then you study and learn, and put in place lessons through 'act'. So, this is NOT: make a plan, do it, check the results against some arbitrary target, then reward and punish! A point here is that SDSA becomes the way of life, the way we do things around here every day.

- **Tony Schwartz**, in Harvard Business Review, discusses how Sony Pictures achieved big productivity gains by allowing employees to 'increase their effectiveness by practising simple rituals that refuel their energy, such as taking a daily walk to get an emotional breather or turning off e mail at prescribed times so they can concentrate'. And by encouraging 'employees to create and stick to such rituals, (organisations) will be rewarded with a more engaged, productive and focused workforce.

- **Malcolm Gladwell** in *Outliers* (and echoed by David Shenk) has discussed how true mastery is achieved by the '10,000 hour rule' of practice, with DNA playing a much reduced, but over-emphasised, role. In short, repetition. Gladwell gives a table of 75 inventors and business people to illustrate his point. It takes time, patience but also persistence. In fact, Samuel Smiles identified these three, in his 1854 book *Self Help* that apparently had a profound influence on Toyota's founder Sakichi Toyoda. As Smiles said, 'genius is patience and persistence'.

- **Ohno** stated that the essence of TPS is developing within each employee a "kaizen consciousness" (opportunity awareness). TPS experts view Lean transformation as changing the thought process of every employee. Becoming Lean to them is about improving organisation performance, seeing problems, solving them the right way, and in doing so continually increasing the intellectual capital and skill of all members of the company. Tapping and evolving the creativity of every employee, if properly cultivated and directed, has unlimited potential.

  But note, Ohno's "kaizen consciousness" is not just doing occasional, or even frequent, kaizen events between which times no improvement takes place. The Entropy principle (every system degrades with time) means that by so doing you will be slipping back. Ohno intended that improvements take place by everyone, every day. This means a continual flow of ideas, nearly all of them very small but having large cumulative effect. A "kaizen consciousness" is a "mindset thing".

This brings us to Kaizen. The literal translation of Kaizen is 'small change for the better'. Real kaizen is about small change. By contrast, many a Western organisation and its managers favour big, bold, dramatic, top down driven change. But it is often not successful.

Why is Kaizen or small change so effective? Because small changes:

- Are non-threatening, to employees and to their managers;
- Are immediate – often, no report has first to be written, or permission obtained;
- Lead to habit;
- Build confidence – employees build their confidence about problem solving and improvement, but so too do managers learn about the good ideas of their staff;

- Linked with ritual – as discussed above, ritual may include daily issue surfacing or developing a 'questioning culture';
- Many small ideas, implemented, lead, over time, to big change;
- Kaizen involves or 'empowers' staff – there is much talk about 'empowerment' but how do you do that? By Kaizen, by the methods outlined above. An announcement such as 'now you are empowered, we expect big things from you' is very threatening and doomed to fail;
- Less fear of failure – if you fail, it is not a 'big deal': learn from your mistakes;
- Reduces stress – it IS stressful for a manager to be required to make big changes or big cuts. So, start small. There is the 'How do you eat an elephant?' story. Certainly not in one bite!
- Encourages experimentation – you can try out small changes, whereas big change may lead to 'paralysis by analysis'. There is the story of the drunk looking for something he has lost. So he looks under the light because, he says, that is where he can see best even though that is not where it was lost. A big change requirement sometimes elicits a looking-under-the-light response.

Robert Maurer, a psychologist and clinical professor, explains in his wonderful little book, *One Small Step Can Change Your Life*, why kaizen works. He shows it this way:

- Large goal > fear > access to cortex restricted > failure
- Small goal > fear bypassed > cortex engaged > success.

Maurer explains that the brain is programmed against big change. The much older mid-brain enjoys priority over the newer cortex. The cortex is where rational thought and creativity lie, but the mid brain is to do with fight-or-flight survival. It sets off alarm bells whenever we want to make a departure from our usual safe routines. Large issues or changes are seen as threatening. A defence mechanism kicks in which over-rides logic. 'Your brain loves small questions' – hence puzzles. But big questions such as 'What new products are needed?' are threatening, and the barriers instantly rise.

What should be done? Building on Maurer and the authors mentioned earlier:

- Ask little questions.
- Set small goals.
- Solve small problems.
- Learn to see small opportunities at the gemba. There is the story of 'What is the colour of the car parked next to yours?' Generally you will get this wrong (panic?) when asked the first time. But when asked every day the correct answer becomes routine. You 'learn to see', as Mike Rother says.
- A Toyota style organisation structure that makes small ideas easy to put forward and implement – as explained by David Mann and Leader Standard Work (LSW).
- Argue against a corporate culture that says that only top-down is worthwhile.
- Learn to anticipate. This is in line with Spear and Deming, above.

- Break work and problems down into segments. Rather than debating yes or no to whether NHS spending should be 'ring-fenced' it is better to collect many small ideas on where savings can be made and where is there waste.
- Small ideas repeated often have much better retention, especially when practised rather than spoken about. Here, think of Western style cramming for exams, only to forget everything soon after.
- Don't keep problems to yourself. Maurer is a clinical psychologist and begins working with stressed patients by getting them to take small steps, like writing in a journal for just two minutes each day and phoning in, and then progressing to more and more contact. Tidy your desk? Too big a change! But can you spend just one minute a day tidying your desk? Much less threatening. Then repetition kicks in and establishes the 'kata' that Mike Rother speaks about.

TWI Job Methods is a proven, effective method for improvement. (The TWI trilogy of instruction JI, method JM, and job relations JR form a systems approach to supervision that is discussed elsewhere in the book). Here every step of a job is listed and Kipling's '6 Honest serving men' questions (what, why, when, where, how, who) are systematically applied. Invariably this leads to a huge number of small improvements. These can be the basis for a 'Kaizen Event', for idea management, or for continuous improvement in general.

Rewards and Kaizen

The problem of extrinsic rewards, especially big rewards, is that they give the impression that only big advances are worthwhile. So give recognition for little ideas. Thanks have been shown to be much more effective than monetary reward, but if you must give an extrinsic reward give a luxury item rather than cash – assuming that basic salary is adequate.

There are several reasons why suggestion schemes are often a failure in the west, but successful in Japan; an important reason is to do with expectation. In the west small ideas are thought to be not good, not worthwhile, only acted on if there is a good return on investment. In Japan there is a culture that says that ALL ideas are good because this encourages even more ideas to come forward. Another reason suggestion schemes may not work is poor ability to communicate and process ideas. Ideas should be progressed quickly, displayed on a board and shared with everybody, and their progress clearly indicated.

Further Reading

David Mann, *Creating a Lean Culture*, Productivity Press, 2005 (Second edition, 2010, is more relevant for office and administration tasks.)
Steven Spear, *Chasing the Rabbit*, McGraw Hill, 2009
Mike Rother, *Toyota Kata*, McGraw Hill, 2010
Tony Schwartz, 'The Productivity Paradox: How Sony Pictures Gets More out of People by Demanding Less', *Harvard Business Review*, June 2010, page 65-69
Malcolm Gladwell, *Outliers*, Penguin, 2008
David Shenk, *The Genius in All of Us*, Icon Books, 2010
Robert Maurer, *One Small Step Can Change Your Life, Workman, 2004*

2.1.3 Waste (Muda)

'Muda' is Japanese for waste. Waste is strongly linked to Lean. But waste elimination is a means of achieving the Lean ideal – it is not an end in itself.

Waste prevention is at least as important as waste elimination.

Value is the converse of waste. Any organisation needs continually to improve the ratio of value adding to non-value adding activities. There are two ways to do this – by preventing and reducing waste, but also by specifically going after value enhancement.

Taiichi Ohno, (or possibly Shigeo Shingo) father of the Toyota Production System (TPS), of JIT, and patriarch of Lean Operations, originally assembled the Seven Wastes, but it was Deming who emphasised waste reduction in Japan in the 1950s. Today, however, it is appropriate to add to Ohno's / Shingo's famous list, presumptuous though that may be. The section after next begins with the original seven, then adds 'new' wastes for manufacturing and service.

But TPS refers to the trilogy of 'Muda, Mura and Muri', emphasising their interconnection. Their interconnection is brilliantly shown through Kingman's equation on queuing – discussed in an earlier section. Mura refers to unevenness. Muri refers to 'overburden' – loading a service operator with excessive work that results in delay and dissatisfaction.

Type 1 and Type 2 Muda: Elimination and Prevention

Womack and Jones talk usefully about two types of waste.

Type 1 Muda is activities which create no value but are currently necessary to maintain operations. These activities do not do anything for customers, but may well assist the managers or stakeholders other than customers or shareholders. Type 1 should be reduced through simplification. It may well prove to be the greatest bottom-line benefit of Lean. Moreover, Type 1 Muda is the easiest to add to but difficult to remove, so prevention of Type 1 Muda should be in the mind of every manager in every function.

Type 2 Muda creates no value, in fact destroys value, for any stakeholder, including customers, shareholders, and employees. Elimination should be a priority. Type 2 tends to grow by 'stealth', or carelessness.

Waste Elimination is achieved, as Dan Jones would say, both by 'wearing muda spectacles', a skill that must be developed since EVERYONE is almost blind to noticing routine, unchanged methods and objects – it is the way that the brain copes with variety, and by kaizen – both 'point' and 'flow' varieties. Elimination or reduction is assisted by 5S activities, standard work, mapping, level scheduling and by amplification reduction. Ohno was said to require new managers to spend several hours in a chalk circle, standing in one place and observing waste. This should happen more frequently in offices, in warehouses, and in factories.

Waste Prevention is another matter. Womack and Jones talk about the eighth waste – making the wrong product perfectly – but it goes beyond that. Waste prevention cannot be done by wearing muda spectacles, but requires strong awareness of system, process, and product design. It is known that perhaps 80% of costs are fixed at the design stage. Of that 80%, a good proportion will be waste. System design waste prevention involves thinking through the movement of information, products and customers through the future system. For instance, questioning the necessity for ERP and the selection of far-removed suppliers from a total perspective, and removing layers in a supply chain. Process design waste prevention involves the avoidance of 'monuments', the elimination of adjustments, and working with future customers and suppliers to ensure that future processes are as waste-free as possible. For instance, incorporating flexible service workers in a flexible layout. Prevention involves much more careful pre-design considerations. It also involves keeping options open via 'mass customisation' and recycling considerations. Of course, pokayoke is a prime technique for defect prevention in service and manufacturing.

In my opinion, waste prevention is likely to assume a far greater role than waste elimination in the Lean organisation of the future – in the same way that prevention in Quality is now widely regarded as more effective than inspection and fault elimination.

Value Added, Non-Value Added; Avoidable and Not Avoidable; Organisation Value Added and Organisation Non-Value Added

In Lean manufacturing the terms 'value adding', 'non-value adding' and 'necessary non-value adding' is widespread, meaningful, and useful. Abbreviate these to VA, NVA, and NNVA. Value added activity is something that the customer is prepared to pay for. In some types of service, for example healthcare and holidays, the customer is certainly prepared to pay for activities, so VA, NVA and NNVA designations are useful.

In other types of service and administration, for example many clerical procedures, you may argue that the customer is not prepared to pay. Yet to call activities NNVA can be both unhelpful (since everything is NNVA) and demotivating to employees. How would you like to spend most of your life doing necessary non-value added work?

In such situations it may be more useful, and clearer, to talk about 'Not Avoidable' and 'Avoidable' work. A problem here is negative connotation, and the abbreviation NA can be confused with not applicable!

Yet another alternative is to refer to Organisation Value Added (OVA) and Organisation Non-Value Added (ONVA). Here it is probably not helpful to talk about Organisation Necessary Non-Value Added – so this will not be used.

Shingo's Seven Wastes

A section on the wastes should begin with a great big warning. Do not go out and look for the Seven Wastes or the service wastes, or whatever, as a checklist. Doing so IS waste! Instead, take time to think about the customer's needs and the purpose of the system – then identify your own appropriate kinds of waste that are preventing the system reaching its ideal state. You can use the lists that follow as a prompt or as a source of some possible ideas.

An important point is that, in reducing waste, we are not concerned with the speeding up or efficiency of value adding steps. Waste is what happens BETWEEN the value adding steps.

Another important point is that waste reduction is about doing things right. But doing things right should always be subservient to doing the right things. As Ackoff, quoting Drucker, said, 'the righter you do the wrong things, the wronger you become'.

Shingo's Seven Wastes were originally for manufacturing. However, they do have application in many types of service. As ever, in translating manufacturing concepts to service – beware!

You can remember the Seven Wastes by asking, 'Who is TIM WOOD?' Answer: Transport, Inventory, Motion, Waiting, Overproduction, Over-processing, and Defects. This idea came from the Lean Office at Cooper Standard, Plymouth, UK.

In all these wastes, the priority is to avoid, only then to cut.

The Waste of Overproduction

Shingo believed that the waste of overproduction was the most serious of all the wastes because it was the root of so many problems and other wastes. In many types of service this remains true. Overproduction is making too much, too early or 'just-in-case'. The aim should be to make or do or serve exactly what is required, no more and no less, just in time and with perfect quality. Overproduction discourages a smooth flow of goods or services. 'Lumpiness' (i.e. making products or working in erratic bursts) is a force against quality and productivity. By contrast, regularity encourages a 'no surprises' atmosphere that may not be very exciting but is much better management.

Overproduction leads directly to excessive lead time, for example when processing and passing on files in batches rather than one at a time. As a result defects may not be detected early, products may deteriorate, and artificial pressures on work rate may be generated. All these increase the chances of defects. Overproduction also impacts on the waste of motion – making and moving things that are not immediately required.

Yet overproduction is often the natural state. People do not have to be encouraged to overproduce; they often do so 'just to be safe'. Often this is reinforced by a bonus system which encourages output that is not needed. By contrast, a pull system helps to prevent unplanned overproduction by allowing work to move forwards only when the next work area is ready to receive it. Hamburgers are only made at a rate in line with demand and clerical operations are most effective when there is a uniform flow of work. The motto 'Sell daily? Make daily!' is as relevant in an office as it is in a factory.

Overproduction should be related to a particular timeframe – first reduce overproduction (or early delivery) in a week, then a day, then an hour.

The Waste of Waiting

The waste of waiting is probably the second most important waste. It is directly relevant to FLOW. In Lean we are more concerned with flow of service or customers than we are with keeping operators busy.

In an office, any time a customer or customer item is seen to be not moving or not having value added is an indication of waste. Waiting is the enemy of smooth flow. Although it may be very difficult to reduce waiting to zero, the goal remains. Whether the waiting is for the delivery of a spare part or of customers in a bank there should always be an awareness of a non-ideal situation and a questioning of how the situation can be improved. Waiting is directly relevant to lead time – an important source of competitiveness and customer satisfaction. However, remember that because an item or customer is moving it does not necessarily follow that value is being added.

A bottleneck operation that is waiting for work is a waste. As Goldratt has pointed out in his book *The Goal*, 'an hour lost at a bottleneck is an hour lost for the whole plant'. Effective use of bottleneck time is a key to regular work, which in turn strongly influences productivity and quality.

The Waste of Unnecessary Motions

Next in importance is probably the waste of motion. Unnecessary motions refer to both human and layout. The human dimension relates to the importance of ergonomics for quality and productivity and the enormous proportion of time wasted at *every* workstation by non-optimal layout. A QWERTY keyboard, for example, is non-optimal. If operators have to stretch, bend, pick up, move in order to see better, or in any way unduly exert themselves, the victim is immediately the operator but ultimately quality and the customer.

An awareness of the ergonomics of the workplace is not only ethically desirable, but economically sound. Toyota, famous for its quality, is known to place a high importance on 'quality of worklife'. Toyota encourages all its employees to be aware of working conditions that contribute to this form of waste. Today, of course, motion waste is also a health and safety issue.

The layout dimension involves poor workplace arrangement, leading to micro wastes of movement. These wastes are often repeated many, many times per day – sometimes without anyone noticing. In this regard 5S (see later section) can be seen as the way to attack motion waste.

The Waste of Transporting

Customers do not pay to have goods moved around unless they have hired a removal service! So any movement of materials or information is waste. It is a waste that can never be fully eliminated but it is also one that should be continually reduced over time. The number of transport and material handling operations is directly proportional to the likelihood of damage and deterioration. Double handling is a waste that affects productivity and quality.

Transporting is closely linked to communication. Where distances are long, communication is discouraged and quality may be the victim. In service there is the rule of thumb that communication falls off sharply beyond about 5 metres. Feedback on poor quality is inversely related to transportation length, whether in manufacturing or in services. There is increasing awareness that for improved quality in manufacturing or services, people from interacting groups need to be located physically closer together. For instance, the design office may be deliberately placed near to the production area.

As this waste is recognised steps can be taken to reduce it. Measures include monitoring the flow lengths of paper through an office or the distance a customer needs to walk while catching a plane. The number of steps, and in particular the number of non-value adding steps, should be monitored.

The Waste of Processing
(or Inappropriate Processing)

Inappropriate processing refers to the waste of 'using a hammer to crack a nut'. Think of a mainframe computer rather than distributed PCs, or a large central photocopier instead of distributed machines. But further, think of a large aircraft requiring passengers to travel large distances to and from a regional airport. Thinking in terms of one big machine instead of several smaller ones discourages operator 'ownership', leads to pressure to run the machine as often as possible rather than only when needed, and discourages general purpose flexible machines. It also leads to poor layout, which as we have seen in the previous section, leads to extra transportation and poor communication. So the ideal is to use the smallest machine capable of producing the required quality, distributed to the points of use.

Inappropriate processing also refers to machines and processes that are not Quality capable: in other words, a process that cannot help but make defects. In general, a capable process requires the correct methods and training, as well as the necessary standards, clearly known.

Note that it is important to take the longer-term view. Buying that large bottleneck 'machine' (photocopier? kitchen? hospital scanner? air terminal?) may just jeopardise the possibility of flow for many years to come, for both customers and employees. Think 'small is beautiful'. Smaller machines avoid bottlenecks, improve flow lengths, are perhaps simpler, can be maintained at different times instead of affecting the whole plant, and may improve cash flow and keep up with technology – buying one small machine per year, instead of one big machine every five years.

The Waste of Unnecessary Inventory

Inventory is relevant in many types of service. Although having no inventory is a goal that can never be attained, inventory is the enemy of quality and productivity. It is so because inventory tends to increase lead time, prevents rapid identification of problems, and increases space, thereby discouraging communication. The true cost of extra inventory is very much in excess of the money tied up in it. 'Push' systems almost invariably lead to this waste.

There are three types of inventory: raw material, work in process, and end items. The existence of any of these is waste, but their root causes and priorities for reduction are different. End items must sometimes be held to meet variation in customer demand, but excessive inventory is waste. It also represents risk of obsolescence. Raw material may be temporarily necessary due to supplier constraints – quality and reliability. WIP or distribution inventories need to move through the supply chain as fast as is feasible. A section in this book is given to inventory considerations.

The Waste of Defects

The last but not least of Shingo's wastes is the waste of defects. Defects cost money, both immediate and longer term. In Quality Costing the failure or defect categories are internal failure (scrap, rework, delay) and external failure (including warranty, repairs, field service, but also possible lost custom). Bear in mind that defect costs tend to escalate the longer they remain undetected. Thus a fault in a microchip discovered when it is made might cost just a few dollars to replace, but if it reaches the customer it may cost hundreds to replace using field service, to say nothing of customer goodwill. So, central themes of total quality are 'prevention not detection', 'quality at source', and 'the chain of quality'. The Toyota philosophy is that a defect should be regarded as a challenge, as an opportunity to improve, rather than something to be traded off against what is ultimately poor management. In service, 'defects' include a variety of types including product defects, errors made by the server, and errors made by the customer.

More recently, 'zero defections' has become a powerful theme, recognising that the value of a retained customer increases with time.

The New Wastes

These may be added to Shingo's original list, and are appropriate in service and manufacturing:

The Waste of Making the Wrong Product Efficiently

This is Womack and Jones' eighth waste. It is really a restatement of the first Lean principle. Doing the right things.

The Waste of Untapped Human Potential

Ohno was reported to have said that the real objective of the Toyota Production System was 'to create thinking people' (TPS = Thinking People System). So this 'new' waste is directly linked to Ohno. The 1980s were the decade of factory automation folly. GM and many others learnt the hard and expensive way that the automated factory and warehouse that does not benefit from continuous improvement and on-going thought is doomed in the productivity race.

Today we have numerous examples, from total quality to self-directed work teams, of the power of utilising the thoughts of all employees, not just managers. Human potential does not just need to be set free. It requires clear communication as to what is needed both from management and to management, it requires commitment and support, because uncapping human potential is sometimes seen as a real threat to first line and middle managers, and it requires a culture of trust and mutual respect which can be won, not by mere lofty words, but by example, interest and involvement at the workplace (Gemba). Basic education is also necessary. The answer to the question, 'What happens if I train them and they go?' should be, 'What happens if you don't train them and they stay!'

Examples: not using the creative brainpower of employees, not listening, thinking that only managers have ideas worth pursuing.

The Waste of Inappropriate Systems

How much software in your computer is never used, not the packages but the actual code? The same goes for MRPII, now repackaged as ERP or CRM systems.

The Lean way is to remove waste before automating, or, as Michael Hammer would say, 'Don't automate, obliterate!' The waste of inappropriate systems should not be confined to computers and automation. How much record keeping, checking, reconciling, is pure waste? Recall the categories of waste.

Recently, for example in the Three Day Car project, the waste of inappropriate systems was highlighted when it was found that typical new car order to delivery time is seven weeks, of which less than a week is for manufacture. It's the order processing system, not the shopfloor, which is the greatest barrier. Often, it's not the operations which consume the time and the money: it's the paperwork or systems. And we now understand a little more of the dangers of demand amplification, of inappropriate forecasting, and of measurement systems that make people do what is best for them but not best for the company. All this is waste.

Wasted Energy and Water

Energy here refers to sources of power: electricity, gas, oil, coal, and so on. The world's finite resources of most energy sources (except sun and wind) were highlighted in a famous report, 'The Limits to Growth', written by the Club of Rome in 1970. Their dire predictions have not come to pass, but nevertheless the true impact of unwise energy use on the world's environments is growing. Wasting these resources is not only a significant source of cost for many companies, but there is also the moral obligation of using such resources wisely.

There is little doubt that this form of waste will escalate sharply up the priority list in the years ahead. Reducing these wastes is likely to have greater and greater financial impact – and moreover enjoys the support of everyone.

Although energy management systems in factory, office and home have grown in sophistication there still remains the human, common sense element: shutting down the machine, switching off the light, fixing the drip, insulating the roof, taking a full load, efficient routing, and the like. By the way, the JIT system of delivery (now used by Tesco) does not waste energy when done correctly: use 'milkrounds', dropping off small quantities to several shops in the same area, or rationalise suppliers to enable the collection of mixed loads daily rather than single products weekly.

Several companies that have 'institutionalised' waste reduction, Toyota included, believe that a good foundation for waste awareness begins with everyday wastes such as switching off lights and printers. You get into the habit.

Wasted Natural Resources

A most severe, and ever-more important waste is that of wasted natural resources. Hawkin, Lovins and Lovins of the Rocky Mountain Institute estimate that 99% of the original materials used in production of goods in the USA becomes waste within six weeks of sale. Robert (Doc) Hall points out that almost everything we own is en route to the tip. Paper is a case in point – the 'paperless office' is still a dream, in part because it has been a low priority. According to Lycra Research 1.5 trillion pages were printed in offices in 2006. In the US each person uses 320 kg of paper annually. Xerox found that Dow Chemical had 16,000 printers, producing 480m printouts per year at a cost of $100m over five years. By contrast Easy Jet is a paperless company – almost. Conservation begins with awareness and measures.

Today conservation of materials is not only environmentally responsible, but is beginning to be profitable. To reduce the waste of materials a life cycle approach is needed, to conserve materials during design, during manufacture, during customer usage, and beyond customer use in recycling. Of course, incentives such as pollution payments, commitment contracts, and voucher swops also have a role.

Seven Customer Service Wastes

Most of the above wastes are seen from the organisation's perspective. What about the customer's perspective? Perhaps an improvement programme should begin with the service customer wastes:

- **Delay** on the part of customers waiting for service, for delivery, in queues, for response, not arriving as promised. The customer's time may seem free to the provider, but when s/he takes custom elsewhere the pain begins.
- **Duplication**: having to re-enter data, repeat details on forms, copy information across, answer queries from several sources within the same organisation.
- **Unnecessary Movement**: queuing several times, lack of one-stop, poor ergonomics in the service encounter.
- **Unclear Communication** and the wastes of seeking clarification, confusion over product or service use, wasting time finding a location that may result in misuse or duplication.
- **Incorrect Inventory**: out-of-stock, unable to get exactly what was required, substitute products or services.
- **Opportunity Lost** to retain or win customers, failure to establish rapport, ignoring customers, unfriendliness, and rudeness.
- **Errors** in the service transaction, product defects in the product service bundle, lost or damaged goods.

Two Service Operations Wastes

Gonzalez-Rivas and Larsson give two types of waste that are pervasive in service and administration, but often go un-noticed.

- **Waste of multitasking,** which involves frequent stop-start. Like changeover in manufacturing, each stop-start involves losses for the stop itself and also start-up loss. Brain research shows each time concentration is broken, it takes around 15 minutes to restore performance to where it was. So each time an email notification flashes on your screen and you respond, restoration time is involved. But that is only the start. Where you work on more than one task simultaneously rather than sequentially, each task is likely to be delayed. Completion of the first will be delayed due to working on the other. A second task will also be delayed if you are also working on a third task. And so on. And it gets worse: some of the 'other' tasks are likely to be low importance, but urgent. These push out the high importance, less urgent. Eventually the high importance tasks have to be completed – but now in a reduced period of time, meaning that quality is likely to suffer.

In manufacturing there is often the temptation to just make another batch while the machine is set up. Some operators believe that this 'makes good sense'. But the consequence is that other jobs are delayed and inventory is built that may not be needed for some time. In service, inventory is information.

- **Waste of high utilisation** as discussed in the section on Muda, Muri and Mura: variation is 'a killer'. If there is no variation, queues do not accumulate. Thus with variation, 'efficiency' through higher utilisation is not effective. Recall delays at Heathrow airport where runway utilisation is in the high 90%'s. Efficiency (or 'savings') due to high utilisation needs to be set against penalties due to long delays. There is an optimal value, and it is well below 100% utilisation.

Fourteen Office Wastes

Office wastes are probably the most pervasive of all types of service waste. They are especially important in professional service functions such as accountancy, law, design and consulting engineering. Office managers need to foster an awareness of these office wastes among all staff, and be responsible for creating an environment where the wastes can be progressively eliminated. Office wastes are not driven out by imposing additional rules, measures and procedures, but by assisting, mentoring and questioning at 'Gemba'. The office wastes are given below. They are not mutually exclusive. Indeed, some are root cause of others. The list below can also be used with the later section on Total Productive Administration. All these wastes are, of course, particularly acute where there are bottleneck resources. The office manager's task, then, is to recognise and protect the bottleneck from these wastes.

- **Sorting and Searching**: looking for documents or computer files that have been temporarily misplaced or poorly located.
- **Inappropriate Measurement**: measures drive behaviour so inappropriate measures will drive inappropriate behaviour. Are the measures primarily to improve the customer system or to mollify the boss? Measures take time to collect, so at best their collection and analysis are necessary non-value added activity. Adding another measure seldom helps the system, but will certainly add to the workload and may encourage cheating and shortcuts. In service, beware of measuring unit costs. If the 'units' include rework and failure demand you may be getting worse when the measure says you are getting better. Moreover if unit cost

becomes a target, then all sorts of undesirable behaviour may be induced – for example a call centre recording a unit when saying, 'Hello and goodbye!'

- **Under-load**: 'Work will expand to fill the time available for its completion' (Northcote Parkinson). But worse, under-load may encourage the imposition of additional work on already busy people who are making a difference to the customer. This happens when under-loaded managers dream up new forms, procedures and measures. Ohno said, 'Excessive information must be suppressed'.
- **Overload**: Toyota's word for this is 'Muri' or overburden. See the section on queuing to appreciate the disastrous consequences in cases where work is fully loaded or even almost fully loaded.
- **Inappropriate prioritising:** Stephen Covey talks about a two-by-two matrix of urgency and importance, and points out the tendency to do the urgent but not important, rather than the important but not immediately urgent. We all get caught with this, and the office manager's role must be to monitor and protect. Many office managers are the source of activities that are urgent but not important.
- **Interference**: a variant on inappropriate prioritising – by emails, excessive socialising, dropping-in, and noise. One way around this is to set aside blocks of time where none of these activities is permitted.
- **Inappropriate frequency** is where activities such as meetings, reports, measures are performed more frequently than is necessary to achieve a good flow of work. Diminishing returns, or even negative returns, may occur with increasing frequency. This is perhaps a re-statement of Occam's razor: 'Entities should not be multiplied unnecessarily'.
- **Start up and End off**: work moves too slowly at the beginning of the day, or even after breaks, and slows down or stops too early at the end. The cause may be inadequate information or instruction.
- **Mistakes, Errors or Lack of Appropriate Knowledge** result in failure demand and so are a major source of reduced capacity. Recall Deming's '94/6 rule': most problems lie with the system, not the person.
- **Misunderstanding or communication errors** are the root of many of the other wastes. See the later section on the 'Gaps Model' where four gaps are described: between customer requirements and manager's perceptions of requirements, between perceptions and standards or instructions, between standards and execution of the service, and between execution and what is promised about the service.
- **Sub-optimisation** or improving the parts but not the whole is the essential 'systems' problem. Seeking to improve individual parts can sometimes make the whole worse. Examples range from installing a new computer system to improve one part, to measuring the calls per hour handled by call centre staff.
- **Waiting** – not customers waiting in a queue, but office staff waiting for decisions, for gate stages, for others, for information. The consequences are particularly severe for bottleneck resources, or elements along the 'critical chain'. See the separate section on this topic.
- **Inappropriate presence:** the waste of attending meetings or activities that have no productive purpose. Meetings should be short and focused, not long and general.
- **Inappropriate trade-off**: Smith and Reinertsen have made the useful point that six tradeoffs are made either implicitly or explicitly between four objectives:

development speed, product or service cost, product or service performance, and development programme expense. In most cases the tradeoffs are not even considered. This results in too much or too little time being spent on such important considerations.

A starting point for office waste reduction is awareness of these wastes. Even better is estimation or quantification, perhaps through activity sampling.

To reiterate: the job of an office manager or an administrator is not to 'check up' on wastes, but to help to facilitate their removal. This is the concept of the inverted triangle, where managers support front line activities, and hence improve the service.

Further Reading

Taiichi Ohno / Japan Management Association, *Kanban: Just-in-Time at Toyota*, Productivity Press, 1985

George Stalk and Thomas Hout, *Competing Against Time*, The Free Press, New York, 1990

James Womack and Daniel Jones, *Lean Thinking*, revised edition, Free Press, 2003

Paul Hawkin, Amory Lovins and L Hunter Lovins, *Natural Capitalism*, Little Brown and Co, 1999

Dominic Rushie, 'Business Reports a Loss on Paper', *Sunday Times Business*, 19 Aug 2007

Preston Smith and Donald Reinertsen, *Developing Products in Half the Time*, (second edition), Van Nostrand Reinhold, 1997

George Gonzales-Rivas and Linus Larsson, *Far from the Factory*, CRC Productivity Press, 2010

Ronald Mascitelli, *The Lean Product Development Guidebook*, Technology Perspectives, 2007

2.1.4 Variation

Variation, or variability, is the Enemy of Lean! Every Lean manager should know and understand that queue length or lead-time is a function of arrival variation, process variation, and capacity utilisation. These are in fact 'Mura' and 'Muri', the root cause of much 'Muda'. This section examines the two types of variation or Mura. Please also refer to the Part 1 on Queues.

Note that we are not talking about variety here. There will always be variety in service. Customers are different and their needs change over time. Variety needs to be absorbed, or coped with, as part of system design. Variation, or variability, however, needs to be limited. But both too much and too little variation cause problems. Both extremes cause failure demand. Taguchi talked about the 'loss function', where the further one moved from the optimal, the greater the loss. The mechanical analogy is that an engine requires tolerance limits – too tight and the engine will be impossible to make; too loose and tolerance stackup will ensure failure.

There are two types of variability: customer-introduced variability and internal process variability. This is similar to Kingman's equation, discussed in Part 4 on Queues, where two of the variables are arrival variation and process variation. A third interacting factor is utilisation.

We should note that the importance of variation is relative not absolute. In Kingman's equation the coefficient of variation (both arrival variation and process variation) is defined as the standard deviation of the process time divided by the average process time. Take two processes each with a standard deviation of process time of one minute, but one having an average process time of one minute, and the other with an average process time of 30 minutes. The coefficient of variation in the first case would be significant, but negligible in the second case.

Customer Introduced Variability

Frances Frei has described five types of customer-introduced variability. But Frei also makes the point that there is a trade-off decision to be made. Don't assume that reducing variability is always the right thing to do. Some customers are willing to pay a premium for increased variability, such as increased menu choice, or for the service provider to help with form filling and clean up. Frei also believes that sometimes it is possible to achieve both low cost and variability accommodation – for example by segmentation of customers that gives only that narrow band of customers the right level of support. This is a potent thought. Here we concentrate on variability reduction.

Frei's five types are:

1   **Arrival variability:** unfortunately customers, whether walk-in or call-in, don't arrive uniformly, and don't place demands on a service system uniformly.

This effect has been widely studied in Queuing Theory (see the separate Box on this topic). It may be possible to influence the demand rate, for example by booking, but many service demands are uncertain, at least in the short term – for example appliance failure, burglary, or house leaks. Over longer periods, arrival rates may be predictable to some extent, for example seasonal car breakdown demands. Service providers should first of all record then study arrival rates. The better you can predict, the better your service offering and capacity management will be. So, break down the 'time series' (the pattern of arrivals) by seeking out:

- Seasonal patterns;
- Patterns by month, by week, by day, by hour;
- Patterns by regular events such as public holidays, Christmas, festivals;
- Relationships with major irregular events, such as flood, a celebrity visit, the launch of a new product;
- Other drivers such as end-of-year buying by central and local government.

Begin simply by drawing a time series graph, dividing it into appropriate time segments, and then annotating special events. It maybe a good idea to draw a control chart with upper and lower limits at plus and minus three standard deviations.

If you can get short-term average rates – for example weekly breakdown rates – you will be able, very probably via the Poisson distribution, to calculate probabilities of x arrivals in y hours.

2   **Request variability**: this is the variability within a service arrival. For instance, customers arrive at a bank in a variable manner, but also have different numbers and types of transactions. You will know the frustration of standing in a queue at a bank behind someone paying in the weekend's cash takings.

It may be possible to manage request variability. Methods include

- having a fast track queue such as the ones you see at supermarkets;
- prohibition of certain types of transaction at certain times of the day, for example, no transactions except emergencies at night;
- limiting choice to menu items.

However, request variability should be tracked. An easy way in many service situations is simply to keep a tally chart. Length of calls can be automatically logged to detect 'special causes'. This is NOT to 'check up' on staff!

Complaints and failure demand in general are an important source of request variability. Not to log these is a major failing. What percentage of front line complaints is recorded and passed on? Often quite low or even nil. Also, on an on-going basis, get staff to record value demand and failure demand. Post these and discuss them regularly around a Communications Board. See separate section under Tools.

3   **Capability Variability**: not all customers have the same skill level. Some require much more guidance than others. Older people, for example, may require more time to resolve a computer problem than teenagers. Clearly, this source of variability is much more important in some settings than others. Contrast a doctor diagnosing a patient (or a technician diagnosing computer problems) with form completion or payment for parking. Allowing time to get to the true cause is much more important. Designing around customer capability variability not only helps the customer, but also improves organisational productivity – for instance having a help desk or key.

Yet in most service situations the competence of customers and technology cannot be assumed. It may be a customer problem, or it may be a technology problem – for example, a failure to read a magnetic strip allowing exit from parking. Capacity considerations should allow for this. But the need for resource capacity can be reduced by

- **Clear signage**: it's surprising how often customers or patients don't know where to go. Follow a sample of customers; don't assume it is obvious. This overlaps with 'Servicescape' (see the separate section). Amazing things can be done with good signs and paint.
- **Reduced choice** also limits customer capability variability. Reduced choice menus are one reason why Benihana restaurant is able to turn around satisfied restaurant customers so quickly.
- **'Over the shoulder' analysis**: Quicken software became famous for its user friendliness – made possible by close observation of customer interaction with its software.
- **Key stroke analysis**: analysing computer key strokes and loops has become a standard practice. One software program builds in a counter that monitors that sections of code are used most frequently – then focuses attention on those.
- **Standard Operating Procedures (SOPs) for Customers!** Why not put as much effort into guiding the customer as is put into guiding employees? If the wonderful photo-guided SOPs now found in industry were standard practice with customers, the level of errors and complaints would surely fall.
- **Quick help guides**: another standard practice is to include a 'quick start' as well as longer guides in cameras, computers, and the like. Online help is also standard. How can the pop-up flag principle that guides computer users be adopted?
- **IVR (Interactive Voice Response) -** beware of this! Failure demand can result from a mismatch between actual customer needs and

management perception of customer needs. Don't even consider it before listening to a good sample of actual calls.

- **Customer training**: Zara 'trains' customers to make immediate buying decisions or lose out.
- And last but not least, **patient coaching** and **friendly explanation** pay off. Resist the temptation for an employee to do the work themselves, especially with a scowl, and more especially where the customer is likely to return.

Reducing customer variation requires effort. Track the rate of errors made by customers. Pareto. Redesign where necessary. This is frequently an unrecognised source of problems, which can persist for years.

4   **Effort Variability** measures the effort that a customer makes to complete the transaction. For instance, does he put the supermarket trolley away or leave it for someone else to collect? Does he place the tray and waste in the appropriate box at Burger King? Does he leave litter? Does he remove shoes and laptop before airport security or wait until he gets to the front of the queue? Of course this may have an impact on cost, and inconvenience other customers.

- What can be done? Shaming and penalties are generally not the way to go. Appeal to the persons' sense of community. Humour can work. So can information about other customers ('80% of residents recycle their newspapers.'). Thank him for doing the right thing. But also make it easy and obvious.

5   **Subjective Preference Variability** is variation in customer opinion. One customer may appreciate a lot of personal attention, another may not. In high intensity situations it may be possible just to ask for customer preferences.

- Some hotels are making a virtue out of this variability by asking customers their preference in pillows, sheets, beds, open windows, and so forth. This may win customers but may also complicate scheduling.

Internal Process Variability

The last section dealt with external or customer variability. This section examines the management of internal variability. This links with 'The Hinckley Framework' for Quality improvement (see separate section). Internal sources are the '6 M's and an I': Man (or people), Machine, Method, Material, Measures, Mother Nature, and Information.

- **'Man' (or people) variability** is a major source of variability. People-induced variation occurs not only between people but also by one person over time. Means of managing people variation include:

- **Standard Operating Procedures (SOPs)** which can be quite negative, de-motivating, and harmful. Note the difference between Standard Work and SOPs. The former are developed by operators for operators. The latter are often imposed. Please refer to the Standard Work section. Standardise only the frequently repeatable. You certainly do not want scores of different standards in an attempt to cater for every service situation. But you do want to get the vital few things correct. So 'pareto' the variety, then again pareto the steps in the process. Some steps will be absolutely vital to do precisely, but these may be only a few. Recall the story of the call centre operator required to ask respondents the same question three times irrespective of their reply. It is important to get through the requirements of the process, whether interacting with a legal client or taking a menu order. But spontaneity and personal interaction are also important.
    - **A Checklist** of items that have to be covered (the 'what'), but leaving the 'how' to the service deliverer.
    - **Training:** airlines are very successful in getting cabin crew to smile and be cheerful. Positive attitude can be built. See the section 'Fun with Moments of Truth'.
    - **Contingency Plans:** common 'what ifs' can be thought through in advance. What if a key member of staff is ill, what if there is an 'unexpected' surge of work, what if the computers go down, and of course Health and Safety – what if there is a fire?
- **Machine** variability reduction is dealt with by TPM (Total Productive Maintenance) procedures. Although TPM can be involved, for office machines simple regular maintenance checks often suffice. Place a board showing tasks that need to be done, who is responsible for doing them, and a sign-off or tick box to show that they have been done. This is particularly important where customers use machines.
- **Material:** consistency of materials can be achieved through policy on purchasing and procurement. A consistent corporate style gives a positive message.
- **Measures** - a big one! Measures are discussed in a separate section. 'You get what you measure' and 'Tell me about rewards, and I will act to maximise my own personal benefit'. You had better believe it.
- **Methods:** regularity and reinforcement are key. SOPs are the means of reducing variability, but need to be appropriate to the level of work. Build in checks, such as valid fields in data entry. And audit, but not with blame or punishment in mind. So much can be achieved with checklists, in every service organisation, irrespective of level. From Queen's Counsel to Clerk, get into the habit of building and maintaining checklists as a way of recording experience. The WWWDD – what went well, and what should be done differently.
- **Mother Nature:** you can't play God, but you can prepare contingency plans for likely events. Virus protection?
- **Information:** standardisation of information and displays can play a huge role in Lean sustainability. Decide what is necessary, ensure as far as possible similarity throughout the organisation, and establish responsibilities for updating and looking at the information.

2.1.5 Runners Repeaters and Strangers: Activity Analysis

How Do People in Service Spend Their Time?

Everyone is in 'service', even if you are in 'manufacturing' or construction. One view is that almost everyone at work can be seen as spending their working day or working week doing a mix of the following activities:

- **Runner activities**: these are activities that take place typically in an office every day and occupy most of the day. The office factory. For example, a person taking calls in a call centre every day, most of the day.
- **Repeater activities**: these activities occur regularly or semi-regularly. For example, an accountant consolidating the accounts once each month, a sales and operations planning (S&OP) meeting, or any regular meetings, running training periodically but regularly. Many service workers have a range of activities that are Repeaters, some done perhaps every day, others perhaps every year. Many creative activities such as design or advertising are like this – as are routine divorce cases or routine hospital operations or seeing patients.
- **Stranger activities**: these are the non-regular activities that are seldom repeated. Major projects or research, non-regular special tasks, complex managerial, legal or medical cases.
- **Waste activities**: these are activities that can be eliminated with very little negative impact. The classic wastes of transport, waiting, overproducing, and errors come to mind. Also included is failure demand (Seddon) – as a result of not doing something or not doing it right the first time.

Of course the areas are not mutually exclusive. Runners, Repeaters and Strangers (RRS), are not neat little boxes. Perhaps it is more useful to think of a continuum of activities.

Runners, Repeaters and Strangers is a well-established classification concept relevant to manufacturing scheduling. In manufacturing it is the products that are so classified; in service it is the activities. In manufacturing RRS provides a guideline into layout and scheduling. In service, RRS is particularly relevant to the way work is organised, and may be relevant to layout.

Classifying Activities

The following four figures taken together illustrate general philosophical points about Lean service and Systems. They give an idea of what a Lean service transformation will look like.

In the first figure the activities in a service area have been transformed. First, note that the diagram reflects a 'systems' view. That is, some activity groups now consume more time, others less, but overall much less time is required to do the work. This reflects Ohno's idea that Activity = Work + Waste. Notice that waste activities have been reduced. But this has not happened by 'taking out waste' or 'waste walk' activities. Such activities do take out some minor wastes, but the big hit is via a transformation in thinking. Particularly powerful is the 'Check' methodology discussed in the second section. What has happened is that the activities have become more regularised. The Runner activities use about the same time, but the big move has been with Repeaters. More activities take place regularly. Greater repeatability drives down the error rate – by better processes, not necessarily by standardisation. There is better regular communication, perhaps around a Communications Board. As a result there is far less rework. The proportion of Stranger activities has also declined because more are done as part of a regular process. This has resulted from work reviews, feedback, checklists and systematic error reduction done every day.

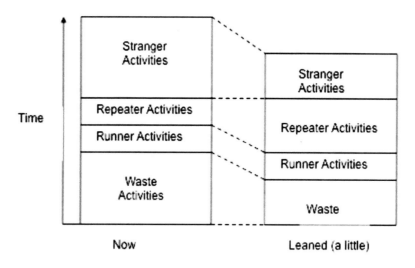

The second figure also represents a systems view. Here more resources are put into 'up front' activities such as understanding customer requirements or moving more experienced people to the front line so as to reduce failure demand. In these 'customer facing' stages, cost and time has increased. But the payoff is further downstream where errors and rework are much reduced. End-to-end time has been saved, even though times for earlier upstream activities have increased. The 'silo' view of measures and costing has been avoided.

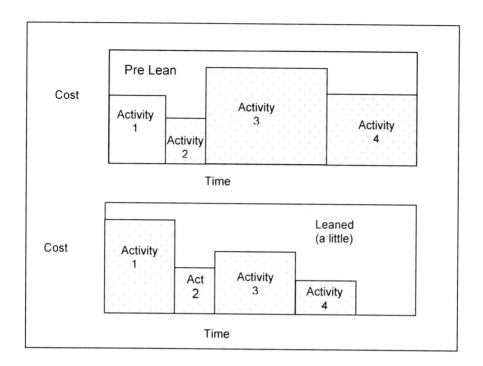

In the third figure we see the Lean concept of pushing down decision making to an appropriately lower level. It is about 'empowering' staff so that they so that they can use their initiative both to create 'delight' and to sort out problems. Most people have experienced the annoying statement, 'I'll have to refer that to my supervisor'. In service it is the front line staff who make the difference, through numerous Moments of Truth, between excellent and poor service – irrespective of the service system design.

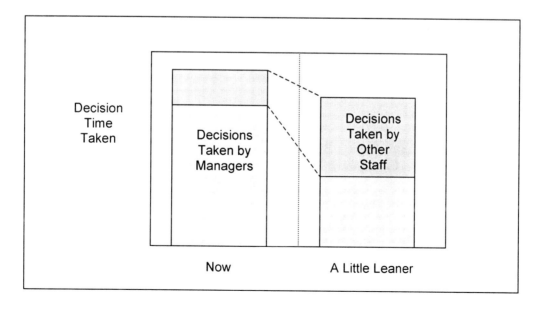

The fourth figure is an adaptation from Roger Schmenner, who maintains that there has been a trend among the best service companies towards what he calls 'swift, even flow' – surely a concise description of Lean. This is being achieved by two changes: reducing variation and reducing throughput time. Note that Schmenner is not talking about variation in the process but about a more focused service offering – solicitors specialising in conveyancing, hospitals specialising in specific areas, the emergence of a variety of fast food restaurants, and so on. Schmenner does not talk about waste and Runners, Repeaters and Strangers, but this is what has made the trend possible.

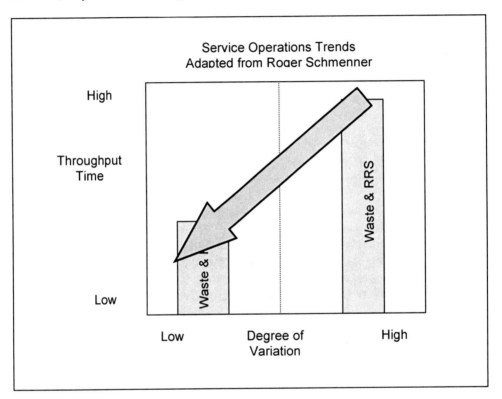

Further Reading

Roger Schmenner, 'How Service Businesses have Survived and Prospered', *Proc OMA – POMS Conference*, Como, Italy, 2003

2.1.6 Little's Law

Little's Law is a deceptively simple equation that describes the relationship between three of the fundamental measures or quantities that are of concern to every service (and operations) manager. Little's Law is

Average work in process = throughput x leadtime

This holds true for <u>any</u> *longer-term, stable* process. Longer term means that the equation may not hold for short term (daily?) fluctuations but will hold over the longer term (weeks?), provided that conditions do not change – no special promotions, new technologies, new employee level, and so forth. So the three entities all need to be longer term averages.

'Work in process' could be customers, work in process inventory, money, invoices, tax forms, prisoners awaiting trial. Throughput is the rate of work – for example, customers per day, deliveries per week, money per month, invoices per period, tax forms per day, court cases per day. Leadtime is the total time including both value adding time and waiting time.

Why is this law useful? Because:

- Knowing any two allows a manager to know the third. If we have an average of 12 projects in hand and complete an average of 2 projects per week, the average leadtime = 12/2 = 6 weeks.

- When a manager aims at one, there are implications for the other two. So if a manager aims to increase throughput this can only be done by increasing work in process or decreasing leadtime. If the manager would like to decrease leadtime to 5 weeks on average, but still completing two projects per week, then the average number of projects in hand must reduce to 2 x 5 = 10 projects.

- A manager can make a quick check on claims. For instance a delivery service deals with an average of 1200 parcels per day, with an average lead time of 14 days. They claim to have an average of 10,000 parcels in process. Is this correct? From the equation, average work in process = 1200 x 14 = 16,800 parcels. So, no, not correct.

There is no way around Little's Law! The entities are linked.

Little's Law is linked to Kingman's equation because Kingman's equation expands on the variables relating to leadtime (or average queue time) – namely arrival variation, process variation, and utilisation.

2.1.7 Plan for Every Task (PFET)

Toyota has a concept called Plan for Every Part (PFEP). See, for example, Conrad and Rooks. This is a fundamental supply chain or end-to-end concept where the PFEP specifies supplier, quantity, packaging, storage points, delivery and routes – consolidating all this data into one place.

In service, the equivalent is Plan for Every Task (PFET) (Locher, 2011). Maybe not *every* task, but certainly every bigger recurring task. A task is a sequence of operations to satisfy a customer, managerial or regulatory requirement. A task does not have to have its own map. Some have tried to do this, only to submerge in paper or data.

Note: A 'Task' is not a major Process. A process is analysed using the methods in Part 3. A task is a supporting activity, but a recurring one. Examples include opening an account, paying invoices, preparing a management report or review, preparing a course, undertaking a performance review, making travel reservations, insurance payment and claims, reviewing an article, and the many, many other activities that together take up swathes of time.

Think of PFET as the 5S of office work.

PFET means that such tasks should have an end-to-end plan. To begin PFET concept, list or brainstorm out all the office activities that are done (say) each month. One way is just to put up a flipchart and ask staff to enter non-trivial tasks. Amazing as it may sound, the full list of tasks is seldom known by any one individual in any office.

Thereafter start the detailed PFET analysis. Begin with the perceived biggest tasks. A Six Sigma-type SIPOC chart (Suppliers, Inputs, Process or Task name, Outputs, Customers / Clients) would be useful – certainly for bigger tasks. Then a list should be developed. This should cover:

- A clear definition of what is required;

- Who requires the task output;

- Where does the information to initiate the task come from;

- When the task should be done – what or who initiates the task;

- Where should the task be done;

- Who will normally do the task, plus a reserve list of people that can do it. (This can be held on a Skills Matrix chart);

- Any equipment needed;

- Where will information be held. Not only physical location, but the appropriate media. Is one location possible or practical?

- How the task is to be done. This could be a flowchart, a list, and for the most involved tasks a job breakdown chart (with major steps, key points, reasons for key points);

- A priority code. For instance, can it be interrupted?

The 3S of PFET are:

Scrutinise: this involves questioning whether the task is needed at all, the frequency with which it is done, who does it and where, and the priority. Remember Steven Covey's matrix of important and urgent: urgent but non-important tasks tend to drive out low urgency but important tasks.

Simplify: go through the usual routine and simplify. Simplification involves reducing unnecessary steps but could involve preparation – for example using templates or standard forms.

Standardise: Who, where, when, how. This could involve documentation, but for tasks should not standard operating procedure (SOP) type detail or entry into ISO 9000! Is a start-up or close down routine (like checks or clean up of desks (including electronic) , data, e mails) a good idea?

Some routine tasks need to done on a standby basis. Examples include telephone and e mail enquiries, and on-call. For this, simply has a schedule board where such tasks are timetabled between various groups.

Without PFET, productivity can be destroyed. Get the office group together and decide on task rules – for instance, no e mails will be answered between 10 and 12, no meetings in the morning, training only on Fridays, coverage during lunch hour.

Finally, PFEP addresses what the late Quality guru, Phil Crosby, referred to as 'Ballet not Hockey'. Ballet ensures every performance is more or less similar, but with (Ice) Hockey the whistle blows and every game is a unique experience. What is your organisation: Ballet style or Hockey style?

Further Reading

Tim Conrad and Robin Rooks, *Turbo Flow: Using Plan for every part to turbo charge your supply chain*, CRC Press, 2011
Drew Locher, *Lean Office and Service Simplified*, CRC Press, 2011

2.1.8 The Inverted Triangle

The Inverted Triangle is a well established concept both from Lean (see Imai, 1997) and from Service (see Vineet Nayar, 2010). It is also in line with the Toyota concept of 'Servant Management' (see Liker and Hoseus, 2008).

The traditional organisation chart places top management at the top apex and the front line at the base, with customers below that. Information flows up to management, and command and control flows down. Everyone looks up to satisfying the goals of 'the boss'. Fear and non-cooperation driven targets is the rule of the day. For customer impact, essentially, the boss gets in the way. As Deming states,

> "....anybody should first and foremost try to satisfy his boss (get a good rating). The customer is not in the pyramid...[and]...thus destroys the system."

This arrogant representation follows the way that many top managers have come to see themselves – as the single top person, deserving of remuneration perhaps hundreds of times more than those on the front line. As Nayer explains, it is illogical that 'employees reported to a manager who could not add value to their job or that people who created little value could wield a lot of power' (often for their own ends).

The inverted triangle reverses this. The front line is at the top, working with customers. The whole organisation is there to support the front line. Information flows up to help the front line. Managers are focused on the gemba and visit it frequently. Measures, not targets, flow downward to help understand the system. This is the 'hot stove' concept – where the supportive family is gathered around the stove (organisation) which provides warmth and a sense of security. There is hierarchy in the supportive family, but the 'moms and dads' do their utmost to bring out the potential of the kids, to coach, to help them overcome problems, and to instil their own values. Parents have the responsibility to provide food, clothing, and to ensure education.

According to Imai (1997), management has two functions: Maintenance and Improvement. Each needs attention. This concept is embedded here.

Nayar describes an interesting concept used at his very successful IT company to reinforce the inverted triangle. It is called the smart service desk (or SSD) ticket. Whenever an employee has a problem, a query, or a work request he or she can open a SSD. The ticket has a deadline date, and is automatically referred to a support manager in an appropriate department. The employee has visibility on the progress of the ticket. The employee must be satisfied with the response or else the ticket remains open. The longer term aim, in line with Seddon's concept of failure demand or Goodman's DIRFIT, is that no SSDs are raised.

Further reading

Maasaki Imai, *Gemba kaizen: A commonsense, low cost approach to management.* New York: McGraw-Hill, 1997

Vineet Nayar, Employees First, Customers Second, Harvard Business School Press, 2010

Jeffrey Liker and Michael Hoseus, *Toyota Culture: The heart and soul of the Toyota way.* New York: McGraw-Hill, 2008

2.1.9 Leader Standard Work (and Building Culture)

Leader Standard Work (LSW) is really about changing to a Kaizen Culture by regularity. LSW has become popular in manufacturing and is growing strongly in service.

According to David Mann, there are four integrating elements:
- Leader standard work
- Visual controls
- Daily accountability process
- Leadership discipline.

LSW is a deployment process with similarities both to Strategy (Policy) Deployment, and to the Inverted Triangle (see the previous section). It also has similarities with TWI's three interacting elements: job instruction, job methods, and job relations. See Part 4. Idea management is also usually an integral part. See also Part 4.

Leader Standard Work (LSW)

This involves building a set of standards that are followed regularly by various levels of management. Leader standards are guidelines not rigid procedures. The standards might be checklists, agendas, or working through the items on a visual display or reporting board. After-action reviews are held to ask what can be learned from past mistakes or implementations.

Problems MUST be followed up. Mann explains this with the analogy of a camp fire, which must extinguished. Extinguishing means both putting out the fire, and coming back and stirring it to ensure that no sparks remain.

Addressing improvement opportunities must also be part of the standard work. The day a manager walks past an unacceptable practice and does not enquire at the LSW meeting is the day that quality and culture begin to slip back. And the day that the manager ignores the standard because he is 'above all that' is the day that the organisation has set out on 'the road to perdition'.

Of course, LSW does not involve 100% of a manager's time. As shown by Imai, the proportion of time given over to LSW decreases with management level. Perhaps 40% at the supervisor level to 5% at senior levels. Obviously this varies with type of service and with change initiatives that are being implemented. The aim, however, is to do less and less 'fire fighting' and more on prevention and improvement.

Visual Controls

LSW takes place at the gemba, not in the manager's office. A regular proportion of LSW time will take place with the group standing around a visual display board. On the board is shown performance metrics, problems that have occurred or remain unresolved, and ideas. This is done in a supportive, or inverted triangle, way. It is not done to 'check up'.

See the section on Communication Boards in Part 4 of the book.

Daily Accountability Process

The accountability process revolves around three tiers of daily meetings:

- Tier 1 - Shift start-up
- Tier 2 - Daily meeting, Supervisor and Team Leader
- Tier 3 - Daily meeting, Value Stream Manager (VSM), Supervisor and Support Team

A 4th tier is possible for plant managers and their support staff.

Tier 1 - The Team Leader's Shift Hand-over Meeting
comprises a standard maintenance focused agenda with defined roles in attendance at Gemba around the team's visual management (VM) board. A pull, not push principle manages the content to avoid information overload. Typical content includes Roster report and people assignments, Previous period / shift performance assessment, and Today's plans and issues.

Tier 2 – The Supervisor and Team Leader's Daily Meeting
is concerned with both maintaining (working in) and improvement (working on) activity to a standard agenda and with defined roles around the department's VM boards at Gemba. Maintenance content would involve:

- The status of key processes with day, week, period and year to date trending;
- Summaries on quality, cost and delivery;
- Follow-up of actions on assigned tasks;
- Noteworthy issues from yesterday and events due today;
- Tracking of achieved pitch, flow, rated speed, etc and the issues.

Improvement activity includes:

- First Line Managers (FLMs) allocated assignments to improve service. Only basic project management skills are needed for these tasks.

- Using a visual task assignment board tasks due on the day are reviewed. Completions on time are flagged with a green symbol and incomplete with red. The colour flags are important because they highlight interruptions to the improvement process and an opportunity to learn.

<u>Tier 3 – VSM's Daily Meeting with Supervisors and the Support Team</u>
using a standard agenda and roles, including Value Stream support team members held at the Value Stream board. The meeting will assess trends. Assignments will be allocated to supervisors and support personnel to investigate root cause of missed targets, negative trends, issues observed on Gemba walks. This institutionalises the DIRFIT methodology as explained by John Goodman.

Tiers 2 and 3 bring into life the 'latent improvement capacity' of leaders and their supervisors that can remain unfocused without the daily accountability process being in place. Small improvement steps are preferable to big ones as this allows detail to be examined. See the earlier section on Kaizen.

Acknowledgement: Thanks to Robin Howlett for this section.

Further Reading

David Mann, *Creating a Lean Culture*, CRC Press, 2010.

2.1.10 The Toyota Rules and 'Chasing the Rabbit'

In a now classic article in *Harvard Business Review*, Spear and Bowen proposed the 'Four Rules of the Toyota Production System'. The article has become immensely influential. It was written following extensive research at Toyota. Steven Spear claims that the four rules capture the essence or DNA of Toyota. Here, the four rules are interpreted for service. Steven Spear has elaborated on the four rules discussed below in his book *Chasing The Rabbit* (now renamed *The High Velocity Edge*).

Rule 1: 'All work shall be highly specified as to content, sequence, timing, and outcome.'

Some people from service take a quick read of this sentence before rejecting it outright, as being applicable only to manufacturing. This is unwise. The rule needs to be interpreted in a wider context. It goes right back to the days of F W Taylor and his 'one best way', and is the basis of Plan, Do, Study, Adjust. But in service, it challenges us to think about the current best-known way, or ideal way, to carry out work and to minimise error. So, what is the best or ideal way to

- do a check-out at your hotel?
- greet a passenger joining a flight?
- produce an annual report?
- collect necessary data from a legal or financial client?
- start designing a component?
- carry out a ward round in a hospital?
- run a university course?

Many of these are simply not specified, or are specified in insufficient detail, to their detriment. In service, we certainly do not want to over-specify and destroy spontaneity, but under-specification is also bad. Think of the waste of duplication of a new employee having to 'learn the hard way' or not benefiting from the accumulated experience of predecessors. Note that in service we are not talking about restrictive, prescriptive, scripted, responses. But we are talking about the things that simply must be done, like a credit check, and must not be done, like serving meals in a ward while a medical round is taking place.

The rule also places the onus on management to see that specifications are developed. If there is a problem it is not good enough to say, 'You must try harder', or 'You must work more conscientiously', or 'We have a motivation problem'. Instead, the process needs to be examined to see why the problem arose in the first place and to prevent it happening again. If there is no standard method, this cannot be done. So, 'Why did the patient get the wrong medicine?' or 'Why was the necessary spare part missing when the repairman called?' puts the emphasis on the process, not the person. This is pure Deming.

Rule 2: 'Every customer-supplier connection must be direct, and there must be an unambiguous yes-or-no way to send requests and receive responses.'

If there is a problem or issue, the single, shortest path of communication must be clearly known and used. In the West we like to reward problem solvers. This is OK as long as the problem is communicated and its solution built into the new standard. But, too often, the problem is solved but hardly anyone apart from the problem solver and perhaps his immediate manager knows about it. The next shift does not know, so when the problem recurs it is 'solved' in another way. Both shifts get rewards for 'initiative', but the fundamental solution remains in the head of the solver. In service, when a customer complains to the front desk, does the front desk person communicate it? Does it get to the source of the problem, or, indeed, to management? Or, more likely, does management sit in a fool's paradise thinking everything is great? Sometimes the communication route is too long – most people have played the children's game of sending a message around a circle. Sometimes the problem is communicated to a 'CRM' or 'maintenance MIS', leaving it to someone else to follow up. And please don't think that having an IVR (interactive voice recognition) system means that you have addressed Rule 2. Sometimes the problem is communicated through many informal networks, thus introducing the possibility of distortion and mischief. Communication channels need to be thought out the other way around – from bottom to top. Moreover, in service, information should flow ahead of the customer, so that the car for service, the patient, the new recruit, the student, is expected and prepared for prior to arrival.

Rule 3: 'The pathway for every product and service must be simple and direct.'

This is about clear value streams. And it is about the minimum steps in the stream. We do not want the spaghetti of the job shop in either manufacturing or service. Simplify the streams, the routings, the priorities. If at all possible, don't have a complex of different people and conflicting priorities for the customer to navigate through. Open that extra till as soon as required. In service, have you ever experienced multi-stage automatic telephone answering – and finally got through to a person (or worse, a machine) who couldn't deal with your 'unusual' request? Try a human. Better still, try a highly knowledgeable human at the first stage. So, value stream map it from the customer's perspective. And remember Stalk and Hout's Golden Rule: 'Never delay a value adding step by a non-value adding step'.

Rule 4: 'Any improvement must be made in accordance with the scientific method, under the guidance of a teacher, at the lowest possible level in the organisation.'

This is about all improvements being done under PDSA (Plan Do Study Act – or the Deming / Shewhart cycle) even if it is only a small improvement. Without PDSA there is little learning. Put up a hypothesis of what you expect, carry out the work, then see if your hypothesis is correct. If it is incorrect, why is it incorrect, and what can you learn for next time? All changes must be tested and reflected upon. The 'lowest level' means both place and organisational level. So improvement must be done at Gemba, by <u>direct observation</u>, probably using the <u>Socratic method</u>. Direct observation is needed for understanding and anticipating problems – not managing by remote control via KPIs that come in too late to make a difference to the customer. The Socratic method asks why; it does not show how.

Note the last part of the rule 'at the lowest possible level'. It is NOT the job of a Six Sigma black belt or industrial engineer or other 'expert' or consultant to tackle every improvement. It is not their job even to approve every improvement. But it is their job to teach the method. 'A3' (discussed in a late section) is a great improvement tool, but an even better mentoring and coaching tool.

Spear and Bowen suggest that the rules are not learned by instruction, but by questioning. The rules are not stated. They are absorbed over time. Challenging questions involve going to the Gemba and asking:

- How do you do this work?
- How do you know that you are doing it correctly?
- How do you know that the outcome is defect free?
- What do you do if you have a problem?
- Who do you communicate with?
- How do you know what to do next?
- What signals cue your work?
- Do you do this in the same way as others?

In fact, it is learning by the on-going use of Kipling's six honest serving men, 'who taught me all I knew; their names are What and Why and When, and Where and How and Who'.

Bear in mind that 'it is not the quality of the answers that distinguishes a Lean expert, but the quality of the questions' (source unknown), and as Yogi Berra said, 'Don't tell me the answer, just explain the question'.

'Chasing the Rabbit' (or 'The High Velocity Edge')

In his later work, Steve Spear builds on these original four rules, especially Rule 4. As he says, 'Greatness is possible' by following the 'Four Capabilities'. These are

1 **Specifying Design to capture existing knowledge and building in tests to reveal problems**
This is an extension of Rule 4. Specify in advance what is expected, and include a check on those expectations. This makes the assumption of humility, that we don't know all the answers and uncertainties and so require a systematic procedure to uncover the problems and to build good practice. This is in line with the Lean philosophy of 'surfacing' problems. It has been said, if you think you have no problems, that is the problem! It is also in line with the quality 'guru' Phil Crosby who used to maintain that one of the greatest shortcomings in both manufacturing and service organisations is management's failure to specify

what is required, but goes further to require testing. Testing need not be a formal scientific test, but simply a comparison between what was expected and what actually happened.

2 **Swarming and Solving Problems to build new knowledge**
Where expectations are not met, 'swarming' is required – that is, an immediate response by an appropriate and often multi-functional team. At one organisation that we have visited, 'swarming' involves immediately calling together an appropriate team who gather around a white board, which has the format of an A3. A3 problem solving is discussed in a later section. The board is on wheels and is moved to the 'gemba' – where the problem has occurred. This, of course, is directly in line with the Lean philosophy that a problem is a treasure, and the root cause should be sought.

3 **Sharing new knowledge throughout the organisation**
Once a better way has been found, communicate it. One organisation we are familiar with communicates better practices via the intranet. Another displays new procedures on the company screen saver. Not by command and control but by making the improved procedures possible – in line with Deming's 94/6 rule where 94% of problems are with the system and only management can change the system. Of course, lawyers have been doing this for decades – it is called precedent.

4 **Leading by developing the first three capabilities**
Not only insisting that capabilities 1 to 3 are done, but making them the way of life. Of course, this cannot be done by edict.

We believe that these four capabilities are exactly in line with the 'Check' methodology described in the next section. In fact, Spear's 'Capabilities' and Seddon's 'Check' methodology are mutually reinforcing.

Further Reading

Steven Spear and Kent Bowen, 'Decoding the DNA of the Toyota Production System', *Harvard Business Review*, Sept-Oct 1999
For a healthcare related perspective on the four rules see Stephen Spear, 'Fixing Healthcare from the Inside, Today', *Harvard Business Review*, September 2005
Steven J Spear, *Chasing the Rabbit*, McGraw Hill, 2009. (A new edition of the book is called *The High Velocity Edge*, 2010)

2.2 Systems Concepts Relevant to Service.

2.2.1 Seddon's Six Stages of 'Check'

'System' is the theme that runs throughout this book. But how do we understand the system? John Seddon's 'check' stage is a powerful orderly way to do this. Here we will use the stages of Seddon's 'Check model', and discuss each one. 'Check' derives from the Deming Cycle – Plan Do Check Act – but begins with Check. Seddon may or may not agree with the comments! In my opinion the six stages of check deserve to be as widely known as the five Lean principles. This is especially the case in service. The six stages of 'check' are:

1   Purpose: What is the purpose – in the view of the Customer or Client?

Purpose is the reason why you are doing the task. It is not 'Vision': Vision is where you want to be. It is often worth stating both Purpose and Vision. Ask 'what is the purpose of the system <u>from the customer's viewpoint</u>?' It is an 'outside in' view, not an 'inside out' view. What Deming said about an aim, could also be applied to Purpose: 'It is important that an aim never be defined in terms of activity or methods. It must always relate to how life is made better for everyone.'

'What does the customer want from the system?' is an outside-in question. 'How can I get these bastards to do more work?' is a (wrongheaded) inside-out question.

This requires taking a 'helicopter' view. Of course there may be several customer categories. If you get a list of things you are probably not high enough in your helicopter. So first seek the overall purpose – then you can get into the lists. You may then decide to home in on the most relevant item on the list – being the system or sub-system of immediate concern. So you will get statements such as

'To pay deserving clients as quickly and easily as possible;'
'To ensure a hassle free air travel experience from A to B;'
'To equip participants with practical Lean Thinking skills.'

Note: the purpose should have a verb and a noun.

Why do this? It is simply an opportunity to stand back and consider why the organisation exists, without getting into organisational functions or departments, an attempt to avoid sub-optimisation, to remain holistic. The purpose statement should lead to the critical measures that enable a judgement to be made on whether the purpose is being achieved. Finally, to quote Seddon, 'While cost reduction is a natural consequence of 'lean', it is not its purpose. The purpose of 'lean' is to increase capacity by designing a system that optimally responds to customer demand.' (Watchoutforthetoolheads – Vanguard education, 2006.)

Note that 'Purpose' is never profit. Profit is one measure of success in achieving the purpose. John Kay in *Obliquity* and Hopper and Hopper in *The Puritan Gift* give numerous examples of failure that has resulted when placing profit as the purpose rather than a result of achieving customer ends.

Some service organisations find it difficult to define who the customer is. In third party logistics, for instance, is it the end customer or is it the company paying for the service? Perhaps it does not matter: both require consideration and the valid requirements of different customer groups to be serviced. Seddon takes the pragmatic view that we need only consider the immediate customer.

Sometimes, the 'customer' is an object like an aircraft or building or pipeline. It can be valuable to put yourself 'in the shoes' of such customers – asking what they would want if they could talk. As a pothole, how many times are you visited and what is done on each visit?

2   Demand: What is the nature of the demand?

Having defined the purpose of the system, now you can consider the demands that are placed on the system by customers. Seddon uses the very powerful concept of Value Demand and Failure Demand. Value Demand is demand that is in-line with the purpose. It is what the system is there to do, what it exists to serve – 'it represents the demands customers make for things they want'. Failure demand, by contrast, is 'demand caused by a failure to do something or do something right for the customer' (Seddon). A demand is any customer action that triggers work in the system. Seddon's Failure Demand is monitored at the system boundary or Moment of Truth. To find out how much Failure Demand there is, it is necessary actually to monitor a sample of demand by listening to calls, going through correspondence, picking up front-line requests at incoming points such as reception, call centre, or points of contact between customers and consulting engineers, or workmen.

Beware! Do not do mapping before you understand demand. You will not know what questions to ask. You may miss failure loops. You may conclude that the process is good, when it is actually generating failure. Your capacity calculations are likely to be wrong. This situation is much less of an issue in manufacturing because there is usually very little external rework imposed on a factory.

Why do this? To understand how much work is being loaded unnecessarily on the system, and hence possibly overloading the system, with severe consequences on response times and generating even more failure. There is little point is studying the flow of work when only a small percentage of demand is should actually be there. Importantly, failure demand also destroys the morale of workers who may see themselves as 'fire fighters'. When workers begin to see their work not as repetitive drudgery but as actually improving the system for customers and themselves, morale can improve more dramatically than by sending them on a hundred motivational courses or by imposing KPI's and hoping for the best. The latter is the classic 'beatings will continue until morale improves'.

There is no point in using sophisticated automatic call analysis systems that record the number of abandoned calls when you do not know how many of these calls are failure demand. Many a service system has believed itself to be overloaded with work, only to discover, as failure demand is reduced, that they have easily sufficient capacity.

This is not simply 'muda' or 'necessary non value added' work. Activities such as 'waste walks' simply will not pick up the extent of failure demand. This is also not the same as Phil Crosby's cost of poor quality concept of failure costs, inspection costs, and prevention costs where all quality-related activities are classified into one of these categories – this is an 'inside-out' viewpoint. Failure demand is like rework, except that rework is internally imposed, but failure demand is externally imposed. Both, however, tie up capacity wastefully.

To understand demand, listen to the actual voice of the customer. Do not do market surveys or questionnaires. Write down what they actually say or write in emails. Note the types. Classify and record the frequency. For instance:

Type and Frequency of Demand	Frequency %	Value/ Failure
I want to make a claim….	41%	Value
What is happening with my claim?	15%	Failure
'Have you received my estimate?'	9%	Failure
Chasing payment / cheque	9%	Failure
Broker chasing claims history/settlement	6%	Failure
'Can I have your fax number / address?'	5%	Failure
Client chasing update on the claim	4%	Failure
Chasing call back	3%	Failure
'I haven't received my letter / claims form'	2%	Failure
Supplier calling for missing information	2%	Failure
'Supplier has not yet contacted me'	2%	Failure
Chasing response to e-mail	1%	Failure
'I am waiting for written confirmation that I can proceed'	1%	Failure

Once you have this very valuable information, you should do two things:
(a) re-design the system to flow the value work more efficiently, and
(b) set up ways, including the root causes, of eliminating the failure demand.

In understanding demand, start at the beginning – at the end customer, at field demand. Do not start with intermediate demand as generated in a depot or intermediate office.

Demand should be classified by source: What are demands? Where are they arising? How frequently? When are they arising? Who is making the demands? Draw run diagrams. Use maps. This is all essential if you are to design against demand.

Ask the question whether the demand is preventable.

In interactive service environments the concept of Moment of Truth (MoT, see the later section on Interactive Mapping) is a powerful concept made famous by Jan Carlsson of SAS airlines. Moments of Truth are applied to every interaction between service provider and customer. The demand analysis described here can be used at major stages of a customer's 'Cycle of Service'.

Preventable Value Demand: there is not always a clear distinction between Value Demand and Failure Demand. In some so-called 'break-fix' systems, where demand is for field service repairs, demand for first time service is value demand. But if the root causes of the problem were adequately tackled through design or preventive maintenance, the demand could be eliminated. Why did the central heating system go wrong? Lack of maintenance? Unclear instruction? A Design fault? Or merely old? It may be useful to distinguish this type of demand from other failure demand. Call it preventable value demand.

3   Capability: *What is the system predictably achieving?*

This sets out to answer whether the system is able to meet the load put on it in a stable, predictable way. Of prime concern are the end-to-end service time and the variation of it. The word 'predictable' refers to the stability of the system – is it 'in control ' or 'out of control'? You will probably need a run diagram or Statistical Process Control (SPC) chart to answer that question. There is a fundamental difference between a system with a response time that on average is OK but that has wide variation, and one with similar average response but highly stable performance. To know whether the system is capable it is necessary to know the purpose, the critical measure or measures. The appropriate measures will have to taken over a representative period of time. Note that the measure will almost always be an end-to-end measure from the customer's viewpoint. Also you would like to know if there are patterns in demand and stability.

A run diagram is also a powerful way to understand the system variation – are there patterns in the variation – period to period, area to area, and how much between customers? If there happens to be a service level agreement (SLA), is the SLA being met?

Why do this? Because if there are special causes at work that are destabilising the system they need to be identified and eliminated. The first priority, and often easiest thing to do, is to eliminate the special causes or special events. To change the common cause variation requires a more fundamental redesign. Analogy: an automobile cooling system. Relatively easy to solve special causes like a hole in the radiator, but complete redesign is required to get the automobile running permanently at a lower than average temperature.

4 Flow: *How does the Work Work?*

Now that there is an overall appreciation from the customer's viewpoint, begin to look at how value is delivered to the customer.

Only now is it appropriate to map the process.

Is there flow? Is customer flow smooth, swift, simple, steady, and slim? Note that we are concerned here with flow that meets the purpose – not just flow for the sake of flow. Don't attempt to flow activities that should not be there in the first place – failure demand. And we are concerned with the customer. If there are stages that don't contribute to the purpose they should not be on the 'main line' of flow. We may recall Stalk and Hout's Golden Rule: 'never delay a customer value adding step by a non value-adding step'. Support activities should be done off-line, in parallel where delays don't bother the customer. Here we may note a pseudo difference between manufacturing and service – manufacturing focuses on the flow of the object, service focuses on the flow of the customer. The ideas of the late Eli Goldratt are also highly relevant – focusing on the bottleneck – to determine the overall rate of flow, and possibly on the drum-buffer-rope methodology. See the section on Goldratt's five steps. However, remember a point of caution: Goldratt appropriately focuses on the bottleneck in a manufacturing system and protects the bottleneck by ensuring that it is never idle and there is always inventory to work on. In a service system, bottlenecks are certainly important but a queue of customers in front of the bottleneck would illicit more concerns than a queue of inventory. So we have to find ways in which we can both maximise the utilisation of the bottleneck AND not delay customers. This leads on to another consideration: the reduction of variation. There is only one way both to maximise utilisation and to reduce the queue, and that is to minimise variation. So levelling demand becomes important as does the reduction of unnecessary variation – through waste reduction and mistake proofing. For more insight into flow, variation, utilization, and constraints, see the section on Queues in Part 4.

Why do this? Because flow is primary to customers – but you cannot understand flow unless you know purpose and capability.

5 System Conditions: *Why does the system behave this way?*

The system conditions are what cause the system to behave the way it does. It is structure, the processes, the measures, the managers and maybe the people. Here, Deming's 94/6 rule is highly relevant: 94% of problems are caused by the system, only 6% by the people. See the section on the Red Bead Game, under Control Charts. So the first reactions should not be to blame the person, call for training, say that they are 'concrete heads', or to complain about 'the culture', but to look at the process or system conditions that are causing the malfunction.

There will very likely be 'dirty data' flowing around the system, and several inappropriate measures. Both of these will cause distortions. To understand these effects will mean:

- Looking at the structure – how many hand-offs are there?

- Looking at the process – how contorted? How long to respond? Are errors recognised? Can the people do anything about them or are they time or function restricted?

- Looking at the measures – do the measures support flow and help to improve the process, or are they primarily there to make management happy? Are the measures end-to-end or exclusively departmental? Is the aim to 'make the numbers' or to solve the customer's problem? Does the costing system support rational behaviour – or is it output driven to cover variances?

- Do problems get passed on, or are they tackled at or near the source?

- Are the workers primarily focused upwards towards management or horizontally towards customers?

- Is the information system or ERP system capable of meeting customer requirements? Does it collect and distribute correct information?

- Is the information 'dirty' (a Seddon phrase)? How much dirty (incorrect/incomplete) data is flowing in the system?

- Is the layout conducive to achieving the purpose? Look at the state of visual management, etc.

John Seddon believes that the most important of these is the measurement system. "Tell me how you'll measure me and I'll tell you how I will behave." You may recall the oft-quoted statement about Toyota – 'we achieve brilliant results with average people working with brilliant processes rather than mediocre results with brilliant people working with broken processes'. This statement captures the right sentiment – but it is a manufacturing statement, and in service many more people are customer-facing so good people are needed too. But good people, cannot be good without good managers, so…

6   **Management Thinking**:

This is the true 'culture' of the system, because the beliefs of the managers flow down into the people. A Toyota saying is that 'the shop floor is a reflection of the management'. In many organisations, you quickly realise whether the managers are primarily focused on satisfying their own managers' (or 'corporate') purpose or whether they are focused on the customer's purpose. That is what has happened in many hospitals, banks, and universities, which are often so focused on meeting targets that the customer is forgotten.

You can get a view of management thinking by looking at the reward packages of both managers and staff – What are the rewards based on? What is promotion based on? (Short or long-term focus? Satisfying customers or achieving corporate KPI's?). 'Tell me how you will measure me and I'll tell you what I will do'. A bonus or reward system, by the way, is frequently a problem in itself – see Alfie Kohn's devastating critique in *Punished by Rewards*.

To what extent are managers and hence the organisation, target driven rather than measure driven? The right measures help to understand the system, particularly end-to-end measures, but targets encourage cheating and dysfunctional competition. You can get more insight by monitoring how much senior managers know about 'The Gemba'. How aware are managers about front line activities?

Managers' attitudes: Frank Devine talks about three groups of employees – the inner-directed, the watchers, and the 'limit testers'. The limit testers are always testing the rules, and the watchers observe managers' reactions – if the limit testers get away with it then a negative feedback loop is established.

7   Study

This final step is not given in the Seddon Check methodology, but the current writer feels that it should be made more explicit. Whereas the 'Check' stage includes studying the situation before the intervention, 'Study' includes recording what worked and what did not work, after or during the intervention. This allows learning and not having to repeat mistakes. Perhaps some critical, repeatable activities could have 'standard work' developed for them – for instance a doctor washing hands, or recording critical information so that the cause of failures can be diagnosed without having to rely on memory. This then would complete the PDSA (Plan Do Study Act) cycle, and lead on to the next cycle.

The Check sequence gives an excellent insight into the system status. A holistic, system design can now begin. Seddon calls this 'making the work work'. By keeping the total system in mind, the sub-processes can be mapped and improved.

Further reading

John Seddon, *Freedom from Command and Control*, Vanguard, 2003
See also the Vanguard web site www.lean-service.com
Alfie Kohn, *Punished by Rewards*, Houghton Mifflin, 1999

2.2.2 CATWOE

Peter Checkland uses a useful series of soft-system concepts, known through the mnemonic CATWOE, to look at systems and sub-systems. They are particularly important in service. They are:

- **Clients**: These are often customers, but the word customer is not always appropriate – for example in a hospital or prison. There may be several groups of clients, not all of them customers, and they may have different needs. A local authority may have to mediate between several groups such as shoppers, disabled, and business, all wanting parking privileges. Meeting the needs of clients is what the system or value stream is there to do. Thought needs to be given to the clients for whom the system is to cater – today's clients, or tomorrow's clients? (And should they be segmented?) Seddon has a pragmatic view that some find controversial. He prefers to look only at the immediate customer, believing that other stakeholder's best interests are met when the customer's needs are met. Hence, the patient not the hospital administrator or the doctors; the hotel guest, not the local community or the environment.
- **Actors**: The participants in the system, other than the clients and owners. They may include employees, suppliers or volunteers. Some actors may not be subject to direct control but may be vital to the working of the system – for example, an internet service provider. Make a list.
- **Transformation**: What the system sets out to do. Usually the clients are 'transformed' in some way. So this stage is about identifying the need that should be satisfied. Try to remain in general terms – 'holes' rather than 'drills' – the former is the need, the latter presumes the solution, perhaps too early. List the inputs and outputs. In Six Sigma there is useful concept called SIPOC: Suppliers, Inputs, Process, Outputs, Customers / Clients. This is a listing under each of these headings. SIPOC is a good way to do the Transformation step.
- **Weltanschauung**: This German word relates to the fundamental beliefs of the system, which often go unchallenged. 'Reducing cost is good', or 'Customers cannot be trusted with a no-questions-asked return policy', or selling a shoe that is not a perfect fit, or 'Unions (or management) are bad', are examples. The weltanschauung may be obvious to the client, but not appreciated by the actors. As an example, some Eastern airline passengers put courtesy and respect ahead of on-time arrival. The other way around may be the assumption in the West. This is a very powerful concept worthy of consideration in every service mapping exercise.
- **Owners**: Who 'owns' the system? Again, this is not always obvious or official. Shareholders perhaps. But perhaps (some) managers or unions. These are influential groups, which can cause a system transformation to crash. They may overlap with the actors. The true aims of the owners must be appreciated, even if they are not stated in words.
- **Environment**: Where does the system boundary lie? What should be considered to be within the system and what in the environment? A system's

environment lies outside the system boundary – a very important concept – see the next section below. The environment beyond the system boundary cannot be controlled easily but may have a major influence. The economy, the weather, demographics are examples.

To these classic CATWOE may be added:

- **Victims**: Are there 'victims' of the present value stream? Will there be 'victims' of the future value stream? An example is call centre working hours that create 'victims' out of the employees' families. If more flexible working arrangements can be found, the turnover of staff may drop. Remember Steven Covey's dictum 'win, win or walk away'. Keep trying to find a way in which everyone wins.
- **Beneficiaries**: Likewise, there will be beneficiaries – intended or not.

Note: Weltanschauung and System Boundary – two of the most powerful system concepts – were introduced by C West Churchman, who with Russell Ackoff, was one of the founders of Operations Research.

2.2.3 System Boundary

System Boundary is one of the most powerful and worthwhile considerations. The system boundary may not coincide with organisational boundaries. Define the system too narrowly and you will sub-optimise. Define it too widely and you will have an unmanageable process. If the system boundary is ill-considered, the transformation will fail.

Do discuss the appropriate boundary – both organizationally and over time. Also examine the measures that are in place within each sub-system and ask if they support the overall system purpose.

System boundary is closely linked to end-to-end. This is often aligned with a customer's experience of using a service. Every customer knows the poor experience of being shunted around between departments or between field service and office operations. End-to-end performance should be measured. In Lean, the concept of the horizontal value stream as opposed to the vertical silo is well established. Likewise the problem of seeking to improve a part but as a result decreasing overall performance is increasingly recognised – as for example with several computer installations or the location of a call centre overseas.

Yet system boundary remains an issue worthy of serious high-level debate. Have you now created horizontal silos instead of vertical silos? Should you involve future customers? Should you treat suppliers as partners? Should you repair a pothole or surface the whole road? Where does the NHS 'free at point of use' end?

Widening the system boundary is one of the key features of Design Thinking.

As a starting point, here is some basic guidance. Generally, activities that cannot be influenced are outside the system. But what is inside the system? A few thoughts:

- **Purpose**: if you use the word 'and' in your statement of purpose, perhaps you have two systems.
- **Shared resources**: if resources are shared (say medical consultants shared with other providers, or shared ERP systems) you will need to consider the influence of these resources. Can you assume they will agree? Would it help to involve them?
- **Customer involvement and 'co-production'**: customers can be useful co-producers. They can deliver value or destroy the effectiveness of the system. What role should they play and what tasks could they take over? To what extent should customers be involved in system re-design?
- **End to End**. We know the system should be end-to-end, but where is the end? Does the fire service start with a fire, or with prevention? Should prevention be considered another, separate system?
- **Supplier involvement and 'co-production'**: it would also be useful to involve suppliers end-to-end, but do you have any influence over them, and how much impact does their involvement have on the system?
- **Loops within the system**: if you can establish some clear 'loops of responsibility', perhaps they should be considered stand-alone systems. Are whole tasks done by one group or split between several groups? For instance, are customers – or files, applications, complaints - sent from group to group?
- **Key resources**: if key resources (managers? unions? support staff?) are omitted from the study, could they sabotage it, directly or indirectly? What is the risk of failure by omitting key resources?
- **Operations, HR and Marketing**: in most Lean service systems you will have to consider marketing (because of the improved performance) and HR (because of the change needed from the people in the system). So even if these two functions are not part of the system, there is a good chance that they should be involved in its redesign.

2.2.4 Requisite Variety

Ross Ashby, one of the founders of modern systems thinking, proposed the 'Law of Requisite Variety': variety is needed to control variety. Hence a rugby team of 15 players should be opposed by another team of 15 players, with both teams playing under the same set of rules. If one player is sent off the other team is more likely to score. In fact, in the Six Nations rugby 7 points is the average score by a team while an opposing player is in the 'sin bin'. In service operations, customer variety must be matched by service variety. Since service customer requests are so varied, a good service system needs to have requisite variety and not be bound by standard procedures that ultimately cause failure and dissatisfaction. This is a warning against the illusion of 'efficiency' through over-standardisation. In manufacturing where products have much less variety and are sometimes almost identical, more rigid standards are much more applicable. However we must not confuse requisite variety with the necessity for error-free performance. There are still key points that have to be done correctly.

In service variety needs to be ABSORBED not reduced. Ashby's law would conclude that any attempt to control high variety with lower variety actions, would be doomed to failure. This is what happens when the number of options allowed in an automated answer service is restricted. The customer makes the closest choice but knows it is not what is required. Failure often results. This is a situation where narrow manufacturing thinking is not only inappropriate, but in some situations such as a hospital can literally be fatal.

A service operator may well have 'standard work' – which is the current best known way to deal with particular situations as developed and improved through operator experience – but such standard work procedures need to be flexible in dealing with the almost infinite variety of possible customer calls. Attempting to standardise every step instead of just the critical stages, can be a disaster. In short, requisite variety is required.

2.2.5 The Viable Systems Model ('VSM')

The Viable Systems Model is a relevant, and long established, way of looking at organisational problems, particularly in messy, unstructured situations. But it is a methodology that many in the Lean community are unaware of. Had they been more aware of it, 'VSM' would have been the accepted acronym for the far older Viable Systems Model rather than the newer Value Stream Map. In this section we will use VSM in the original sense.

VSM originated with the eminent systems thinker Stafford Beer in the early 1970s. It uses a framework similar to that of the human body. It takes the stance that it is far more useful to look at any organisation or system in terms of the VSM rather than the traditional organisation chart. The late Peter Scholtes called the organisation chart the "train-wreck" chart. When the organisation chart was invented its purpose was clear: it was to assign blame and responsibility. The assignment of responsibility would enable "prompt detection of derelictions of duty ... and point out the delinquent." Exactly the opposite of what a system aspiring to improve should be doing!

There are five organisational processes or 'levels' necessary to create a 'viable system'. These five act on the 'primary activities' the organisation delivers in order to survive. In Lean language the primary activities are the essential direct value adding activities. The primary activities would not include what would be called in Lean 'necessary non value adding activities'. The five levels are:

- **Co-ordination** activities act to ensure the coordination of primary activities. A schedule or timetable would be an example. Where they are unclear, delays and conflicts result. Are the bottlenecks, the flows, the capacity, the value delivery processes understood in relation to the work that is supposed to be done?

- **Monitoring** activities check what is happening in the primary activities. Are they in control or out of control? This should be a higher-level audit check that things are going to plan. To be effective monitoring must bypass filters introduced by intermediate levels. Avoid micromanaging. These are the measures. Are they appropriate?

- **Cohesion** activities link primary activities so that synergy results – the whole is greater than the sum of the parts. They are concerned with inside and current activities. Cohesion needs to monitor and to coordinate. Alignment and resource allocation are major concerns. This is a tricky area because there must be an appropriate balance between autonomy and the fear of loss of control. Avoid micromanaging. If synergies are not being obtained, why is that function there or what is going wrong?

- **Intelligence** activities are concerned with monitoring the environment and adapting to changing circumstances. They are concerned with outside and future activities. Preparing the organisation for the future: planning, research, training.

- **Policy** activities are concerned with the future direction of the organisation: the strategy. This needs to interact with Intelligence activities and to guide Cohesion.

All five levels are necessary for a viable system to continue.

Within each sub-system, there is 'recursion'. In other words, systems contain sub-systems each with the characteristics of the higher system. A corporation has these five levels. So do its divisions. At the overall level, some or all of the prime activities may be organisational divisions each of which has these five levels within itself. And the division may have functions or departments or value streams each with the five levels.

This is the way the body works. Monitoring, coordination, cohesion takes place at (say) organ level. They run themselves. But there is coordination, monitoring, and cohesion between organs. Intelligence is gathered at each level, and information flows up or down only when thresholds are breached or policy changes.

The VSM methodology first involves 'unpacking' the system, organisation or problem into the primary activities. These are listed and grouped. Each group has a boundary – like an organ in the body. The groups are in turn linked together. Having drawn the basic diagram, an audit or discussion can begin as to the effectiveness or existence of each of the five levels that are needed. Finally, gaps are identified or suggestions made as to improvements.

2.2.6 Peter Senge's Systems Laws

To know about a system, you have to know not only the entities or objects but their context – like the notes in a piece of music. The properties of water cannot be understood by studying the properties of its components, hydrogen and oxygen.

Peter Senge, an influential systems thinker from MIT, has proposed 10 systems 'laws' that not only help us to understand systems better, but which are also an excellent aid to avoiding implementation pitfalls. The laws are set out below, with some additional comment on the relevance for service and administration.

- 'Today's problems come from yesterday's 'solutions''. This could be a re-statement of the 'push down, pop up' principle. Attack one problem, stemming from past actions, and another pops up. This is the fundamental problem of reductionist rather than holistic thinking. In administration, using a new target to solve the problem often leads to unexpected behaviour.
- 'The harder you push, the harder the system pushes back'. Or, 'systems bite back'. Most systems are in a state of natural balance. When a factor is altered others compensate. Hence the rapid growth of wildlife when predators are removed, but then stabilising due to food shortage. This happens in organisations also. People react to change in direct proportion to the amount of change. Senge calls this 'compensating feedback'.
- 'Behaviour grows better before it grows worse'. The wildlife story in the last point is an illustration. Management is often deluded (and rewarded!) by short-term results. Why? Because the whole system is not appreciated.
- 'The easy way out usually leads back in'. There are many quick and easy solutions to problems in organisations – and they are all wrong! Juhani's law states that 'the compromise will always be more expensive than either of the suggestions it is compromising'.
- 'The cure can be worse than the disease'. Help may induce dependency – ask Africa!
- 'Faster is slower'. Perhaps the supreme implementation law! Take time to achieve buy-in. The essence of what strategy deployment should be about.
- 'Cause and effect are not closely related in time and space'. If there is a problem in the office, the solution lies in the office.... Very likely not so!
- 'Small changes can produce big results – but the areas of highest leverage are often the least obvious'. Malcolm Gladwell in *The Tipping Point* talks of 'mavens' in an organisation that have great influence despite their apparent lowly status. Find them! Likewise, timing is critical. Goldratt's 'conflict resolution diagram' may be useful to help to find these influential points.
- 'You can have your cake and eat it too – but not at once'. The essential aim of Lean – you can have short leadtime and high quality and low cost – but it takes time to achieve. TRIZ (the Russian originated theory of inventive problem solving) believes that finding 'contradictions' is the starting point for innovation. Like Lean, it seeks 'AND' not 'OR' solutions.

- 'Dividing an elephant in half does not produce two small elephants'. Again, a warning on reductionism. Focusing on improving the point, but ignoring the whole, may make things worse. Improving throughput in an operating theatre may clog the subsequent beds. Rewarding one department whilst ignoring others may lead to overall decline.
- 'There is no blame'. Senge's point here is similar to Deming's preference to start with the process rather than the person. Deming said 'Drive Out Fear'. And Covey says 'win, win – or walk away'. Seek ways in which both sides will win. There IS a way. This is the basis of much of the superb Harvard Negotiation Project studies.

Further reading on Systems

An overview of many of the significant figures in the systems movement, and their ideas, over the past century is given in
Magnus Ramage and Karen Shipp, *Systems Thinkers*, Springer / The Open University, 2009
Peter Scholtes, *The Leader's Handbook*, McGraw Hill, 1998
Stafford Beer, *The Heart of Enterprise*, Wiley, 1979
Patrick Hoverstadt and Diane Bowling, *Modelling Organisations using the Viable Systems Model*, Royal Academy of Engineering, May 2002, Available from
www.fractal-consulting.com
Peter Senge, *The Fifth Discipline* (revised edition) , Randon House, 2006
Malcolm Gladwell, *The Tipping Point*, Abacus, 2000

For the sceptics, and for amusement at the behaviour of real systems, but also much profound material, see
John Gall, *The Systems Bible*, General Systemantics Press, 2006

See also the section in Part 4 on Variation, Mistakes and Complexity in Service: Why Problems Occur, for further discussion on system failure.

A Case of Failure Demand

In 2007 a leading UK bank advertised a financial product with a very attractive interest rate. Investors were required to complete an application form and existing account holders were required to have the investment funds available in their account. A large number of applications for investment followed.

The office processing the applications was overwhelmed. Many applicants were still outstanding one month after completing the application form. Many enquiries were made - failure demand. Enquirers were told that the investment would be backdated to the application date. After six weeks many potential investors had taken their money out of their accounts.

When these applications were processed the transaction could not be completed -failure demand - because the funds were not available. Letters were then sent out requesting re-application with sufficient funds - more failure demand, but this time internally generated. Many customers had already invested elsewhere.

A failure to resource the office adequately – or to monitor the flood of applications and adjust resources accordingly – led to a huge amount of unnecessary work as well as loss of customers – some probably permanently.

Caution: On Repetitiveness and Experience

Every service or administrative job, or customer that is dealt with may seem to be unique. But almost every piece of service work has repetitive elements – for instance the stages of writing a report or conducting a meeting – even though the report or meeting is unique.

The quality guru, Phil Crosby, spoke about 'ballet, not hockey'. In a ballet, they rehearse, adjust and learn what works and what does not. Then they fix the performance and every show is the same, allowing for a degree of 'poetic license' and the possibility of using an understudy.

In ice hockey, every game is different, even though the rules are followed. Hockey is fun, but is it good management? Hence, Crosby asked, is your company more ballet-like or more hockey-like? This is 'horses for courses' again, but in Lean we must attempt to be more ballet-like if possible.

Ballet is, of course, a creative process but manages to have many transactional features. More 'ballet' is possible, even in hockey. Good ballet and good hockey (or football), like good service, has the right blend of repetitive elements that can be analysed, rehearsed, improved and fine-tuned, but can still be adaptive.

There is the story of championship-winning golfer Gary Player who when asked about his luck said, 'Yes, I do have good luck, and you know what? The more I practice the luckier I get!' Similarly in good service – it's not luck, it's careful analysis, preparation and execution. In all these, mapping can help.

Don't be misled by the old story of 'I have 25 years experience!' Ask if, instead, the person has had one year's experience 25 times.....

2.3 Design Thinking Concepts Relevant to Service

2.3.1 Introduction to Design Thinking

In his famous book *The Design of Inquiring Systems*, C West Churchman gave an early but profound insight into what our book refers to as Design Thinking. He said that 'design has the following characteristics:

1. It attempts to distinguish in thought between different sets of behavior patterns.
2. It tries to estimate in thought how well each alternative set of behavior patterns will serve a specified set of goals.
3. Its aim is to communicate its thoughts to other minds in such a manner that they can convert the thoughts into corresponding actions which in fact serve the goals in the same manner as the design said they would.'

So think of designing an airport, bus service, or call centre. What are the likely behavior patterns? (Tourist, Businessperson, Tax free shopper, Student - each having different age groups, different sexes, and time – and hence different behaviour patterns.) Are these behavior patterns commensurate with the goals of the system? What needs to be communicated in order that the goals are served? Recall the opening of Heathrow Terminal 5. An excellent physical design, but a start-up disaster. Apparently a failure to understand and communicate the behaviors of passengers, staff, and the baggage handing system.

Service Design offers huge opportunity for widespread involvement. Unlike much product design, which is often highly technical and introverted, service design can and should be much more participative. However, there are conceptual similarities between Lean product design and Lean service design.

The section below draws heavily on the work of IDEO, perhaps the world's most prominent service design organisation. The section also draws on Austin and Devin's concept of 'Artful Making', Eric Reis' concept of 'Minimum Viable Product', and blends in relevant concepts from Toyota design practice.

Eric Reis' concept of 'Minimum Viable Product' (from Lean software development) would appear to have much in common with Toyota's design methodology and with the Steven Spear/Deming Learning cycle, but adds to them. The Minimum Viable Product is 'the version of a new product (or service) which allows a team to collect the maximum amount of validated learning with the least effort …. It is a test of a specific set of hypotheses with the goal of proving them or disproving them as soon as possible.' So it is a Lean, experimental design approach that tests a concept with the least number of features to get a market or customer reaction.

The story is told about Google Maps. Senior Managers were impressed at the initial presentation. But the team considered it still an early prototype. Larry and Sergey, so the legend goes, simply said: "It is already good enough. Ship it." The team complied, despite their reservations and fear. Adjustments were made on the fly, rather than seeking up-front perfection. And the rest is history: Google Maps was a huge success. This success was aided by the fact that it did just one thing extremely well –its lack of extra features emphasised its differentiation. Shipping sooner accentuated this difference, and it took competitors a long time to catch up. Ask what is the minimum needed to test the product or service in the market?

Contrast the 'Waterfall Model' of design with the Agile or Minimum Viable Product Model. The former goes through sequential stages of Requirements, Design, Implementation, Verification, Maintenance. It moves from a known problem to a known solution. The Agile model goes from a known problem to an unknown solution, but sets out to test a string of small hypotheses and thereby adjust into the right solution by iteration. Insights include: 'Ship early and ship often', 'test and feedback', 'Learn, find out and prevent bugs', '5 why: why did we not catch that – what did we not understand?' Answer all of these and proceed by learning, rather than adopting the high risk procedure of putting forward a fully developed, detailed design which may then fail.

Similarly, Austin and Devin use the analogy of developing a theatre production, and say that "any activity which involves creating something entirely new requires artful making." Artful making is an emergent process involving cheap and rapid iteration to search for a valuable outcome. Cheap and rapid iteration (the reconfiguring of a process) is key to artful making, allowing experimentation to create form out of potentially diverse materials. Thus the production of a good Shakespeare play or a movie builds on the strengths of, and allows adaptation by, the principal actors. It involves a blend of top down direction and 'bottom up' innovation. This emergent process differs from industrial making "which emphasises the importance of detailed planning as well as highly specified objectives, processes and products". It is important not to try solving artistic problems (read many 'service problems') with industrial methods. You can't 'supervise' talented actors (read 'good service workers').

The Artful Making concept accepts variation within known parameters (release), allows discussion and contribution by all without prejudice (collaboration), believes the whole is greater than the sum of its parts (ensemble), and that quality is exhibited through interaction between members of the business and ultimately between the business and the customer (play or fun). This is maintained through collaboration that implies appreciation of the capabilities, skills and characteristics that each member of the team brings to the table and appreciates all for their uniqueness. Artful making is a belief that the process, through iteration, will deliver value.

Tim Brown of IDEO sees service design encompassing a wide spectrum from tackling some of the world's most challenging problems such as reduction in obesity to the detailed design of a hospital waiting room. It is the customer experience that is the most telling point in all these case studies. In every case there is the opportunity for turning all employees into design thinkers.

A service design exercise has many of the characteristics of a Lean Kaizen Event. These are held on-site, over a few days, with the staff and supervisors from the area as well as others such as people from quality, service improvement, IT and accounting. Events comprise direct observation and analysis, followed by brainstorming and idea generation, and then actual implementation and trial. Asking 'why?' is expected. There is no rank. Just do it.

There is similarity with the 'OODA' loop (John Boyd). Observe, Orient, Decide, Act. Observe means direct observation; Orient includes interpreting against experience, tradition, evidence, culture, and others; Decide includes hypothesis; Act includes testing the hypothesis.

There is also similarity with the '3P' process used in Lean manufacture. This 'production process preparation' uses concepts such as

- laying out the actual components, materials, and tools on a table;
- insisting that several alternative ways are generated for doing every process;
- brainstorming in separate groups to reduce 'groupthink';
- using scale models;
- using simulation – computer simulation or physical simulation or both;
- testing against various scenarios;
- homing in on the best solution gradually, but keeping options open until some decisive factor leads to a rejection of that path, but not the whole project;
- eventually, using full-scale mock-up prototypes.

IDEO typically uses the following stages: Observation, Synthesis, Idea Generation, Prototyping, Refinement, and Implementation (Bhavnani, 2006). However, like Lean product design, these are not definite steps separated by 'stage gates' but blend into one another, loop back, and evolve. Austin and Devin's analogy with a theatre production is useful. Although there is a framework or script, a play evolves through interaction between the actors, each bringing their own skills and interpretation, through experimentation and adjustment. Hence, all Shakespeare plays are different when performed and are interpreted in new and innovative ways.

IDEO's Tim Brown talks about moving through three overlapping spaces – the inspiration space, the ideation space, and the implementation space. This is non-linear and overlapping. And, like writing a Masters dissertation, it passes through phases of optimism, uncertainty, panic, and confidence.

But first the team......

Team

Service design thinking is not elitist. In fact, the involvement of the front line that comes into daily contact with customers is essential. It is also multidisciplinary. You may need service improvement specialists, maybe engineers, and often ergonomists. But you will also benefit from the insights of the full range of customers, including children when they are important customers. Software geeks and gamers may be useful. In fact IDEO likes to have 'fringe' users who may bring a future, as yet non-conventional, view of different needs and requirements.

Toyota and IDEO are similar with regard to follow-through responsibility. Toyota's 'shusas' (or chief engineers) are responsible for a new model from concept to use. If the car fails in the market, the shusa has failed – irrespective of the technical competence or the on-time launch of the car. So the shusa must study markets and customers as well as being in touch with technical developments. IDEO likes several team members to follow through to implementation stages.

Design Philosophy

The focus is on the **complete customer experience**. Widening the boundary. Not just the design of a seat for a railway carriage but the full cabin. This is systems thinking, with the recognition that it is the whole package, all the 'moments of truth', that make up customer satisfaction and delight.

Service design uses **a 'human-centred' systems approach**. There is much in common with socio-technical design – the emotions of staff and customers, as well as 'technical' delivery. Tim Brown asks, 'Does it inspire a new behaviour that will be forever associated with it?'

'Fail early, fail often' is used. Generate many ideas. Experiment and experiment again. It is not waste to reject ideas early on. It *is* waste to stop development at an advanced stage. This is similar to Toyota's 'set-based design' and 'bookshelving'. Set-based design gradually narrows the options, keeping many open as late as possible. For instance, start with 6 engine types and gradually narrow them down to the most suitable three. This is where 'bookshelving' comes in. The rejected three are not thrown away but are retained for possible future modification and use on another model. In service, and at IDEO, the record might be a sketch, a video, or a model. Bookshelving also results from blue-sky research studies on car components that are kept on the shelf for unspecified future use.

IDEO uses a 'Tech Box' – literally a Pandora's box of objects, gadgets, tools, materials, devices that are there to spark creativity.

Tolerate risk. Experiment. New service design involves risk. So, experiment. A famous service example is Harrah's Casinos, which continually experiments with new tables, layouts, one-armed-bandits, and so on, always seeking out better ways. But doing these as randomised trials – with old and new side-by-side - collecting data on usage and takings, over comparable time periods. This is similar to Darwin's survival of the fittest

Some relevant quotations from Austin and Devin's book *Artful Making* (2003) follow: "The experimental imperfections in the artful making approach are a primary source of innovation, a vital part of making anew. Artful makers respect and even treasure their 'mistakes'. These experiments are never deleted, a library of 'mistakes' builds which can be instantly accessed." And the "inclusion of past actions into the materials of creation is the force that drives emergence."

Gaining control by giving up control – another phrase from Austin and Devin – is of great relevance to service managers. "Compliance mechanisms, no matter how cleverly designed, inhibit exploration of paths that managers cannot understand". So, "control by release. Control by turning loose within well-understood parameters," as Austin and Devin put it. This is much like the military 'rules of engagement' that specify what can and can't be done but allow great flexibility within those rules.

The manager in artful making (read service design) believes that the iterative exploratory process will create good ideas of value to the customer without the need to exert control and direct events but rather to coach the team through the many multilayered and often diverse interactions.

This sentiment is echoed in a *Harvard Business Review* article about Sony Pictures where significant productivity gains were made by introducing two changes:

- 'Stop expecting people to operate like computers – at high speeds, continuously, running multiple programs at the same time – and recognize that human beings perform best and are most productive when they alternate between periods of intense focus and intermittent renewal.'
- Recognise people's 'core needs' – physical health, emotional well-being (arising out of feeling appreciated), mental clarity (ability to focus), and spiritual well-being (arising out of a feeling of serving a purpose beyond profit).

So, don't try to control every minute. Social interaction is good for productivity and health.

Get 'professional' help. Here, a professional is not necessarily someone from an established profession such as accounting, engineering or medicine: a professional here may be a skateboarder, frequent flyer, health centre user or hiker, or computer nerd. In short, anyone who makes good use of the service and knows a lot about what is needed. Extreme users are best! These are the people who are most likely to have *latent* needs.

Top down AND bottom up. Relying exclusively on top-down SWOT analysis, guided by consultants is a bad idea. Especially, beware of target driven improvement that is very likely to result in incremental improvement (if any!) rather than radical innovation. Good service design blends bold concept with 'devil in the detail'. Ask Apple computer!

2.3.2 The Service Design Methodology

What follows uses the service design methodology of IDEO as a framework. The IDEO methodology uses the following steps: Observation, Synthesis, Idea Generation, Prototyping, Refinement, and Implementation.

The steps below are presented as a sequence, but in practice flow back and forth until a good service design emerges.

Direct Observation

An established principle in Lean is direct observation at 'the gemba' or place of action. This is the starting point of Lean Service Design. To this can be added direct listening to customers, for example in a call centre or at a help desk. Cambridge philosopher Ludwig Wittgenstein said, 'Don't think. Look'. Do not rely on market surveys, which often aggregate the needs of existing customers. As Ford said, 'If I had asked customers what they needed they would have said a faster horse.'

While observing, ask why? Why do African women have to carry water in a drum on their head? Why not pull a rotating drum with a handle attached to each end? Why is a room numbering system so confusing? Some software developers use 'over the shoulder' observation to see where customers spend time and experience problems.

IDEO has interesting stories about direct observation. For instance, observing how difficult it is for passengers carrying luggage to insert a ticket into an automatic barrier, leading to redesign of ticketing and entry systems for a subway. Another: observing the stresses, needs, and confusion of patients in accident and emergency leading to redesign of waiting rooms and procedures.

Web site and phone IVP (where you get a choice: select 1 if...) should also be tested by direct observation of customers. How often do you phone an IVP and get exactly what you want, first time? Navigating a web site can be extremely frustrating.

Direct observation may include the following:

- Simply stand, watch and listen at 'the gemba' – the point of service delivery.
- Record the actual words used by a customer at the first point of contact – a classic call centre approach, discussed under 'Demand' in the Check methodology section. Listen and classify into value and failure demand.

- Following the customer journey – this is similar to the cycle of service/moments of truth mapping methodology explained in the mapping section of the book.
- Fly on the wall – Xerox used to use copy centres where customers could come in to make photocopies. Customer behaviour could then be studied.
- Shadowing – following a customer. Better still, asking to walk with him or her.
- Mystery shopping, or self-service. Here an employee of the service company pretends that she is a customer or applicant.

The following are not direct observation but are other IDEO innovations:

- Draw your own concept. Often used with children, this simply asks children to draw what they would like to experience.
- Extreme user interviews. This deliberately targets non-mainstream users (Geeks? Teenagers? Pensioners? Students?), who would make use of the service in a different way and may therefore reveal hidden opportunities. Other examples: Springbok rugby fans requesting South African beer, students wanting cut down versions of textbooks containing only relevant material.

Then, of course, there are traditional surveys and market research. But here focus on those customers who are not using the service or who have defected.

Synthesis

Synthesis involves bringing together the information collected during the observation phase. The idea is to assemble a 'rich picture', appreciation, or understanding of the situation. Methods include:

- Drawing a 'Rich Picture' systems diagram or cartoon. Essentially, assemble a montage. Draw the players and their interactions. Use bubbles with actual quotes. Use symbols for computers, phones, and artifacts. Add photographs. System boundary lines are drawn around logical groupings. These may not correspond with organisational boundaries.
- A variant on rich picture building is to use a form of 'affinity diagram'. Here, statements, conversations, comments, conversations, and sketches are first written on sticky notes and then assembled on a big board in logical groupings.
- Storytelling: tell stories of experiences. Especially effective if emotion or acting can be brought in.
- Scenarios: a scenario is a 'what if' of a possible future situation, typically done by writing a story about a future event. A scenario is not a forecast, but should be based on reality not fantasy.

Idea Generation

Ideas are generated in all stages of service design, but this stage is concerned with specific idea creation. More than one of the following may be used:

- Brainstorming – conventional brainstorming is often effective, but here are some checkpoints:
  - Before throwing ideas forward, allow five minutes of silent, individual thinking.
  - Have participants write their ideas on sticky notes. This has the effect of clarifying ideas.
  - Begin by going around the group, one by one. This prevents domination by powerful personalities. Participants offer up their stickies.
  - No criticism; focus on volume.

- Heuristic problem solving. Karl Albrecht believes that effective problem solving is not a linear stepped procedure, but an interaction between five zones:
  - The Neutral Zone where ideas meet, accumulate and where the problem is defined and re-defined.
  - The End Zone – where the group will get to.
  - The Data Zone – or zone of evidence and facts.
  - The Ozone – the zone where idea generation and brainstorming take place.
  - The Judgment Zone – the place for critical evaluation.

Albrecht believes that effective problem solving involves moving the group through the various zones, backwards and forwards, but always making clear what zone the group is in. Maybe you start in the neutral zone, move to ozone, back to neutral, then end zone, then data, then judgment, then back to ozone, end zone, and so on. Keep going. Refine, narrow down or expand. We have personal experience of this highly effective iterative method.

- **A3**: classic Toyota A3 is described in a section in Part 4. Note that this is iterative, developmental, and consensus building. Never done alone. John Shook says 'it takes two to A3'.

- **The Why:** this is again classic Lean and is usually part of A3. But do ask why and why not. For example, 'Why can't we run an eye hospital, or do heart surgery, like a production line?' (as in hospitals in Russia or India respectively) or specialise like Shouldice hospital in Toronto which only does hernia operations?

Prototyping

IDEO does prototyping for service design. This has an equivalent in Lean product development called '3P' – production, preparation, and process. Essentially it is

- Build a mock up, or prototype, preferably full scale. But do this cheaply and flexibly. Use cardboard boxes, wood, or 'crayform'
- Emphasise that the participants will have the chance to influence their own working environment or service experience – present or future.
- Get users to simulate using the design prototype. This may involve role-playing. But do it, experience it, don't talk about it.
- The participants discuss, adjust, and do it all again.
- Write up the standard, recommended ways of operating.
- Keep a flip chart handy. Get participants to write ideas on the chart. A flip chart can be followed through to actual implementation.

Implement

The implementation stage flows naturally out of prototyping. Because there has been involvement of actual users in several of the earlier stages, but particularly during prototyping, there is ownership and there should be no 'change management' or implementation barriers. John Seddon refers to this as 'roll in' rather than 'roll out'. A good systems thinking maxim is 'slower is faster'.

Further Reading

Ritesh Bivani, *IDEO: Service Design (A)*, INSEAD case Study, ECCH, Case number 606-012-1, 2006
Tim Brown, *Change by Design*, Harper Business , 2009
Roger Martin, *The Design of Business*, Harvard Business Press, 2009
Tony Schwartz, 'The Productivity Paradox: How Sony Pictures Gets More out of People by Demanding Less', *Harvard Business Review*, June 2010, page 65-69
Venkat Ramaswamy and Francis Gouillart, Buiding the Co-Creative Enterprise, *Harvard Business Review*, October 2010, p100-109
Karl Albrecht, *Practical Intelligence*, Jossey Bass, 2007
BBC TV Series, *The Genius of Design*, 2010

Part 3:   Service Analysis and Mapping

3.1   Overview of the Lean Service Approach

This section gives an overview and relates to the flow chart below. What is attempted here is an overview applicable to most administrative and service situations. The vast range of such situations means that the overview and flowchart can never be totally satisfactory. However, the intention is to provide general guidance and to raise a few relevant considerations. The main concepts follow from Part 2 of this book. Detailed tools that may be applicable are described in Part 4 of this book.

Begin at what is here called '**Level 1**'. This is the big picture, the high level overview.

A starting point is to decide if the area you are working with should be centralised or decentralised. It is an organisation question, which may not be relevant to all. Some offices and functions serve multiple product or service streams (in other words they are a central support function), while others are integrated with service delivery or manufacturing. If the former is the case, a good consideration is whether the function should be moved closer to the prime process. For example, should a call centre be decentralised to be closer to field service, or should accounting and planning be moved from a central function into a 'focused factory' located next to the shop floor? Or the other way round? This question is a vital one. You can proceed without answering the question immediately, but bear it in mind.

Then consider the range of tasks that are undertaken. Often there will only be one main task, like a call centre supporting field operations. Other times there may be a range of functions such as accounting, undertaking cash flow, credit checks, ledger, invoicing, measures, and so on. Of course there will always be secondary tasks, such as appraisals and training.

Consider the Runners, Repeaters, Strangers (RRS) concept. For example, are there Runners that take place all the time, and Repeaters that happen regularly but not continually? Do a Pareto of the activities. It is an important way to organise resources, and to prioritise analysis activity. You may come out with a two dimensional chart: main tasks against RRS categories.

Then attempt to define in concise terms the purpose or aim of each task or sub-system. Purpose should be from the customer's viewpoint, preferably end-to-end. Profit is not a purpose, it is a measure. The complete task. Look at the existing measures and ask if they support the purpose, or actually work against it. You are likely to find several measures that do the latter.

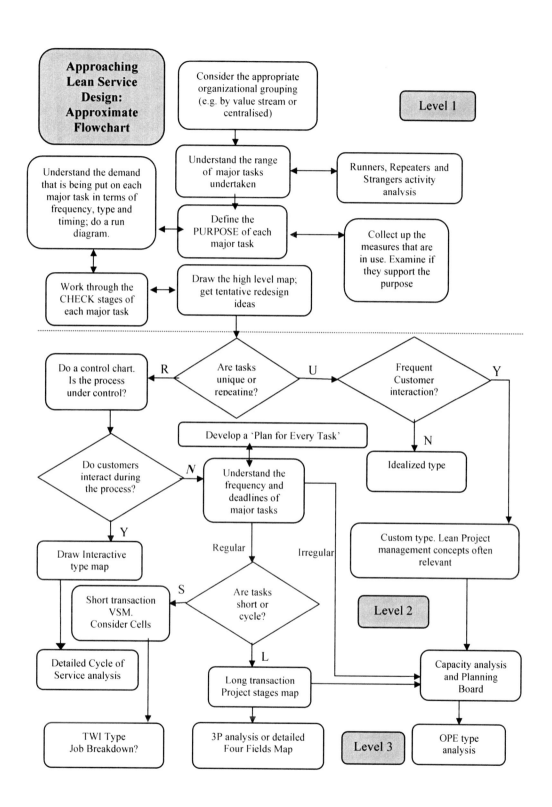

Approaching Lean Service Design: Approximate Flowchart

Consider the appropriate organizational grouping (e.g. by value stream or centralised)

Level 1

Understand the range of major tasks undertaken

Runners, Repeaters and Strangers activity analysis

Understand the demand that is being put on each major task in terms of frequency, type and timing; do a run diagram.

Define the PURPOSE of each major task

Collect up the measures that are in use. Examine if they support the purpose

Work through the CHECK stages of each major task

Draw the high level map; get tentative redesign ideas

Do a control chart. Is the process under control?

R

Are tasks unique or repeating?

U

Frequent Customer interaction?

Y

Develop a 'Plan for Every Task'

N

Idealized type

Do customers interact during the process?

N

Understand the frequency and deadlines of major tasks

Custom type. Lean Project management concepts often relevant

Y

Draw Interactive type map

Regular

Irregular

Short transaction VSM. Consider Cells

S

Are tasks short or cycle?

Level 2

Detailed Cycle of Service analysis

L

Capacity analysis and Planning Board

Long transaction Project stages map

TWI Type Job Breakdown?

3P analysis or detailed Four Fields Map

Level 3

OPE type analysis

Once you have defined the purpose of the system, think, propose and discuss the ideal way in which the service should be delivered.

Keep in mind that the most effective thing you can do to improve the effectiveness of an existing system is to free up capacity. This enables response time to be improved and initiates a virtuous circle of improvement that steadily eliminates problems. And the most effective way of freeing up capacity is to reduce failure demand – demand that should not be there in the first place.

Understanding the demand on each task is critical. Major categories are Value Demand (first time demand) and Failure Demand. Quantify these. Often, this will involve listening to customers' actual words. Demand also needs to be understood in terms of frequency (load) and timing across an hour, a day, a month. A run diagram will be a powerful aid.

Having defined the main tasks, draw out a high level map for each task. Just the broad stages, no detail. 'Where is the system boundary?' is an important consideration. As the map is drawn, carry out the six 'Check' activities as described in an earlier section. These Check activities are likely to refine the map and to re-quantify the demand situation. The outcome should be some tentative ideas on change. Perhaps some radical ideas. You are after high level wastes here. The detailed Seven Wastes are not really applicable at this level – it is broad level wastes that are of concern.

You will have got into some detail already, but now **Level 2** detail process analysis begins. An early point is to distinguish between unique and repeating tasks. This is not clear-cut. In service few tasks are ever the same, at least at the detail level. Dealing with complaints, bookings, repairs, reconciliations, property registrations, hernia operations, is repetitive, but designing a new building or defending a criminal case is not repetitive to the same degree. It is a judgment call.

Assuming repeating tasks, an early consideration is to use control chart theory to have a look at tasks that are 'out of control' and to explore the reasons. Maybe customer response goes walkabout when Joe goes on leave. List these 'system conditions' for future attention because they can have a devastating 'knock-on' effect.

Now look at whether customers interact during the process, or whether interaction takes place largely at the beginning and end. This is a fundamental distinction: where customers are involved the service needs to be more flexible. Customers are part of the process and the extent of their involvement is a consideration, they can make errors that are not fully under your control, and front line staff interaction is more critical. By contrast, in low interaction situations a staff member may never deal with an existing customer.

If the service is Interactive, the Service Blueprint or Cycle of Service methodology is a powerful approach. This looks at value enhancement primarily, efficiency secondarily.

If the service is not Interactive but repetitive. and where the tasks have regular deadlines and are generally short cycle, we call it Transactional in this book.

Both Transactional and Interactive approaches will benefit in a major way from the earlier Level 1 analysis. To 'jump in' directly to this stage risks sub-optimisation. You will never know what has been missed!

Where repetitive transactional activities are generally short cycle – say less than an hour - this would be the only area where some manufacturing-type value stream mapping MIGHT be applicable. Possibly the service is more of a 'service factory'. Cells may be relevant here, but are sometimes challenging to implement in service.

Long cycle activities are better dealt with by some project management concepts. Time management considerations are always important, but particularly so in what are called 'Custom environments' in this book.

Where tasks are unique, a question is whether critical resources (mainly people, sometimes facilities) are shared. By a 'shared' resource we mean the degree to which a person works alone or as part of a team. Perhaps no-one works completely alone, but it is the sequence dependencies that are the issue – to what extent critical resources are dependent on the completion of activities by others. Also of relevance is whether a critical resource works on several tasks simultaneously – perhaps a senior accountant, engineer or computer systems analyst whose expertise is required on several projects. Not good practice, but sometimes unavoidable. Where they are shared, sequencing and scheduling are simpler, but not necessarily very simple. Where they are not shared, the establishment of cells is easier. In Custom environments, 'Critical Chain' concepts are often helpful.

Level 3: the micro detail level. In repetitive environments, particularly short cycle, a TWI-type 'Job Breakdown Chart' is often useful. This simply involves creating a table with the main steps, (ignore steps like 'pick up pen' that will be done anyway), key points (a key point is one that makes or breaks a job, may injure the worker, or makes it easier to do), and the reasons for the key points. The reasons are particularly important. 3P type analysis is useful in several environments, but particularly in the Custom or project management type. Detailed Four Field mapping can be used to get right into the detail. In many professional service environments, Overall Professional Effectiveness (OPE) concepts can be very powerful.

Once again, beware of leaping into detail much too early. You risk shifting the deck chairs on the Titanic. Worse, you may completely 'turn off' staff by micro analysis, like silly 5S, time studies or activity sampling that is done way too early when 'everybody knows' that there is huge waste out there. This is not to say it is useless – ten seconds taken out of 50k activities per year is not trivial.

Sometimes you may stop work after Level 1. The insights and gains may be sufficient. It could be that you have taken out 50% of the time or waste. Similarly at Level 2.

3.2   A Service Mapping Framework

Why Map? Because a map fosters understanding amongst participants who would like to improve the process or system. In particular, a map fosters understanding of the relationship between elements. An example is the famous map of the London Underground. This allows an easy understanding of how to travel around London, used by millions of people. But the London Underground map is not a geographic map that can be used by walkers. It has the minimum necessary information needed for tube travel, and shows this complex information in a superbly clear way. That is what a map should aim to do.

It is tempting to leap in and begin to map or 5S or do a kaizen event virtually on day one of a Lean implementation. This may be a reasonable, even a good thing to do in early days of Lean, for the sake of sending out a positive message to all levels of staff, top to bottom. This type of activity may be referred to as 'Lean Light' as opposed to 'System Lean'. Lean Light can switch on the light, highlight the vast number of opportunities, enthuse the staff for a while, and may even teach a few Lean tools.

However, Lean Light does have its dangers: a piecemeal approach, a considerable risk of sub-optimisation, not much impact on the bottom line, and sustainability issues when staff at all levels begin to realise these points.

You may think you are doing great things by 5S activity up front. Perhaps you are. But you are more likely to be arranging deck chairs on the Titanic.

So, move into System Lean quite rapidly – although not necessarily at the very start of a Lean implementation.

For Lean Light, skip Level 1 as described below and move directly to Level 2 – but be aware of the risks. Remember, Lean Light is the mark of the inexperienced, though enthusiastic, Lean practitioner. It is much better to approach mapping on three levels as discussed below.

Level 1: This is the Big Picture or Systems view where the purpose of the system is understood. It should be more strategic, led by a senior manager or, at the very least, fully supported and endorsed by a senior manager.
Level 2: This is the process value stream map level at which the end-to-end process is mapped in current state maps (note plural), and most often a future state map and action plan is proposed. In Level 2 four generic types will be presented.
Level 3: The detailed process activity map aimed at some sub-processes. This level is not always done, particularly for some types of value streams.
The three level concept is shown in the following figure. The Flowchart and accompanying text give an outline of the process.

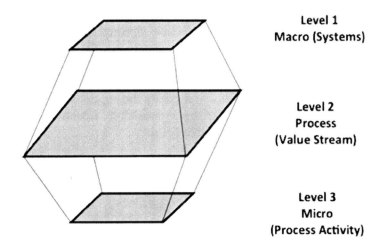

Level 1
Macro (Systems)

Level 2
Process
(Value Stream)

Level 3
Micro
(Process Activity)

At the top level is the macro map, applicable in most service situations. This is the 'big picture' or Systems view. It is presented in the next section. Below that is found the mapping typology with the four types. This will be referred to as Process Mapping – although for two of the types, mapping in the usual sense of the word is less useful. Each of these four types is presented in a later section. Below that are 'micro' maps where, if necessary, the detail can be explored. The micro maps are the traditional 'industrial engineering' process activity maps or 'four fields mapping'. At the micro level, the '3P' process and concepts like Overall Professional Effectiveness are relevant in some situations. These are covered briefly in a later section. In many situations, but certainly not all, 'mapping' at all three levels is appropriate. However, such mapping may not be end-to-end. It is appropriate to map, or at least analyse, end-to-end at the macro level, but often mapping will only be partial if at all at the micro level.

All four types can be used to design and redesign a service delivery system. However, the Idealised and Custom types are applicable in specific design environments.

	Goals	Design or Structure	Management/ Measures
Organisation Level			
Process Level			
Job (Task) Level			

Another but similar view draws on Rummler and Brache (1990), who suggested a hierarchical improvement matrix, as shown in the table above.

What is suggested in this book is that the 'System' or purpose be examined at the macro or organisation level, then the process level be explored in greater depth after the system purpose is understood, and then only in some cases the task or detailed job level be analysed.

However, the macro or systems level is not necessarily the organisation level. It may more commonly be a major grouping within the organisation. Levels 2 and 3 then follow appropriately. This is shown in the table below.

Organisation	Macro Level (Level 1: System) examples	Process Level (Level 2) examples	Micro Level (Level 3: Task) examples
Local authority	Housing, leisure services	Housing repairs, leisure centre management	Detailed visit process, swimming
Healthcare	A&E, patient operations (both end to end)	A&E patient flow, operation cycle of service	Detailed scheduling, ordering supplies
Bank	Personal banking, small business support	Account management, business advice	Opening an account, processing a loan
Consulting Engineer	Project management	Design	Preparing a contract
Field Service	Product support	Maintenance cycle of service	Ensuring correct parts

3.3 Level 1: System Considerations and Macro Maps

This section contains the stages necessary for macro service mapping and analysis. These basic concepts are applicable in every service situation and should precede the more detailed focused analysis undertaken in Level 2.

Acknowledgement

Parts of this section draw heavily on John Seddon's *Freedom from Command and Control*. However, the views presented here are not necessarily those of John Seddon.

Starting out on Lean Service Improvement

The methodology for Lean service improvement presented here starts at the System level. This is in marked contrast to almost all publications on Lean mapping, whether manufacturing or service, which generally start with the identification of families and then dive straight into process level mapping. Very little or no discussion is typically given about understanding the wider system. For example, see Keyte and Locher – a good book on what are here called 'service transactions' – and Drew, McCallum and Roggenhofer, whose Step 1 is 'Create value streams by grouping similar products or services'. Moreover, these books consider demand much later. This is acceptable in manufacturing but seldom in service.

A starting point in Lean service improvement is to identify the system of concern. Generally, at the macro level, this will be known. You will know that your concern is, for example, in Accident and Emergency or Field Maintenance. Where there is some uncertainty is with the system boundary – where the system of concern begins and ends. Note that this is different from the classic manufacturing value stream mapping approach, which breaks the overall area into families using a matrix of products or customers against major process steps – trying to identify appropriate groupings.

Looking at the system or big picture helps to avoid sub-optimisation. Or, as Stephen Covey advises, 'Start with the end in mind'.

The following procedure should be worked through by a high level team before actual Lean improvement begins.

Step One: Clarify the System

List and classify the major service delivery systems with which the organisation is concerned. These are the transformational processes that the organisation is primarily involved in delivering.

If you are lucky the area may have only one clear major activity that everyone works on all day, except, for example, when training, interviewing or appraising. But some administrative functions do several major tasks, such as an accounting function that does cash management, ledger, and payments. A university may do both research3 and teaching. If this is the case, these tasks or sub-systems need to be defined and clarified. The purpose of each needs to be defined. A useful way in is to use a matrix with tasks and Runners, Repeaters and Strangers, as shown below.

If you know the system of concern you can skip over the following and jump straight to system boundary considerations below.

	Major Task 1	Major Task 2	Major Task n
Runners	Sub process prime Sub process support		Etc
Repeaters	Sub process support	Sub process prime Sub process support	
Strangers			

There are two types of system:

- **Primary (or Core)**: a series of activities, which deliver customer value in terms of a product or service. In a hospital, a primary mission may be concerned with transforming a sick patient into a reasonably well patient. But this would have to be broken down into the main core systems such as A&E, adult surgical, and outpatient care. Generally, primary systems deliver value to real, external customers. Call centre activities, together with any related field service activity, are primary. A creative process such as design or research may best be regarded as primary, insofar as value is delivered to future external customers.

- **Support**: a series of activities, which are necessary to support the prime systems. A support process does not generally deal with external customers. The recruitment process is an example. Do not get into an argument about support processes being value added or non-value added. To label support processes as 'non-value adding' can be demotivating, if not insulting. The distinction between primary and support is not always clear-cut. There are 'grey' areas between them – examples are invoicing and a university library. If in doubt classify it as 'support' because the doubt reveals that it is at least not in the front rank of prime customer value.

Begin by listing the primary systems.

- Carry out a ranking exercise that aims to arrange the processes in terms of importance to the current and future business. This can simply be done by voting on a one-to-five basis. A 'smarter' way is to do pair-wise comparison whereby every candidate process is ranked against every other on the basis of more important (+1), same (0) or less important (-1). Simply add up the point scores for each process.

- Rank the systems in terms of perceived ease of implementation.

- Plot the processes on a matrix showing importance against ease of implementation. You will often give priority to processes in the 'important/easy to implement' category.

- Discuss which systems should be considered for the first tranche of Lean improvement.

Then repeat the exercise with the support processes. There may be good reason to start a Lean improvement exercise with support activities, since you may want to develop some experience with mapping before getting into core processes. You may, of course, wish to do all the prime processes in an area together because they overlap so much.

At this stage you will want to select the team to do the exercise. A good team size is around eight, including an experienced facilitator, some staff from the actual process and, essentially, front line management from the process. They do not all have to be full time.

Step Two: Go though the 'Check' Stage

The six stages of The Vanguard 'Check Model' are described in the second section of this book. They are very powerful. Working through the steps is important. It is also recommended that consideration be given to the CATWOE characteristics as discussed in the Systems section.

Why do you want to do this? First, because it clarifies system issues. Second, because it gives an insight into the proportions of 'value' and 'failure' demand. Ideally, failure demand should not exist, but it may be tying up large chunks of resource, driving away loyal customers, and preventing potential customers from being served. Third, because the step gives valuable insight into what the process is actually dealing with as opposed to what management thinks the process is dealing with.

Staff and managers from the process should both be involved in the 'Check' stage because involvement in the discovery of problems and issues is the most successful way of bringing about change. Both managers and staff often have fixed ideas about what 'the problems' are. Listening to customers' actual words helps to change minds. Staff and managers both see the problems, they design the solution, they get it going. Then it is sustained.

This step may seem like a waste of time when the team is most anxious to 'get in and start analysing or mapping'. Don't be deluded. Don't fall for 'We know our customers', or 'We know what the problems are'. The step is likely to be a time consuming one, so the team needs to be split up to cover a range of customers and situations. But it is time well spent.

Get the team to 'go to the Gemba' (the place of action) and collect a sample of actual demands on the process. The start is the entry point for customers into the process. It may be the call centre, the front desk at a hotel or library, the A&E entry point, or the point at which orders are taken. This point may not always be in an office: it may be in a field emergency vehicle, at a check-in counter, or at home collection points. If possible, walk the first few steps with the customer. In a 'professional service' process this step may present some difficulty in terms of time or confidentiality. If so, ask the front line professional to make notes after each interview as to the nature of the request, but excluding personal detail.

A representative sample is required. This will require discussion. For example, the team may wish to cover types of customer, times of the day, service types, size of request, or urgency of request. What is not needed is an 'activity sample' (see later separate section) but simply an appreciation of the situation. As a rule of thumb, collect 200 observations or calls.

The team should record verbatim, as far as possible, what customers actually say. If requests for work are written, note them down. Use the actual words, but reduce the remarks to a sentence or a phrase or two.

Then the team should transfer the phrases to large (12.5 cm x 7.5 cm) post-its.

The Affinity Diagram is the next stage. First colour-code each post-it with a large green or red dot for Value Demand and Failure Demand respectively. Value Demand are 'first time' requests. Failure Demand are requests that should not happen if the process is working well.

Categorise the 'Top 10' demands. Seek logical groupings. For example, these may be product, service, age, complaint, location, time, or gender related. Collect similar post-its and group them into areas. This may involve more than one iteration.

Then group the post-its into two columns, Value Demand and Failure Demand, and as many rows as necessary. For example, the rows may be by contact type: walk-in, telephone, internet, post. There will invariably be one or more Paretos (dominant groupings). For example, 65% of demands arrive by phone, and 80% of failure demand arrives via the internet. Although not statistically valid, this will be very useful information. You may decide to collect up more information to give the conclusions more statistical validity, but for most processes the value will already have been gained.

The groupings will form a valuable insight into how the process should be mapped and which are the important issues.

Understand the System Capability (Variation and Delivery)

Capability is part of the Vanguard Check Stage. Here we elaborate further. Time and variation are vitally important factors in service. Lead time is very often the major differentiating factor, or the greatest source of dissatisfaction in service delivery.

As discussed in Part 1, there are three variables that influence lead time (or queue time) – arrival variation, process variation, and utilisation. You cannot understand service lead time without some grasp of where you are with respect to all three. Which is having the greatest influence? Variation is particularly important where there is high utilization. Arrival variation and process variation both play a role – so ignoring one whilst focusing on the other is folly.

The ability of the system to meet current demands in time is important. Time-series data need to be collected on the end-to-end system performance. Note that 'end-to-end' should be from the external customer's viewpoint, not the organisation's viewpoint. At least use an external factual measure, not a subjective measure: the time from placing the order to actual receipt, not the time from booking the order into the scheduling system to the promised (or re-promised?) delivery date. The time series should cover at least a month, but the period will need to be discussed, particularly if seasonality is a factor.

–   Select an appropriate end-to-end measure from the customer's viewpoint.
–   Measure: note that customer end-to-end times are very likely to cross departmental boundaries and will sometimes cross managerial or organisational boundaries.
–   Draw a run diagram, covering a reasonable horizon.
–   Establish the control limits for the chart. Use statistical process control software, or software such as Minitab. If this is not available, calculate the mean and standard deviation and draw the upper control limit as mean plus three standard deviations.
–   Examine for variation. See if the process is 'in control'. Are all points between the control limits, or between the upper control limit and 0? If they are, it is a good sign – the process can be improved without bothering about special circumstances. If there are points that plot beyond the control limits, it indicates that there are 'special causes' beyond normal variation. The cause of such situations needs to be identified if possible because they are unusual events that may de-stabilise the process. It is not always easy to go back and identify the reasons for some out-of-control plots, but do discuss them with the service team. Perhaps there are repair jobs that are shelved because an unusual spare part is not available, or the location is hard to get to, or the customer's credit rating is unacceptable. Whatever the reasons, you will need to think if these merit special attention.

See also the separate sections within the Tools section on Variation and Control Charts.

End-to-end delivery response time is often an important differentiator in supply chains and in service processes. Drawing out the run diagram will allow the team to make comparisons with competitors and to identify opportunities. For instance:

- How do healthcare end-to-end response times compare between hospitals?
- How do they compare against patient needs?
- What additional business would be generated by shorter response times?
- How do actual response times match with service level agreements?
- What percentage of completions fall within customer expected delivery times?

Look out for unsatisfactory actual end-to-end response time even though the currently measured response time is satisfactory. A classic example was doctors having an unofficial queue, but adding patients to their official queues only when the wait time was under-target.

If the end-to-end times are unsatisfactory, then one consideration has to be, which part of the end-to-end process should be tackled first? It is a judgment call as to whether system redesign will result in dramatic time reductions to bring the process within acceptable times, or whether the process needs to be 'chunked'. If the process needs to be 'chunked', where is the greatest potential for time saving? The Three Day Car Study showed that typical wait time for medium price cars in 2002 was 40 days, but actual manufacture and delivery times together were three or four days. The opportunity therefore lay in the order entry and scheduling system, not in manufacture.

Next consider CATWOE. See Part 2. Work through the CATWOE stages – they will give huge insight.

Step Three: Redefine the System and System Boundary

Now the team is in a better position to redefine the system or process boundary. What is to be included and what excluded is an important consideration. You will usually want a process to be 'end-to-end' – a complete 'cycle of service' – for example, the complete cycle from wanting a car to be serviced to the service being satisfactorily concluded. However, you may want to modify your earlier analysis if you find, for example, that the availability of spare parts is a major source of complaint. In the Custom type service category (see later) the team will want to consider what third parties to involve, if any. In the Interactive category there are sometimes several third parties who can 'spoil the party' – cleaners in a hospital or restaurants at an airport.

Step Four: Draw the High Level Map

This step would have started in Step 2 – check. Now it can be refined. The broad outline map of the process shows only the main steps or players. The purpose is to clarify the system that is being dealt with. The input and output should be shown in generic terms only – for instance, 'Customer Demand'. Show only the main stages and main interactions. This is not the actual mapping exercise, but it will form the framework for broad scale analysis and for detailed mapping. Two examples will be shown.

A Level 1 map should not require the process to be walked or physically mapped. That comes later. The Level 1 map, unlike Level 2, may require some discussion but will be known to almost everyone. Managers should be able to write down the outline. To this outline map will be added the information from the 'Check' stage. This will generally not be known beforehand.

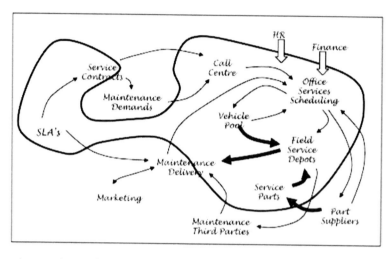

To the map shown above should be added:

- **Value and failure demand information**. In the example it was found that about 40% of calls were failure demand.
- **Rework loops**. In the example about 25% of calls were aborted due to incorrect parts, client not available, incorrect information e.g. model number. These were Pareto-analysed.
- **A run diagram or control chart** showing delivery performance over time. In the example the system was found to be generally 'in control', but end-to-end time was between one day and 25 days. The SLA was 48 hours.
- **Measures**. The various sections each have their own performance targets; call to fix time is not measured.

The high level map is a prime tool for management discussion. Often senior management will not wish to dive into the detail of the subsequent maps to be described, although they will want the broad conclusions from such mapping. The high level map is also a prime tool for concept re-design. Strip away the detail and get to the essence of the system. A high level map will often be drawn several times as more is learned about the current system and about future system possibilities.

Sometimes it is adequate simply to show the main activity groupings and their interactions. An example for a field service operation is shown.

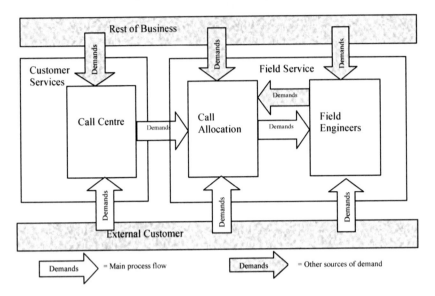

From James Carr, MSc Dissertation, Cardiff Business School, 2007

Step Five: Examine the Current Measures

Having defined the purpose and the appropriate system boundary, it is important to examine the current measures of performance to see if they support or conflict with the purpose. An example from a call centre supporting a field service operation is shown.

What is not being measured can be as important as what is being measured. Is it end-to-end or overall performance from the customer's standpoint that is being measured?

Be particularly concerned with measures and especially any targets that are likely to drive deviant behaviour. First, superimpose on the high level map 'loops' that show the organisational boundaries. Then write down the main KPI's that are in operation within each loop. Finally, critically examine each KPI grouping to see if they conflict and if they support the overall end-to-end purpose of the system.

Numerous examples of conflicting or counter-productive KPI's from the British public service are given in the amusing, worrying, but very useful book *The Tiger That Isn't* by Blastland and Dinot, Profile Books, 2007.

Measure	Focus	Support the Purpose?	The Effect
Productivity	Internal,	No	Calls can be dropped

(calls per hour)	efficiency based		or customers given inappropriate attention, resulting in failure demand
MTBF	Reflects the reliability of the machines supported	Yes / partly	Does not drive improvement, but may relate to preventable demand
Number of repeat calls	Attempts to measure the effectiveness of the field service	Maybe…	Games can be played by booking into another job number. May be the customer's fault
Calls waiting	The number of calls in the queue at any time	Partly	The number of abandoned calls is not known

The Creative Phase in Level 1 Mapping

With the high level map and the available 'check' and systems data – including a succinct statement of purpose – the team should consider whether the existing system is capable of meeting the purpose in the easiest, most simple way.

This is the stage where the Service Design methodology should be employed.

Radical, bold, high-level systems thinking is required – not detail tinkering with the existing process. When you get into the detail during Level 2 analysis, you may find some good reasons why the redesign is not possible – but start out from the ideal, from what could be, and not from the negative 'why it can't be done' viewpoint.

Start out from a 'blank sheet of paper', from the ideal, and work backwards rather than forwards from the detailed current state. Give a vision of what might be.
In the earlier example, why not:

- Allow customers to contact field service deliveries directly?
- Allow field service to fix the actual repair times at the customer site?
- Distribute vehicles among field service depots?
- Give field service direct responsibility for spare parts?

Sketch the ideal state. Discuss it with the system owners. Perhaps, for some situations build a Prototype like IDEO and get users to actually use the prototype. Iron out the bugs by direct observation. This is participative design.

Now you are ready to get into the detail using Level 2 mapping and redesign. You will not always need to do a map at Level 2. If you have a radical new concept or if you are designing a new system Level 2 mapping may not be appropriate.

Having obtained a new view of the system, the team may decide to map the whole system at Level 2, or only a part. That is one of the bonus features of the three-level analysis – you only pursue that which is seen to be necessary or effective.

On Selecting Priorities

A useful framework at this stage is PICK analysis. Simply list the options or alternatives and plot them with post-it stickers on the framework below.

		Ease of Implementation	
		Easy	Hard
Impact	Small	Challenge	Kill
	Large	Implement	Possible

Acknowledgement: Thanks to Danny Platt for this framework.

3.4 Level 2: Process Maps

The Service Mapping Typology

The range of possible service processes is huge. It is simply unrealistic to believe that there is one type of map to cope with all service situations. Two common characteristics or axes will be used to distinguish the service mapping types.

Repeatability

This is to do with the repetitiveness of customers or transactions that go through the value stream. Repeatability refers to similarity by stage rather than by individual customer. It is from the organisation's viewpoint, not the customer's viewpoint. While every patient with a broken arm in a hospital may be different, and a patient may only have one broken arm in a lifetime, the stages that they go through in a hospital to get well are broadly similar. This does not necessarily apply end-to-end. A patient may be moved to a hospital in a variety of ways, and as an outpatient may have very different recovery paths, but in the hospital the process steps are very similar. Low repeatability, by contrast, again from the organisation's viewpoint, would occur infrequently: for example a consultant working on the new Wembley stadium.

While the broad stages may have high repeatability, the detail work done may be very dissimilar.

Low repeatability may also mean zero repeatability, or a task that that has never been done before.

Customer Involvement

Customer involvement refers to the frequency with which front line service providers come into contact with customers. By 'Customers' we generally mean external customers. Low intensity service providers may only meet the customer by means of a single briefing or a completed form. High customer contact involves frequent contacts and adjustments. On the whole, 'front office' operations are high intensity and 'back office' are low intensity. Beware, however, of assuming front office and back office thinking – this is another form of silo thinking! A 'middle office' is probably a bad solution also.

Customer involvement does not refer to the length of the contact but to the frequency. Remember (see separate section) that a high degree of 'failure demand' to sort out a problem that should not have happened in the first place does not constitute high customer involvement.

The Mapping Typology

Customer Involvement

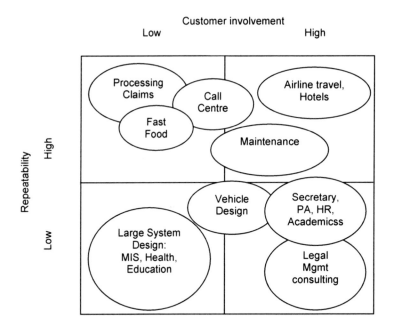

These two axes give a four-cell typology. But the cell boundaries are fuzzy. In fact, both axes are better represented as spectrums.

An end-to-end value stream may cover more than one cell.

It is important to remember that in service, as opposed to manufacturing, it is common for an individual to work part of the time in one type of process and part in another. This is because one person may work in more than one value stream. For example, a solicitor may do relatively repetitive work, such as conveyance, for part of the week, and then change to a court case or briefing a QC during another part of the week.

Idealised Type

The Idealised Type typically occurs in large system design situations. A service system is being designed or re-designed. It is normally high-level. There may well be a period of intense briefing with external customers while the project is being sorted out, but thereafter the next contact with external customers is towards the end of the process. For example, a security system, a distribution system, a course curriculum, a transport system, or an information system. Innovation is critical. Takt time is not relevant.

Custom Type

A classic Custom type occurs when an architect or consultant works with a client to solve a problem. The goal may be clear but exactly how to get there is not. Many PA or administrative tasks are of this type. Frequent adjustment is common, as, for example, when a travel agent works through an itinerary with the client. Many examples will be of the project management type, so project management theory and practice will be useful. This type has the following characteristics:

- Excellent understanding of customer requirements is important;
- There is open-ended scope for customers and work. A consulting engineer may seldom design a similar artefact although similar basic disciplines and tools may be used. A surgeon will have to examine each patient individually before deciding on a course of action.
- Innovation is a differentiator.
- The process can only be specified in broad outline. The framework to allow effective, creative work is the focus.
- Times can be estimated but there is great uncertainty. Takt time has little meaning.

Transactional Type

The Transactional type is the closest to manufacturing – the paper factory, some call centres. There is a low degree of customer contact – maybe none face-to-face, only by telephone, letter or internet. Insurance and banking so-called 'back office' operations are classic areas. Production scheduling is often of this type. Someone in HR may work part-time in a creative value stream, and part-time in a transactional value stream. Takt time may well be meaningful, but needs to be treated with caution where there is a danger of generating poor quality work. In this type, decisions have to be made, but typically only within limited parameters such as Go/NoGo, the amount of money, or by referring to an enquiry system or flowchart.

A dental receptionist taking regular appointments may be of this type because many routine appointments (but not dental surgery) involve approximately the same steps. But visiting a dental surgery would be better mapped using Interactive maps.

Interactive Type

This type has the following characteristics:

- Frequent interactions with customers, often by several 'players' along the value stream. These 'players' may come from several departments or even several organisations.
- The customer builds satisfaction not through just one transaction or 'product' but through the accumulation of experiences or Moments of Truth, sometimes over an extended period.
- Front line delivery by service staff is a differentiator. There is a great deal of difference between an efficient but scowling check-in clerk and one who greets guests by name and with a sincere smile.

The four types of service will be used to position different types of tools for Lean service – particularly value stream mapping variants.

Once again, this is not to suggest that a service employee spends all his or her time in one segment. It is quite possible for an employee to work in two or three segments during a short period. An admin manager may work part of the day helping to set up a conference (Custom type), then do a spell of processing expense claims (Transactional administrative work), then talk with potential new hires (Interactive type).

Likewise, within a value stream the types may change. In a typical major hospital value stream involving an operation, there will certainly be a macro system design phase. Then, when the patient consults the doctor the process may be improved by Custom type mapping. Hospital administration and keeping track of the patient's paperwork may be improved by Transactional mapping. And the pre-op and post-op stages may be improved by Interactive mapping.

Working in Mixed Environments: Runners, Repeaters and Strangers and Time Management

Four service system types have been presented. In practice, many service workers do not work 100% of their time in one environment. This is a major difference between service and factory shop floor operations.

The proportion of time where the work is repeatable will seldom be zero. It may be that a manager's day is seldom the same but nevertheless there are weekly meetings, monthly reviews, and an annual budget cycle. Advantage should be taken of any repetition. Regularise where possible.

Regularity is a good Lean technique. It is line with levelling the work. Do a Runners, Repeaters and Strangers (RRS) analysis on office work. Runner work is done most of the time. Repeater work is done periodically – some (?) daily, some weekly, some monthly, some yearly. Stranger work is fairly unique or unpredictable. This work is primarily creative (which is not to say that work in other segments is not creative).

Please refer also to Part 1 where RRS is discussed in more detail.

Splitting your activities into RRS categories is good time management and an effective management style in itself. Steven Covey recommends a 2 x 2 matrix for urgency and importance. It fits well with Lean thinking. Low urgency, low importance work should be avoided if possible. High urgency, high importance work always enjoys priority attention, so does not require much debate. The problem lies with high urgency, low importance work that tends to waste (or at least misapply) huge chunks of potentially good time. Such work must be deliberately managed to reduce waste. Examples are emails, meetings with agenda items of low relevance to some, and bureaucratic administrative procedures. Effective time management begins with recording and classifying. Is this 'mapping' or just good time management?

How to reduce the amount of low importance, high urgency work:

- First, examine the activities in terms of value demand and failure demand. As ever, try to eliminate failure demand activities or, better still, their root causes.
- Second, group the activities and try to do them in blocks of time, regularly but as infrequently as possible.

Use the following Lean Time Management Matrix:

	Runner Activity	Repeater Activity	Stranger Activity
Value Demand Activities	Use Transactional or Interactive principles.	- Use Creative principles. - Set aside time blocks. - Establish work time protocols. - Regularise visits, meetings. - Comms Board - Standard work & procedures	Group and move to time slots. Fit around the Repeater activities.
Failure Demand Activities	Priority elimination	Eliminate	Eliminate root causes.

- **Time Blocks**: creative work requires longer periods of concentration, not broken up into smaller segments with frequent disturbances from email, telephone, people dropping in, and so forth. Research has shown that the human brain needs 'settle down' time for productive work.
- **Work Time Protocols** allow the blocks of time to be established and to work. For example, all may agree that no emails will be answered in the morning. Except emergencies. Everyone knows this.
- **Standards**: these are the broad standards for Repeater activities. For example, all meetings will be concerned with ONE topic only, minutes will be written in a standard format, A3 sheets will be used for reports and signed off by all concerned, communication boards will be updated daily by specific individuals, a tidy desk policy will be in operation (although no taping up specific locations!), computer files will be organised (broadly) in a standard way, etc.
- **Regularise visits**: many Lean managers (taking a leaf out of Toyota) have taken the notion of 'Gemba' to heart and decided that regular shop floor or office visits are essential. Do not try to fix appointments between 8 and 11, because that is Gemba time. The CEO of the Eden Project in Cornwall requires all managers to meet and greet 20 others before they start work.
- **Communications Board**: this is the essential tool for communication, problem solving, teamwork, and improvement. The daily or regular meeting is simply not optional. See the separate section on the use of this board. It is one of the three boards essential in a Creative environment.
- **Ideas Board**: any ideas should be posted up on a prominent ideas board. Do not have a suggestion box. There are four columns: Proposed, Agreed to, In Progress, Completed. Post-its progress across the board, and progress is discussed at the daily meetings.

Establishing the Daily Routine

In Transactional systems, and especially where there are Repeater actions, 'Leader Standard Work' should be established. This helps establish the 'culture' of the organisation. 'It's the way we do things around here.'

Every morning, without fail, a 10 minute meeting is held around the Communications Board with the immediate supervisor or manager facilitating the meeting. Yesterday's performance is reviewed, ideas are reviewed and fed back immediately, problem progress and any difficulties are established, and a brief is given on anything unusual to be expected today.

This repeatability establishes the norm or 'Kata' of improvement. Trust is built up. Communication channels are opened. Immediate and visible feedback is given. Learning takes place. Pathways of practice are built in the brain. Please refer to the section in Part 2 on Service, Kaizen, Leader Standard Work, and Kata.

Brown Paper Mapping Conventions

Brown Paper mapping is a method that can be used in all four categories of the Level 2 map. Some guidelines are presented.

Use a long roll of brown paper, set out along a wall.

Add post-it notes.

Colour-coding the post-it notes is a good idea. For example:
> Yellow: the main activities;
> Green: data boxes;
> Red: queues of paper or customers waiting;
> Light blue: computer system and IT communications.

Add bold red dots to each post-it note to indicate if the activity is VA or NVA (or OVA or ONVA).

Some suggested icons are given on the Icon Sheet, but feel free to add or invent your own.

For some value streams, the person icon can be coloured to indicate similar people or similar team members.

Demand data is particularly important in service, so devote a special Demand Data Box to this topic. Show it at the top left side. The most important demands come from external customers. In the case of a sub-process, the demands may come from an internal source such as the number of expense claims sent in.

The data box should contain:

- a run diagram of typical total entry demand across a day or shift – whether value or failure demand;
- an indication of value and failure demand using different colours;
- if possible, indications of the upper and lower bounds of demand along the run diagram;
- demand categories.

Work Shift Patterns should be shown in a Work Time Data Box on the top right hand side. Sometimes a run diagram (graph) showing numbers at work throughout the day will suffice.

Existing measures of performance should be listed in a bottom left hand side box. Measures are often the source of failure demand and rework.

The resources – principally human resources, but also any critical machines that need to be shared or that break down – should be shown in a box at the bottom right hand side of the sheet. List the names and their working hours if they differ. Note people who work in other value streams, and estimate how much time is available to the current value stream. Consider whether it is worthwhile writing down a critical skills matrix.

Consider early on whether you are going to use 'swim lanes'. The swim lanes idea is that each department or organisation has its own lane in which its activities are drawn. This can certainly emphasise handoffs and rework loops, but it may be better to use a separate Handoff Map (see separate section). Often it is not warranted. Sometimes lanes are reserved for other characteristics such as standards or quality – these can be added later.

Be particularly concerned with 'dirty data', the effect of which will escalate as it moves through a process. As a result, the elimination of 'dirty data' upstream is highly cost-effective. There are different types of data problems: data entry errors (caused by customer or employee), missing data, erroneous data, and clarity errors. Some of these overlap. Aim to eliminate or reduce these problems as close to the source as possible, because all subsequent stages may be affected. Start at the upstream end and estimate the extent of errors by sampling. If sampling is impractical (perhaps because the true state is not known), ask how much time is spent on correcting upstream errors or omissions. The data error rate should be written on the map. A most effective way of addressing such 'dirty data' is by 'failsafing' (or pokayoke) methods. See the later section on this.

Link the activities with lines drawn with flip chart pens.

Where there are decisions or branches, use a diamond.

Add appropriate actual documents along the bottom of the brown paper map.

If the level of activity is high enough, and it generally should be, the layout of a Brown Paper map could reflect the actual physical layout.

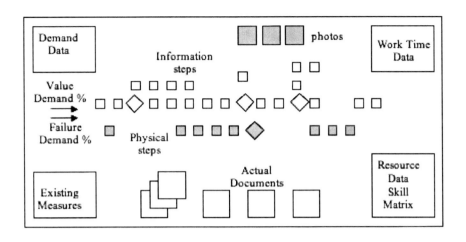

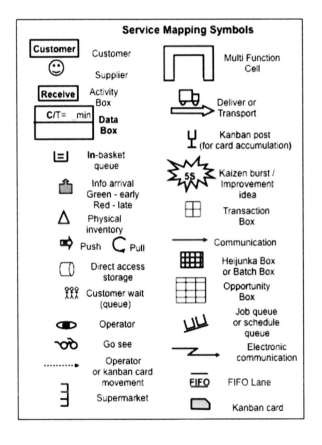

3.4.1 Level 2: Transactional Mapping

Low Customer Involvement; High Repeatability

Typical situations

- Repetitive office tasks in general;
- Order processing;
- Warehouse operations;
- Some maintenance and repair tasks.

General observations

This type of mapping is most like the 'Learning to See' (Rother and Shook) manufacturing mapping. It may also be known as MIFA (material and information flow analysis) mapping. Differences with standard 'Learning to See' maps include:

- Variety of tasks is often greater – tasks are more dissimilar than in typical manufacturing.
- Activity times are much more variable. Some are uncertain, as in maintenance.
- There are almost always more rework loops than in manufacturing – not because of worker incompetence but at the root, because of system design.
- Routings may vary to a greater extent than in manufacturing. This means that resource loadings are less predictable. A route may visit one person several times.
- Activities are more often by people rather than by machines, so capacity analysis needs special calculation – sometimes involving queuing theory considerations.
- Tasks may change volume much more frequently than in typical manufacturing. Volumes are quite likely to change during the course of a day.
- The supplier and customer may be the same person.
- Decision points or branching often need to be included.
- And, as is often the case in service, some work cannot be inventoried – at least not for long – although of course paper and customer queues are common.
- In short, have you ever seen an administrative process like 'Acme Stamping'? I haven't! Come to think of it – there aren't too many factories like Acme either!

This section discusses short cycle Transactional service, with activity times of, say, less than one hour. Longer activity times have some features in common with Custom environments and the reader's attention is drawn to that section.

Drawing the Current State Map

Two examples of a Current State map are shown – one for an administrative process and another for a maintenance process. These illustrations are the formal maps that are redrawn after actual mapping to document the current state. During the mapping exercise, the map is made by the team using post-its assembled on a large sheet of brown paper. See the box on Brown Paper Mapping.

Caution on using Manufacturing 'Learning to See' Value Stream Type Maps in a Transactional Service situation

However useful they may be, always bear in mind that such mapping tools were primarily developed for repetitive manufacturing.

- Simply adding the process activity times given in the data boxes to give an estimate of the end to end time is likely to be totally incorrect! Why? Because rework in service frequently involves the customer starting at the beginning again. If the customer experiences failure and has to begin again, the end-to-end time is double. And so on. The only true measure of end-to-end time is to track individual customers.
- Error rate percentages for each stage may be useful, but remember this is the view from the organisation's perspective, not the customer's perspective. It is frequently meaningless to multiply the percentage good at each stage to conclude with an overall percentage good. Why? Again, because customers re-start when failure occurs.
- Do draw feedback loops where transactions have to re-start the process for whatever reason. These are seldom shown in Learning to See maps, but give important insight in service.
- Demand and Load: unless you distinguish between Value Demand and Failure Demand, all subsequent calculations will be misleading. Why? Because failure demand is not true demand, and can be eliminated.
- Takt time could also be misleading unless failure demand is separately considered.
- Variation: there is significant variation in many service operations – in both demand and activity times. Using an average figure is misleading if not dangerous. Hence show a record of both arrival variation (demand) across a representative period, and get an idea of process time variation.
- Shared resources: many service workers work on a variety of jobs during the course of a day, week and month. It is unusual to find a dedicated resource as in a manufacturing operation. The percentage of time used should be shown. Moreover if the value stream only works at certain times of the week or month, this needs to be shown.
- Measures: measures have a significant impact on workers performance. They need to be included.

An Administrative Process

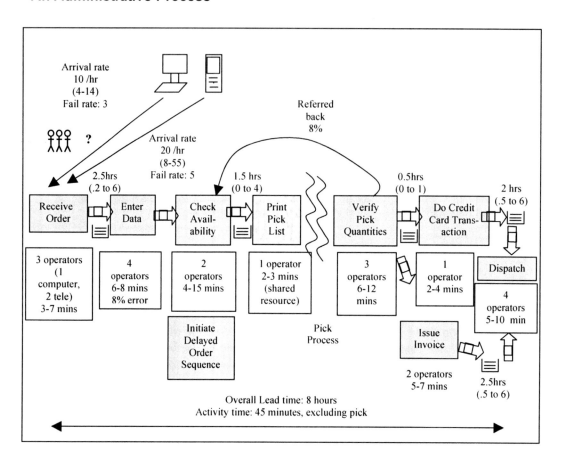

Layout

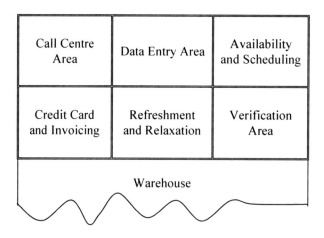

Features of note:

- The **Customer Icons** appear at the top of the page, one for each customer type or source of demand.
- Note Well: the **lead-time** should NOT be derived from adding up the process times and wait times. This does not account for rework loops, and therefore may not represent the customer experience. The only valid way of tracking customer lead-time is to measure it specifically with a good sample of real customers.
- The **variation** is given so that queue lengths and utilisation can be estimated – see the sections on variation and queuing in the Tools section.
- Often, **transactional system** activities are not worked on all day. There may be meetings or other streams to be worked on. So discuss and estimate how much time is taken up by this task each day or each week. Often the workload will not be uniform across the month. In this case, note the peak and average demand rate.
- **Activity boxes** run along the centre of the map.
- **Data boxes** appear below activities, including:

    - Number of people per stage;
    - Unit processing time or rate per stage (minimum, maximum and typical);
    - Batching information;
    - Error data. An estimate of the percentage of errors made. This is particularly important in earlier stages. You may also like to estimate the input error rate and the output error rate. That is, what percentage of (say) documents contains errors when the step is started, and what the percentage is after the step. The input error rate will accumulate as the document moves downstream, unless it is corrected.

- **Failure Demand** is indicated.
- In this case the actual number of customers calling in is unknown because the interactive voice response system (IVR) does not accept more than ten customers waiting at any time. The management measures of waiting time are an illusion. Beware! IVR systems are often classic industrial-type thinking inappropriately applied to service. Efficiency is assumed to increase, but the reverse may result because of failure demand.
- **Tagging**: to obtain activity and queue times it may be possible (if times are not excessive) to obtain estimates by 'tagging' either a sample of customers or a sample of documents. A customer may be physically tagged or monitored in the case of a walk-in process, or electronically tagged where an IT system is used. Where documents are flowing though the process, the tag can be a stapled note requesting each stage to fill in arrival and departure times of the document. Of course, it is not necessary to follow a customer or a document from end to end. Part flows can be monitored simultaneously and then collected up.

- At the entry point have a **data box** in which is written a note on the extent of 'dirty data' entering the process. 'Dirty data' may or may not result in rework.
- **Queue symbols** (either in basket or customer queue symbol) are shown between activity boxes. Minimum, maximum and typical queues are shown. In practice these times will often have to be estimated or obtained by questioning staff.
- **Rework loops**: show these looping back to the appropriate stage. Show the range of rework activity loops – the minimum and maximum number of times a document or customer goes around the loop. These are very important.
- **Decision diamonds** are shown.
- **Time line**: along the bottom of the map is the time line, using the standard Lean convention showing both total time and 'value add' or activity times. In most offices there are three types of time to consider. It is useful to estimate all three:

  - **The Process Time**: this is the actual work time at each stage.
  - **The Stage Time**: this may be the same time as the process time where there is one-piece flow, but this is unusual. It is more likely to be the time for a batch to go through a process – including queue time during the batch and sorting or collating time. Often a batch is worked on for a period of time, then there is a gap when other work is done or meetings take place.
  - **The Inter-Stage Time**: this is the time between stages that may include transport, postage, or, most commonly, accumulation time, where for instance a batch is worked on once per day.

- **Total Time** is the sum of the average times. **Activity Time** is the sum of the activity times. Adding these up, using the typical times, will give an indication of the cumulative lead time – but only for right first time customers. It is very important to include an estimate of the time variation – minimum, most likely, and (say) 95% completion time. (Not 100% or maximum because there may be special causes.)
- **Shared resources**: whether these are people or machines, they need to be specially identified because they are barriers to flow. Shared resources need to be scheduled or prioritised, and hence smooth flow will not always be possible.

Loops as sub-systems

This step divides the value steam into sub-systems or loops. It will frequently take place after the Current State has been mapped, but for complex value streams it may be considered up front.

In the example, there may be two loops – before and after order picking.

In mapping terms, the sub-systems can be shown as 'loops'. Within each loop, a set of resources aims to achieve a particular purpose. They are a logical set. Loops or sub-systems can be used to break down a complete value stream. It is, however, important to note that constructing the end-to-end value stream is not the same as 'optimising' each sub-system. The parts must remain subservient to the whole. Loops may be focus for kaizen events if the complete value stream is too large to tackle. Loops may used to sequence the transformation to the future state.

Loops or sub-systems may also be a way of breaking down the mapping project itself. One sub-team to a loop.

The classic Lean way is to start downstream and work backwards. In a manufacturing-oriented process this makes sense because the customer is downstream. The single 'pacemaker' (see later) is usually well downstream, allowing upstream steps to be pulled. In a customer-intensive value stream, this is not the case. Prioritising the loops should be related to the impact on value or satisfaction.

Wastes and System Conditions

From the current state maps it is useful to draw up a table of the effects of the current system showing the 'System Conditions', which cause the waste or effect. A partial call centre example is shown. The analysis team should work through the table before attempting to draw a Future State.

Waste / Effect	System Conditions	Caused by
Cheating on targets and measures. Management is deluded.	Manager measures	Inappropriate measures and targets
Hanging up on callers; customer dissatisfaction	Monitoring of call lengths	Targets
Excessive customer wait time	Waiting queue not measured; system does not allow more than 10. Management deluded; customers dissatisfied	Technology of the call monitoring system
Duplication	Dual data entry; customer annoyance	System design
Handoffs	Departmentalisation, skill shortages	Capacity issues
Customer required to give policy number. Delay, annoyance	IT system record entry point	IT system design

Analysing the Map and Creating the Future State

The aim of the Future State exercise is

- to get work flowing more steadily, more quickly, more predictably, and more accurately. Note the word FLOWING.
- to achieve the system purpose.

Achieving Flow

Flow is destroyed by interruptions. Interruptions are caused by rework, by lack of good data (or 'dirty data'), by batch and queue, by waiting for other data, and by lack of continuity of work caused in turn by breakdowns of equipment or stoppage of work due to telephone calls, emails, meetings and briefings. These fall into two categories: external to the process (meetings, socialising etc), and internal to the process (rework, batch and queue etc).

There are questions to ask on flow. These questions can be tackled in a kaizen event (or improvement event) over a few days. Kaizen events are described briefly in Part 4 of this book. Guidelines are:

- If you were designing the process from scratch, how would you do it to make achievement of purpose as quick and as hassle-free as possible?
- What are the causes of failure demand and rework loops? What would it take to eliminate these?
- Do the measures lead to unaligned behaviour? In other words, do the ways in which people try to meet their measures conflict with the purpose of the system? Example: monitoring call centre productivity may generate failure demand.
- Does each packet of information travel ahead of the work, or can it be made to travel ahead so that activities are adequately prepared and failure demand or rework is reduced? For example, is there a way in which a maintenance man can know what to expect before he gets there, so that he can bring the appropriate tools and spares?
- What is the best way to organise the work? In terms of Runners, Repeaters and Strangers? Can work be better grouped or blocked each day so that Runners can be done in a block (say) every two hours, Repeaters be done on regular days, and Stranger activities be arranged so they cause the least disruption?
- Where can work be flowed, one piece at a time?
- Is a work cell possible? In offices, as opposed to factories, cells are often difficult across processes that have more than one manager, and may even be difficult within an office because of people's reluctance to share their workspace. But the advantages can be huge for lead-time reduction and for quality. Some incentive may have to be given, or the advantages demonstrated through simulation. If a 'full-blown' cell is not possible, think of various 'half-way houses', such as rearranging desks, taking down barriers, and improving visibility.

- If physical cells are not possible, consider workflow technology. But beware – do not automate waste.
- Can you have a one-stop process?
- Does all work have to travel along the same path? Is a fast track possible? For example, in mortgage applications do 'blue chip' customers have to go through the same route? Are all jobs of equal complexity?
- If not, can more simple jobs be dealt with by less experienced staff?
- Can you untangle the 'spaghetti' – either physical or informational?

Once the system conditions have been identified, the new design can proceed. Everyone needs to understand that the prime task is to do the work – including whatever it takes to eliminate repeat (failure) demands. The second task is to improve the system. There are no other tasks. In other words, a virtuous cycle needs to be established – eliminating failure reduces waste and frees up capacity, thereby enabling more failure categories to be systematically addressed. Start with the top ten categories and work down. Demands that are received but do not fall within the top ten need to be dealt with by a more experienced worker or manager. By definition, such demands will constitute a very small proportion of the total cases.

Don't have inappropriate measures (and especially targets) that stand in the way of doing this. Allow the workforce to solve the customer's problems, don't prevent them from so doing by restrictive rules or 'standards'. This can be a liberating experience for employees, and a loyalty creator for customers.

A Maintenance Process (or 'Break Fix' Process)

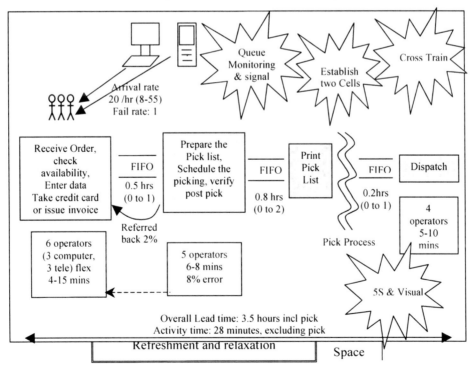

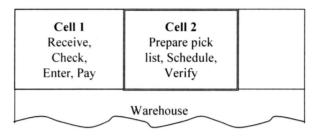

Points of Note on the Future State Map:

- Note that the maps both have an associated layout diagram. This is very common in Transactional mapping. Refer to the section on layout and cell design in the Tools section.
- Note that the lead time should NOT be derived from adding up the process times and wait times. This does not account for rework loops, and therefore may not represent the customer experience. The only valid way of tracking customer lead-time is to measure it specifically with a good sample of real customers.
- To develop the future state map, the participation of people from the area is required.
- The future state map must be consistent with the overall system concept developed in Level 1.
- Maps should also have time line performance data.
- In the current state, customer queuing was unknown. In the future state, queues are specifically monitored.
- Capacity is adjustable. If the queue length goes above a certain length – four in this case – an operator moves from Cell 2 to Cell 1. This may necessitate a physical move because of equipment.
- Cross training will be required.
- Failure demand has fallen because most issues are sorted out at the front end. This front-end-loading is good practice in many transactional situations.
- Push icons have been replaced by FIFO lanes. A push system is not necessarily first-in first-out, but a FIFO lane is. A FIFO lane should have a designated maximum length that would trigger a warning (light?) to indicate a non-normal situation.
- Kaizen bursts show necessary changes. An Action Plan for implementation must be developed from the map.
- The detail of the actual procedures for taking credit cards, what to do if stock is not available, the compilation of the pick schedule, etc, is detailed in Level 3 mapping. Such detail is not appropriate here, where the broad process is being established.
- There is a need to put in place an end-to-end measure. At least this is now possible.

Transactional and administrative mapping can proceed in two stages. An example is shown. First, draw the high level flow diagram.

High Level Flow Diagram

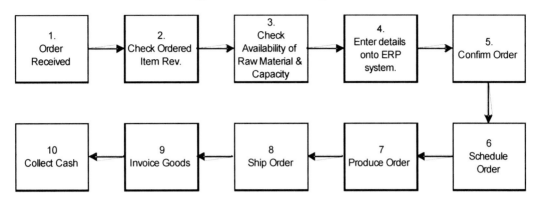

Then add the detail relating to the actual capability of the system as follows:

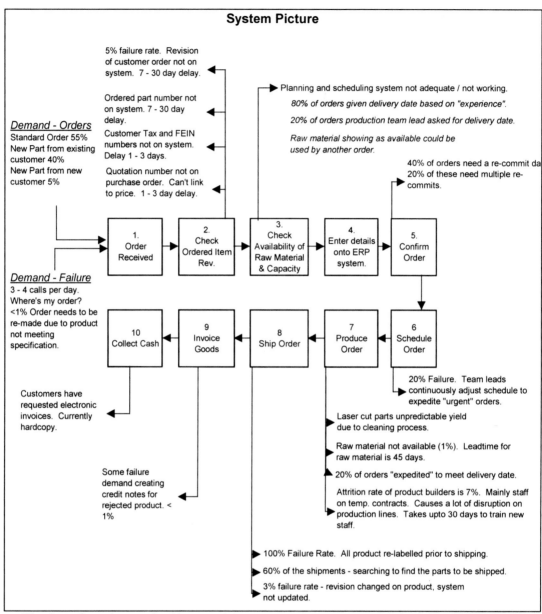

System Picture

5% failure rate. Revision of customer order not on system. 7 - 30 day delay.

Ordered part number not on system. 7 - 30 day delay.

Customer Tax and FEIN numbers not on system. Delay 1 - 3 days.

Quotation number not on purchase order. Can't link to price. 1 - 3 day delay.

Demand - Orders
Standard Order 55%
New Part from existing customer 40%
New Part from new customer 5%

Planning and scheduling system not adequate / not working.
80% of orders given delivery date based on "experience".
20% of orders production team lead asked for delivery date.
Raw material showing as available could be used by another order.

40% of orders need a re-commit da
20% of these need multiple re-commits.

Demand - Failure
3 - 4 calls per day.
Where's my order?
<1% Order needs to be re-made due to product not meeting specification.

| 1. Order Received | 2. Check Ordered Item Rev. | 3. Check Availability of Raw Material & Capacity | 4. Enter details onto ERP system. | 5. Confirm Order |

| 10 Collect Cash | 9 Invoice Goods | 8 Ship Order | 7 Produce Order | 6 Schedule Order |

Customers have requested electronic invoices. Currently hardcopy.

20% Failure. Team leads continuously adjust schedule to expedite "urgent" orders.

Laser cut parts unpredictable yield due to cleaning process.

Raw material not available (1%). Leadtime for raw material is 45 days.

20% of orders "expedited" to meet delivery date.

Attrition rate of product builders is 7%. Mainly staff on temp. contracts. Causes a lot of disruption on production lines. Takes upto 30 days to train new staff.

Some failure demand creating credit notes for rejected product. < 1%

100% Failure Rate. All product re-labelled prior to shipping.

60% of the shipments - searching to find the parts to be shipped.

3% failure rate - revision changed on product, system not updated.

(Thanks to Steve Langan for this example)

Further questioning of Transactional Maps

The aim is to reduce time and waste. It is essentially a creative process. Preferably the people involved in the process should be used in its analysis and improvement. Bold thinking is a requirement, not piecemeal adjustment. The title of a classic 1993 article by Michael Hammer in *Harvard Business Review* gives the clue: 'Reengineering work: don't automate, obliterate!' That is the type of thinking that is required. The same *Harvard Business Review* article tells of how Ford used to have 400 accounts payable clerks compared with just seven people at Mazda. Although Business Process Reengineering has become somewhat discredited since the mid 1990s, due to its association with job cuts, don't throw out the baby with the bathwater. Many valuable insights remain.

The basic step is to examine the process chart and to split the activities into those that add immediate value for the customer and those that don't. Refer to the Seven Wastes for guidance. The concept is to achieve the added value benefit for the customer as soon as possible. Therefore try to make every value-adding step continuous with the last value adding step, without interruptions for waiting, queuing, or for procedures which may assist the company but do nothing for the customer. George Stalk of Boston Consulting Group refers to customer value sequence as the 'main sequence'.

Questions concerning the sequence of activities include the following. Note however, that these questions are really prompts for the team *at gemba* doing the work, not for the system designers working on high from remote process maps.

- Can the non-value adding steps be eliminated, simplified, or reduced?
- Can extra work be done early to prevent delay later on in the process?
- Can any activity that delays a value adding activity be simplified or rescheduled?
- Are there any activities, particularly non-value adding activities, which can be done in parallel with the sequence of value adding activities?
- Can activities that have to be passed from department to department (and back!) be reorganised into a team activity? Better still, can one person do it? What training and backup would be required?
- Where are the bottlenecks? Can the capacity of the bottleneck be expanded? Do bottleneck operations keep working, or are they delayed for minor reasons? To quote Eli Goldratt, 'An hour lost at a bottleneck is an hour lost for the whole system', and 'An hour lost at a non-bottleneck is merely a mirage'. Are bottleneck operations delayed by non-bottleneck operations, whether value adding or not?
- What preparations can be made before the main sequence of value adding steps is initiated to avoid delays? For example preparing the paperwork, getting machines ready.
- Can the necessary customer variety or requirements be added at a later stage? For example doing the basic 'vanilla' service but adding the 'flake chocolate' as late as possible.

- If jobs are done in batches, can the batches be split to move on to a second activity before the whole batch is complete at the first activity?
- Can staff flexibility be improved to allow several tasks to be done by one person, thus cutting handing-on delays?
- What is the decision-making arrangement? Can decision-making power be devolved to the point of use? Can the routine decisions be recognised so that they can be dealt with on the spot? Perhaps 'expert systems' can be used.
- Where is the best place, from a time point of view, to carry out each activity? Can the activity be carried out at the point of use or contact, or must it really be referred elsewhere?
- Do customers enjoy a 'one stop' process? If not, why not?
- If problems do develop, what will be the delays and how can these delays be minimised?
- What availability of information will make the value adding sequence smoother or more continuous? Is there more than one source of information, and if so can this be brought to one place? A common database perhaps? The long established MIS principle is to capture information only once, and let everyone use the same data.
- As a second priority, can the time taken for value adding activities be reduced?

Yet more useful thoughts from process reengineering come from the originator, Michael Hammer, who identified the essential characteristics of BPR as follows:

- Several jobs are combined into one: 'Is it essential to have a qualified accountant do that?' 'Does it really have to go to another person?'
- Workers make decisions: 'Why does that decision have to be referred to the boss?'
- The steps in the process are performed in a natural order: can process steps be overlapped? Is that non-customer benefiting task necessary?
- Processes have multiple versions: one simple route for the routine many, another for the complex few, rather than all going the same way.
- Work is performed where it makes most sense: on the spot if possible, rather than referring it back to a specialist.
- Checks and controls are reduced: inspect and fix defects immediately, cut out the waste of unnecessary checks.
- Reconciliation is minimised: build supplier partnerships with trust; a case manager provides a single point of contact; customers don't get shunted around.
- Hybrid centralised/decentralised operations are prevalent: make use of common information systems, but decentralise decision-making authority.

Managing Critical Resources

In the Transactional area, when creating the Lean operating system, there will frequently be resource-balancing issues with critical resources. Please refer to the section 'Managing Critical Resources' under the Custom Environment section.

See also the possible use of Cells and one-piece Flow in the Tools section.

Takt Time

Of the four service types used in this book, the manufacturing concept of takt time is mostly (only?) applicable in the Transactional segment. Even then it must be treated with caution lest it lead to unexpected behaviour. On the other hand, takt time can be very useful when applied in the right application with the right attitude. What is takt time? It is the time available for work divided by the amount of work in that period. So, it is expressed in time units, typically minutes in service, and is the customer-driven drumbeat rate of work – one every so many minutes. Work units may be orders that are picked, files or cases processed, maintenance tasks undertaken, calls received or made, or possibly even lines of code written. Of course, most of these will be highly variable and therefore caution is appropriate. Particularly in service, takt time must never be a 'stick' for productivity. Rather it must be seen as a tool to aid planning and to highlight issues.

$$\text{Takt time} = \frac{\text{Total available work time}}{\text{Average demand}}$$

Note that it is available time in the formula, not the total time. Available time comes after deducting time for breaks – formal and informal – and for morning meetings, routine tasks such as clean up (5S?), and the like. Perhaps also short interruptions, for example answering the phone as a routine part of the day.

Very often in Transactional service it is appropriate to have more than one takt time during a day, so takt time can be segmented. In other words you can have (say) three takt times during the day – low takt during the first few hours to cope with the morning peak, midday takt to cope with lunch time demands, and high takt time in the afternoon.

Why may takt time be useful in Transactional service?

- As a way of calculating the required resources;
- As a way of monitoring work with a view to improvement. But be careful, takt can be a disaster in service if it is used to monitor and control;

Takt time can be used to determine the necessary resources via the formula:

$$\text{Required people} = \frac{\text{Sum of activity times}}{0.8 \text{ of Takt time}}$$

So as takt time decreases, the number of resources required increases. And why the 0.8? First, 0.8 is an estimate, but it is there to allow for variability – this is further explained in the Tools section, and in the introductory section on 'Muda, Muri, Mura' showing the exponential relationship between utilisation and lead time.

In service there is usually much higher variability than in manufacturing situations. Hence it is appropriate to use a lower percentage of the takt time when calculating the required resources. Calculating the number of people and improving the flow in a short cycle Transactional environment are often done using Yamazumi (or Work Balance) Board concepts. This is explained in more detail in the Tools section.

Standard Work

Like takt time, standard work in Transactional systems is often useful but needs to be treated with caution. First, standard work is developed by the service staff themselves, maybe in cooperation with system designers or managers, to capture and retain the best way found thus far - the how. Work standards, on the other hand, are what the system designers require to be done – the what and when. A standard is not a hard and fast rule in service. It is a guideline. But it also should contain key steps that must be done correctly if failure is to be avoided. Standardise only the frequently repeatable.

In service, over-standardisation can lead to poor service, but under-standardisation can be equally problematical. Getting the right level of detail in standard work is a real skill. Do not try to standardise every task. And even tasks that have Standard Operating Procedures (SOPs) should only have standards relating to the vital few critical steps. Office people generally don't like working in a highly specified office factory where almost every keystroke is specified and every location is specified – 'over the top 5S'. Nor is this necessary. The big gains are often, as usual, in system or process design: for example, screen presentation and sequencing, avoidance of duplication, office layout, and form design.

Don't forget to go back to purpose and customer. Are those forms, copies, reports what the customer actually wants?

Standard work applies in other category types. See the separate section on this important topic.

A less intimidating, more participative type of standard work is the TPA idea of 'best of the best'. Thus if six office workers are doing the same job, ask them to compare their methods. One may be better at one activity, another at another activity. Ask them to share best practice. This may involve detailed observation, timing or simply discussion. This level of detail is Level 3.

List of Related Tools

- Total Productive Administration/OPE
- 5S
- Spaghetti and Layout Diagrams
- Activity sampling
- Cell design
- Muda Muri Equations
- Capacity
- Variation
- Quality tools
- Queuing
- TOC/DBR
- CONWIP
- Kanban
- Servicescape
- Measures
- TRIZ – free perfect now
- Service level inventory

3.4.2 Level 2: Interactive Mapping

High Customer involvement, High Repeatability

Typical situations

- in general, a customer 'cycle of service', or an end-to-end journey by a customer through a service provider
- visit to a restaurant
- airline check in and subsequent flight
- hospital visit or dental surgery visit
- car servicing
- university registration

Drawing the Current State Map

The current state map here builds on the 'Service Blueprint' originally developed by Shostack in the 1980s. It uses the 'swimlane' approach to show the role played by various parties in the service delivery process. The method developed here is a considerable expansion on earlier versions. See for example, Womack and Jones, 2005, and Zeithaml, Bitner and Gremler, 2006.

The central stream of an Interactive map is the 'cycle of service' – concentrating on the experiences of customers as they move through the process. This is an important distinction from 'Learning to See' value stream type maps where the customer is shown only at the beginning and end. Here it is all the customer's experiences, or Moments of Truth, that accumulate into the overall degree of satisfaction. A Moment of Truth is an occasion where a customer comes into contact with a service deliverer (person or object) and experiences a good, neutral or bad reaction. The Moment of Truth concept was originally proposed by Richard Norman of Harvard Business School, but it was made famous by Jan Carlsson of Scandanavian Airlines in his book and in his airline management.

The Interactive map is used principally to enhance the *experience* of the customer, rather than on cost cutting or organisational waste removal. Customer waste removal – such as delays that waste the customer's time are very much of concern in an interactive map. Of course an interactive map can be used to identify organisational waste, but the prime purpose is to redesign the system for improved customer flow. If customer flow is achieved, waste in the form of failure demand, delays and defects will be reduced.

Some organisations may use interactive maps as a *customer experience audit*, tracing the step by step impressions that a customer may gain during a visit or journey. This could lead directly to prioritising any negative experiences.

Takt time has limited or no use in this type of map.

One immediate question about Interactive maps is – what customers do you select? No problem if there is only one customer type. Customer selection depends on customer need. So an interactive map for a library visit, for example, may have to consider book users, web users, quiet readers, and audio-visual users. This is a judgment call. Consider the following:

- Group customer needs into a generic visit. All customers will not visit all stages, but the lessons to be learned from mapping will be retained.
- Decide on the dominant customer types. Map this as the main stream. Then add supplementary portions of other supporting maps. For example, most customers come in for routine car servicing, but some have special needs – minor or major repairs. These two can be added as supplementary maps.

The Moments of Truth (MoT) in a Cycle of Service should be expressed in the words of the customer, these are often requests or desires, NOT in what the manager thinks each step should be. Thus, in visiting a cinema, the MoTs might be 'how do I find out what is showing at what time', 'I want to buy a ticket', 'I would like to buy some refreshment before the show starts', etc., and not 'determine what is showing', 'queue', 'buy ticket', 'buy drinks and popcorn'. So, follow the customer and seek to determine their requirements. At the high level of the Cycle of Service, the customer's MoT's or desires are independent of any organisational arrangement that the service provider may have.

This 'voice of the customer' is entirely consistent with the activity of understanding customer demands by listening, undertaken in the 'Check' stage.

Each high level MoT can then be broken down into a series of more detailed considerations, at this stage by function. For example 'how do I find out what is showing at what time' could be broken down into MoTs for newspaper, web, TV, and physical displays. These detailed MoTs may never be articulated but nevertheless have huge influence on behaviour. More detailed customer MoTs would be to do with ease of finding out, clarity of information, speed, appearance. 'I want to buy a ticket' would have MoTs for web, on-site ticket sales, signage and physical arrangement, queue management. More detailed customer MoTs would be to do clarity of direction, with ease, delays or queuing, convenience, friendliness, and physical appearance.

Each detailed MoT could then be prioritised using the Kano model (see separate section) into Basics, Performance factors, and Delighters. Basics just have to be provided without compromise. Performance factors offer some latitude, but their impact may be significant. Delighters are possible differentiators. For each detailed Mot there is either a hard of soft standard. Hard standards are clearly spelled out. Soft standards allow creative initiative and behaviour on the part of staff to help customers meet their needs. Broad guidelines are specified.

A part example for a Women's fashion clothing store is given.

Customer MoT	Function	Detailed MoT	Kano category	Standards
'This store looks like it may have what I need'	Store Management	Visually attractive	Performance	Hard
		Clean	Basic	Hard
		Opening times	Performance	Hard
		Good layout	Performance	Soft
		Music	Delighter?	Hard/soft
		Temperature	Basic	Hard
		Well lit	Basic	Hard
	Merchandising	Well presented	Performance	Soft
		Clear displays	Performance	Soft
		Key brands visible	Delighter?	Soft
	Retail operations	Shelves stocked before opening	Basic	Hard
'It feels as though I can get what I want'	Store Management	Customers welcomed	Delighter?	Soft
		Ability to communicate	Performance	Soft
		Credit card facility	Basic	Hard
		Staff well groomed	Performance	Soft
		Friendliness	Performance	Soft
	Merchandising	Well stocked	Performance	Hard
		Size guide available	Basic	Hard
		Good branding	Performance	Soft
		Clear pricing	Basic	Hard
	Retail operations	Staff knowledge	Performance	Soft
		Change rooms	Basic	Hard
		Checkout queues not long	Basic	Hard

(Thanks to Alex Speciale for this example.)

Structure of the Interactive Map

The basic map has six horizontal swim lanes. From top to bottom they are typically:

- **The Tangibles**: this is the physical environment. Along this lane notes are written (or digital pictures are added) of signs, web screen appearance, physical layout and appearance. This is known as the 'Servicescape', a phrase used by Zeithaml and Bitner – see Layout in the Tools section. Tangibles have the effect of what Berry and Benapudi refer to as 'evidence-based management', so that customers 'clue in' to signals by things and people. Make sure that your facilities provide evidence of the story you want to portray.
- **Customer Moments of Truth**: this is the most important lane, following the customer's journey and experiences.
- **Communication Line**: this line is used to separate the customer from the organisation, but it is also used for communication links. Symbols, such as phones, will often appear.
- **Organisation or Service Provider Lane**: this shows the sequence of actions taken by the organisation to respond to customer requirements.
- **IT Lane**: this lane is reserved for activities and interactions with the IT system. Information should ideally travel ahead of the customer.
- **Measures**: along this lane, note any measures that are used, for example call wait time.
- The boxes with four squares serve as checks for the Service Transaction Box elements (arrive, wait, serve, depart). See the Tools section for details.
- The twelve-box symbol at the bottom right is a reminder to look through the Opportunity Box. See the Tools section for detail.

See the example on the next page

Beware!

The classic Service blueprint or interactive map includes swimlanes for 'front office' and 'back office'. This pre-judges the solution and, in the worse case, can lead to inappropriate 'silo thinking' or 'manufacturing thinking'. A back office, created for 'efficiency' may lead to just the opposite through failure demand, communication breakdown and sometimes a 'them and us' attitude.

There will inevitably be an error rate in transferring work from 'front office' to 'back office'. Worse, a customer may have to re-explain.

'Streaming leading to downstream specialisation, may sometimes be effective for example in a hospital. But it carries the risk of allocation to the incorrect stream. This in turn may lead to considerable failure demand and variation increase. Far better then to place experts at the front line to absorb variety, to handle some cases directly, and where not possible, to make correct streaming allocation decision. This is counter-intuitive for traditional managers who think that experts need to be 'protected' by front line staff.

Another problem is using a mapping process to determine end-to-end time. This would be done by simply adding up the process times and queue times to calculate overall lead-time. But, it ignores rework loops and customer re-starts. In effect, the clock is re-set every time the customer goes back. Of course, the customer's clock is not re-set: it is the end-to-end completion time that counts. This time can be determined by recording individual customer journeys, and if possible individual re-starts.

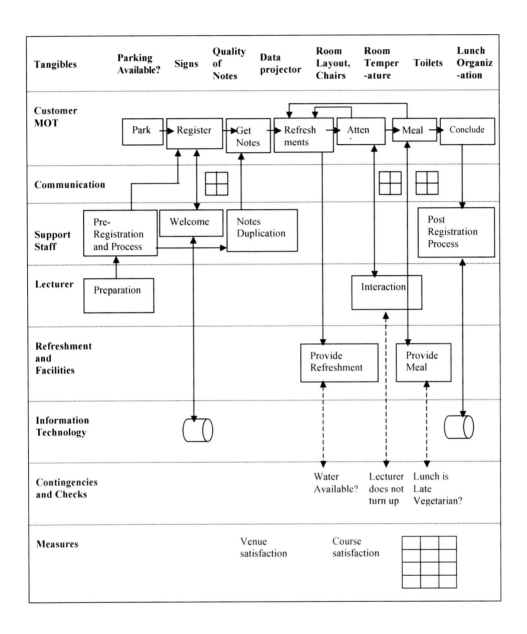

Tangibles	Parking Available?	Signs	Quality of Notes	Data projector	Room Layout, Chairs	Room Temper-ature	Toilets	Lunch Organiz-ation

Customer MOT: Park → Register → Get Notes → Refreshments → Atten → Meal → Conclude

Communication

Support Staff: Pre-Registration and Process, Welcome, Notes Duplication, Post Registration Process

Lecturer: Preparation, Interaction

Refreshment and Facilities: Provide Refreshment, Provide Meal

Information Technology

Contingencies and Checks: Water Available?, Lecturer does not turn up, Lunch is Late Vegetarian?

Measures: Venue satisfaction, Course satisfaction

Steps in Mapping

- If possible start at the pre-map stage, and end at the follow-up stage. See note on 'The Wider System' below.
- Determine the entry arrival rate of customers. Often, draw a graph of arrival rate, customers per minute for example, against time. This is critical for good customer service analysis.
- It will often not be possible to follow the customer through a value stream as you might follow a product through a value stream, because the customer may not be physically present for some of the stages or because there are long gaps of inactivity on the part of the customer – as in car service or a hospital visit. But a typical customer's interactions can be followed.
- Some customer actions cannot be observed, but a simulated trial can be made. For example, ask someone to log into the website as a 'pseudo-customer' and look for the product or service. Or make an emergency call, or look up the company in the Yellow Pages. Get the pseudo-customer to go through the full process.
- Where possible, follow and observe actual customer experiences.
- Capture the broad activities, not the detail. 'Book the order', not 'Enter name and address'.
- Where activities follow in a sequence with little interruption, write these one below the other.
- Start a new column of activity where activities are separated by delays or queues.
- The sequence of activity may jump from customer to service provider and back. There may also be parallel paths, for example where a customer is enjoying a coffee or shopping at an airport while the aircraft is being loaded.
- Show the queues or delays by means of a suitable icon – in-basket, queue of people.
- Estimate or observe the activity times. Maximum, minimum and normal. It is particularly important to try to obtain service times because this will have a direct impact on queue time. See the separate section on Queuing.
- Where there are queues, note the queue 'discipline'. That is:

    - Single queue, multiple queues or multiple single queues
    - FIFO, or priority customers;
    - If queuing takes place on the phone, note the type of messages that are given out;
    - Sometimes queues are joined by other customers from other streams – such as for airport security or for a hospital operating theatre. Here, note the queue size and question the staff about maximum and minimum queues and delays.

- Note the number of resources employed by the service provider at each stage. Also note which department or organisation they belong to.
- If there is physical inventory, such as spare parts as opposed to electronic files or human queues, show these as inventory triangles. The existence of physical inventory that is inherent to the process, not peripheral to it, means that a whole

raft of Lean related concepts may be possible. Integral inventory would be spares in a maintenance system, peripheral inventory would be paper or other consumables in an ordinary office. Integral inventory can make use of Lean concepts such as kanban, supermarkets, runner systems, partnership purchasing and vendor managed inventory. Peripheral inventory is often best managed by visual management methods, 5S, and re-order point methods. These are briefly discussed in separate sections.

- Note whether customers are treated in batches or one at a time.
- Finally, indicate the Customer Critical Path. This is the sequence of activities that a customer will have to wait for in order to complete the service end-to-end. Normally the path will start with the customer, go to the organisation, may well return to the customer and to the organisation a few times, and finally end with the customer.
- Show failure demand rework loops in another colour. Don't forget these – most Interactive value streams have failure demand.
- Add 'process owner loops'. This is often a better alternative to adding more swim lanes for each of the departments involved. Process owner loops can be drawn on transparent plastic to cover the map. Simply draw bold lines of different colours to surround activities in similar departments.

The Wider System

Sandra Vandermerwe suggests that the 'customer activity cycle' has three phases – pre, during, and post. While mapping is usually concerned with the 'during' phase, Vandermerwe suggests that a great deal of value adding opportunity exists by looking at the other two phases – closing the big loop.

The pre phase is before the experience begins, 'when the customer is deciding what to do to get the result'. In this phase there are opportunities to issue advice (on a mortgage loan), to collect information (about a forthcoming car service), to pre-book a slot (in a hospital), to give guidance (on a forthcoming holiday), to warn of delays (en route or when the customer arrives), to issue pre-reading for a course, and so on. Some of these may be revenue-earning activities, perhaps with partner organisations, others may attract or lock in customers. The pre phase should be seen as a major opportunity for creating customer delight, immediately or later. The customer path can be smoothed and delays avoided.

The post phase is after the experience, 'when the customer is maintaining the result or keeping it going – receiving, extending, upgrading and updating'. In this phase there are also opportunities to solicit feedback, to follow up on repeat purchases, to impress customers with excellent service if things go wrong (such as a Lexus recall that not only explained the need in detail but also gave gifts and checked over the vehicle), to join a 'fan club' or alumni group to maintain networking, to provide an upgrade or newer model on good terms, and so on. Again, some may be direct revenue-earning, others may attract future business, yet others may simply build reputation.

Analysing the Map

Several tools or concepts are available:

- The Kano model
- Standards
- Mistake Proofing (Pokayoke)
- Service Transaction Box if relevant
- Information Travel
- Value and Failure Demand
- Layout and Cells

Each one is described in a separate section. However, <u>it is important that each concept is considered step by step, and not applied to the map as a whole.</u> A systematic approach is key.

An illustration is shown for the first four steps

MoT	Kano Basics	Kano Perform	Kano Delighter	Standards	Fail Safe?	Trans-action Box ?
Park	Available	Suffic-ient space?	Designated parking	Car Size; spaces/ delegate ratio		Maybe
Register	Name tags available; signs; in attendance	Friendly; wait time	Online pre-registration	Max wait time	Photo? Sign in?	Yes
Get notes	Available	Quality & read-ability	Colour; extra documenta tion	Slides per page, font		No
Refresh-ment	Tea & coffee avail; water on tables	All day? Variety? Fresh? Sweets?	Danish pastries; fruit	On time at specific times	Signal if empty; checks	No

General points to consider:

- Always consider the purpose of the overall process. What is it there to do? And how can it be done more simply, with less customer hassle, and less error? The process must be consistent with the Level 1 analysis.
- How can information flow around the process? Does it travel with the object or customer or ahead or behind? If information does not travel ahead there are likely to be delays and problems when service providers discover that something is missing. Like a customer forgetting to bring in his passport.

Like discovering that the repair cannot be done because a part is not available. Like finding a customer not at home when the delivery calls. So how can information be made to flow ahead? Can more relevant information be collected and transferred before the customer physically arrives?

- Do customers or information travel in batches? Is one at a time feasible?
- Is one-stop possible?
- Are parallel operations possible?
- Can expertise be put on the front line to reduce or eliminate failure demand? Failure demand is a John Seddon idea, explained in *Freedom from Command and Control*. This concept is further illustrated by the case study of the Portuguese car dealer Simao, carried out by Cardiff Business School and explained in Womack and Jones' *Lean Solutions*. Here all necessary information is extracted from the customer before he arrives for his car service, thus ensuring a hassle-free non-repeat visit with all spares available. Queue time is minimised. This is also an illustration of information flowing ahead of the customer.

List of Related Tools

- Opportunity Box
- Service Transaction Box
- Cycle of Service
- Kano model
- Standards
- Failsafe/Pokayoke
- Layout and visual management

Further Reading

Valerie Zeithaml, Mary Jo Bitner and Dwayne Gremler, *Services Marketing*, 4th edition, McGraw Hill, 2006. Chapter 9 covers service blueprints.
Lynn Shostack, 'Designing Services that Deliver', *Harvard Business Review*, Jan/Feb 1984
Leonard Berry and Neeli Bendapudi, 'Clueing in Customers', *Harvard Business Review*, February 2003
Sandra Vandermerwe, *The Eleventh Commandment*, Wiley, 1996, Chapter 13
James Womack and Daniel Jones, *Lean Solutions*, Simon and Schuster, 2005, Chapter 4
John Bicheno, M R Gopalan, V S Mahesh, 'Extending the Effectiveness of Service Mapping', *Management Review*, Indian Institute of Management Bangalore, Vol 11, No 1, March 1999
John Bicheno and Matthias Holweg, *The Lean Toolbox 4th Edition*, PICSIE Books, 2009

Fun with Moments of Truth

Moments of Truth can be made memorable, and add to the customer experience.

The following is extracted from an anonymous email sent to the author on 16 September 2010, by Frank Sperotto

Kulula is an Airline with head office situated in Johannesburg. Kulula airline attendants make an effort to make the in-flight "safety lecture" and announcements a bit more entertaining. Here are some real examples that have been heard or reported:

- On a Kulula flight there is no assigned seating, you just sit where you want; passengers were apparently having a hard time choosing, when a flight attendant announced, "People, people we're not picking out furniture here, find a seat and get in it!"
- On another flight with a very "senior" flight attendant crew, the pilot said, "Ladies and gentlemen, we've reached cruising altitude and will be turning down the cabin lights. This is for your comfort and to enhance the appearance of your flight attendants."
- On landing, the stewardess said, "Please be sure to take all of your belongings.. If you're going to leave anything, please make sure it's something we'd like to have."
- "There may be 50 ways to leave your lover, but there are only 4 ways out of this airplane."
- "Thank you for flying Kulula. We hope you enjoyed giving us the business as much as we enjoyed taking you for a ride."
- As the plane landed and was coming to a stop at Durban Airport , a lone voice came over the loudspeaker: "Whoa, big fella. WHOA!"
- After a particularly rough landing during thunderstorms in the Karoo, a flight attendant on a flight announced, "Please take care when opening the overhead compartments because, after a landing like that, sure as hell everything has shifted."
- From a Kulula employee: "Welcome aboard Kulula 271 to Port Elizabeth ... To operate your seat belt, insert the metal tab into the buckle, and pull tight. It works just like every other seat belt; and, if you don't know how to operate one, you probably shouldn't be out in public unsupervised."
- "In the event of a sudden loss of cabin pressure, masks will descend from the ceiling. Stop screaming, grab the mask, and pull it over your face. If you have a small child travelling with you, secure your mask before assisting with theirs. If you are travelling with more than one small child, pick your favourite."
- Weather at our destination is 50 degrees with some broken clouds, but we'll try to have them fixed before we arrive. Thank you, and remember, nobody loves you, or your money, more than Kulula Airlines."
- "Your seats cushions can be used for flotation; and in the event of an emergency water landing, please paddle to shore and take them with our compliments."

- "As you exit the plane, make sure to gather all of your belongings. Anything left behind will be distributed evenly among the flight attendants. Please do not leave children or spouses."
- And from the pilot during his welcome message: "Kulula Airlines is pleased to announce that we have some of the best flight attendants in the industry. Unfortunately, none of them are on this flight!"
- Heard on Kulula 255 just after a very hard landing in Cape Town: The flight attendant came on the intercom and said, "That was quite a bump and I know what y'all are thinking. I'm here to tell you it wasn't the airline's fault, it wasn't the pilot's fault, it wasn't the flight attendant's fault, it was the asphalt."
- Overheard on a Kulula flight into Cape Town, on a particularly windy and bumpy day, during the final approach, the Captain really had to fight it: after an extremely hard landing, the Flight Attendant said, "Ladies and Gentlemen, welcome to The Mother City. Please remain in your seats with your seat belts fastened while the Captain taxis what's left of our airplane to the gate!"
- Another flight attendant's comment on a less than perfect landing:
  "We ask you to please remain seated as Captain Kangaroo bounces us to the terminal."
- An airline pilot wrote that on this particular flight he had hammered his ship into the runway really hard. The airline had a policy which required the first officer to stand at the door while the passengers exited, smile, and give them a "Thanks for flying our airline". He said that, in light of his bad landing, he had a hard time looking the passengers in the eye, thinking that someone would have a smart comment. Finally everyone had got off except for a little old lady walking with a cane. She said, "Sir, do you mind if I ask you a question?" "Why, no Ma'am," said the pilot. "What is it?" The little old lady said, "Did we land, or were we shot down?"
- After a real crusher of a landing in Johannesburg, the attendant came on with, "Ladies and Gentlemen, please remain in your seats until Captain Crash and the Crew have brought the aircraft to a screeching halt against the gate. And, once the tire smoke has cleared and the warning bells are silenced, we will open the door and you can pick your way through the wreckage to the terminal."
- Part of a flight attendant's arrival announcement: "We'd like to thank you folks for flying with us today. And, the next time you get the insane urge to go blasting through the skies in a pressurized metal tube, we hope you'll think of Kulula Airways."
- Heard on a Kulula flight: "Ladies and gentlemen, if you wish to smoke, the smoking section on this airplane is on the wing. If you can light 'em, you can smoke 'em."
- A plane was taking off from Durban Airport. After it reached a comfortable cruising altitude, the captain made an announcement over the intercom, "Ladies and gentlemen, this is your captain speaking. Welcome to Flight Number 293, non-stop from Durban to Cape Town. The weather ahead is good and, therefore, we should have a smooth and uneventful flight. Now sit back and relax... OH, MY GOODNESS!" Silence followed, and after a few minutes, the captain came back on the intercom and said, "Ladies and

Gentlemen, I am so sorry if I scared you earlier. While I was talking to you, the flight attendant accidentally spilled a cup of hot coffee in my lap. You should see the front of my pants!" A passenger then yelled, "That's nothing. You should see the back of mine!"

3.4.3 Level 2: Custom Process Mapping

High Customer involvement, Low Repeatability

Typical situations

Custom environments include engineering and architectural design, advertising, media, computer programming and systems analysis. Project management activities.

Many office functions are of this type. They deal with an endless stream of mainly small projects, and some larger ones. A proportion of the jobs has some repeatability, and frequently involves high customer interaction – with both internal and external customers. Administrative secretaries, HR practitioners, professors, consultants, trainers are examples.

Takt time has little or no meaning. This is a high variety process and, as Seddon has said, the system must be designed to absorb variety. Therefore, standard work in the detail sense also has low applicability. Not so in the wider sense, however.

In this situation, particularly where there are design projects involved, concepts from service Design Thinking frequently will be useful. See Part 2.

Mapping in Custom Environments
79

Academics to zoologists, with consultants, engineers, and solicitors in between, may think their work fits exclusively in this category. Often, they would be wrong. Please read the sections on Runners, Repeaters and Strangers and on Level 1 Service Mapping, if you have not already done so. They are highly relevant to this type of process. The classic 'Learning to See' mapping tool is seldom appropriate in Custom environments such as illustration design, senior management, universities, creative arts, and cooking, but before rejecting mapping as an inappropriate tool in this type of environment, be aware that many creative environments have repetitive elements that can be mapped using conventional mapping tools, combined with what follows. Examples are engineering design, administration, management consulting, medical services, insurance claim visits, research in a laboratory, many hotel tasks, and many marketing activities.

Custom Environment Mapping is not 'mapping' as such. Rather it is establishing a supporting organisation, environment and principles that will allow the process to flow with low waste and low lead-time.

In this type of environment, if good work has been done at the macro level mapping and analysis stage, the system will be well understood and what remains is detailed management and procedures.

Some general guidelines for Custom Environments:

Generally, three parallel displays (rather than 'maps') are required – one dealing with the **overall process** in broad terms, another with **resource analysis**, or how the creative resources (people) allocate their time, and the third a **'Communications Board'** to keep track of progress. These three make up an excellent interactive set.

The Overall Process Board: A diagram or map of the main process or project stages should be on display. This may be:

- The stages or gates in a new product introduction process;
- The project stages in a civil engineering or architectural design project;
- The stages in a consulting project;

(All of these may be linked in with standard project management software.)

- The stages in a legal process;
- The month-end financial reconciliation and reporting cycle;
- A physician consulting patients with health concerns;
- The annual policy deployment process.

(These last four may also be regarded as Transactional. It is a judgment call.)

These are not maps in the analysis sense as used in other sections, but a display or precedence diagram of the main process steps.

A professional service organisation or function may have several parallel processes going at the same time, or they may be done as and when the need arises. Projects may vary considerably in scope or duration but may all still follow the same broad steps. For example, management consulting or market survey.

In all these cases it is usually only necessary to have one overall process map per type on display. Display the generic process to aid understanding.

For a large project, for example design engineering, where the project is the main or only focus of activity during an extended period, the actual precedence network may be shown.

Establish the main stages of the process. This will involve a high-level block diagram rather than detailed stages. The diagram should show key interdependencies – where a resource needs to wait for completion by another resource.

Please note that the Stages/Gates are not supposed to mean that a 'stage-gate' approach should be used in all cases. Stage/Gate represented a great advance over traditional new product development when it was introduced some twenty years ago. This approach uses formal gates through which the product or project must pass or be aborted. Gates may be set up, for instance, for technical, market, and financial viability. The approach was consistent with 'concurrent' engineering where several functions worked simultaneously on the project and came together at the gates. It may be suitable for larger projects, but it is certainly 'over the top' for many office and administrative Custom processes. Even in some new product development, the stage-gate approach is being superseded by the Toyota style 'Set-Based' approach. See later.

Draw in swim lanes to represent the different departments or sections that participate in the process. In these cases, the diagram will be similar to the Four Fields Map described in Level 3 – except that the level of detail will be far broader.

- Together with representatives of the various 'players', draw out the block diagram or precedence diagram. This is standard practice in many engineering projects.

- An important point is that the Overall Process Board should not be regarded as a one-off exercise to establish the stages. It should be regarded as a 'working board' on which ideas are posted and comments made. Checklists should be accumulated and built on in every Custom process, so the Overall Process Board should facilitate this process by having a column where 'Lessons Learned' can be added. It is expected that lessons learned will be added regularly. If they are not being added to, this is an indication that management of this type of process is lagging.

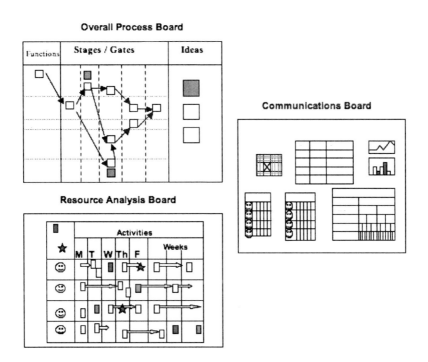

Resource Analysis: these boards (typically whiteboards) are concerned with resource allocation – how key resources (people or teams) are spending their time. The idea of the board is to load level and flow the work. In that respect it is a form of Heijunka. The group manager will use the board for overall management, not chasing. He will be concerned with releasing work, moving some projects ahead and de-expediting others. A possibility is that the equivalent of the Resource Analysis Board may be kept on the computers of everyone in the group, perhaps on Excel. This, of course, allows for updating and communicating the status by computer network. However, it is not so good for communication. So, even if the Resource Analysis Board is kept on computers, do keep a physical board as well.

The steps are:

- Identify the key resources or resource categories: perhaps engineers and technicians; barristers, solicitors, legal clerks; specialists and nurses; accountants and sub-accountants. Teams which normally work together are shown as one category, otherwise individuals are shown. 'Key resource' means a person or team having the core skills needed for completion of a task or project. Thus a print room, canteen, or mail delivery are not core skills even though they may be important.
- Set up two Resource Planning Boards: the first concerned with weekly activities, going out four to six weeks ahead, starting next week, and the second concerned with daily activities for this week. The week-by-week board is shown horizontally with activities going from left to right, and each row representing a key resource. The Weekly Board typically uses planning divisions of a week with activities shown in days. The Daily Board uses planning divisions of days where activity units are hours. Activities are simply written in the appropriate period, or post-its are added.
- A task should be broken down into its smallest sensible element, particularly if it involves work done by a critical resource. See the section on Cells in the Tools section.
- Each week, regularly, the boards are updated by each resource (person or team). The resource simply indicates by drawing in blocks what activities they plan to work on (part) day by (part) day for the next week, and week by week for the following four (?) weeks. These are shown in the appropriate swim lane. Colour coding is used, for instance:
  - Blue for individual activities, not dependent on others;
  - Green for team-working activities, not dependent on others;
  - Red for activities where commencement of the activity depends on another key resource, either internal or external to the group;
  - Yellow for unoccupied, spare capacity.
- This is ideally a voluntary, participative process, not a top down check. The purpose is smooth flow, problem solving, time management, not chasing.

A typical outline of the Resource Analysis Board is shown.

The Communications Board is the third element. This is described in a separate section in the Tools section of this book. The Communications Board has wide applicability outside the Custom service area.

The Communications Board is the 'glue' that holds the Process Board and Resource Analysis Board together. Use of the three boards together can be assisted by good time management and good Lean project management. See Lawrence Leach and Ronald Mascitelli respectively.

Together the three boards allow managers to address the critical concerns of capacity and time management.

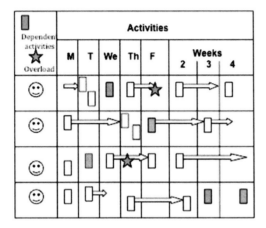

Managing with Critical Resources

Critical resources are of course found in Transactional and Interactive environments but they are generic in Custom environments. In the first two they are generally easier to manage because they are more stable over time, whereas in Custom environments resource loadings change all the time. A key resource may also be a machine – in a hospital a bed, a CAT scanner, an operating theatre.

This section should be read together with the section on Cells in the Tools part of the book.

The management of the critical resources, and their smoothed flow of work, is the prime task of managers in Custom or project environments. This is often not sufficiently appreciated, and is probably a major reason for both client dissatisfaction and employee stress. In multi-project environments – a hospital, a design office, a legal practice – the management of critical resources is very challenging, but the point is that the manager needs at least a basic understanding of the problem.

In Lean manufacturing the supervisor, or preferably the team, balances the work using the Work Balance Board (also referred to as the Yamazumi Board). The same activity may be found in Transactional service environments, except that in manufacturing the team would balance to perhaps 90% of takt time whereas in Transactional service they would balance to perhaps to 80% of takt. In project or Custom environments a similar activity should take place, but with the following modifications:

- In this section the term 'resource' will be used. In office and service environments a resource is typically a person or a group with similar skills, rather than a machine. There may, however, be situations where the resource is a machine or vehicle, such as an operating theatre, ambulance, room, or print shop. In Ordnance Survey the resource is the plane used for map photography.
- Only the critical (or Drum) resources need to be balanced. Be aware, however, that loading of critical resources in custom environments tends to be erratic, and the critical resource can change over very short periods.
- Balancing is a regular activity because new projects arise all the time, and there is little repetition.
- Where there is sequence dependency of activities – as in a multi-resource project – a network or Gantt chart or precedence network should be drawn (even if sketched in outline only) to understand the dependencies and to estimate when critical resources will be called upon. In complex environments the use of a package such as Microsoft Project will certainly assist. Where there are no sequence dependencies the task is much simpler, with critical resources merely having to show on the chart what they will be working on and for how long. Non-sequence dependent activities may also include meetings and training. In many situations, of course, a critical resource will be involved in both sequence dependent and non-sequence dependent activities.
- Balancing is on a much broader time scale – perhaps days or even weeks, sometimes hours, certainly not minutes. So the balancing activity is against the days or hours available, not against a takt time, which generally has no meaning in Custom environments.
- When critical resources are loaded is determined both by the project network or Gantt charts and by non-sequence dependent activities. Both types should be moved earlier or later so that the load on critical resources is not exceeded. This is easier said than done, given that some activities may be fixed in time and others are sequence dependent, so that adjusting a critical resource will have knock-on effects on other resources whose activities may need to be expedited or postponed. Most project management computer packages have a resource-levelling feature that can assist, but this, of course, requires that all activities are on the system.
- Nearly always the best method of load balancing is not to rely on a computer package (although a package may provide useful input), but to discuss the loading in a team setting with all critical and near critical resources present. The team could meet (say) once a month for broad guideline purposes, with the manager taking routine decisions between the meetings.
- The Lean 'pull' system (or CONWIP – constant work in progress – or Drum in Goldratt's Drum Buffer Rope system) should also work. That is, it should 'pull' work into the system depending on the utilisation of critical resources. Never launch new work until there is capacity available to do the work. The

Drum Buffer Rope system says that work completed by the critical bottleneck allows new work to enter. If work is not completed, none enters. The Rope is the connection between the critical bottleneck and the entry point. The (time) Buffer protects the bottleneck from uncertainty.

- The critical activities should be loaded to perhaps 80% of full capacity, to allow for variation and uncertain task duration times. The 80% figure is an estimate and each individual service organisation will have to determine its own satisfactory figure.

- Time buffers (called 'feeding' buffers in Critical Chain project management) should be allowed where there are sequence dependencies that relate to critical resources – in other words where a critical resource may be held up by a non-critical activity.

- If work has to be completed by a particular time, Critical Chain instructs that a project time buffer be located at the end of the project but that no 'slack' or 'float' be allowed for anywhere else in the project except in front of sequence-dependent critical activities.

- The critical resource should not work on simultaneous projects – see Hal Mather's ship story in the Capacity Tool section. One at a time is good Lean practice, in any environment.

- Another valuable idea comes from Lean Construction or 'The Last Planner'. This is the idea that critical resource activities should be subject to a checklist of requirements which is gone through before the activity is due to start. Checklists are not necessary for all activities, only critical activities. Checklists should include everything that might prevent the activity proceeding smoothly and in an error-free way. A critical resource checklist for an operating theatre (surgeon) would include all the instruments, supplies and availability of support staff. A critical resource checklist for a court appearance (solicitor) would include adequate briefing, clothing, coordination of all involved including witnesses, support staff availability, and travel arrangements to get there. This is very similar, of course, to the checklists that Toyota designers use. Last Planner checklists need to be built up by experience, as with any checklist, but the point is actually to keep, use and improve the checklist. The checklists become very valuable documents.

In so-called agile (or Lean) software development the concept is to break down the product into usable chunks ('chunking') and to try to ensure that the deliverables are completed in a continuous levelled stream. This is exactly like the TPS concepts of Heijunka and mixed model scheduling. It is also compatible with the ideas of kaizen. In agile software development the emphasis is on completing a working deliverable as soon as possible, and then going back and improving it – rather than going for the big, complete, perfect solution presented at the end. This is also similar to the Toyota 'set-based' new product development approach. So why not use these powerful concepts in Custom service or project environments – particularly the Interactive kind? It is surely advantageous for clients, who can then fine-tune the deliverable together with the service provider as they work through the project – whether it be a law suit, a new building, a university course or tutorial, or a new product advertising campaign.

A Note on Critical Chain Project Management

The phrase 'Critical Chain' originated with the late Eli Goldratt, who wrote a revolutionary book with the same title. Unlike critical path project management, the Critical Chain looks at both sequence dependencies and resource usage. The Critical Chain will normally not be the critical path. The Critical Chain is the longest path through the network after levelling the critical resources. Note the plural here. It is frequently the case that one resource is overloaded early on, another resource is overloaded later, and yet another later still.

Managing the project focuses on the critical resources. There will always be just a few of them or perhaps only one. These resources must be identified and utilised well:

- a time buffer (called a feeding buffer) after non-critical resources that lead into critical resources – so as to reduce the likelihood that the critical resource will be delayed;
- a project buffer at the end of a project; then monitoring progress in two dimensions – the percentage of the critical chain complete versus the percentage of the time buffer that has been consumed.

Critical Chain project management aims to overcome two weaknesses in conventional project management:

- **Parkinson's Law**: activity expands to fill the time available;
- **The Student Syndrome**: waiting until the last possible moment, when the due date is imminent, to begin an activity, so that any delay will then mean that the task will be late. Perhaps, as many students will attest, the start date is already too late to complete the task at the normal rate of work, so that overtime (or non-Lean lumpy) work will be required.

Readers who are in full-time project management and who may not be familiar with the following references are highly recommended to read:
Eli Goldratt, *Critical Chain*, North River Press, 1997 (a novel, like *The Goal*)
Lawrence Leach, *Lean Project Management*, Advance Inc., 2005

Toyota's 'Obeya' and Design Management

What is described above may be found, with suitable modification, in a small design group, a solicitor's office, a university academic or administrative department, or any office that undertakes a series of small projects.

The design of a major engineering artefact such as an aircraft, car, or major bridge will of course be far more complex. Nevertheless, it can be built up from modules set up on similar principles.

For example, at the overall product level, Toyota's design system is far more comprehensive, but it does use a chart room. The room is referred to as the 'Obeya' (big room). Around the walls are placed diagrams, flowcharts, plans, designs, resource allocation charts and the like – everything that pertains to the progress of the design. Toyota, of course, is concerned with bringing new vehicles to market and this is top-level project engineering. The project manager or 'chief engineer', as he or she is called, has a small team but meets regularly with functional line managers in the Obeya.

Obeya is just one element of Toyota's Design Management system. The key elements of the process are summarised by Patricia Panchak as:

- Test first, then design – not design, then test;
- Customer interest is the engineers' job, not the sales and marketing team's;
- Capture the knowledge developed during the process.

Other elements include:

- A strong 'chief engineer' who has the task of translating customer requirements of values to the new design. He or she has responsibility for the success of the entire project but does not have authority over the line managers whose teams actually do the technical design work.
- 'Set-Based' Concurrent Engineering whereby the design team tests several concepts for each sub-system, gradually narrowing the choice. The specifications slowly converge. This is in contrast to the stage/gate approach where the whole project may be abandoned at any stage, resulting in big waste. The Toyota way simply 'bookshelves' concepts that may be not feasible at the time, but may well be useful next time around.
- The 'set-based' approach also involves delaying decisions as late as possible. A form of 'postponement', or variety as late as possible, as found for example with Dell and Benneton.
- A system of coaching for new designers that involves them working in several departments and on the line, but then being mentored by a senior engineer.
- A system of checklists that captures best practice.
- A3s are used to standardise knowledge capture. Capturing the knowledge and lessons learned is important, but making it easy to access next time is just as important.
- The functional teams are experts in their own technical area, and are supposed to pursue leading-edge developments. These 'bookshelved' developments may be brought out at a later stage.

List of Related Tools

- Overall Professional Effectiveness
- Control Charts
- Information inventory

- Kaizen and Knowledge Management
- A3 problem solving
- Activity Sampling

Further Reading

Ronald Mascitelli, *The Lean Design Guidebook*, Technology Perspectives, 2004
Ronald Mascitelli, *The Lean Product Development Guidebook*, Technology Perspectives, 2007 (a really excellent review of many concepts relevant to Custom environments – not just product development)
A full description of the Toyota Design management process can be found in Allen Ward's *Lean Product and Process Development*, Lean Enterprise Institute, 2007.
Lawrence Leach, *Lean Project Management: Eight Principles for Success*, Advanced Projects, 2005
James Morgan and Jeffrey Liker, *The Toyota Product Development System*, Productivity Press, 2006
Peter Hines, Mark Francis and Pauline Found, 'Towards Lean Product Lifecycle Management: A Framework for New Product Development', *Journal of Manufacturing Technology Management*, Vol 17, No 7, 2006.
Patricia Panchak, 'Teledyne Benthos Adapts the Toyota Product Development System', *Target*, Third Issue, 2007
Herman Ballard, *The Last Planner System of Production Control*, PhD Thesis, University of Birmingham, 2000

3.4.4 Level 2: 'Idealised' Mapping

Low Customer involvement, Low Repeatability

Typical Situations

- Unstructured, typically 'messy' problems in 'human activity systems'
- Change management
- Design of a system such as an airport terminal, an investment in a new facility in China, or a university course
- Some Information Systems design, transport system design
- Organisational design
- Some Research and Development
- Writing a book, thesis or publication

In all of these there is low repeatability, but not necessarily low repetitiveness. Thus a scientist may seldom repeat an experiment or piece of analysis, but the sub-processes are likely to have repetitive stages. This is a less structured environment than the Custom type. Here we design the plant, in the Custom type we design the products that are made in the plant. Many of these situations overlap with project management, so material from the last section may also be relevant.

This is a situation where many of the concepts from service Design Thinking will be useful. See Part 2.

What is discussed here is the process design level. If, for example, you are designing a new facility in China, much further work will be needed at the micro design stage.

In this type of environment takt time is not applicable. It is also a fairly high variety process and, as Seddon has said, the system must be designed to absorb variety. Therefore, as with the Custom type, standard work in the detail sense also has low applicability. Not so, however, in the wider sense.

Drawing the 'Map'

Improving this type of process draws heavily on systems thinking, particularly that of John Seddon, Peter Checkland and Russell Ackoff, and on ideas from Goldratt's Theory of Constraints. As in other quadrants, the analysis begins with the macro (big picture) systems analysis.

An important idea here is 'back from the future'. In other words, design the ideal state and then move backwards to understand what barriers are in the way.

Checkland's soft systems methodology (SSM) was designed to tackle 'soft' problems, that is to say problem areas where quantification is not appropriate and the problem area is only loosely defined. Russell Ackoff refers to this as 'a mess', with the idea being to move from 'a mess' to 'an improved mess'. In fact this is consistent with the Toyota view that they do not try to design the perfect system first time, but rather implement an imperfect system and improve it over time.

The problem is often to find the problem. A manager may know that 'things are not what they should be' but finds it hard to pin down the problem due to a complex of interacting factors (in other words, a system).

SSM was developed by Peter Checkland and has been explained in several books. It has been used in many parts of industry, services and government. It is a tool for improvement rather than solution, since 'solutions' are seldom found in unstructured situations. It is referred to as 'soft systems' methodology, because 'hard' quantification is often not possible. However, 'soft' does not mean easy; the soft stuff is often the hard stuff.

The Rich Picture

SSM begins with the rather vague activity of building the rich picture. Recall that Seddon calls this 'Check'. The idea is to build up a rich understanding of this 'thing' we are about to analyse. This may take many forms: going to the Gemba and simply listening, market research, briefings by managers, inputs from customer focus groups, trends and projections from specialists and consultants, historic data, published information, and simply walking around. This part overlaps with the previously discussed high level analysis. Valuable insights can be obtained from

- **Value and failure demand**: this means listening, categorising, and quantifying;
- **Variation analysis**: this may involve drawing a run diagram or control chart (a) to identify 'special cause' events and see if the process is in control, and (b) to identify patterns of variation – trends, seasonality, cycles – and in the case of parallel processes such as more than one training course, how much variation is within the process and how much between processes;
- **The RATER dimensions**: which of these dimensions has the biggest gap?
- **Capacity and Constraint analysis**.

All of these are discussed further in the Tools section.

Reference Projections, Scenarios and Feedback Loops

The first two of these were suggested by Ackoff. Both represent a challenge to the status quo. Scenarios have been used by organisations such as Shell to look into risk and to challenge thinking. They are not a forecast but a description of a possible future state. Today many companies test future plans and policies against scenarios.

A reference projection is an extrapolation from the present, assuming that nothing will change in the wider environment. For example, market share is currently 30% and is growing at 5% per year. A reference projection would say that in ten years time, market share will be 80%. How likely is that? Probably something has to change. In that sense, this is similar to Goldratt's Theory of Constraints, which states that there is or will be at least one constraint – marketing, people, capital, skills, capacity, or whatever – in the way. Break or relieve the constraint and you will break through to a whole new plane. Reference projections are also a way of bringing 'an uncomfortable truth' home to managers, unions, and employees. For example, our costs are increasing faster than inflation. One reference projection for the British Health Service is that healthcare will absorb most of GDP by 2050.

Feedback loops are a powerful way to represent the dynamics of a problem. Such dynamics are hard to capture on a conventional map. See the Tools section.

Input-output diagrams

The first specific step is to draw one or more input-output diagrams. These diagrams show the 'transformations' with which the system is concerned. They are known as SIPOC diagrams in Six Sigma – Suppliers, Inputs, Process, Outputs, and Customers. For example, using people, machines, money, components to produce products. It is clearly possible to be much more specific, and the more specific the better. Begin by identifying the process that undertakes the transformation. Name it. Now add all the 'inputs' into the process and all the 'outputs' from the process. It is often useful to distinguish between the actual outputs and the desirable outputs. Also, distinguish between those inputs and outputs over which there is control and those over which there is no control. A useful question may be to ask who are the 'victims', 'beneficiaries' and customers. Drawing these diagrams forces you to think about just where the system begins and ends; this does not necessarily coincide with the organisational groupings. Input/output diagramming is really an attempt to clarify the process or system with which the team is dealing. Of course it is possible to think in terms of a hierarchy of input/output diagrams. There may be an overall transformation within which several interacting transformations are located. But often, at this stage, it is not necessary to think through the detail. As a rule of thumb, do not have more than four sub-input/output diagrams.

Purpose

The next step is to write down a statement. Checkland refers to this as the 'root definition', but here it will be called 'Purpose'. This is not the aim or objective but a description of what the system does or hopes to do <u>for the customer</u>. It may begin with the words, 'a system to ....'. Ackoff calls this 'the mission statement'. Ideally it should be a challenge to excite and inspire the players or employees.

Whatever it is called, Purpose should attempt to capture the essence and richness of the situation. The root definition may run to several sentences and include mention of the customers, the people (or 'actors') involved, the transformations (inputs to outputs) that it seeks to achieve, the 'world view' or philosophy of the system, the 'owners' of the system or the problem, and the environment in which the system operates. Checkland uses the mnemonic CATWOE to recall these features (see the section on System). The reasons for the existence and continuation of the system are usually incorporated.

Some prefer two versions of Purpose, one short and snappy and the other longer and more detailed. An example from health (Accident and Emergency): 'A patient quick-response system', or the longer version, 'A hospital system to receive and process patients in need of short-term care, in line with the patients' relative needs, with minimum delay and hassle'.

Conceptualisation

From the Purpose comes the system conceptualisation. Ackoff calls this 'Idealised Design'. Checkland's view is that this is put together by asking, 'What are the minimum necessary activities for this purpose?' How can this purpose be achieved as simply as possible? We are concerned with activities, so use a verb and a noun (e.g. 'transfer information'). These activities should be the minimum necessary. It is very important to note that these activities are derived directly from the Purpose or root definition and not from the actual situation. Conceptualisation is an opportunity for creative synthesis, for 'what might be', not a description of 'what is' at the moment. The reality of the real situation must be kept apart. The only guidance is from the Purpose itself.

But on a more down to earth level, Conceptualisation simply means developing the concept as if there were no restrictions of resources or organisational politics. Just pretend that the current organisation or system burned down today, and you have to start all over again. However, 'no restrictions' does not mean sci-fi way-out futuristic design. It is design with today's implementable, available technologies.

Although it is 'blue sky' thinking, it is also useful to think 'Blue Ocean'. This concept comes from a book of that title by Chan Kim and Renée Mauborgne, who challenge you to think about a strategy that would enable you to be placed so that you would not have any competitors. Quite a few have tried this, a recent one at the time of writing being Tesco's Fresh and Easy grocery chain in the USA.

Many formats can be used to present the ideal conceptualisation. Service blueprints and value stream maps, as discussed in this book, are certainly possibilities. The conceptualisation should show the interactions between the parts. Usually a diagram is drawn with the activities written inside activity boxes or 'balloons', and the interconnections between balloons are shown by means of arrows. Different types of arrow may be used to denote information, materials, customers, and other flows. A boundary may be drawn around all the balloons to indicate what is inside and what is outside the system. Then the flows into and out of the system are drawn – people, money, materials, customers, satisfaction, etc. It is useful to show where these flows come from and where they go to. Also identify on the diagram what the major external influences are. The measures of performance used by activities or by parts of the system may be included.

To summarise, the conceptualisation is a creative synthesis showing the activities, boundaries, interconnections, flows, and influences. An important idea is that the concept is holistic; it does not seek out specific improvements to sub-systems before the full concept is complete.

Comparison and Recommendation

Conceptualisation is an abstract exercise. Now comes a systematic comparison with the actual situation. The team 'returns to the real world' and begins to list what changes are feasible and practical. What activities are shown in the concept and what are found in practice? Do the information flows correspond? Are the organisational groupings correct?

In the 'real world' structures commonly evolve which result in product or information flows that double back on themselves, or responsibility for a task being split between several sections. The conceptualisation can be broken down into sub-systems that work together more closely than with other sub-systems. Because the conceptualisation has proceeded from the root definition it should overcome the problem of artificial boundaries that may exist within any real organisation. For quality management this is often very important: for instance, should purchasing be part of manufacturing? Should design work closer with marketing? These queries should benefit from the analysis, insights, creativity, and holistic nature of the previous stages, leading to a list of suggestions for change.

The strength of this methodology, as against a pure creativity exercise, is the disciplined structure that the analysis brings. The ideas generated are not random, but are seen in context with other requirements and constraints.

A Methodology for Developing the Future State

The methodology integrates the experience of conventional Lean value stream mapping with years of experience from the 'Soft Systems' approach developed by Peter Checkland. The steps are:

1   Understand the nature of the administrative or service system – primarily to do with the frequency of customer interactions and the degree to which the transactions are essentially routine or essentially creative. Repetitiveness is another useful dimension;
2   Select the appropriate type of mapping tool, or combination of mapping tools;
3   Develop the current state map – 'what is';
4   Build the rich picture of the system;
5   Develop the 'what might be' conceptual design of the product service bundle or 'ideal state';

6   Decide on the appropriate focus of people and process;
7   Compare 'what is' with 'what might be';
8   Develop the list of feasible, desirable changes;
9   Develop the Action Plan.

'What Might Be'

Once the particular value stream has been identified, the customer must be the starting point. Not only today's customers but also tomorrow's. Both the needs ('holes not drills') and the do-not-wants are required. This gives a 2 x 2 matrix – although it may well be useful to segment customers by, for example, spending category. A useful segmentation is to think of customers you want and customers you do not want. Begin by listing – through brainstorm, focus group, market research, direct observation, or all of these – the fundamental customer needs. The Kano model of Basics, Performance factors, and Delighters is useful here. Try to focus on ultimate needs to avoid short-term myopia: needs are sustainable, but wants may reflect current technology or current solutions. Then think about tomorrow's customers: will they be different in terms, for example, of age, spending power, education, expectations, free time and so forth? Then once again list the needs and do-not-wants of tomorrow's customers.

The Kano model, Brainstorming, and the Focus group are useful tools.

An understanding of customers requires an understanding of the product service bundle. Note the words 'product service bundle'. Every administrative task or service is a bundle of product and service. They are products in the sense that they transform an input into an output – or, as in the previous section, they fulfil a need. But they will have service elements insofar as there will be customer Moments of Truth. An airline aims to deliver passengers safely on time but the customer experience can be very different. Two insurance companies can both meet claims within the same time period, but with varying degrees of customer satisfaction through, for example, ease of use, friendliness and lack of hassle. Another way of looking at it is to use the Zeithaml *et al* RATER dimensions: The 'R' – reliability – is mainly the product; the 'ATER' – assurance, tangibles, empathy, responsiveness – is mainly the service. The product service bundle can be summarised by 'the "what" and the "how"'. The 'what' is the product: you buy a broadband service, but how is it installed and supported?

Develop the product service bundle concept in a workshop with the use of two colours of post-it sticker, one colour showing the product and the other the service. This is the ideal state. This stage should be done without considering practical constraints, but nevertheless avoiding science fiction by considering only what is possible today or in the very near future.

Prioritising

The next stage is to prioritise the process-people mix. Begin by positioning or debating the position of the value stream on an adaptation of Peter Wickens'

'Ascendant Organization' matrix. Peter Wickens is the former HR director of Nissan UK.

- The process axis should reflect the current state of processes in relation to the ideal state. Indicative (though not foolproof) measures would be 'hard' measures such as on-time performance, defect rates, rework, failure demand percentage, lead time in comparison with competitors. It should also include the skills of the workforce, rather than the effective use of those skills – you may have a highly skilled but demotivated workforce.
- The people axis should reflect the current state of employees (or 'actors') who are delivering the product service bundle, state of morale, willingness to adapt and change, commitment, friendliness, 'culture' (a dangerous word!).

It is NOT correct to equate process with 'product' and people with 'service'.

Of course the ideal is the 'ascendant' quadrant with high focus on both people and process. Wickens says that this is seldom the case, and many organisations are either 'anarchic' – focused on people but with poor process capability, or 'alienated' – the reverse. Virtually all publications on mapping ignore the people aspect. This may just about do in some manufacturing organisations but certainly will not fly in administrative and service organisations, particularly those with high customer interaction.

Several hints as to the extent of people focus can be found from the following questions:

- Are measures focused on customer requirements or on managers' requirements?
- Is there trust or fear?
- Is there pride in work?
- Is a clear vision known to everyone – not just senior management?
- Are problems welcomed?
- Are managers seen regularly at the Gemba?
- Is feedback sought from customers?
- Does feedback reach those who can make a difference, or is it ignored?

Positioning the process on the Ascendant Matrix just described should indicate where to begin the change process – with people or with process. Remember Deming and Ohno. Deming's '94/6' rule implied that 94% of problems lie with the process – the responsibility of management – and only 6% with the people. Ohno said that Toyota gets brilliant results from brilliant processes and 'average' people, rather than average results from brilliant people with poor processes. There is considerable evidence that it is easier to change the processes first and then the people, rather than the other way round. Change happens when people see that the new processes actually work and have the commitment of management behind them. On the other hand, there have been remarkable service transformations, which have focused in the first instance on people aspects. Examples are Scotrail (differentiating itself from British Rail), and Air Seychelles and SAS airlines, both of which focused on Moments of Truth improvements through their people.

Wickens says, '…with all the talk of eliminating waste and increasing labour productivity, the one element that is left out of the equation is the impact of ever-reducing waste and ever-increasing labour productivity on the people who are subjected to it! Most companies dress it up by talking about "working smarter, not harder" but the reality is that as waste is eliminated … and people move towards spending greater time adding value, the pressure on them can, in fact, increase even though each individual activity may be less strenuous' (Peter Wickens, *Energise Your Enterprise*, Macmillan, 1999, p 60).

The important message is that a good Lean service or administration future state needs to consider both process and people. People aspects – including the attitudes and behaviours of management and the measurement system – need to be compatible with the process.

Comparison and Developing The Action Plan

The Action Plan comes out of a comparison between the 'what is' current state map, and the insights from the 'what might be' exercise, including the discussion of the product-people focus. The Action Plan should include people assigned to specific milestones. The planning horizon would normally be six months.

Further Reading

Russell Ackoff, Jason Magidson and Herbert Addison, *Idealized Design*, Wharton School Publishing, 2006
Peter Checkland, *Systems Thinking, Systems Practice*, Wiley, Chichester, 1981
Brian Wilson, *Systems: Concepts, Methodologies, and Applications*, Wiley, Chichester, 1986
Peter Checkland and Jim Scholes, *Soft Systems Methodology in Action*, Wiley, Chichester, 1990
Peter Checkland and Sue Holwell, *Information, Systems, and Information Systems*, Wiley, Chichester, 1997

3.5 Level 3: Detailed Mapping

Level 3 mapping is particularly appropriate for Transaction mapping, is sometimes used in Interactive mapping, but is unusual in Custom or System Design areas.

It would be unusual to use Level 3 mapping detail for an end-to-end process. This is what old-style industrial engineers attempted to do. Much of that activity would be waste, because in the earlier Levels it is likely that whole swathes have been modified or scrapped.

Three methods will be described here: the application of the '3P' method in service, the Six Sigma mapping method, and Four Fields Mapping.

The '3P' Method for Service

The Toyota 3P – or Production Process Preparation – is a methodology for exploring different ways in which a product should be built. It is a manufacturability review, following the design – or more correctly done in parallel with the design. There seems to be no good reason why a 3P should not apply in service design, following a Level 2 consideration.

3P is considered vital because the decisions made at this detailed level may affect waste and flow for years to come. Having done a great job in Level 2, don't now throw much of it away.

A 3P uses a multifunction team. An important idea is to consider a range of ways in which the product might be made or the service delivered. Toyota, probably for provocation, likes to consider at least seven ways to make a product. A 3P is usually conducted as a mini kaizen event – possibly over a one or two day period. Many of the detailed options the team comes up with will need further investigation – but note that this is done subject to the designs that have been decided in Level 2. It should not be a ponderous process: multidiscipline is preferable, including the presence of front line service delivery staff, perhaps aided by experts in particular fields. The idea is to work through a range of possibilities. In many cases, this will also include a visit to the Gemba and an evaluation process to consider any tradeoffs between, say, cost, quality, speed, and customer satisfaction. Also, of course, there is the important point that the chosen alternatives should be compatible with one another.

So your team has come up with a good service delivery concept in Level 2, taking out much unnecessary waste and failure demand. Nevertheless, within your future state concept there remain many possibilities. Consider a few:

- **Queues**: a single queue leading to multiple servers, or multiple queues, or priority queues for certain customers? If a queue builds up, what action, if any, should be taken? If it decreases, what action should be taken?

- **Signs**: what signs should be erected, their appearance, their wording? Bear in mind that too many signs can confuse.
- **Equipment selection**: what equipment (hardware) should be used – computers, internet, displays, but also desks, chairs, lighting and so on? Should present equipment be used? New is not necessarily better.
- **Software**: although the choice of computer software may be beyond the scope of the team, at least the displays, ease of use, capabilities, and requirements for both staff and customers should be covered.
- **Automation**: what should be automated, if anything? Should automatic voice answering be used?
- **Signals**: what signals are appropriate for staff and for customers? For example, should customers be informed about long waits? Should the wait be estimated? How should system conditions be signalled – lights, digital displays, computer flags? Should signals of poor performance be automatically escalated?
- **Records**: how should they be kept – or should they be kept at all?
- **Front desk presentation and appearance**.
- **Health and safety issues**.
- **General decoration**: even if an interior designer is used, (s)he should be involved in the event.

For each one of these, don't rush in and accept the first option that comes to mind. Time taken here is very well spent.

The power of 3P is that multidiscipline views are brought to bear. The outcome is 'their' design, not one imposed from on high.

Six Sigma Detailed Mapping

There are a number of variations in the way Six Sigma organisations perform the detailed mapping tool.

The sequence below shows a six-step approach, which builds the map into a detailed state ,which can be revealing and useful when analysing the variables that affect the output.

1 Identify process steps within the project boundaries.
2 Identify Output variables and add them above the appropriate operation.
3 Identify Input variables and add them below the appropriate operation.
4 Partition variables into C,N,X categories.
5 Add customer specifications.
6 Highlight value-adding activities.

The C,N,X approach is a useful method employed for partitioning Input variables. If there are variables that require holding constant in order to achieve the desired output or reduce variation, these are labelled 'C'. You would often expect these to have a Standard Operating Procedure (SOP) or 'Something On Paper'. They may also be guided by standard steps given by a computer screen. Those variables that are not currently controllable (often because the resource provision is outside the system boundary) are labelled 'N'. Finally, those variables that can be changed to various settings are labelled 'X' for experimental purposes. Not all processes have Xs but there may be a desirable experiment to run with Cs in the future.

The map below shows the process steps necessary to make a cup of tea.

What seems a fairly straightforward task, which many of us carry out without a second thought, can be built up into a useful map for understanding the process, its inputs, outputs and current controls. If the six-step process is completed on this example, then the process owner would see immediate improvement opportunities to reduce variation through the introduction of standards (with adherence audits) and to failsafe (pokayoke) all designs.

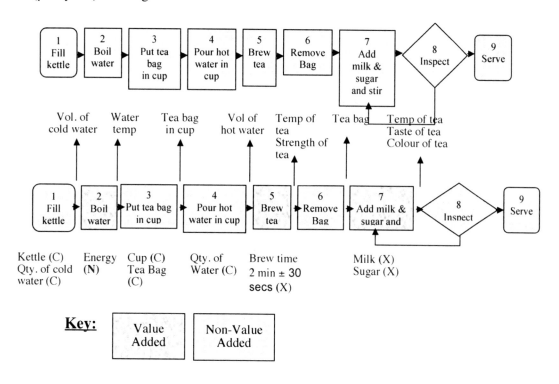

Four Fields Mapping

Four Fields mapping is a swimlane map with some features similar to the Service Blueprint discussed under Level 2 Interactive mapping. However, a Four Fields map is far more detailed and is generally used internally for administrative processes rather than for following a customer, as is the Service Blueprint.

The four fields (or columns) are:

- **The functions, departments, participants**: each of these is shown under its own swimlane and the activities to be performed within each swimlane are indicated; classic IT or computer programming symbols, such as activity box, document, decision point, data storage, etc., are used.
- **Time**: the time for the activity is written next to the activity; variation is not usually given, but this would be an improvement; delay times are also included.
- **Resource**: the times taken by critical resources are written in this column: if there is more than one critical resource, more columns can be added.
- **Standards and criteria**: if there is a standard this is recorded, otherwise, the criteria used for making the decision are given.

It is also common to record the stage of the process in the far left column.

Note the last two columns could be replaced by:
- Measures that relate to that particular stage or activity;
- Customer satisfaction with the stage – either by showing a rating out of five or with a happy or sad face icon.

The value in a Four Fields map is that it is inter-functional. So the functions should all participate in drawing the map. Wasteful activities are picked up by the team, and opportunities identified.

In practice, Four Fields mapping is done using the above format but with post-it stickers. It therefore resembles Brown Paper mapping described under Level 1.

Further Reading

John Bicheno and Philip Catherwood, *Six Sigma and The Quality Toolbox*, PICSIE Books, 2005, for more in Six Sigma, including many tools
Ronald Mascitelli, *The Lean Product Development Guidebook*, Technology Perspectives, 2007

Reference

Sarah Lethbridge, 'Four Fields Mapping', MSc Lean Operations Notes, Cardiff Business School, 2010

Part 4: Tools for Lean Service Systems

4.1 DIRFIT and Learning: Goodman, Argyris and Spear

A number of powerful concepts come together in this first 'Tools' section. They are the 'Do It Right the First Time' model from John Goodman, Root Cause analysis from Kaizen, Learning from Chris Argyris, and the improvement loop from Spear and Deming. Together these improve both numerator and denominator of the service utilisation ratio, and reduce variation, thereby enabling faster, more efficient service.

Recall the queue curve in the section on muda, muri and mura. All customers desire less delay and more effective service. Queues (or delays through a system) are directly related to both variation and utilisation. The lower the variation, the lower the delay. And the lower the utilisation (or load) the less the delay. Utilisation is the ratio is load (i.e. work) to capacity. But there are two types of load: value demand and failure demand. And capacity (or activity) is work + waste. Hence seek to reduce failure demand and to reduce waste. And reducing failure demand is about getting 'it' right the first time. 'It' (or value) must be clearly understood. This leads to effectiveness which is efficiency x value.

First is the 'Do It Right the First Time' (DIRFIT) concept. This, explains John Goodman, is THE way to maximising service customer satisfaction and building loyalty. Of course, given changing customer expectations, service complexity and changing technology, it is exceedingly difficult to build a service system to perfection and continuing perfection. What is needed therefore is a feedback loop (or PDSA) procedure to:

- monitor customer activity;
- identify any deviations from satisfactory outcomes on the part of customers - complaints by whatever means, out of spec response times, repeat calls, returns, incidents, unexpected questions, sources of possible dissatisfaction identified by employees, customer safety incidents, others;
- respond immediately and unreservedly, including apology;
- put in place countermeasures at local level, including authorisation to make small changes;
- if local countermeasures do not look likely to be a permanent fix, escalate the concern;
- put in place a root cause procedure;
- prevent future occurrences – eliminate future failure demand, by changing the system or exploring failsafe (pokayoke) methods (see separate section);
- implement the new system.

A system must be designed to do this. It is exactly in line with the Lean concepts of 'surfacing' problems. Employees are not going to highlight customer problems, concerns or deviations, unless:

- it is easy to do;
- it is expected to be done, not done on a whim;
- there is no fear (Deming's 'Drive out Fear');
- measures and targets do not conflict with this activity;
- there is no penalty – financial, time, promotion, or work. Here the three questions from Mager and Pipe are very useful:
  - Is performance punishing?
  - Is non-performance rewarding?
  - Does it make a difference?

IT can play an important role here, as can the Lean concepts of visual management and leader standard work. The latter may, for instance, include daily review meetings and a built-in escalation procedure. In fact, this is also similar to the 'Viable System Model' advocated by Stafford Beer – see separate section.

Of course, management needs to give active support to the principle of surfacing problems. Hence the idea of the 'inverted pyramid' whereby the focus at all levels is on supporting the front line, rather than the standard pyramid whereby all are focused on reporting upwards to achieve KPIs.

Steven Spear has a four step 'capability', as explained in the earlier section The Toyota Rules and Chasing the Rabbit. This overlaps with this feedback (PDSA) loop. To repeat, Spear gives the four capabilities as

1   *Capturing the best collective knowledge and making problems visible;*
2   *Building knowledge by Swarming and Solving Problems;*
3   *Spreading Lessons Learned to the Whole Organisation;*
4   *Leading by Developing Capabilities 1, 2 and 3 in others.*

There are similarities with Argyris' single- and double-loop learning. Single loop learning is adjusting the thermostat. Double loop learning is determining the most suitable temperature in the first place. Argyris points out how difficult this is for employees (and managers) who have grown up being expected to defensively solve not escalate, to 'remain in control', and to 'maximise winning not losing'. To change this behaviour requires senior managers to have the opportunity to practice these new skills.

Learning by deliberate experimentation is now much easier using IT and statistical packages – perhaps also six sigma. For instance Harrah's casinos famously conducts many experiments with gaming tables. Google and Amazon are also deliberate experimenters.

Further reading

John Goodman, *Strategic Customer Service*, AmaCom, 209
Steven Spear, *Chasing the Rabbit*, (now renamed *The High Velocity Edge*) McGraw Hill, 2009
Chris Argyris, 'Teaching Smart People to Learn', in Joan Gallos (ed), *Organization Development*, Josey Bass, 2006
Ian Ayers, *Supercrunchers: How Anything Can be Predicted*, John Murray, 2007

4.2   Queues (and Kingman's Equation)

Kingman's equation is about queues. We need to understand queues, not only because they occur so widely but also because they increase the lead-time, reduce competitiveness, annoy customers, work against quality (through reduced error detection time), and take up space. Generally, service process times, especially in professional services, are much longer than in manufacturing. And, in service, people (customers) wait in queues rather than products waiting in a buffer. So queues are generally more important for customer satisfaction in service than in manufacturing.

Kingman's equation is $AQT = ((c_a^2 + c_p^2)/2) (\rho/(1-\rho)) t_p$

where

- o   AQT is the average queue time
- o ρ Is the utilisation, expressed as a decimal. ρ is arrival rate / service rate.
- o $c_a^2 + c_p^2$ are the arrival variation and process variation coefficients
- o t_p is the process time

There are three variables (arrival variation, process (or server) variation, and utilisation) that influence the queue (or wait) time, or cycle time through the process.

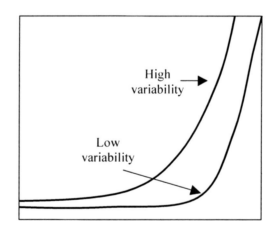

Average Utilisation ρ

This exponential graph can be demonstrated easily in a few minutes with a dice game having servers and process players. For a description see 'The Lean Games Book'.

The Service Systems Toolbox

As long as the utilisation is less than 100%, if <u>both</u> types of variation are zero the queue is zero; if utilisation is 100% or 1, the queue is infinite. And if utilisation tends to zero, the queue tends to zero because there are no customers or orders. Also, of course, queue length and wait time is relative to the mean time of the process. If a process takes an hour, 5 people or jobs in the queue will mean an expected delay of 5 hours; if the process takes a minute, 5 people in the queue will mean an expected delay of 5 minutes. Generally, the longer the average process time, the more important is queue length. Obvious, but worth stating.

In the Toyota system variation is 'mura', and utilisation is roughly equivalent to 'muri' or overload.

Utilisation is load / capacity (or arrival rate / service rate in service, or demand / time available for the work to be done, in manufacturing. Let us look at this formula.

- Note that there are three types of demand – value demand, failure demand and rework demand. Value demand is first-time demand. Failure demand is externally generated repeat demand caused by 'not doing something or not doing something right' (Seddon). Rework demand is internally generated demand caused by errors that are corrected internally without the external customer knowing about it.
- The time available for work to be done is reduced by wasteful activity. In fact, as Ohno said, 'activity = work plus waste'.
- Cutting failure demand and rework reduces the load, sometimes significantly.
- Reducing waste (or muda) also reduces the load. Waste can cause both rework and reduce capacity, thereby affecting both numerator and denominator in the utilisation equation.
- Toyota's 'muri' or overload applies to people and machines. Note from the graph and the equation that overload begins at less than 100% utilisation.
- Reducing failure demand, internal rework, and waste should be a priority for any service and manufacturer.

So, Kingman's equation incorporates
- The Toyota view of 'muda, muri and mura';
- The Six Sigma view of reducing variation;
- The Seddon insight of eliminating failure demand.

After reducing these three, there remain value demand and value added time. Each has variation - arrival variation and process variation. Variation, in turn, is of two types – common cause and special cause. Special cause variation is, in general, easier to identify and eliminate whereas reducing common cause variation may require system redesign. This comes straight out of Deming's 'Profound Knowledge'.

Kingman's equation is universally applicable to operations. Highway engineers understand the implications. For example, the counter-intuitive step of slowing down motorway traffic to improve flow is adopted on the M25. Why? Because it reduces 'process' variation and hence reduces queues. Likewise, access control is used to feed cars onto a highway such that arrival variation is reduced. We have all experienced the effect on queues that closing a lane on a motorway has at busy times. But at midnight, closing a lane makes no difference. This is an illustration of the exponential effect of utilisation.

Frances Frei, in a Harvard Business Review article, expands on arrival variation by saying that there are five types of 'customer-introduced variability': arrival variability (that is between arrivals), request variability (within arrivals), capability variability (customer skill), effort variability (how much effort has the customer made – say before airport security), and 'subjective preference variability' (simply different customer expectations). This is useful because it lists out what is really required in a six sigma variation reduction project. Frei's types of variation are discussed in more detail in the section on Variability in Part 2.

Likewise process variation is subject to many or all of the classic 6 M's: man, machine, method, material, measures, mother nature.

But, we need to explore further....

- Utililsation is the big one. If utilisation is low – say 50% or less - arrival variation and process variation will have small impact. If utilisation is high – say above 80% - arrival and process variation will be of high importance.
- If you aim to have short delays or queues then either variation or utilisation must be small, assuming that you have already reduced failure demand.
- We may note the implications of aiming at both high utilisation and low queues. This is only possible with very low arrival variation, very low process variation, and very little rework or failure demand. Impossible?
- If utilisation is high, reducing the utilisation (say by 30%) will have a big impact, but reducing the process variation will have less impact despite being more difficult to achieve. Even if you are able to reduce process variation to zero (near impossible in service) you will still have the influence of arrival variation.
- Of course, if you attempt to run your process at 100% utilisation, your queue time will be infinite! But 100% utilisation is not possible, at least over the longer term. No process is known that runs at 100% utilization forever!
- In manufacturing, the cost of extra capacity is typically high. Hence the option of reducing lead-time by reducing utilisation by, in turn, adding capacity is often not taken. Manufacturing managers may prefer to reduce variation – hence the popularity of six sigma and standard work. But in service, and sometimes manufacturing assembly, extra capacity may frequently not be expensive and can be added incrementally by, for example, adding an extra employee or moving employees between functions.
- Capacity adjustment is a good solution where demand cannot be influenced. In a supermarket, shelf stackers man the till when queues build up. But this option is not as good in, for example, a call centre where failure demand may be an important constituent of total demand.

- It follows that actions to reduce utilisation should be the first focus. A priority should be to reduce failure demand or to have a responsive procedure that adjusts capacity when utilisation (or queues) increases.
- Reducing failure demand is more of a 'root cause' action that permanently decreases the load on the process, and hence decreases utilisation. You MAY be able to reduce resources in this way, but the first priority should be about improving service through reduced queue time. Beware of getting into the vicious cycle described by Hopp and Spearman:

  - sufficient capacity is provided to reduce queues;
  - management notices that at times utilisation is well below 100%;
  - Management cuts resources ;
  - utilisation increases;
  - queues build, service declines;
  - management is forced to provide more resources or to cut demand;
  - the cycle begins again.

- Arrival and process variation are measured by the coefficient of variation, c_a and c_p. In the equation, the terms are c_a^2 and c_p^2. c_a and c_p are given by σ_a / t_a and σ_p / tp. σ is the standard deviation and t is the mean (or average) time – or mean inter-arrival time in the case of t_a. This makes intuitive sense: if the standard deviation of process time is 1 minute and the mean process time is also 1 minute, variation will be much more significant than a process where the standard deviation is 1 minute, but the mean process time is 20 minutes.
- From this it follows that, since many service processes are longer than manufacturing processes, variation is generally more tolerable in service than in manufacturing.
- Uncertainty of queue length increases rapidly with increasing utilisation. At low utilisation, the effects of variation are small – because in Kingman's equation the variation term is multiplied by a small number. Hence queue length uncertainty is small. But at high utilisation, the effects of variation are much larger because a larger number multiplies the variation term. So, you may have a long queue or a short queue. In other words customer wait time, and hence customer satisfaction, is a matter of chance at high utilisation levels.
- Taking the points about utilisation and variation together, it is much more effective to focus on reducing failure demand whilst allowing for moderate variation, than it is to try to cut variation – especially when doing so actually increases the load due to the generation of failure demand. Hence many six sigma efforts may be misdirected.
- Likewise, attempts to remove all variation through standardisation is counterproductive for two reasons:
  - as stated, even if all process variation is removed, arrival variation would still remain;
  - over standardisation may easily result in the generation of failure demand.

- As Seddon has said, a service process needs to be able to 'absorb variety'. This is another way of saying that a process needs to be able to self-adjust or else failure demand is likely.
- It is interesting that the TWI (Training Within Industry) approach to Job Instruction, through the 'job breakdown chart' put emphasis on getting the 'key' activities correct, but ignores standard times. This can now be seen to make a lot of sense, because time variation is less critical than utilisation. Utilisation is affected by errors – generating failure demand or rework.
- Arrival variation is often ignored, but it has equal influence to process variation. A steady arrival pattern will lead to lower queues and delays than lumpy. Can this be influenced? Maybe by informing customers of peak demand times. Most service centres experience uneven demand with peaks on Monday, payday, early morning, and lunchtime.
- The work release behaviour of processes immediately upstream of a bottleneck is important. If it releases work steadily the bottleneck queues will be on average shorter than if the upstream resource releases lumpy work.
- Little's Law always applies. This is: the average queue time = number of customers in a queue / average process rate. This applies to both whole systems and to individual processes. If 2 customers are processed per hour and there are 10 customers in the queue, the average queue time will be 10/2 = 5 hours.
- And writing the equation the other way around: Number of customers in a queue = Average queue time x average process rate. But average queue time is Kingman's equation.
- Often, in service, we know the average completion or process rate (say customers per hour) and the number of customers in the system. We can then predict the average queue or delay time. This can compared with, for example, promises made to customers about delays or, in a project environment, used to calculate the cost of delays.
- 'Queue discipline' can be very important in service processes, especially professional service. A FIFO (first in, first out) basis is often assumed. This may be a mistake in queuing. Important or critical jobs should often go to the front. If you have several jobs of equal priority, you can minimise the average wait time by doing the shortest jobs first.
- A standard tool used in manufacturing, is the 'Line of Balance'. In Production Planning it is known as the Cumulative Capacity Planning Chart. In Queuing, there is a most useful equivalent. Plot Cumulative demand and cumulative completions on the vertical axis, and time on the horizontal axis. The clock starts running at the origin. The first arrival is plotted against the elapsed time. And so on for all arrivals, to form the cumulative arrival line. Draw the line of best fit. The first completion is plotted after the elapsed time. And so on for all completions, to form the completion line. Again draw the line of best fit. Now we have a useful graph with a cumulative arrival line and a cumulative completion line.

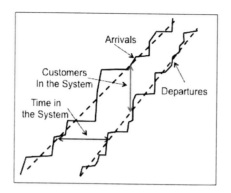

Cumulative Customers

Elapsed Time

- The slope of the line of best fit through the arrival line gives the average arrival rate.
- The slope of the line of best fit through the completion line gives the average completion or service rate. Note that this is not the same as the capacity rate.
- The vertical distance between the lines at any time gives the number in the system (queuing plus being served). The average can be estimated by inspection. In manufacturing, the vertical distance is the amount of inventory in the system.
- The horizontal distance between the lines gives the time in the system (queuing plus service time). The average can be estimated by inspection.
- (In production or capacity planning the arrivals line is forecasted demand, the completions line is the anticipated production rate. The vertical distance between the lines (or inventory) may be constrained by storage space; the horizontal distance between the lines may be constrained by the storage time or shelf life, and the slope of the production rate line may be limited by actual capacity.)
- The slopes of the lines can be used in Kingman's equation.
- The graph can be a good general guide to Lean implementation. The arrival and completion lines should converge, until the distance between them is less than the lead-times (or queue time) that customers expect. At the same time variation in both the arrival rate and completion rate should reduce. See Figure 3. In the figure the arrival rate changes because of greater customer satisfaction.
- Plotting the lines is an excellent way to monitor a service or manufacturing process. Diverging lines give an immediate indication of a problem.
- With regard to 'buffers' against variation, there are only three kinds: inventory buffers, time buffers (customer queues or waits), capacity buffers (or less than 100% utilisation). Of course, if inventory cannot be held, as in some service, there is a straight trade-off between capacity and queue time. If customer wait time cost can be estimated, there will be optimal level of capacity. Note the

typical flat-bottomed nature of the total cost curve on the upside of the optimal point. This means that it is less risky and wise to err on the side of greater capacity. Note, however, that if the process step is a bottleneck as opposed to a constraint, the economics are different – because, to quote Goldratt, 'an hour lost at a bottleneck is an hour lost for the whole system'.

• If you attempt to 'protect the constraint' by a time buffer, as in TOC, this can reduce arrival variation. But it does nothing for process variation. Remember that you are making a trade-off – the increased throughput from the bottleneck against the cost of delay (of customers, or inventory). If you know these – and if not you should try to find out – then there is an optimum utilisation rate. Sometimes it will be more cost effective to provide extra capacity than to increase the constraint buffer.

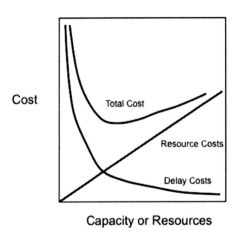

Cost

Total Cost

Resource Costs

Delay Costs

Capacity or Resources

In Service:
Delay costs are mainly with customers waiting (Often ignored!)
Resource costs may be able to be varied in the short term.
In Manufacturing:
Delay costs are often with inventory buffers
Resource costs may be associated with hard resources such as machines

Note the flat-bottomed Total Cost with increased capacity

• TOC advocates the 5 steps of improvement – a procedure that has been successfully employed numerous times. The steps are Identify, Exploit, Subordinate, Elevate, and Repeat. Kingman's equation adds insight:
  o To identify the constraint, it is simplistic to just examine the load and compare it with demonstrated capacity. What we know through Kingman is that overload begins at less than 100% utilisation and knowledge of variation is particularly important at high utilisation. For instance, a resource loaded at 85% of capacity may be more of a constraint than a resource loaded at 90% but having much lower process variation.
  o Exploiting the constraint should include variation reduction in addition to other traditional methods such as protecting it with buffer.
  o Subordinating other resources should include looking upstream of the constraint to examine arrival variation coming onto the constraint.

Making Queuing Less Painful

Of course, from a Lean perspective you would like to avoid any queue. So this should be the first priority. But since variation is so endemic, some queues may be unavoidable. Then the other half of the question is the psychology of queuing, or making queuing less painful. Several researchers have studied this aspect. In general improvement is 'low cost/no cost', once you are aware of the situation.

- Pre-process waits feel longer. It is the time to the first contact that is most important. Once customers feel that they are 'in the system' they relax a little. So, at A&E in a hospital the waiting time to get to the initial point of contact is more important than the subsequent wait to be seen by the doctor. So have an early greeting process, even if subsequent waits are longer. Can this be done in call centres?
- Unoccupied waits feel longer. If people have nothing to do, the wait feels longer. So:
    - distract: provide reading material, computer games;
    - provide mirrors so people have something to look at while they are waiting: this works!
    - amuse: as at Disney;
    - let them know that they are not forgotten: play music while callers are waiting in a telephone queue, or better still, give a countdown (see next section);
    - prioritise: allow customers to do other tasks (shopping) by picking up a number and displaying the number of the next customer to be served;
    - prioritise 2: call restaurant customers on their mobile (cell) phone when their table is ready.
- Uncertain waits feel longer. So:
    - inform: Disney informs customers of the length of time to get to the ride if you are standing at a particular point – but then also deliberately overestimates the wait time;
    - keep appointments: the previous section showed the folly of booking to 100% of utilisation. Inevitably there will be delays, so build in buffer time.
- Unfair waits feel longer. The British feel strongly about perceived queue jumpers. But sometimes it is necessary to give priority. So:
    - most important, always try to have a single queue rather than multiple queues: there is generally no excuse for parallel queues;
    - have a separate entrance or queue where there are different priorities.

The Poisson Distribution

It is generally unwise to assume that demand rates and service rates will be normally distributed. Much research, and common experience, show that the Poisson distribution is a far better assumption, certainly for customer or job arrival rates. The Poisson distribution often has a long tail. Common experience suggests that 'buses arrive in twos' and that service times in queues are unevenly distributed; just as you think the queue is moving steadily, the person immediately in front will inevitably have numerous transactions! Both these situations arise because the distribution is Poisson, not normal. Maintenance work invariably arrives according to a Poisson distribution. Design work also has this characteristic – some small jobs take a very long time.

The Poisson distribution goes from zero to infinity. For instance, in a bank there is no chance of getting less than zero arrivals in an hour, and a small probability of getting 1000 arrivals in an hour. For customer arrivals or product breakdown rates, if there is theoretically an infinite number of arrivals it is a Poisson distribution. If there is a finite maximum number of possible arrivals, it is a Binomial distribution. Arrivals are usually Poisson distributed.

The good news is that the Poisson is characterised by only one figure – the average rate. There is no standard deviation. The average rate can sometimes be found by looking up the records of the number of arrivals or product breakdowns or events per day, week, hour or whatever. With caution you can convert to the required time interval. For example, if you work a six-hour day and usually get 36 calls, you can say that you get six calls per hour provided that calls are more or less uniform throughout the day.

Once you know the average demand rate, then you can predict the probability of a certain number of events in any time period. For instance, if you know that the average product failure rate requiring service is four per day, then, if failures follow Poisson – and they usually will – you can easily calculate the probability of there being exactly 0, 1, 2, 3, 4, 5, 6, etc. failures on any day. This will help to determine the appropriate capacity to service the failures. The probability can be found from the Poisson function on Excel, or by using the formula:

$$P(x) = e^{-\lambda}\lambda^{x} / (x!)$$

where λ is the average rate of arrivals over the time period in question, e is the base of natural logs (found on most calculators), and x is the number of arrivals in the period. x! means the number multiplied by all successive numbers below that number to 1, for instance

$$4! = 4 \times 3 \times 2 \times 1 = 24.$$

Relating to Kingman's equation in the last section, the Poisson distribution, has a coefficient of variation of 1 because the mean λ is equal to the variance (or σ^2).

Many texts on statistics or operations management list the Poisson cumulative distribution – that is, the probability of that number of arrivals or less in the period. For instance, if the average arrival rate is six per hour, the probability of six arrivals or fewer is 0.61, and the probability of twelve arrivals or fewer is 0.99.

Where the average number of arrivals or events per period is greater than 20, the Poisson becomes unwieldy and the normal approximation to the Poisson can be used. This can be done quite easily by taking the mean (μ) of the normal distribution as λ and the standard deviation (σ) as $\sigma = \sqrt{\lambda}$. Thereafter use the usual properties of the normal distribution.

The z value, where $z = (x - \mu)/\sigma$, can be used to calculate any probability.

Of course, for an important process it is worth checking whether the Poisson assumption is valid. For automated processes, such as using an ATM, assuming the Poisson is likely to be incorrect. Note that the exponential distribution, related to the Poisson and also available on Excel, can be used to model the time between events.

For arrivals, the Poisson is generally a good assumption. The Poisson uses the average rate of arrivals, and calculates the probability of the number of arrivals in a time period. The probability of the time between arrivals is given by the related exponential distribution. The average inter-arrival time is the inverse of the arrival rate. So if the average arrival rate is five per hour, the average inter-arrival time is $1/5 = 12$ minutes.

Relating the Poisson Distribution to Queues

Queues are widely found in service, so understanding their characteristics is important.

A headache in administration and service is that service capacity usually cannot be stored or inventoried – it is perishable. This is a major reason why it is simply not good enough to provide the average capacity. If there are no customers, service capacity is lost forever. But customers will continue to arrive at the average rate, so a server working at the average rate of arrivals will fall further and further behind.

The ratio of arrival rate to service rate is important for service management. The ratio is known as the utilisation factor ρ (called rho), where $\rho = \lambda / \mu$ and λ is as before the arrival rate – say in customers per hour – and μ is the service rate also in customers per hour. ρ can take on values between 0 and 1. Where ρ is zero there is no queue. As ρ increases, queues grow very slowly at first, then rapidly above a ratio of about 70% or 80%. The lower the variation, the later the 'take off' point. If there is no variation then the queue is zero as long as the arrival rate is less than the service rate, but as soon as the arrival rate exceeds the service rate, even minutely, the queue will grow to infinity. In practice there is always variation, so the queue starts to increase rapidly above, say, 70%.

The shape of the Poisson distribution, particularly at low values, has a long tail. This is in line with everyone's experience of waiting in a queue at a bank or post office: most people have very short transactions, but a few have very long transactions. The same applies to arrivals. See the figure as an example. This is the Poisson distribution for an average of three arrivals during a period of time. So, for example, there is some chance of no arrivals and a very small chance of nine arrivals during any period.

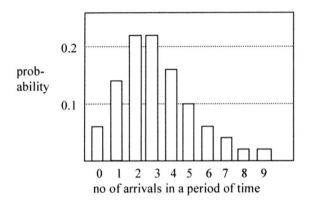

4.3 Capacity Management in Service

Capacity management in service varies with the type of service system – particularly the flexibility of resources and time to acquire or train resources. In some service situations, for instance a supermarket, it may be easy to react to demand by shifting people from shelf-stacking to tills, whenever demand grows. This is capacity management by short-term pull. In other situations non-flexible resources may have to be recruited or trained – or capital resources like aircraft or hotel rooms acquired.

There are some guidelines.

The most important guideline is to decide on the purpose of the service system before deciding on the capacity. In one classic case a government department thought that they were hugely overstretched, only to discover some months later that they had a surplus of staff when the system was redesigned – not by a piecemeal waste reduction exercise, but by a fundamental re-think as to what the process was actually there to do and then asking what would be the best way to do the task.

In another case, when the true requirement of the customer was defined as 'power by the hour' rather than selling engines, the whole business changed, including thinking about the required capacity.

Then ask how much failure demand and waste there is in the process. Failure demand should be eliminated or massively reduced. See the separate section on value and failure demand. Capacity that is there to cope with failure demand may have to be re-deployed. Why are there all those re-work loops? How much waste is there in a design office, perhaps doing designs that are subsequently scrapped, or shelved and then substantially re-done? How many service calls are abortive?

Lastly, consider Capacity. A useful, if not essential, starting point is Kingman's equation. Please refer to the earlier section on Kingman.

Capacity and Demand

A big differentiator between service and manufacturing is the variability of demand. This is accentuated by the fact that demand, in the form of queues or waits, is often intolerable to customers. Some service demands have to be met on demand or at very short notice, or else failure in the form of defection or dissatisfaction (even death) will result. This is made worse by the fact that 'buffer stock' cannot be kept. Most administrative and service systems experience demand variability from customer to customer, from hour to hour, from day to day, and by season.

John Seddon of Vanguard Consulting suggests that any service analysis begins by determining if the system is 'in control' from a statistical process control point of view. In other words are there 'special causes' at work or is variation 'natural variation'?

Why is this important? Because, if the process is 'out of control' it means there are unpredictable elements at work that disrupt smooth flow of work and lead to poor and erratic customer service. Such out of control elements need different treatment from processes that are in control and where 'common cause' variation is at work. Using a car analogy, the temperature may vary on hot and cold days and when climbing or descending a hill. This is common cause variation in control. But if the fan belt breaks or the radiator springs a leak, this will cause 'special cause' variation and is out of control. If you are trying to improve the performance of the car, you do not want these out of control conditions to be present.

The example shows the time for completion for repairs by a field maintenance service in two regions of the country.

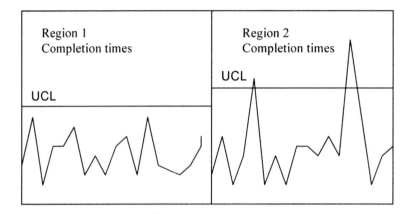

The first region is largely in control. Not so the second region. Here there are some unexplained high numbers. We don't know what happened here, but we do know that the variation is too high. There must be some special causes at work. Possibilities are vans going out with the wrong tools or information, untrained staff, confusion over work leading to long delays, or even workers 'goofing off'. Further probing reveals a potential special cause: shortage of parts leading back to the appointment of a new spare-parts manager who was adopting new policies to try and reduce inventories.

To find out if a process or system is in control, first determine the critical customer requirement or measure of the overall end-to-end system response. Examples are

- order to delivery time;
- number of forms processed per day;
- number of calls handled per day;
- response time for repair;
- new product introduction time;
- mortgage approval time;
- ambulance response time.

But note that the measure should be largely under the control of the system, not outside the system. Thus the wait time for a category of patient is a valid parameter, but overall time for a cure is not. The greater the number of events outside the control of the system, the more likely is an 'out of control' signal.

Plot the system response measure on a run diagram. For example, calls per day on the vertical axis against days on the horizontal axis. Calculate mean and upper control limit (UCL) – three standard deviations above the mean. Many statistical packages, such as Minitab, will do this task. If all plotted points are below the UCL, the system is 'in control' and variation is 'natural'. If there are points above the UCL, these require special examination. Determine the specific circumstances for each. This is just like your car's temperature gauge showing red – you need to stop and investigate. These 'out of control' points are a warning sign of special events, which need to be specifically addressed – preferably eliminated but otherwise specially catered for. The 'special causes' above the control limit may be things that can easily be remedied, such as too many people on leave at the same time, but they may also be systemic, such as an inherent flaw in the scheduling system.

Predicting Demand

Demand should be managed, but will still need to be predicted in order to provide the right amount of capacity. Some service organisations believe that demand is difficult or impossible to predict. However, in many situations demand can be predicted by segmenting.

- Graph the total demand. If data is available for a minimum of two cycles – perhaps two years – it should be possible to detect trend and seasonality, if any. Several statistical and forecasting packages are available to assist with this, but do plot the data series before diving into the statistics – there is no substitute for the eye of an experienced manager. If there is trend and seasonality, these effects will have to be removed from the series first so that only the 'noise' remains. Of course, if there is trend or seasonality in the data, the mean and standard deviations are not useful.

- Produce an analysis of demand by events per time segment. Start wide and gradually narrow the time interval. The data series plot is the starting point. Examine this series carefully to identify time groupings. For example, is there usually a difference between the first and last weeks of the month, between Monday and Friday, between morning, lunchtime, and afternoon? Plot the number of events or customer arrivals per day – not as a graph of events against days of the month, but the number of days during the month when there were exactly 0, 1, 2, 3, ... arrivals. Then repeat by day, for example Wednesday and Friday, or morning and afternoon, depending on what the examination of the data series has revealed. Then (possibly) home in by hour, and so on.
- See if demand follows a Poisson distribution over the various time horizons explored above. If it does – and this is very likely in service and administration for at least one of the time segments – then you have a

powerful piece of information which will enable you to design a good, Lean response system and to assess the risk of unmet demand at various staffing levels.
- Classify demand:
    - predictable, semi-predictable, non-predictable;
    - capable of being influenced, or not capable of being influenced;
    - urgent and non-urgent: a critical activity or event ideally requires an immediate response, it must have priority.

Examples of predictable demand:

- routine maintenance;
- insurance renewals;
- direct debit instructions;
- shut down periods;
- routine events (Christmas, Easter, Thanksgiving);
- planned promotions;
- pre-booked events.

Examples of semi-predictable demand:

- car service distance intervals;
- events related to the main interval (like brake shoe replacement every second service);
- lunchtime demands;
- service or extension demands related to prior purchases (likelihood of purchasing an upgrade x months after a computer is purchased);
- some consumable repurchases;
- repeat visits by businessmen visiting a hotel (this can be asked for, or an incentive given);
- weather-related services (accidents, drinks, leisure);
- lagged demands, for instance, after a new house or office is occupied or started to be built, or after the sale of a new car;
- statistical, for example the probability of a bird hit every 1000 flights, or knowing that arrivals follow a Poisson distribution with average rate of y per week.

Examples of demand which can be influenced are

- price incentives;
- warnings of delays;
- upgrade incentives;
- reminders for service.

Calculating the Load

Load is the amount of work coming on to a particular resource (person, group, facility) in a time period. Calculating the workload on resources is necessary to identify those resources that are critical from a capacity point of view. In manufacturing this can be done relatively easily by assembling the routings for each product, multiplying the volume of the product by the unit time spent on each resource, and collecting up the sum of the total times spent by all products on the resource. This is generally done ignoring variation. In service, calculating the load is similar in principle and is discussed in the next section.

Calculating load, when done correctly and supportively, can have the added benefit of a time management exercise.

Shared Resources

Some manufacturing value streams and a few administrative and service value streams can get away with ignoring the impact of shared resources. If you are lucky enough to have resources that are dedicated to a value stream full-time, or for a known proportion of time, the problem is considerably simplified. In this case, average load can be determined by volume multiplied by average unit processing time.

The next easiest problem to solve is where there are clear priorities. For example, when an emergency call comes in, all routine tasks are abandoned and the resource is devoted to the value stream. In this case the load is calculated as above, and shared resources can be ignored except where there may be several priority demands from different value streams – for example, a call centre or administrator being shared across more than one value stream. In the latter case, see the next section. It is unwise to ignore other activities that are not part of the value stream in question, but that have an impact nevertheless on the load on a critical resource in a value stream. For example, the call centre or administrator may be subject to seasonal time demands that result from another value stream.

The objective is to get the value stream to flow. But in order to allow flow, the total load on critical resources must be determined because the resource may be a bottleneck, or effectively overloaded – also called 'overburden' by Toyota. We have learned that to load a resource above about 80% of nominal available capacity courts disaster in the form of sharply escalated delays. The 80% figure is a typical guideline dependent on variation both of customer arrivals and of service time.

Assuming that we do not have the simple case and that critical resources are shared between several value streams, it is necessary to estimate the average load.

- Decide on a suitable period. This may be a half-day for a repetitive transactional process such as order picking, making meals, hotel check-in. A day may be suitable for a semi-repetitive administrative or repair process, a week for many office tasks where deadlines are known well in advance or for longer-cycle maintenance, an even longer period for some professional or creative processes.

- List the range of tasks typically undertaken during the period.
- Estimate the length of tasks. This is often done by voluntary recording or tagging. Times for short cycle tasks may be found by direct observation. Tagging is suitable for long cycle tasks – simply have a traveller form going around with the document or ask people to record activities during the day on a piece of paper. Remember to explain the reasons for recording. Short cycle tasks can be recorded by video, but this is undesirable unless the video is made and analysed by the operators themselves, perhaps to be used as a follow-up kaizen activity.
- Estimate the time split between tasks and, crucially, how much the time split varies. Is the resource heavily loaded one week, lighter the next?
- Estimate the likelihood of the resource being overloaded, and under what circumstances. For example, an accountant working in two value streams is heavily loaded by one of the value streams for the last four days of the month. Are the delays on both value streams tolerable, or does capacity need to be adjusted by overtime, temporary work, or secondment?
- Decide on the necessary actions, if any.

Capacity, Takt Time, and the Yamazumi Board

In repetitive service situations – in some offices and warehouses, even if for a part of the day – you may be able to use takt time. What follows applies to repetitive short cycle activities – that is, where most activities take less than (say) fifteen minutes, and are done by a group all doing approximately the same general task. Activities accumulate into jobs, perhaps passed from person to person.

Relevant formulas are:

Takt time = available work time / demand

Cycle time for an office = .8 x takt time

No. of workers required = sum of the activity manual times/cycle time

Applying this:

- Before you even start timing or looking at activities, you need to look at the activities themselves. Are they really necessary from the customer's perspective?
- Do a 'paper kaizen'. That is, take out the ONVA (Organisation Non-Value Added) activities. Redesign for flow using the checklist above. The sum of the activity times should decline sharply, and as the times decline so will the

number of resources. Of course, other work will have to be found for the extras (an opportunity to expand customer service).

- And before calculating activity times, the work should be examined for waste and the existence of failure demand. Both should be removed as soon as possible – and as they are removed so the work content will fall and so will the number of workers needed. As this happens, they should be reassigned not fired. A map and a Spaghetti Diagram would be useful.

- The available time is the time available for processing work, after meetings, kaizens, and all breaks. This need not be a full work day – perhaps the task is worked on only in the morning.

- In an office or warehouse with flexible workers who can be moved around, the takt time can be calculated every day and the appropriate number of workers assigned daily. In fact, the number of workers can be altered during the day – if, for example, there is a heavy workload in the mornings but a much smaller workload in the afternoon. Workers could, for instance, work on order picking in the morning and then some of them could be assigned to work in the dispatch bay in the afternoon.

- Cycle time is taken at 80% of takt because of variation (discussed above). The factor 0.8 is a matter of experience. In practice it may be found too high or too low, but 0.8 is an excellent starting point.

- The sum of the activity times is the total manual work content to complete one piece of work from start to finish in the area – assuming that workers do not stand and watch printers, photocopiers and the like. Of course times will vary and will have to be observed or estimated. The best way is to get the workers themselves (nurses? clerks? engineers?) to time a number of operation cycles. Then exclude any 'way-out' times – high or low – and take the lowest repeated time.

- The 'profile' or histogram of times for an activity is interesting in itself. Refer to the figure below. The lowest observed times should not be taken; they are 'flukes'. There is a strong case for taking the second or third times as the activity time. Perhaps average these two. The distribution is bi-modal. Why is that? Could it be that there are two levels of skill, or that what is regarded as an activity has not been adequately thought through? In either case there is an opportunity for improvement. There are also some 'outliers' on the right – what has happened in these cases could be looked at.

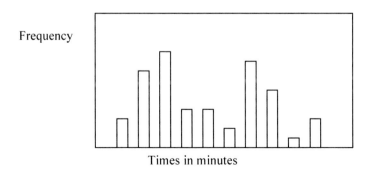

Frequency

Times in minutes

- In the figure above there is evidence of good practice and not so good practice. There is an opportunity to learn from the best. What is it that those recorded on the left are doing differently from those on the right – assuming that they are all doing similar tasks? Incidentally, it is not always necessary to time activities to find this out: let office or service workers study one another.
- If rates of demand change significantly over the day it is good practice to consider having several takt times over the day. Perhaps the demand for correspondence is highest in the morning, and invoices have to be completed in the afternoon. Perhaps you can use this takt time calculation for only part of the day – the remainder of the day being given over to less repetitive work.
- If an activity takes longer than 80% of takt it must be done in parallel: for example two people working on an activity that takes twice as long as 80% of takt.
- There is also a concept called the 'Drop-off rate' (not to be confused with the term used in economics or HR hiring). This is useful because it relates to the completion rate – i.e. total demand less failure demand. A completion rate is, of course, the inverse of takt time. This is possibly a better rate to use in future state system design, when the aim is to eliminate as much failure demand as possible. The 'Drop-off' rate time will be greater than takt because the demand is less – so you will need fewer people.
- Then comes the Yamazumi Board or Work Balance board. Refer to the figure below. The idea is to allocate the activities between the workers.

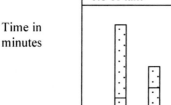

Time in minutes

0.8 of takt

Persons 1   2   3   4   5   6

- At the outset the Yamazumi calculation is far looser than the manufacturing equivalent. Take (perhaps) 80% of takt time. Then balance the activities between the people so that 80% of takt is not exceeded. In the figure above persons 1 to 3 both do two jobs. Person 2 is lightly loaded, but for the moment nothing can be done about it. Person 4 does one activity. Persons 5 and 6 do the same activity, but it has an activity time longer than 80% of takt so each person does every second activity. Possibly, if the work content of activity 5/6 could be reduced, or if the work content of person 2 could be reduced, then one person could be saved (reallocated to another group).
- You may be able to use a Heijunka System. Please refer to the later section on Heijunka.

- It is good practice to balance for several rates of work (takt times) while you are about it. Then if or when the rate changes, the appropriate work allocation can follow.
- The calculation for the current resource rate serves as a useful check. It should work out at about the present resource staffing level. If the calculated resources are much more than currently employed, you may have missed some work that is being done or your activity times are loose. If the calculated resources are much less than currently employed, you may have been misled as to amount of work that is being done, or your times are too tight.
- The calculation for the number of workers will probably not yield a nice round number. This is then a judgment call: if the fraction is 0.8 or above probably ignore, if the fraction is 0.6 or below it may be worth considering assigning a worker to work only half the time in the area and the other half on some other activity.

Cells and Bottlenecks: Drum Buffer Rope and FIFO Lanes

There are many situations in service and administration where there is a sequence of operations or stages, one stage of which may be regarded as a bottleneck. Virtually all multi-stage queuing situations are of this type. Examples include the administrative stages of an order fulfilment process in general, a sequence in a call centre, many sequences in hospitals – from accident and emergency to the sequence of stages in a medical operation, multi stage government processes such as tax or passport application, airline check in, and registration at a university. These are sometimes referred to as 'replenishment' systems.

In all these examples there is likely to be a heavily used resource – the bottleneck. Strictly, a bottleneck is a stage that limits the amount of money that can be made – but here we will consider a bottleneck as the most heavily loaded resource. It is better to use the more general term on 'constraint' – but this is not as widely understood as the term 'bottleneck'.

Managing such systems through Drum Buffer Rope is far more efficient than attempting a multi stage kanban system and, where there is a clear bottleneck and high variation, Drum Buffer Rope is often far better than attempting to install a balanced cell.

The late Eli Goldratt, author of the bestselling book *The Goal* and father of Theory of Constraints has made numerous breakthrough contributions in the management of bottlenecks. Here we consider one application.

Goldratt says, 'an hour lost at a bottleneck is an hour lost for the whole system, but an hour lost at a non-bottleneck is merely a mirage'. Non-bottlenecks can catch up, but time lost at a bottleneck is lost forever. On the management of bottlenecks, reading Goldratt and Cox's classic novel *The Goal* is recommended for any service manager having sequential tasks, even though it is manufacturing based.

Where there is bottleneck stage 'drum buffer rope (DBR) and first-in-first-out (FIFO) lanes are very useful concepts. DBR is a concept from Eli Goldratt, and amounts to a multi-stage kanban or pull system. A version of the DBR concept, modified for service and administration, has wide applicability in sequential service operations.

The Drum is the bottleneck. This is the resource to focus on. A bottleneck resource needs to be 'protected' from being under-utilised through waiting for work. That is where the Buffer comes in. The buffer protects the bottleneck from running out of work. Particularly in service situations, work at each stage before (or upstream of) the bottleneck is variable, even highly variable, so the flow of work to the bottleneck can be erratic. Hence the bottleneck needs to be protected by the buffer. The buffer is a timed target quantity of work, rather than a number of items. The buffer could be a FIFO (first in, first out) lane. The buffer could be an accumulation of files perhaps arranged on a gravity-fed chute, or a 'lazy susan' that swings around when full. Remember, an in basket is not a FIFO lane; it is a LIFO arrangement, and not good for flow. The extent of the Buffer – that is the maximum length of time that work in the buffer must cover, should be estimated from the likelihood of the Drum running out of work due to problems and variation in the activities between the first operation and the Drum.

Note the important point that there is no necessity to keep permanent buffers of work between every stage – buffer is only necessary in front of the bottleneck.

The Rope connects the Drum to the first workstation. As an element of work is completed at the Drum, a corresponding element is let in at the first station. This stabilises the lead-time through the process. Work that has accumulated in front of the first workstation is immediately apparent. The queue of work in front of the bottleneck is regularly monitored. Typically, zones are used. Think of work accumulating along a FIFO lane – first in the red zone, then the yellow zone, then the green zone. Each zone would represent a time buffer. When, through variation in flows, work fills the red and yellow zones and overlaps into the green zone, no action is required. If the yellow zone is exposed, there is a small danger that the bottleneck may run out of work. Monitor the situation, but probably take no action. If the red zone is exposed, earlier (upstream) stages must accelerate their work (or add resources) so that the bottleneck does not run out of work.

In many service situations, however, it may not be possible or desirable to prevent customers coming into the system. So, the DBR system needs to change to that shown below. In this situation the number of resources manning the bottleneck is assumed to be variable and flexible – like adding or removing people in the short term, or changing the shift pattern. Here, two queues of work need to be monitored.

First is the queue in front of the bottleneck: again, use red, yellow, green zones (often virtual rather than physical) in front of the bottleneck – but this time reversed. The green zone is closest to the bottleneck. A queue in the (notional) green zone would indicate a high level of service and would call for a reduction in resources used at the bottleneck. A queue in the yellow zone indicates no necessity to take action. A queue in the red zone indicates that queues or delays are becoming excessive and extra resources are called for in the short term. Again, the 'rope' principle is used whereby work completed at the bottleneck triggers the release of work into the system at stage one.

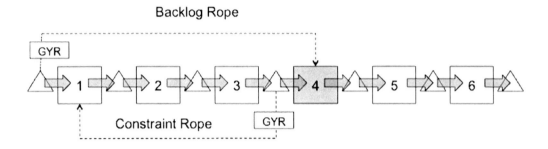

(This figure is adapted from John Arthur Ricketts, *Reaching the Goal*)

Second is queue of work waiting to come into the system. This could be the queue of calls waiting at a call centre, or the amount of work waiting to be done by field service operations. In the former case use the number of calls, but in the latter case it would be preferable to use estimates of time to carry out the work. Again, use Red Green Yellow monitoring. Queues in the green zone indicate a satisfactory waiting situation, red would be unsatisfactory. If the queue is in the red zone then the resources at the bottleneck need to be increased to allow for greater throughput.

The system works best, of course, where resources can easily be switched into bottlenecks. A variant is Tesco, where checkout queues are monitored and extra staff are drafted in from shelf stacking and other activities when queues build up.

More on Capacity: Bottlenecks

As a result of variation in server times, arrival times, and customer requirements, it is vital that capacity be sized accordingly. In other words, there must be a cushion of extra capacity, a cushion of customers or a queue or very short-term flexibility of resources to switch into high load areas. A critical resource generally means a person but could be a machine such as a CAT scanner.

However, it is insulting to assume, by asking customers to wait, that the customer's time is free, particularly when customers observe the critical resource wasting time doing things that should have been done beforehand, or should be done by someone else.

In relation to key resources in particular, there are obligations on the part of the service provider to do the work efficiently but there are also obligations on the part of the customer. In some service and administration situations, equipment is involved. This must also enjoy priority to make sure that it is working when needed. So there may be three components required for effectiveness: the provider, the customer and the equipment. See the section on Overall effectiveness.

In service and administration, as in manufacturing, be guided by the late Eli Goldratt's five steps:

- identify the constraint (or critical resource);
- exploit the constraint;
- subordinate the constraint;
- elevate the constraint;
- do it all again.

- **Identify** the constraint means recognising the most heavily loaded or critical resources. The bottleneck is usually the stage in the process that takes the longest time. Note, however, that if more than one person works on the stage, then the time for the stage should be divided by the number of workers. So in fact the longest operation may not be the bottleneck. The bottleneck may also be a skill bottleneck: it may be that someone with unique skills or authority is not available to work all day, so work tends to accumulate in front of the stage. Of course, a bottleneck may also be a machine like a copier that is in constant use. This may sometimes be the case where the machine is a shared resource. In service it is very common for the bottleneck to be 'floating', i.e. not at one single constant point. In this case the following may apply to more than one 'bottleneck':

  There is a fundamental distinction between critical and non-critical resources. <u>A critical resource is one that delays a customer from finishing earlier</u>. When seeking to identify critical resources, bear in mind that a good rule of thumb for administration is to allow 20% extra capacity for administrative activities and 30% extra capacity for service activities for variation.

- **Exploit** means to make best use of the available capacity at those critical resources. Make sure that critical resources are used to good effect. For example:

  - Establish a signalling system to direct customers to the available under-utilised, but critical, resource such as a checkout point, the next available check-in counter at an airport, a just-become-free doctor.
  - Ensure that no time is wasted by the critical resource during the service encounter.
  - Make sure that all work arriving at the bottleneck is defect free (i.e. no 'dirty data'), and complete as needed. Is the paperwork waiting for you when you need it? Perhaps put in an inspection operation before the bottleneck.
  - Protect the bottleneck from running out of work. It should never be idle waiting for work. This may mean establishing a buffer (in-basket? patient queue?) in front of the bottleneck.
  - Can the bottleneck work longer hours without incurring extra expense? This may mean arranging the work schedules of existing staff.
  - Look at the operational efficiency of the bottleneck resource. Are there 'micro wastes' due to poor layout, poor 5S, or poor access to data?
  - For a true bottleneck resource, a time buffer of customers may be appropriate.
  - Ensure that customers are adequately briefed before the encounter. This means giving customers adequate notice: 'Have your passport ready for inspection'; 'Remove your coat before you get to the actual airport security point'; 'Make sure your form is completed in every respect before handing it in'; 'Check that all items in your supermarket basket are priced'. Sometimes it is worth having a pre-checker. The manufacturing equivalent is placing the inspection point in front of the critical resource.
  - Ensure that the work cannot be done by a non-critical resource: the nurse rather than the doctor (or vice versa!), a junior engineer rather than an experienced, highly creative, design engineer.

To summarise, Stalk and Hout spoke about the Golden Rule of Time-based Competition: 'Never delay a value adding activity by a non-value adding activity'.

- **Subordinate** means that the flow of work to a critical resource should enable that critical resource to work effectively. Thus a surgeon should have everything ready to go before the operation starts. The pit-stop analogy is appropriate: do the maximum amount of preparation before the grand-prix car drives into the pits. It sounds trite to say that it is the critical resource that is critical, but so often the critical resource is held up as a result of failure by non-critical activity. For example, the already-checked-in airline passenger who then delays a flight departure while shopping; or the car service customer who has to return because a part was not available, when the information could have been gleaned at the phone-in stage.

So, is all accompanying paperwork there on time? Is there batching at a prior operation which means that work arrives at the bottleneck in erratic batches? Can one-piece flow of files or patients be arranged? If room service is the bottleneck, is there an efficient communication system with checkout? Is the anaesthetist there when the surgeon needs to start work?

- **Elevate** means break the constraint. The exploit and subordinate stages are often low cost or no cost. But elevate can cost money. So don't hire an additional critical resource before you have exploited and elevated.
    - From a Lean perspective, the ideal is to have flexible capacity that can switch into high load activities at short notice. An example is the British supermarket chain Tesco, which continually monitors checkout queue lengths and opens up extra checkout stations at short notice. The extra checkout staff are drawn from specially trained staff who work in 'back stage' activities such as shelf-packing and who can catch up load in off-peak times. To this end, a table such as a skills matrix can be helpful.
    - One company I know uses a combination of flexitime, annualised hours, drawing on other operational staff, and finally drawing on office staff, to address variable capacity requirements.
    - Then comes the possible trade-off between extra human resources (in-sourced or out-sourced) and technology such as ATMs or self check-in at an airport, check-in via the internet, or even auto-scan shopping trolleys.
    - 'Self' is a powerful word in service. It is both a way to address capacity issues and a way to improve flow and efficiency. Can the customers take on some of the work themselves – for example, via online airline check-in at home? Self-inspect, self-check, self-serve. Sometimes customers really love this aspect of self-service. At other times it is seen as simply offloading work onto the customer. You have to know which of these is the case.

- *Do it all again. Avoid Inertia*. When the bottleneck has been broken another bottleneck is likely to arise.

The Service Systems Toolbox

More on Capacity: Forecasting and Adding Capacity Incrementally

If capacity (people, machines such as buses) takes time to acquire, you will need to forecast demand. 'The only thing you know about a forecast is that it will be wrong', and 'a forecast is lucky or lousy'. A forecast is not a prediction, it merely sets out the bounds of uncertainty. So:

- A forecast should be three numbers: average, upper and lower bound. According to Paul Saffro, they form an expanding 'cone of uncertainty'.
- Know at what stage the product or service is in the life cycle. There is much more uncertainty early on, so adapt the forecasting method.
- Use 'Sales and Operations Planning'. In other words, use the collective expertise of sales, marketing, operations and any others.

You can mitigate forecast uncertainty by adopting the good Lean principle of 'small machines'. In other words select the smallest, simplest machine possible. Multiple small machines have multiple advantages over larger machines – not least a reduced risk of oversizing. This principle extends to people too. Beware of a highly specialist person. Consider instead a home-grown multifunction worker who is happy working in several areas.

Be aware, however, of *The Black Swan*. Only white swans were observed for a thousand years or more, and on that basis Europeans believed that all swans were white. Then a black swan was found in Australia. Nassim Taleb in *The Black Swan* quotes Bertrand Russell's 'problem of inductive knowledge' with his story of the chicken that is fed every day and comes to believe that the general rule of life is to be fed regularly and be cared for by humans. Then on the Wednesday before Christmas something unexpected happens. It has huge consequences for the chicken. These 'catastrophic' events are much more common in service than the occasional 9/11 – and because of their huge impact it can be unwise to rely on the comfortable assumption of the normal distribution.

More on Capacity: Influencing and Smoothing Demand

In service there are widely adopted ways of smoothing demand, including price hikes at peak times, discounts and offers during off-peaks, making customers queue at peak times, and informing customers of anticipated delays. In some service businesses, more than might be expected at first glance, it is possible to build ahead of demand, for example by pre-preparing legal documents (see the section on service inventories), and making sure that the customers' path is smoothed by working through the service blueprint ahead of time. Ask at each Moment of Truth, but particularly at bottleneck stages, if and what it is possible to pre-prepare. A checklist? In general, of course, service is perishable and cannot be stored, but do question this assumption. See the inventory section.

Smoothing demand and flow is, of course, the essence of the Toyota system. It is called Heijunka. The ideal system is smoothed end-to-end flow, not erratic batch and queue, stop and start.

Further Reading

Richard Metters *et al*, *Successful Service Operations Management*, Thompson, 2003
Paul Saffro, 'Six Rules for Effective Forecasting', *Harvard Business Review*, July-August 2007.
Eli Goldratt and Geoff Cox, *The Goal*, STG, 1985
John Arthur Ricketts, *Reaching the Goal*, IBM Press Pearson, 2008

On the management of bottlenecks, reading Goldratt and Cox's classic novel *The Goal* is recommended for any service manager having sequential tasks, even though it is manufacturing-based.

4.4 Variation, Mistakes and Complexity in Service: Why Problems Occur

C Martin Hinckley in his excellent book *Make No Mistake!* proposed a framework for looking at the causes of problems. The categories are variation, mistakes and complexity.

Here we extend Hinckley's idea to incorporate ideas from Deming, Seddon and the amusing (if it were not so tragically true) book, *The Systems Bible*.

Variation: this is due to the inherent inconsistency of service operations. This book has extensively examined variation through Kingman's equation that identifies demand variation and process variation as causes for delays and queuing. See the section on Queues. Variation is particularly important where a process is 'out of control'. This also has been discussed, the analogy being a car's temperature gauge. When the car is running normally ('common cause' variation, or 'in control') the driver is unconcerned about the temperature even though it may vary with outside temperature and road conditions. But when the gauge goes into the red zone a special cause is indicated and the driver should stop and investigate. The driver or garage can usually fix the problem – by perhaps replacing the fan belt or fixing the radiator leak. But if you would like the car to run consistently at a lower temperature a complete cooling system redesign is required. Specialist help is often necessary. So it is with service processes. For more detail, please refer to the section on Statistical Process Control (SPC).

Mistakes are caused not by process variation but by errors, often human errors. Using the car analogy, the driver may forget to top up the radiator with anti-freeze (omission) or may use the wrong anti-freeze (selection). There are other types of mistakes also – for example information errors, mis-operation errors, and counting errors. All are common in service. Notice that mistakes are different from variation. The system may be in control but mistakes still occasionally occur. Also, SPC (frequently used for variation) is about detection, not prevention. Hence the concept of mistake proofing or pokayoke. See the section on this.

The third source of problems is **Complexity**. This is simply where a process is so long, so involved, that customers and users are dissatisfied. Essentially, a system problem. This is a focus for both systems thinking and for Lean concepts, especially waste reduction, but also other related concepts such as bottleneck management. Another source that could be listed under complexity is simply the complexity of human beings themselves. Please refer to the sections on systems, waste and mapping.

'Complexity' refers to both product and process, both from the customer's viewpoint and from the service provider's viewpoint.

- From the customer's viewpoint, service product complexity refers to the ease of use of the service, and the ability to understand the service product. For example: how easy is it for a customer to understand the benefits and dangers of a pension plan? Service process complexity refers to the number of steps required to obtain the service, or the number of handoffs that the customer must pass through.

- From the provider's viewpoint, service product complexity relates to the training that is required to deliver the service satisfactorily. Service process complexity refers to the number of operations, the number of handoffs, and the difficulty of each operation.

What is here called the Hinckley Framework for Service (an extension of that proposed by C Martin Hinckley) is a very useful checklist for looking at why problems occur. It is based on the 3 sources and the 6 M's plus one:

	Variation	Mistakes	Complexity
Men (or people)	Training, standards	Omission, selection	Individual differences
Machines	(for example print quality due to printer)	Use of machines (for example ATMs, phones)	Can't understand or carry out operating procedures
Material	(print quality due to paper), restaurant food	Selection or omission of items in a recipe, or hotel room	The use of replacement parts or consumables at home or work
Method	Customer variations	Forgetting a step in the process	Confusion (perhaps attempting to train for every possibility)
Measures	Leading to unexpected, but rational, behaviour	Reporting errors, clarity of measures	Too many measures – some conflicting?
Mother Nature	Room temperature for customers	Forgetting to set controls; to warn about safety	(for example teOhnmperature controls)
Information	Sources of data collection	Misinterpretation of instructions, signs, data entry	Complexity of forms

Further reading

C Martin Hinckley, *Make No Mistake!*, Productivity, 2001
Gary Fellers, *Why Things Go Wrong*, Pelican, 1994
John Gall, *The Systems Bible*, General Systemantics Press, 2006
Alfie Kohn, *Punished by Rewards*, Houghton Mifflin, 1993 and 1999
Daniel Pink, *Drive: The Surprising Truth about what Motivates Us*, Canongate, 2010

Tools to Address Variation, Mistakes and Complexity

Relevant tools are given in the table below. Notice their overlapping, or synergistic nature.

	The Service Product	The Service Process
Complexity	Focusing on customer purpose, Kano model, Value Analysis and FAST	Layout ('Servicescape'), 5S, Mapping, Value Analysis and FAST
Variation	Six Sigma, DFSS	Six Sigma, visibility, SPC, TPA, 7 Quality Tools, 5S, SOPs, Guidance notes
Mistakes and Errors	Pokayoke (mistake proofing)	Pokayoke, 5S, SOPs, visibility

- **Purpose analysis**: to clarify what the system is there to do, and what it is not there to do, is a huge aid to simplification. Does this sound obvious? Perhaps – but many service systems are in practice there to meet some imposed target or some manager's measures. The purpose must be an end-to-end purpose. Sub-systems often have their own local goals that are in conflict with the end-to-end purpose.

- **The Kano model**: clarify the basics that must be done, the performance factors, and possible delighters. This helps to establish priorities. See the section on the Kano model.

- **Value Analysis** is a long-established series of methodologies that aims to deliver system functionality in the most beneficial way. This can follow from Purpose and Kano. Value in value analysis terms is function/cost. Function Analysis System Technique (FAST) is a team-based methodology that breaks down a product or service, such as making tea, into its basic functions, and then seeks to improve them through innovation by, among others, asking the Five Hows, and Five Whys.
  - FAST can be used with service products by breaking down the product into its elements, defining the purpose of each element (using verb plus noun, like 'provide security'), then using creativity tools to look at alternative ways in which the function could be provided better at the same cost, or the same at lower cost.
  - For service processes, FAST uses a map – a VSM or service blueprint is a good starting point – but expressed in verb plus noun terms, beginning at the left hand side with the purpose and expanding on the Hows.

How-Why questions are applied along the map, typically in an expanding tree structure, to show alternatives, until suitable alternatives emerge. Creative thinking is required to generate alternatives. A full description of Value Analysis and FAST is beyond the scope of this book, and the reader's attention is drawn to the excellent texts available.

- **Layout, 5S and Mapping** are all discussed at length in this book. Layout and 5S in Part 4, Mapping in Part 3.

- **Design for Six Sigma (DFSS)**: DFSS uses a defined set of steps called IDDOV (Identify, Define, Develop, Optimise, Verify) similar to the DMAIC steps in Six Sigma. It also uses a similar project organisation with Champions, Master Black Belts, Black Belts, and Green Belts.

The Identify and Define stages aim to clarify the customer and his or her needs. Typical tools are the Kano model and Quality Function Deployment. The Develop stage involves brainstorming and identification of alternatives, and their evaluation. Techniques include TRIZ, Pugh analysis (Concept Screening), and FMEA (failure modes and effect analysis).
The Optimise stage is not as robust in service design as it is in product design, which typically uses the Taguchi methodology for design optimisation. In service design the concentration is on prevention of defects and maximisation of customer benefit, rather than on detection and reduction of defects.
Finally, the verify stage involves looking at the capability of the service process, by looking at required skill levels. Notice that, as with Six Sigma, a lot of attention is given at the front end. It is appropriate to take care at early stages to define the customer, the purpose, the environment, and the usage.

Many of these tools are described in Bicheno and Catherwood, *Six Sigma and the Quality Toolbox,* and other publications on Six Sigma.

4.5 Deming's Profound Knowledge and more on Why Things Go Wrong

Related to the Hinckley Framework is W Edward Deming's 'Profound Knowledge'. Deming stressed that profound knowledge does not require an advanced education, but simply applied common sense. Deming said that absence of application of Profound Knowledge was the major source of managerial problems. The four aspects of Deming's Profound Knowledge are

1. **System**: a misunderstanding of the systemic nature of many managerial and societal issues. This includes the failure to understand feedback loops, to assume system boundaries are the same as organisational boundaries, and a failure to understand the interacting parts of a system. In short, a failure to be a 'systems thinker'. Sub-optimisation is the result. Examples are numerous: a manager awarding himself a bonus whilst freezing the pay of employees. Replacing plastic bags with paper bags for 'environmental' reasons. Paper does decompose faster than plastic, but also uses much more energy to produce and to transport. Recycling also is more problematical. This last example illustrates that systems thinking is not always so easy to do, but should be attempted. See the sections on Systems and Seddon's 'Check' methodology.

2. **Variation**: a failure to understand that variation is endemic, and to distinguish common cause from special cause variation. For example, paying a salesman or banker a bonus when performance is simply the result of common cause variation. Nassim Taleb has written extensively on the latter in *Fooled by Randomness*.

3. The **'Theory of Knowledge'**: this is to do with the failure to learn by, for example Plan Do Study Act. 'Without a theory, experience has no meaning' according to Deming. Repeated observations are necessary. A one-off snap shot (like a case study) is invalid. One observation does not validate a theory, but a single observation can invalidate a theory. Please refer to the section on SDSA and Learning.

4. **Psychology**: this is concerned with intrinsic and extrinsic motivation. According to Deming, extrinsic 'carrot and stick' rewards are not effective, especially over the medium and longer term. Intrinsic motivation is often harder, requiring participation and recognition. Many psychologists support Deming in this view, but unfortunately management practice is still widely oriented towards extrinsic rewards. See, for example, Alfie Kohn's *Punished by Rewards*, and Daniel Pink's *Drive*. The latter says there is a case for extrinsic rewards only where there is repetitive, less creative work.

Gary Fellers, had extended this in his book *Why Things Go Wrong* which systematically uses all of Deming's 14 points.

John Seddon, in a similar vein to Deming, talks about 'three big mistakes' in service:

1. Failure to understand the nature of demand

This is the failure to distinguish value demand from failure demand. Failure demand ties up huge amounts of capacity doing work that should not be done at all, leading to overload and poor response. Do it right the first time. Do whatever it takes to eliminate failure demand. Also, demand is largely predictable in service. Not the next demand, but the causes of demand. So, seek it out. See the 'Check' methodology section.

2. 'Assuming that workers can be held accountable for work that they do'

Deming spoke of the '94/6' rule. About 94% of problems are due, fundamentally, to the system, only 6% due to the workers. Therefore start with this assumption, rather than starting with blaming the people. This is also very Toyota-like. Managers apologise to workers that they – the workers – did not understand or were inadequately trained or equipped. There is a need to recognise variation, and to distinguish common cause from special cause. This problem is frequently linked to blame and rewards, making the situation even worse. Common cause variation requires complete system redesign to improve matters – and only managers can bring this about. Special cause variation often involves short-term actions that can be dealt with by appropriately trained workers themselves.

3. Management acts in ways that affect a systems ability to absorb demand

This is Ashby's Law of Requisite variety – only variety can absorb variety. Service systems have huge variety – customers do all sorts of unexpected things and make unexpected requests. Therefore a full set of standard operating procedures is a forlorn hope. Instead, design the system to cope with variety. Maybe front line staff is trained to deal with the 'top ten requests' but are also trained to recognise when a request is not a top ten type, and know who to pass it on to. Then learn the 11th, and so on.

Finally in this section, let us consider just a few of John Gall's often-hilarious insights into Systems. These are tongue-in-cheek, but often profound. Gall builds on Northcote Parkinson, the Peter Principle, Occam's Razor and more, but adds much. They certainly add a warning about thinking that we understand systems. Here are a few favourites, some of which have been added to:

- Complex Systems exhibit unexpected behaviour. Gall tells of the failure of systems that are there to prevent failure, and hence lead to failure of the first system. Backup failsafe systems for nuclear plants, or NASA's space vehicle preparation shed built against wind and rain, but that generates its own weather including rain!
- Systems bite back. The Aswan dam built to generate energy now has so much silt that a large proportion of energy must be used to clear it. email supposed to communicate, but leading to less face-to-face rich communication.

- Information rarely leaks up.
- Pushing on a system doesn't help – or the corollary, adding manpower to a project makes it later.
- Almost anything is easier to get into than get out of – telephone contracts?
- Things in a System are what they are reported to be, but not what they are. 'Flying is not flying' (as in I am flying to New York), the chart is not the patient, and the bed is not the hotel visitor.
- Do it without a new system if you can. Why? Because a new system will bring its own overhead like HR, IT, accounting, and strategy – even Lean experts! Soon these attract consultants themselves or develop their own big problems. Think NHS IT. 'Big fleas have little fleas on their backs to bite 'em, and little fleas have lesser fleas and so ad infinitum'.
- Great advances do not come out of systems designed for great advances – nor from the current major players. Take cars that were supposed to add to transport flexibility but end up in traffic jams. London's average speed is slower than a century ago? Universities are supposed to champion 'universitas' but often end in compartmentalized specialisation. Major players? Take Microsoft and Apple, or ecological research versus backyard Gaia theory by James Lovelock.

4.6 Standard Work and Standard Operating Procedures in Service

Standard work is somewhat controversial in service. This should not be the case. It is a question of degree. Nobody questions the need for correct procedures in the case of a heart attack. Or checklists used by airline pilots. And there are certainly better, standard, ways of conducting meetings, of communicating with the workforce. In service it is said that 'punctuality is the courtesy of kings and the stern duty of business people'. Punctuality is standard.

First, 'standard work' should be developed by the service staff themselves, maybe in cooperation with system designers or managers, to capture and retain the best way found thus far – the how. Work standards, on the other hand, are what the system designers or managers require to be done – the what and when. A shorthand is to think standard work is bottom up: standards are 'top down'.

In Ohno's book "Taiichi Ohno's Workplace Management," he writes:

- "If you think of standards as the best you can do, it's all over. The standard is only the baseline for doing further kaizen."
- "Standards are set arbitrarily by humans, so how can they not change?"
- "When creating standard work it will be difficult to establish a standard if you are trying to achieve "the best way". This is a big mistake. Document exactly what you are doing now."
- "Without some standard you can't say "We made it better" because there is nothing to compare it to, so you must create a standard for comparison."

Note: In the quotations above, the word 'standards' is used. What should be used is 'Standard Work'.

A general rule in service is to standardise (or develop checklists for) only the frequently repeatable. Some of these frequently repeatable activities will be critical – such as a surgeon washing hands and using sterile gloves. For activities like these, there should be no argument about standard work or using a checklist. Using a checklist, as Gawande has pointed out, is not a question of poor training but simply an aid in complex and stressful situations.

An important aspect is to help people understand their roles – emphasising the sense of purpose so people are motivated to do the right things. You cannot 'control' people – command and control is not a workable model. You have to create systems and processes that encourage kaizen. And these systems (or standardised work) don't mean that we stop thinking, as Verble said: "Standardization doesn't mean routinizing everything."

(The above statements are adapted from David Verble, a former Toyota USA HR and OD manager who teaches at Lean Enterprise Institute, USA.)

Three useful quotations set the scene:

'To standardise a method is to choose out of many methods the best one, and use it. What is the best way to do a thing? It is the sum of all the good ways we have discovered up to the present. It therefore becomes the standard. Today's standardisation is the necessary foundation on which tomorrow's improvement will be based. If you think of "standardisation as the best we know today, but which is to be improved tomorrow" - you get somewhere. But if you think of standards as confining, then progress stops.'

(Henry Ford, *Today and Tomorrow*, 1926)

'In a Western company, the standard operation is the property of management or the engineering department. In a Japanese company it is the property of the people doing the job. They prepare it, work to it, and are responsible for improving it. Contrary to Taylor's teaching, the Japanese combine thinking and doing, and thus achieve a high level of involvement and commitment.'

(Peter Wickens, former HR Director, Nissan UK)

'A proper (standard) procedure cannot be written from a desk. It must be tried and revised many times in the production plant. Furthermore, it must be a procedure that anybody can understand on sight.

For production people to be able to write a standard work sheet that others can understand, they must be convinced of its importance.'

(Taiichi Ohno)

From the first quotation we learn that standard work is not static, but improves over time. From the second we learn that a standard is not imposed from on high. From the third we learn that standards are inherently practical. A good standard comes out of a bottom-up questioning culture, ever seeking a better, simpler, safer way to do a task – not a top-down imposed way of working. If you have no standard you cannot improve, by definition. So standards are part of PDSA (Plan Do Study Act).

Standard work should not be there to 'catch you out', but to enable. This is like a tennis or golf lesson. You don't hide your weaknesses from the coach, you bring them out because you want to improve. That is the essential spirit that needs to be fostered.

Moreover, especially in service, standard work is actually a force for empowerment, for liberation, for creativity, rather than being restrictive. This has been described by Adler as 'The Toyota Paradox'. The military uses 'rules of engagement' to direct the modern soldier in fluid situations where 'thinking on your feet' is vital to success. The soldier knows that if he stays within the broad framework he will have the full weight of his government, or indeed the UN, behind him. He may shoot to kill if fired upon. He must treat prisoners within certain parameters. These are standards. Similarly, the maxim used by the Ritz Carlton Hotel group, 'We are ladies and gentlemen serving ladies and gentlemen,' is a superb short statement of standard.

Why is it then that standards are controversial in service? Because they can be mis-applied by unwitting, unthinking management. A 'standard' that requires a call centre worker to handle a call within three minutes, or not to take 'no' for an answer first time around, or not to use initiative to solve customer problems, is misapplication. Ohno, the great Toyota champion of standards, would have been appalled.

John Seddon believes that 'standardisation stops the system from absorbing variety'. This is a serious and valid consideration. Certainly OVER-standardisation prevents a system from adapting to the infinite variety of customer requests. This is what is so wrong with many menu-driven answer machines and with standard forms sent out in all cases. It just adds to failure demand. So, be warned. But then 'don't throw the baby out with the bath water'.

The best and most sustainable standard or checklist should be so good, so obvious, that doing the task any other way is seen as just plain silly. This may have to be demonstrated. But that is the end state, the vision to strive for.

Any standard that generates failure demand – causing the customer to do it all again, but this time with less good will – should be scrapped. So should a standard that becomes confused with a target and generates silly behaviour, such as an ambulance driving around the car park so that the patient will not join a measured queue. Another poor use of a standard is where it becomes confused with an accounting or costing standard – especially with absorption costing, where failure to meet the budgeted rate of work leads to under-recovery of overhead and hence pressures to over-produce to 'recover' the overhead. This is plain nonsense in the context of Lean. Similarly, requiring office workers to tape standard locations for pens and folders on their desks. On the other hand, procedures in an accident and emergency room need to be much more carefully specified. Not top-down imposed, but discussed, reviewed and updated by the people doing the job for the people doing the job. In some cases, such as medicine, help in establishing the standard may be required from an expert.

So, a balance needs to be sought. There is a double Pareto. First, not all processes in service need a standard procedure. Perhaps only the 'Top 10' recurring processes in an area require one. Second, within those processes, only a few critical steps need to have standard requirements – typically to ensure quality and reduce failure demand. By contrast, how on earth can a service worker work with 50 or more standard procedures? Much less learn them?

Note that 'standards' does not mean the rigid, workstudy imposed, job specification that is associated with classic mass production. Such standards have no place in the world of Lean, and especially in service. For such 'jobs' industrial sabotage and absenteeism are to be expected. Beware, however, of the human relations based reaction against 'work standards', which are often confused with workstudy. Allowing standards that are too loose on critical aspects may lead to no standards, which in turn leads to decreased safety and productivity.

In service a standard may be a written Standard Operating Procedure (SOP). But it may also be a checklist, or simply an understanding about methods with your colleagues. The second type may be the most enduring. But it should not be left to chance. Get the groups to discuss their standards formally, at standard intervals. Group norms then kick in. In any case, it is not necessary to cover all the steps. Only the main or critical steps need development.

So, in service, a standard might just be a checklist of the essential steps or data that must be covered. The rest is left open.

Also, beware of thinking that standards have no place in non-repetitive work such as maintenance, service, design, or senior management. Good, flexible maintenance and service work are built by combining various small standard work elements. Good design comes out of creativity combined with standard methods and materials, adhering to standard procedures and gateways. At Disney Florida, for example, visitors to Universal Studios walk through section by section. Within each section, the section time is divided into blocks and in each block certain loosely-scripted material must be covered by the artist. Do visitors notice this? No, they enjoy the professional but personalised delivery.

Management standards should exist for meetings, communications, budgets, and many other activities. Strike the right balance of detail.

Spear and Bowen in a classic article discuss the apparent paradox of TPS that activities, communications and flows at Toyota are at once rigidly scripted yet enormously flexible and adaptable. They conclude that it is the specification of standards and communications that gives the system the ability to make huge numbers of controlled changes using the scientific method. Without standards and the scientific method, change would amount to little more than trial and error.

Peter Wickens, former HR Director of Nissan UK, explains that for an 'ascendant organisation' there must be both concern for the people and control of the processes. Without concern for people you have an 'alienated organisation'; without concern for the processes you have 'anarchy'. This is a good way of thinking about standards in service. Both dimensions are needed.

Despite what some people think about Frederick Taylor, there remains 'one best way', with available technology, to do any task, which will minimise time and effort and maximise safety, quality and productivity. To some this may sound like boring repetition, but the 'new' standards are about participation in developing the best and safest way, mastery of several jobs, and the ability to adapt to changes in the short term.

Below is another way of looking at service standards.

	Value Demand	Failure Demand
Special cause variation	Problem solving standards	Eliminate these sporadic problems; standards not applicable
Common cause variation	Appropriate standards or checklists covering critical points	Eliminate 'chronic' common case problems; could have standards for service recovery failure.

Deming, proposing the PDCA cycle, saw improvement moving from standard to standard. Juran emphasised the importance of 'holding the gains' by establishing standards following a process improvement, rather than allowing them to drift back to the old ways. Recently the concept of the 'Learning Organisation' has become fashionable, including 'knowledge harvesting' from everyone in the organisation. How is this to be achieved? By documenting experience, in other words by establishing standards from which others may learn. Supervisors should have prime responsibility for maintaining and improving standard work.

Too many service operations-based organisations delude themselves on standards. It is tempting simply to impose work standards by getting industrial engineers or workstudy people to do the work and to post standards at workstations, or, which is worse, to keep them in a file. Then, of course, there is no buy-in, no foundation for continuous improvement, and worst of all a great likelihood of large process variance. So the quick way turns out to be the least effective way and often a total waste. Traditional 'Taylorism' is suitable only in the sweat shop. It is far better to work through the few critical stages, get the workers to know why these stages are important, but leave the rest alone.

One good bottom-up way of establishing standards is to get service workers to discuss their methods of doing a task among themselves. Differences emerge. But then let them discuss and develop the 'current best known way', or 'best of the best'. The same thing applies to 5S activities: the fact that everyone may not use the same files, tools, computer systems, filing, layouts, greetings, room cleaning sequence, and so on, indicates that there is possible room for improvement. Not by imposition – that soon falls apart – but by open discussion. Even then, there must be allowance for individual differences.

In new product development, design, and product launch, do what Toyota does and accumulate checklists of things to look out for. The checklists become the accumulated knowledge of the company. This is Knowledge management. If you don't do this simple thing, you are doomed always to 'learn the hard way' and to 'start from scratch'. What a waste!

Standards in Different Environments

Hall and Johnson, distinguish different process types on a 2 x 2 matrix. The axes are the process environment (high or low variability) and the value of the output variation to customers (negative or positive).

'Mass processes' fall in the quadrant of low variability, where consistency is important to customers. This would be a typical manufacturing operation and many transactional service environments. Here, work standards are much more closely specified. It is 'science'.

At the opposite side lie high variability process environments where customers value output variation. These are termed 'Artistic Processes'. It is 'Art'. In this book the quadrants that correspond to Artistic Processes are called Professional services and Interactive services. Here, detailed standards are less appropriate.

Austin and Devin, in Artful Making, describe similar environments to Artistic Processes described by Hall and Johnson. Austin and Devlin use the analogy of a theatre production. There is a script, but different actors bring their own interpretations as does the director. A successful production blends these together, building on the skills of the various parties. But the director has an overall concept, so there is mutual adjustment. But, finally the production settles down into an agreed-on performance that is repeated with minor adjustment night-after-night. This is an excellent way of thinking about appropriate standards.

Standard Work and TWI Job Breakdown

Training within Industry (TWI) has an unparalleled history of success with literally millions of workers having been trained by TWI methods since WWII. It is the foundation of the Toyota system. Its use in service, particularly in transactional situations can only grow.

TWI Job Instruction (JI) makes use of the 'Job Breakdown Sheet'. This is now beginning to be extensively used in healthcare, and in some local authorities and universities. In hospitals JI is used for many tasks, from washing hands correctly to inserting a drip. In manufacturing, particularly in medical device companies that have to comply with extensive regulatory procedures, job breakdown charts are beginning to be seen as a useful supplement to detailed SOPs.

Job Instruction breaks down any job into three stages:
- Important steps – a step where the work is advanced. Verb plus noun. Within each important point, there may be several....
- Key points – these are specific detailed points that either

- o Make or break a job – if not done correctly
- o Injure the worker
- o Make it easier to do
- Reasons for key points. This is to foster understanding by the worker, as to why the steps are necessary.

A job breakdown sheet is a concise description of the task. Whereas a detailed SOP may run to many pages, the corresponding job breakdown chart may be on a single page.

Job Breakdown does not cover every single step, or every task, but only the key or important tasks and within these only the key steps. A job breakdown chart is developed by close observation of experienced workers.

Note that JI is but one part of a trilogy that is considered essential for any person in direct charge of others. The other parts are Job Relations (JR - concerned with effective interpersonal relations) and Job Methods (JM - how to improve any job).

Leader Standard Work

Leader-level standard work is a very powerful concept that has become well established in manufacturing over the past decade. Evidence shows its great potential in service and administration. Essentially, a routine is established involving visual management, review at the gemba every day, and routine follow up. This institutionalises PDCA at the first line manager level. It fits in very well with TWI's three essential tasks of the front line supervisor. See the previous section.

Leader Standard Work is a core concept, rather than a tool and is discussed in Part 2.

Further Reading

Robert W Hall, 'Standard Work: Holding the Gains', *Target,* 4th Quarter, 1998, pp. 13-19

Taiichi Ohno, *Toyota Production System*, Productivity Press, 1988

Charles Standard and Dale Davis, *Running Today's Factory*, Hanser Gardner, 1999

Spear and Bowen, 'Decoding the DNA of the Toyota Production System', *Harvard Business Review*, Sept/Oct 1999

Joseph Hall and M Eric Johnson, 'When Should a Process be Art, Not Science', *Harvard Business Review*, March 2009.

Rob Austin and Lee Devin, *Artful Making*, Prentice Hall, 2003

Patrick Graupp and Bob Wrona, *Implementing TWI*, CRC Productivity Press, 2011

4.7 5S

5S housekeeping is probably the most popular tool in Lean service. There is good news and bad news. The good news: it is easy to do, may have a positive impact on quality and productivity, and sends out a powerful message that Lean 'has arrived' and is for everyone. The bad news: 5S can be a diversion from real priorities, can be seen as merely tidying up, and can give Lean a bad name though over-zealousness.

First, give thought to Captain Mannering's statement in *Dad's Army*: 'Of course it's a good idea Wilson. It'll look as if something is being done.'

The real objectives of a 5S program should be:

- to reduce waste, particularly time spent searching and time lost due to poor layout;
- to reduce variation;
- to improve productivity.

5S programs work well in situations where the need to achieve these three objectives is well known and 5S is seen as the way to do it. It does not work when it is seen as 'tidy up'. If the office is a mess, have a tidy up event, but don't call it '5S'.

Don't do 5S as an independent activity. It will not be sustained. Do 5S because everyone recognises that to meet the purpose of the system, to meet customer demands effectively, a change in the way work is laid out is required.

But 5S is also a mindset thing, changing attitudes from 'I work in an unorganised, messy office' to 'I work in a really well-organised office where everyone knows where everything is and any out of place or missing item is noticed immediately'.

Please see the section on Plan for Every Part (PFEP) in Part 2. This is the activity equivalent of 5S.

The classic 5Ss are:

SORT

Throw out what is not used or needed. The first step is to decide, with the team from the area, the sorting criteria. For example, the team may decide that items to be kept at the workplace are

- items that are used every week;
- items that are needed for important quick customer response;
- items for health and safety,

whereas the less frequently used can be located firstly in cupboards, and secondly in the storeroom.

Then the team needs to classify exactly according to the sort criteria. Touch every item systematically. If it is to be kept at the workplace, is the quantity correct? If never used, or in doubt, then red tag or throw out. A 'red tag' is a label with the date; if no one accesses the item within a specified period it should be thrown out, recycled or auctioned. An auction is a meeting with the whole team who decide together on red tagged items – what to throw out, what quantity to be kept at various locations, and the locations. The sort stage should be done regularly, say once every six months, but as a regular activity not as a re-launch of 5S. You know a 5S programme is not working when it is really a frequently repeating sequence of 2S or 3S activities.

Be careful of over-zealousness and over-the-top. Permit some personal items to be kept at the workplace within reason. Also permit personal discretion and some location choice. Readers may recall the case, rightly reported with some ridicule in *The Times* of December 2006, concerning a taped-up location for a banana on a desktop. If that is your manager's idea of what Lean is about, resign immediately!

Some offices have been known to use Feng Shui to get the 'vibes' right. Is this also OTT?

SIMPLIFY
(or Set in Order or Straighten)

Locate what remains in the best place. A place for everything, using shadow boards, inventory footprints, trolleys or items the right height, and colour-matching equipment to areas – or simply good sensible locations. Like a kitchen where the family knows the location of cutlery and plates and doesn't have to be told. Are drawers and doors really needed? The best location is the obvious one, such that it is silly to put it anywhere else. And everything in its place. Something not in place and not in use indicates a problem. The standard is 'The Dental Surgery'. Why? Because everyone can relate to that standard of excellence, and knows the consequences of failure.

Locate items by frequency to minimise stretching and bending. Repeat this stage whenever products or parts change. Use a Spaghetti Diagram for analysis. Ergonomic principles should play a role here, and an ergonomic audit may help. There are many excellent, inexpensive books on office ergonomics – there is no excuse not to use them.

All this may sound like a waste of time, but, to quote an NHS booklet, it 'releases time to care'. Spend time up front organising the workplace, and benefit from the time and errors saved thereafter. The same booklet makes the point that it all begins with the team leader, by personal demonstration.

SCAN
(Sweep or Shine or Scrub)

Keep up the good work. This includes physical tidy up, on an on-going basis, and 'visual scanning' whereby team members are always on the lookout for anything out of place, and try to correct it immediately. Some companies adopt a 'five minute routine', where people work out a five minute 'get organised' routine for each day of the week so that by the weekend everything has been covered the required number of times. Designate exactly who is responsible for what and what the standard is. This stage will require suitable cleaning equipment to be suitably located and renewed. There could be a sign-off chart for routine cleaning, such as computer screens and notice boards that cleaners might otherwise miss.

'Cleaning is Checking,' means that these are integrated. You don't just clean up, you check for any abnormality and its root causes. The garage analogy is to clean up first: this enables oil leakage to be identified. Continue to clean up any leakage that occurs. But then ask why leakage is occurring, and decide what should be done for prevention. You don't check oil, water, tyres, and tyre pressure on your car every time you drive, but you do check them when you clean your car. Same principle.

Scan may also include calibrating, keeping track, observing, monitoring, looking out for wastes, lubricating, dusting, computer monitor cleaning, and routine servicing.

It would be good to engender

- the 'Mary Poppins' effect – making clean-up fun, or
- the 'Tom Sawyer' effect – demonstrating to others that they are really missing out by not tidying up!

STANDARDISE
(or Stabilise or Secure)

Only now is it possible to adopt standard procedures. This is the real bottom line for 5S. See the sections on Failsafing and Standard Work. But 5S standards also need to be maintained. So develop standards for the first three Ss.

Standardising also includes measuring, recording, training, and improving, and may include work balancing.

SUSTAIN
(or Self Discipline)

Everyone participates in 5S on an on-going basis. Sustaining is about participation and improvement, about making the other 5S activities a habit. Carry out regular audits on housekeeping. Some award a floating trophy for achievement. Others erect a board in the entrance hall with current 5S scores. Yet others have a weekly draw out of a hat and then all first line managers descend on the chosen area to have a close look.

Some companies add a sixth S: **SAFETY**. Although it is good to emphasise safety, a good 5S program should stress it as an aspect of each of the five stages. It may confuse to list safety separately. Safety procedures and standards should also be developed, maintained and audited as part of the programme. The removal of unsafe conditions should certainly be integral to 5S.

An alternative for 5S is CANDO – Cleanup, Arrange, Neatness, Discipline, and Ongoing improvement.

Some companies adopt regular walkabout audits and competitions. See the section on The Communications Board. The first line supervisor audits daily, the area manager weekly at random times, the section manager monthly, and so on.

5S as Root Cause

5S lies at the root of many issues in service. All staff need to be sensitised to this fact, and to be encouraged to make improvements as soon as possible – not to have to wait for some kaizen event. For example:

- when a nurse arrives at a patient, or a repairman arrives at a site, and discovers that there is something missing – it is a 5S issue;
- when a document cannot be found – it is a 5S issue;
- when a surgeon encounters an unfamiliar layout in an operating theatre – it is a 5S issue;
- when customers have to ask for the location of an item in a supermarket or shop – it is a 5S (or visual management) issue;
- when lecturers can't find working flipchart pens – it is a 5S issue;
- when a stationery store runs out of paper – it is a 5S issue;
- on and on….

In all these cases it is no good just to correct the error. The situation must be highlighted and a simple non-bureaucratic procedure put in place to solve the problem permanently.

5S Sustainability

Many companies now claim that they are doing 5S but are in fact doing 2S sporadically. Having no 5S sustainability is a waste, and the programme requires increasing effort to re-energise. The real productivity and quality benefits of 5S are in the later S's, particularly standardisation, not the relatively easy-to-do first two.

Hirano suggests a host of 5S activities, carried out at various frequencies: among others:

- A 5S month, once a year (?), to re-energise efforts;

- 5S days, one to four per month including evaluations;
- 5S seminars by outside experts – with lots of photos;
- 5S visits to leading outside companies;
- 5S patrols, following a set route;
- 5S model workplaces (this has become popular in NHS hospitals);
- 5S competitions;
- 5S award ceremonies;
- 5S exhibits;
- 5-minute 5S each day.

Doing all this sounds like overkill, but putting a few in place has proved helpful in sustaining 5S.

The TWI (Training Within Industry) methodology teaches workstation layout as part of JI (Job Instruction). TWI does not discuss 5S specifically (it pre-dates the 5S concept) but 5S-type layout becomes part of the job. This is the most sensible way to sustain 5S.

Further Reading

Productivity Press Development Team, *5S for Operators*, Productivity, 2002
Hiroyuki Hirano, *5 Pillars of the Visual Workplace*, Productivity, 1995
Karen Kingston, *Clear Your Clutter with Feng Shui*, Piatkus, 2002
Nick Downham and NHS Institute for Innovation and Improvement, *Releasing Time to Care: The Productive Ward*, NHS, 2007

Extending the 5S Concept

The 5S concept can be applied more widely, especially in service. Four areas are given in the table. There are probably many more applications.

	Inventory	Suppliers	Computer Systems	Costing Systems
Sort	Throw out all dead and excessive stock.	Select the best two suppliers in each category. Scrap the rest.	Delete all dead files and applications.	Do you need all those costs and variances? Prune them!
Simplify	Arrange in the best positions.	Cut all wasteful, duplicate transactions.	Arrange files in logical folders, hierarchies.	Cut transactions. Review report frequency. Incorporate overhead directly.
Scan	Regularly review dated stock and ABC category changes.	Improve supplier performance by supplier association & kaizen.	Clear out inactive files regularly.	Audit the use made of costing reports and transaction size & frequency.
Stabilise	Footprint, standard locations	A runner system, payments	Systems, formats	Adopt reporting standards.
Sustain	Audit ABC, frequency of use.	Audit performance.	Audit perform & response.	Review and reduce.

4.8 Control Charts for Service and 'Fooled by Randomness'

Control charts are an important tool in service:

- to distinguish between common cause and special cause variation;
- to understand the extent of the natural variation;
- to know when a process is 'out of control'.

Here we will consider the use of control charts in service but will not get into a technical discussion on setting up a control chart. For this the reader is referred to one of the many books in the area such as Bicheno and Catherwood, and to Statistical Process Control (SPC) software such Minitab.

Deming was fond of saying that many managers do not understand variation and therefore often draw wrong conclusions about performance. In Deming's famous Red Bead exercise a group of six people take turns to scoop out beads from a box containing red and white beads, using a paddle. The paddle contains 50 spaces for beads. Red beads represent defects. Of course there is no way of controlling the number of red beads – it is a matter of natural variation. But the number of red beads is interpreted by the manager as representing good or bad performance. The 'good' are praised, the 'bad' fired. You realise the farce of the situation. But of course in the real world salesmen, managers, stockbrokers, and many others do get rewarded and punished when the performance is due merely to chance – good or bad 'luck'.

For a devastating critique of this kind of behaviour see Taleb's book *Fooled by Randomness*, and Alfie Kohn's *Punished by Rewards*.

This is just one instance where a control chart would be useful. Calculate the upper and lower control limits within which 99.7% of natural variation occurs. The upper and lower control limits are set at the average plus and minus three standard deviations respectively. Only if a point falls outside these limits is a 'special cause' signalled. The process may then be 'out of control'. Otherwise it is 'common cause' variation, and 'in control'. This is much like an engine temperature gauge on an old car. The temperature does vary on hot and cold days and on going up a long hill, but as long as it stays within the green zone (the limits) there is no cause for concern. If, however, it goes into the red zone you stop and investigate: perhaps the fan belt has broken or you have a radiator leak. It is a 'special cause'.

Control charts are called statistical process control charts, not statistical product control charts, because the intention is to control the process, not the products or services that come out of the process. If the process is in control and capable, then the products (or services) that come out of the system will be good.

Why is this relevant in Lean service? First, if you ignore variation you may fall into the red bead trap. It's like drowning in a river of an average depth of one metre.

Second, because you don't want to go chasing after common cause variation. Third, you would like to know how much variation is due to common causes. Fourth, you would like to investigate only those specific special causes. So, for instance, if you have a service level agreement (SLA) to meet a maintenance time target, first understand whether the process is 'in control'. The point is, if the variation is such that the process is 'out of control', it doesn't matter whether the SLA target is being met – it is inherently unpredictable and unstable. The special causes must first be investigated. On the other hand, if the process in control, then you can begin to shift or redesign the whole process, confident in the knowledge that there are no unseen 'bombshells' at work. Note that a process may be 'in control' but still not meeting the SLA. And further, in drawing the control limits, you can get a feel for how variable the process is and ask if this is acceptable. Two processes may have the same average performance, but be very different in terms of customer satisfaction.

Beware: a SLA may have no relevance to a customer, but may be there simply because a manager has decided it is a good idea.

Note also that control limits are not specification limits. Control limits relate to the natural variation of the process, while specification limits are what the managers or customers would regard as being the bounds of acceptability. In the case of an SLA, the SLA would be the upper specification limit and the lower limit would be zero. A process is out of control when readings go beyond the control limits, not the specification limits.

Many control charts, especially in product-based systems, are sampling charts – in other words samples are taken every so often to monitor the process. But you can also have a control chart which is essentially a run diagram monitoring every occurrence.

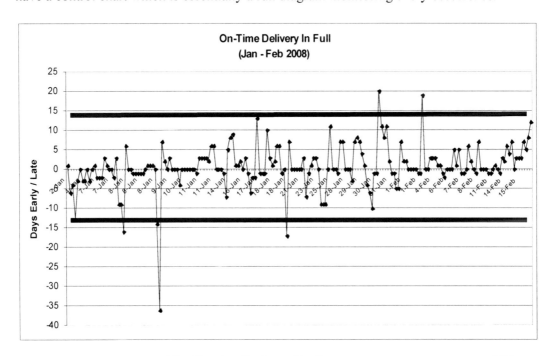

Note that there are a few points above the upper control limit, indicating that there were a few special events that warrant looking into.

A further use of control charts is to monitor the process and to detect shifts. For instance, a call centre uses a control chart to monitor the length of calls. Samples are taken a number of times each day. Then a new product is introduced. Soon afterwards the call length monitoring system indicates that call length is increasing – it has gone beyond the previous control limit. Is this due to inadequate instructions issued with the new product? Is it because the new product is more complex? Or what? The point is that the shift might have been missed if the call lengths were not being recorded on the call centre control charts. Note here that the control chart is used for problem detection and NOT for 'checking up' on the performance of the staff. Everyone needs to understand this.

There are various 'out of control' signals other than a point plotted beyond the control limits. For instance, seven successive points plotted above the average indicates an out-of-control condition.

Attribute Charts

The charts just discussed are 'variables' charts, meaning that the observations can take on any value. By contrast 'attributes' charts have only two states, good or bad, pass or fail. So, for example, customers either complain or don't complain. They are therefore a little less powerful than attributes but they are still very valuable, especially in service. There are two types: **proportion** (p-chart) or **number** (c-chart). Both share the same general formulas for upper and lower control limits, namely average plus and minus three standard deviations.

An easy-to-remember value for the standard deviation of a number – say the number of complaints in an airport where the number of possible points of complaint is indeterminate (so proportion has no meaning) – is that the standard deviation is the square root of the average. So if there were 49 complaints on average per week before the improvement programme and 35 on average afterwards, can we say that an improvement has taken place? Answer: the lower control limit is $49 - 3$ standard deviations of the average $= 49 - 3*7 = 28$. So on the evidence of one week we cannot say that a real improvement has taken place – it may just be random variation. Of course, if complaints persisted at around 35 we could conclude after three weeks that a real change has taken place.

Zone of Tolerance

Statistical Process Control thinking has been extended into the service area by, among others, Zeithaml, Bitner and Gremler, Berry, and Johnston and Clark. All recognise that service is a variable entity – it is never absolutely consistent. And customers perceive service delivery differently. All these authors refer to a 'zone of tolerance' roughly equivalent to the distance between the upper and lower specification limits (not the control limits) on an SPC control chart. The difference here is that beyond the control limit on one side indicates satisfaction and on the other side indicates dissatisfaction.

Johnston and Clark refer to a customer satisfaction 'zone of tolerance' located between 'zones of delight' and 'dissatisfaction'. Zeithaml *et al*'s 'zone of tolerance' falls between zones of desired service and adequate service – meaning that there is a grey zone between the minimum acceptable level of service and the 'zone of delight'. These conceptual models are useful in thinking about the bounds of service quality.

The 'zone of tolerance' model can be used with performance measurement or mapping. Just like traditional SPC, samples of perhaps five random customers are taken through time for

- waiting in a queue at a supermarket;
- response time for maintenance work;
- levels of satisfaction at a hotel, on perhaps a 1-10 scale.

First, however, if we are to use 'zone of tolerance' in a quantitative sense we need to establish

- the upper and lower specification limits – perhaps by questioning managers or customers;
- the upper and lower control limits – derived from previous performance records.

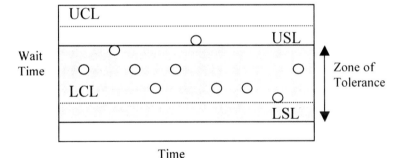

The figure shows that the process is 'in control': the average of the samples falls between the control limits, and all samples except one fall within the 'zone of tolerance'. The point outside the 'zone of tolerance' indicates that there may be some dissatisfaction among customers – in this case wait time is being plotted so above the specification limit is inadequate service. So here there are no special events at work, but the process is nevertheless not capable of always delivering adequate service.

Strictly speaking, if a variable such as wait times is being monitored with samples, a range chart should also be shown. The range chart shows the difference between the highest and lowest values in each sample. A range chart is necessary because two samples may have the same average but different ranges.

Both sets of authors make the point that the zone can shift depending on the importance of the factor and on prior experience. Thus the zone is wider for first-time buyers but narrows for service recovery situations. The level of interest and commitment may also affect the size of the band.

Johnston and Clark use the 'zone of tolerance' concept much like an SPC control chart, maintaining that various 'transactions' or Moments of Truth can be plotted in the chart. A succession of points plotted in the 'dissatisfied' zone leads to the equivalent of out-of-control conditions (a dissatisfied customer) but several points above the zone result in 'delight'. Some behaviour may be compensatory: a poor experience may be compensated by several satisfactory experiences. A poor experience may also shift the 'specification limits' upwards, making the customer even more demanding, but a great experience may lower the zone, thus making it easier to achieve further delight.

Zeithaml and Bitner have done interesting work identifying the factors that shift the specification limits (although they don't refer to them). The upper limit of the zone (leading to desired service) is influenced by implicit and explicit service promises, by word of mouth and by past experience. The lower limit is influenced by

- 'service intensifiers', where, for example, an anniversary dinner might imply reduced tolerance;
- service alternatives: where there are fewer options there is more tolerance;
- the degree of influence that a customer has on the service provider;
- factors that are perceived to be out of the service provider's control;
- the predicted service.

So control charts can be useful on both a practical and a conceptual level. They can be linked into mapping – under the 'check' stage, into measures, and into loyalty considerations.

Further Reading

Valerie Zeithaml, Mary Jo Bitner and Dwayne Gremler, *Services Marketing*, 4th edition, McGraw Hill, Boston, 2006, Chapter 4
Leonard Berry, *Marketing Services: Competing through Quality*, Free Press, New York, 1991
Robert Johnston and Graham Clark, *Service Operations Management*, FT/Prentice Hall, Harlow, 2001, Chapter 4
John Bicheno and Philip Catherwood, *Six Sigma and The Quality Toolbox*, PICSIE Books, 2005
Nassim Taleb, *Fooled by Randomness*, Random House, 2004
Alfie Kohn, *Punished by Rewards*, Houghton Mifflin, 1999

4.9 Mistakes and Pokayoke

The Hinckley framework discusses improving quality through variation, mistakes and complexity. See above. Here we discuss mistake-proofing. Mistakes are a 'big deal' in service: Stephen Spear quotes a figure of 98,000 deaths a year in US hospitals due to errors, and Gawande gives numerous examples of error reduction using checklists.

Mistake-proofing (Pokayoke)

The late Shigeo Shingo did not invent mistake-proofing ('pokayoke' in Japanese, literally mistake proofing), or failsafe, but he developed and classified the concept, particularly in manufacturing. Mistake-proofing in services has developed more recently. The classic work is Shingo's book *Zero Quality Control: Source Inspection and the Pokayoke System*. More lately C Martin Hinckley has made a significant new contribution through his work *Make No Mistake!*

A mistake-proofing device is a simple, often inexpensive, device that literally prevents defects from being made. The characteristics of a mistake-proofing device are
- it occurs 100% automatically – a true pokayoke would not rely on human memory or action; moreover this removes judgement;
- involves an inspection activity;
- either stops or gives warning when a defect is discovered. One example is a cell entry in an Excel spreadsheet that has been set up to take only specific data such as a number or a date. Amazon will not allow you to complete an order online before all data have been completed, and some of them checked. Note that a pokayoke is not a control device like a thermostat or toilet control valve that takes action every time, but rather a device that senses abnormalities and takes action only when an abnormality is identified;
- is low cost.

Shingo talked about 'little' pokayoke and 'big' pokayoke cycles. 'Little' is where the mistake is stopped. 'Big' investigates why it arose in the first place. Both of these are necessary. But from a system viewpoint there is an even bigger cycle, and that is to look at the whole system and ask if the entire process or system can be failsafed – or, as Ackoff says, if the problem can be 'dissolved' from an end-to-end perspective. Remove the root cause from the system. Design it out.

Shingo distinguishes between 'mistakes' (which are inevitable) and 'defects' (which result when a mistake reaches a customer). The aim of pokayoke is to design devices that prevent mistakes becoming defects. Shingo also saw quality control as a hierarchy of effectiveness from 'judgment inspection', where inspectors inspect, to 'informative inspection', where information is used to control the process as in SPC, to 'source inspection', which aims at checking operating conditions 'before the fact'. Good pokayokes fall into this last category.

According to Shingo there are three types of mistake-proofing device: 'contact', 'fixed value', and 'motion step'. This means that there are six categories, as shown in the figure with service examples.

	Control	Warning
Contact	Parking height bars; bar coding on patients, and wrist bands on babies	Staff mirrors; shop entrance light beam; Disney queue warning signs, allergy warnings.
Fixed Value	French fry scoop; pre-dosed medication; valid ranges in Excel spreadsheet.	Kit carts with indentations; shadowboards; ink warning on printer; hamburger age flag;
Motion Step	Airline lavatory doors; 'Pick to light' warehouse picking system	Spellcheckers; beepers on ATM's; tax form completion checks; manager visit display board. Checklists.

This Table was developed from an original by Case and Stewart, 1995.

The **contact type** makes contact with every product or has a physical shape that inhibits mistakes. An example is a fixed diameter hole through which all products must fall; an oversize product does not fall through and a defect is registered.
The **fixed value method** is a design that makes it clear when a part is missing or not used. An example is an 'egg tray' used for the supply of parts.
The **motion step type** automatically ensures that the correct numbers of steps have been taken. For example, an operator is required to step on a pressure-sensitive pad during every assembly cycle, or a medicine bottle has a press-down-and-turn feature for safety. Other examples are a checklist, or correct sequence for switches that do not work unless the order is correct. McDonald's is famous for its large number of failsafe devices – from timers, to flags, to French fry scoops.
A **warning type** may be an outline diagram of a patient's body showing which bits need which type of attention – this may prevent cutting off the wrong arm or applying ointment to a cut instead of a burn where the patient has both!

Shingo further developed failsafe classification by saying that there are five areas that have potential for mistake-proofing: the operator (Me), the Material, the Machine, the Method, and the Information (4 Ms plus I). An alternative is the process control model comprising input, process, output, feedback, and result. All are candidates for mistake-proofing.

Shingo says that pokayoke should be thought of as having a short action cycle, where immediate shut down or warning is given, and a long action cycle, where the reasons for the defect occurring in the first place are investigated. John Grout makes the useful point that one drawback of pokayoke devices is that potentially valuable information about process variance may be lost, thereby inhibiting improvement.

Hinckley has developed an excellent approach to mistake-proofing. He has a classification scheme consisting of five categories of mistakes – defective material, defective information, maladjustment, omission, and selection errors. The last four have several sub-categories. For each category, typical mistake-proofing solutions have been developed. Thus, having identified the type of mistake, you can look through the set of possible solutions and adapt or select the most suitable one.

Pokayoke with Near Misses

If you were a patient in a hospital, what would you prefer: (a) being in a ward where many mistakes are reported, or (b) being in a ward where no mistakes are reported? Think about it. Is (b) because they are so good, or is it because they are so fearful or fed up with reporting problems about which no-one does anything? Would your prefer a pilot not to go through a pre-flight checklist in order to get going sooner?

Preventing mistakes also means anticipating mistakes. Near-miss analysis is a vital part of this. Aviation authorities have a well-ordered near-miss investigation sequence. There is a lot to learn from this. Bates, quoted by Spear, says that for every death due to medication error there were ten injuries and 100 instances where harm was averted. In health and safety there has been long-standing recognition of unsafe acts and unsafe conditions. Near-misses need to be routinely recorded and analysed in a 'no fears' environment.

- In hospitals, we assumed that the critical procedure had already been done but luckily found out that it had not, or we had to delay the operation when we discovered that the medication had passed its 'use-by' date.
- In restaurants, we nearly cooked sirloin rather than fillet, or nearly allowed nuts to get into the dessert.
- In consultancies, we nearly sent out the wrong report version, or disclosed confidential information.
- In a bank, we nearly allowed confidential credit card information to go out with the regular garbage.
- In maintenance, we just happened to have the right spare available, otherwise a repeat trip would have been necessary.

A near-miss is also spotting a situation where a customer could have complained but did not. Remember the rule of thumb that only 10% of customers actually complain.

Making complaining easier is a part of this. But begin from Deming's 94/6 rule that 94% of problems are due to the process, only 6% due to the people. So, what is it in the process that has led to the problem? Once again, Ackoff's maxim that trying to dissolve problems is better than trying to solve them is relevant.

So a near-miss procedure needs to be easy to record, non-threatening, no-blame and either addressed immediately or as part of a routine process – perhaps around the daily Communications Board meeting or the weekly review. It may need to be built into an established, visible Concern, Cause, Countermeasure (3C) procedure. Please do not rely only on Standard Operating Procedures – a SOP simply cannot anticipate all situations. Setting up a near-miss procedure is the responsibility of management. Otherwise near-misses will simply go on for years, until a near-miss becomes a hit with possibly severe results.

Admitting to Mistakes

Admitting mistakes to customers has been shown to be a very effective thing to do, to retain customer loyalty (Goodman). It turns out that customers are often more loyal if a company admits its mistakes and apologises than if no problem has arisen in the first place!

And allowing for customer mistakes and company mistakes by allowing a 'no quibble' returns policy is also good both for inning customers and for retaining them. This famous policy was adopted by Marks and Spencer, and is now widely copied.

Pokayoke with Cycle of Service

Pokayoke is one of the standard considerations used with 'Interactive' mapping. See the section on Interactive Mapping. Here the customer's Moments of Truth are followed through stage by stage, and each stage is checked to see if the step can be mistake-proofed. But 'cycle of service' should, of course, begin with the 'pre' stage, follow through with the 'during' stages, and conclude with the 'post' or follow up stages. Godfrey *et al*, working in healthcare, have suggested useful ideas that can be linked into Interactive mapping but also extended to wider service.

Much of the following overlaps with 5S and visual management activity. Gwen Galsworth, talking about four levels of visual management, gives the analogy of a railway road crossing: passive (a warning sign), assertive (a flashing warning), aggressive (a physical barrier or lifting gate), and assured (a bridge separating road from rail).

Pre-Stage – Elimination: this is where the possibilities for accidents and errors are eliminated even before the routine work begins. Examples:
- Remove sharp objects, locate shadow boards and identify standard locations as part of a 5S activity. For example, a shadow board located near the point of use (perhaps on a trolley in a hospital) not only makes it apparent when an implement is missing but prevents the wrong implement being used by having to fetch it from another location.
- Eliminate handoffs to create a one-stop service.
- Eliminate the need for multiple data entry.

- Eliminate unsatisfactory human work conditions through ergonomics, leading to errors and injury.
- Eliminate sources of noise and reasons for eye protection. Many video and record shops have far higher levels of noise than are found in many factories requiring ear protection.

Pre-Stage – Replacement: replacing human actions by automated actions for safety and error reasons. Examples: automatic smoke or gas detection, automatic air extraction, safety belt warnings, warning lights on office equipment, message waiting on answer phones.

During Stage – Facilitation: make the work easier to carry out and less error prone. Examples: valid ranges in a spreadsheet, checklists, colour coding, traffic light data presentation rather than numbers, ergonomics in general, provision of ear and sign protection.

During Stage – Detection: examples: kit carts, non-completion of required fields in data entry, workplace audit boards showing that various levels of management have visited the area, monthly reporting boards.

Post Stage: Mitigation*:* reduce the effects of an error. Examples: cross checking, double-checking, asking air passengers to check for items left behind or hotel guests to check for their room key. Several lecturers on service management courses tell the story of the hotel concierge chasing after them because they hadn't been reminded to check their room before departure. Have flipcharts for recording types of problem so that they can be addressed by future kaizen activity.

In a more general context, many of these actions can be seen as 'Fitting the Task to the Human' rather than the other way around. This has long been a quest in ergonomics. The attention of the reader is drawn to the many good books on ergonomics, such as that given in Further Reading, which discuss issues such as workstation design (chairs and table heights), lighting, vision, noise, vibration, fatigue, lifting, and even stress and eating habits at or before work.

Pokayoke and Customer Mistakes

Customers also make mistakes – and may then blame the product or service! Stephen Tax quotes the World Health Organization that has identified the failure of patients to take prescribed medications correctly as a major problem. Customers should be thought of as 'co-producers', according to Tax. Vanguard Consulting, working with the UK police, has shown that a very high proportion of '999' calls are not emergencies as defined by the authorities, such as assault or heart attack, but are in fact events that can be given much lower priority.

Customer mistake-proofing can be a matter of attitude on the part of the service provider. Start with the assumption that customers want to succeed and are not lazy, rather than simply blaming them for being stupid or lacking motivation, or even benefiting from their 'mistakes' (such as taking out gym membership only to give it up after a short while). Customer punishment is the often-adopted explicit or implicit solution. This is like Theory X and Theory Y. So what can the organisation do to help the customer to retain the gym membership, to use the useful features on a phone, to attend on time, to stick to the diet, to avoid the lost receipt, or to pay on time? Tax *et al* point out that this can be a source of real competitive advantage.

Customer failures may not be apparent in a superficial mapping study. But customer failures should be apparent if you conscientiously adopt the 'check' stage advocated by John Seddon and described in the high level mapping Tool section. 'Check' looks out for Failure Demand by noting the actual words used by customers when they call in or make demands on the system.

A suggested methodology is:

- Listen to customers' actual words during routine Moments of Truth, when demands come into the system. Sampling is usually necessary. This is by far the most powerful source of data because the comments are unsolicited. Separate failure demand from value demand. For definitions of value and failure demand see the separate section.
- Question existing customers about their experience in using the product or service. Questionnaires are useful, but their interpretation and use is different from the usual. Often questionnaires are used for evaluation or market survey purposes. Here they are used to help to identify causes of failure.
- Question lost customers. Why did they leave?
- Collect complaints – not only formal written complaints, but also verbal complaints which need to be collected by front line staff in a blame-free, 'no-fears' problem-solving environment. Do not use complaints only to look at internal processes, but also use them to look at why the customer failed to do what was expected by the organisation.
- Observe customers using or attempting to use the product or service. Xerox copy centres used to do this. Quicken software was developed by 'over the shoulder' methods. This may include following a new patient in a hospital, a new customer in a bank, and monitoring keystrokes.
- Monitor what John Seddon calls 'dirty data' – incorrectly filled-in forms and the like.
- From all these sources, group the failures into categories, using the Affinity Diagram, where post-its are grouped together. Be particularly aware of customer 'failures' or complaints.
- Then, seek the root causes of customer failure. Why did the customer make the mistake, why did he get lost, why did she use the service incorrectly? Use the Five Whys and the fishbone diagram. Do a self-test: put yourself in the shoes of a customer or ask a member of your staff not concerned with the process to use it.

- Solutions come in many forms: 5S, simplification, training, and technical. On creative thinking in general see books by Roger von Oech. For more technical solutions refer to Martin Hinckley and, of course, TRIZ.

Peter Willmott, doyen of UK practitioners on Total Productive Maintenance, gives more than 20 checks that everyone can carry out on their car with no technical skill but using only their 'God-given senses'. Pointing out these checks to new car purchasers would certainly end many mistakes as well as prolong the life of the car and perhaps the life of the user. Why not extend this practice to many types of product and service?

To summarise: the greatest problem with mistakes is recognising the problem in the first place. This must be followed by the right attitude to its solution: that the customer's problem is in fact your problem.

Further Reading

Shigeo Shingo, *Zero Quality Control: Source Inspection and the Pokayoke System*, Productivity Press, 1986
C Martin Hinckley, *Make No Mistake*, Productivity Press, Portland, 2001
Richard Chase and Douglas Stewart, *Mistake-Proofing: Designing Errors Out*, Productivity, 1995
An impressive, award winning, web site with numerous examples and pictures is at: http://csob.berry.edu/faculty/jgrout/pokayoke.shtml
Atul Gawande, *The Checklist Manifesto*, Profile Books, 2010.
A Blanton Godfrey *et al*, *Healthcare Focused Error Proofing*, North Carolina State University, 2005
Stephen Spear, 'Fixing Healthcare from the Inside, Today', *Harvard Business Review*, September 2005, pp. 78-91
Stephen Tax, Mark Colgate, David Bowen, 'How to Prevent Your Customers from Failing', *MIT Sloan Management Review*, Spring 2006
K Kroemer and E Grandjean, *Fitting the Task to the Human: A Textbook of Occupational Ergonomics*, (5th+ edition), Taylor and Francis, 2000
Gwendolyn Galsworth, *Visual Management*, Productivity

4.10 A3 Problem Solving and Reports

The A3 method has grown hugely in popularity among Lean organisations in recent years, and with good reason.

A3 refers to the standard sheet of paper: two A4 portrait sheets, side by side. The story is that it was the largest size of paper that could be conveniently faxed.

There is the George Bernard Shaw story where he writes to a friend but apologises for writing a long letter because he had no time to write a short letter! That conciseness is an aim of A3. We don't want a multi page report that few might read. We want a concise document in a format that we are all familiar with.

On the face of it, A3 is simply a useful problem-solving framework. But it is far more than that: it is a powerful mentoring and development tool.

John Shook says 'It takes two to A3'. By this he means that an A3 should go back and forth between analyst and mentor / manager several times. The first attempt at solution is very likely to have missed important points. A 'quick and dirty solution' or a way of justifying an idea that an analyst already holds, is NOT what A3 is about.

Rather, it is a tool to explore, to question, to probe, to get to the true root cause. John Shook's excellent book on A3 is presented in an unusual way. On each pair of pages there is the analyst's view and the mentor's view. The solution to a problem begins with the analyst presenting what turns out to be an ill-thought-out proposal. Through mentoring and probing by the manager or sensei, eventually a much deeper solution emerges that reveals the true root cause. The final solution is vastly different to that originally proposed.

As John Shook says 'True A3 is a team sport'.

The mentor should probe whether the problem is clearly defined, whether the goals are clear, whether the root causes have been sufficiently explored, whether the data is valid, amongst others. He should probe about implementation, validation of results, and follow through.

But there is even more: A3 is a consensus building tool. As discussion and mentoring takes place commitment from both analyst and manager grows. Others may be involved in building the implementation plan. It becomes 'our plan' not 'his plan'. Implementation can then begin without further justification. Typical of Lean-style 'nemawashi' or taking longer to build consensus but then much shorter and smoother in the subsequent implementation phases.

In this regard, A3 is frequently used as part of the Strategy Deployment process.

The Technical Detail of A3

A3 is:
- a standardised problem-solving methodology incorporating the PDSA cycle;
- a standard report format. Rather than a multi-page report that may come in various formats depending on the whim of the writer, A3 forces the writer to be concise;
- a standard documentation and easy-filing method.

A3 is actually a family of report formats, used for planning, budgeting, communication, and problem solving. Here we consider only the generic problem-solving type.

The general format of A3 is current state analysis on the left hand side and future state and implementation plan on the right hand side. There is often space along the bottom for 'sign off', for people who have seen or agreed to the analysis.

The standard layout is shown in the figure below. You can see that the left hand side is Check and Plan, and the right hand side is Do, Act and again Check.

A good A3 has a collection of graphics including graphs, figures, fishbones, bar charts and cartoons. It does not have multiple words reduced to a font size that no-one can read! In the following section the various headings in the figure will be explained.

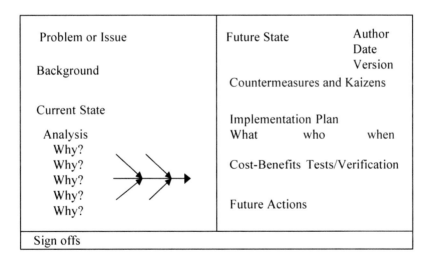

Top right corner: the author or team, the date and the version number.

The Problem or Issue: a statement of the problem. One sentence.

Background: how did the problem arise? This is often a clue to the solution. Also, set the situation in the context of the wider value stream. A short statement of history. Two sentences maximum.

Current State: can take various forms. A process map, possibly with kaizen bursts. A cartoon. A sketch of a product part. A data table. Try to make the current state lively and interesting. Invent icons. Draw happy and sad customers. Try to remain focused on the data, the facts – so bar charts, pie charts, and graphs are the norm.

Analysis: a standard approach is to use either the Five Whys methodology or a fishbone diagram. When using Five Whys there may be several answers to each Why. So prioritise by circling the most likely answers. Similarly on a fishbone diagram, circle the likely causes. Sometimes a run diagram is useful. In fact, any of the classic Seven Tools of Quality can be used. These should be addressed to the first two of the classic 3C approach: Concern, Cause, Countermeasure. Countermeasure is dealt with on the right hand side.

Future State: same comments as for the current state.

Countermeasures and Kaizens: these should be short sentences, arranged in a table. Prioritise. It is good to have short and long term (permanent) solutions in mind. The kaizens may be short, focused actions – 'point kaizens'. Include verb plus noun to indicate the actions. 'Erect sign to direct customers'. In technical problems, a small sketch could be added.

Implementation Plan: simply a list of actions, together with by whom and by when. A more complex case may include a simple network diagram to indicate the sequence.

Cost Benefits: not a great ROI or discounted cash flow analysis, but a simple outlay of actual cash and expected money benefits in the immediate period ahead. State the aim clearly as in £1000 saving within 12 months. Not all improvements generate cash, so include the other benefits: quality of work-life, happier customers.

Tests and verification: after the countermeasures have been implemented, the new solution should be expected to produce various results. State these, so they can be verified later. They should be related to the cost benefits.

Follow up: wider issues might have been raised. What are the envisaged next steps? In Lean there is always the idea that a change always leads onto more opportunities for further change and improvement. A never-ending cycle.

Sign off: often, along the bottom various line managers concerned with the issue should see and sign off the A3. They could, of course, annotate and discuss with the team.

The figure below shows a classic Toyota-type A3 applied to a problem in a coffee shop. Notice:

- the preference for using diagrams, graphs, tables, cartoons, and other graphics rather than many words;

- the 'gap' is clearly identified;

- pareto-type analysis is applied;

- the location of the problem is found by tracing the stages of the of the process forward until the problem is found, then backwards to locate the source. A run diagram is often useful in service situations to find the time and location of the problem;

- 5 why analysis is used, in this case combined with the classic 'M's of fishbone analysis (manpower, method, machines, materials, measures, 'mother nature').

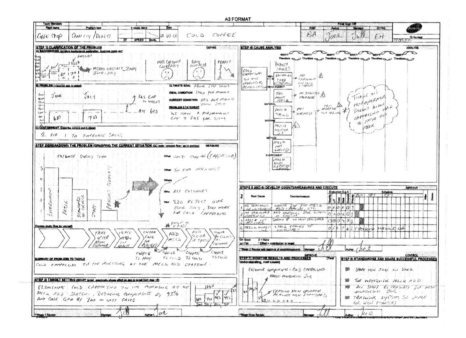

Acknowledgement: Thanks to Justin Watts for the A3.

An A3 can be used at several organisational levels. It is used:

- for routine problem solving – point kaizens;
- as a supplement to mapping;

- as a tool and record for kaizen events. One company places kaizen event A3s on the wall near the relevant area for a standard period of twelve months;
- as a supplement to strategy deployment;
- as a test to evaluate a new employee.

Further Reading

John Shook, *Managing to Learn: Using the A3 management process...*, Lean Enterprise Institute 2008
Durward Sobek and Art Smalley, *Understanding A3 Thinking*, CRC Press, 2008

4.11 Kaizen and Knowledge Management

Kaizen is the Japanese name for continuous improvement. As such it is central to Lean operations, whether in manufacturing or service. The word stems from Kai (to change or take apart) and Zen (to make better). It brings together several of the tools and techniques described in this book and a few more.

Although FW Taylor is a hero to many industrial engineers, the writer included, he did separate the thinkers from the doers. This is exactly opposed to the spirit of Kaizen. In many Western companies the FW Taylor view persists. Consider that most new innovations come from R&D, and that salaries of top managers are huge multiples of those of front line staff. In Kaizen, everyone is a knowledge worker. It is about bottom-up innovation. But more than this: it is about the 'Knowledge Creating Company' where 'tacit' knowledge is tapped. Tacit knowledge is 'know-how', 'the way we do things around here', based on years of practical experience, much of it not written down. This is opposed to 'explicit' knowledge that is written down in codified formulas, procedures and principles. So there are two 'worlds': front line staff and operators exchange 'tacit to tacit' knowledge and some explicit knowledge, while engineers, managers and academics exchange 'explicit to explicit' knowledge. One strength of kaizen is that it sets out to bridge the gap by moving knowledge from 'tacit' to 'explicit', thereby exposing whole rafts of ideas and enabling them to be explicitly incorporated. And 'explicit' knowledge can become 'tacit' by force of habit. Is this why Toyota doesn't send its people on MBA programmes?

According to Imai, author of the original book on Kaizen, it comprises several elements. Kaizen is both a philosophy and a set of tools.

The Philosophy of Kaizen: Quality begins with the customer. But customers' views are continually changing and standards are rising, so continuous improvement is required. Kaizen is dedicated to continuous improvement, in small increments, at all levels, forever. Everyone has a role, from top management to shop floor employees.

Imai believes that without active attention, the gains made will simply deteriorate (like the engineers' concept of entropy). But Imai goes further. Unlike Juran, who emphasises 'holding the gains', Kaizen involves building on the gains by continuing experimentation and innovation.

According to Imai there are several guiding principles:

- **Questioning the rules**: standards are necessary but work rules are there to be broken and must be broken with time;
- **Developing resourcefulness**: it is a management priority to develop the resourcefulness and participation of everyone;
- **Trying to get to the Root Cause**: try not to solve problems superficially;
- **Eliminating the whole task**: question whether a task is necessary;

- **Reducing or changing activities**: be aware of opportunities to combine tasks.

The following are essential features.

- **Kaizen is continuous**: this indicates both the embedded nature of the practice and also its place in a never-ending journey towards quality and efficiency.
- **It is usually incremental in nature**, in contrast to major management-initiated reorganisations or technological innovation (for example, the installation of new technology or machinery).
- **It is participative**: it entails the involvement and intelligence of the work force, generating intrinsic psychological and quality of work life benefits for employees.
- **Its solutions are 'low-cost, no-cost'**: not about installing equipment or systems, but about improving present systems.
- **It taps into the 'tacit' knowledge of all staff**, surfacing this knowledge to make it explicit.

The Kaizen Flag

The Kaizen Flag is a famous diagram developed by Imai and widely copied and adapted. The flag portrays the three types of activity with which everyone in a Kaizen organisation should be involved. These are 'Innovation, 'Kaizen', and 'Standardisation' against organisation level. An adapted version is discussed below.

In the original, senior management spends more time on 'innovation' to do with tomorrow's products and processes, less time on 'kaizen' to do with improving today's products and processes, but also a small proportion of time on 'standardisation' (following the established best way of doing tasks). In top management's case this could include policy deployment and budgeting, but also Leader Standard Work (LSW). See the separate section on LSW. A standard method is the current best and safest known way to do a task, until a better way is found through kaizen.

Middle managers spend less time than top managers on innovation, about the same time on kaizen and more time on standardisation. Operators spend a small, but significant, proportion of time on innovation, more time on kaizen, and most time on standardisation.

Kate Mackle, former head of the British Kaizen Institute and now Principal in the consultancy Thinkflow, explains that innovation is concerned with preventing waste from entering tomorrow's processes, kaizen is concerned with getting waste out of today's processes, and standardisation is concerned with keeping waste out.

The version of the flag presented below is based on Imai's original, but takes into account both experience and the ideas of the decision process developed by Ilbury and Sunter.

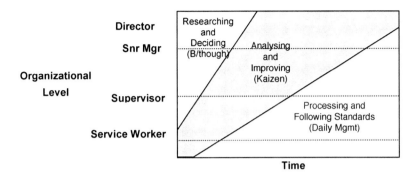

Here 'processing' is following the current standard best and safest known way.

Kaizen and Experimentation

In manufacturing there is the famous Lean 'water and rocks analogy'. The water, or inventory, covers the rocks, or problems. So you deliberately experiment by reducing the water level (take out inventory) to expose the rocks (problems). Not just any problem, but the most pressing problem. Reducing the inventory is supposed to be a 'win-win' strategy: either nothing happens, in which case you run tighter, or you hit the prominent problem, which is good because it is exposed. This is one form of point kaizen. It is also SDSA – plan, do, study, act.

In service, you should also deliberately experiment. The nice thing is that the scope for experimentation in service is vast and the evaluation much faster than in manufacturing. How so? Because there are numerous parallel activities in service: hotel rooms, flights, bank or shop branches, insurance claims, on and on. Why not, therefore, set up trials with, say, room make-up in a quarter of hotel rooms, trial menus at particular locations, or claim procedures for 10% of claims? Then get your customers to help to evaluate?

This kind of experimentation could be part of the Level 2 or Level 3 redesign process. You will need to collect ideas for the trials from employees or customers, or ideas coming out of the mapping process. This concept is by no means new. Google allows new ideas to be posted on their intranet and voted on by employees. IDEO undertakes controlled experimentation: many small failures but a few great successes. Harrah's Entertainment experimentation in Casinos is described in a case study. Harrah was able to conduct experiments, each involving a control group and an experimental group of customers who were given different incentive packages, with the location of slot machines, and with different staff training programmes.

Experimentation, of course, is not enough. The better ways need to be spread and incorporated.

Further Reading

Maasaki Imai, *Kaizen: The Key to Japan's Competitive Success*, McGraw Hill, New York, 1986

Maasaki Imai, *Gemba Kaizen*, McGraw Hill, New York, 1997

Ikujiro Nanaka, 'The Knowledge Creating Company', *Harvard Business Review*, 1991, reprinted in *HBR* July-August 2007

Jeffrey Pfeffer and Robert Sutton, *Hard Facts, Dangerous Half Truths and Total Nonsense*, Harvard Business School Press, 2006

Rajiv Lal, *Harrah's Entertainment Inc.*, Case 9-502-011, Harvard Business School / ECCH

4.12 Kaizen Events or Improvement Events

Kaizen events are useful if not essential supplements to on-going individual-based improvement activities. They can incorporate all the types of mapping described in this publication, and implement many of the improvements over a very short period of time.

At the outset we should say that kaizen events have developed from manufacturing where the focus is on the internal process – it is inward looking. This is still the thinking in many service organisations. But there is another opportunity: the customer-focused kaizen event. Here the focus shifts to solving (or dissolving!) the customer's problems or improving the customer's effectiveness. This means putting yourself in the shoes of the customer. It means redefining the system boundary to include the customer. Of course many processes, like the Custom type and the Interactive type, have strong customer involvement all the way through so it is only natural to include them.

Mike Rother, well known for his seminal books on manufacturing (Value Stream Mapping, and Toyota Kata) has stated that he believes that kaizen events started in the USA because of the availability of Toyota Sensei's coming over from Japan for short periods of time.

Be careful. <u>It is very tempting to rush into a kaizen event</u>. It may even produce good results and make everyone feel good. But what happens if the process is the wrong process? Then the event is simply rearranging deckchairs on the Titanic. So it is essential to do an overall system evaluation first. What is the purpose of the system? Will the event contribute to the best overall solution from the customer's point of view? Only then....

Given that the right theme has been identified, a company and its customers could be benefiting within a week from a leap in productivity in one area of its plant or office. Events are about 'going for it', about a preference for doing it now and reasonably rather than later but perhaps never, even though it could be done better; they are about learning by doing, by trial and error. They are also about involvement in office and service processes by office and service people. They are about real empowerment to 'just do it' without asking for permission to make every little change. A well planned and followed through event has a good chance of sustaining its improvements over an extended period. Poorly planned and executed events, however, have frequently slipped back to the original state – and given such events a poor name in some organisations.

Today, 'Kaizen Blitz' (the name used by the US Association for Manufacturing Excellence) is well proven in both service and manufacturing companies. In the UK, Industry Forum (IF) has adopted kaizen events as a standard approach originally for automotive suppliers (referred to as the Master Class process). The IF methodology has spread to aerospace, the metals industry and construction, among others. Some consulting groups such as TBM and Simpler have developed their own versions.

The IF methodology was aimed at rolling out the kaizen event process. Each event would also have the aim of training more facilitators to be able to run more events and introducing the concept to supervisors and others from areas intended as targets in the future.

An appropriate quote to introduce kaizen events is:

> 'Whether you believe you can,
> or whether you believe you can't,
> you're absolutely right.'
> (Henry Ford)

Today we recognise that successful kaizen events require a great deal of preparation and follow up to be successful. The IF methodology, for instance, consists of several stages.

- A one-day pre-diagnostic to select the area, discuss expectations, and review measures and the measurement systems that are in place.
- An initial preparation period during which measures and basic quality and demand data are collected. This is the scoping stage.
- After about two weeks, a three-day Diagnostic event takes place. The aim here is to establish and clarify what is to be the aim of the event itself. The team is chosen. Mapping is typical here, as is basic education on the Seven Wastes and the Seven Tools of Quality. The chosen team makes a presentation to management and everyone concerned on what they aim to do during the event. Objectives are agreed, and all necessary authorisations made. During the event, you do not want to have to seek permission to make changes. Assurances must be established on possible reduction in manning levels. Sometimes a Lean game is played by the team and perhaps by the operators from the area.
- A further period of preparation takes place over the next few weeks. The measures are firmed up. Final preparation takes place. This may include, for instance, building ahead of schedule to ensure continuity of service during the event, and warning support staff such as maintenance and electricians to be on hand for the event. Any foreseen resources such as tools, tables, boards, racks, and post-its must be acquired.
- A check day takes place during this period for any final arrangements.
- The event itself is a five-day workshop. The idea is to go round the PDCA cycle a few times, ending with some tested, standardised changes. The workshop is facilitated by an IF engineer. Measures are taken each day. On the last day a presentation is made. Follow up actions are given to specific people.
- After the five-day workshop, three one-day follow up sessions are held at monthly intervals. These are to ensure that changes, which could not be put in

place during the workshop, are in fact implemented. Examples are moving a machine embedded in concrete or targeting a quality issue that was not 'cracked' during the workshop.
- Finally, the IF engineer stays in contact with the organisation for an extended period to check sustainability.

A kaizen event can target different aspects. Layout and 5S often come first. Safety may be chosen in an environment with difficult union issues. Later, follow-up events can address lead time and manning.

Below is a proven methodology.

Generally:

- The workshop itself is the easy part. The harder and longer parts are the preparation and follow-up.
- The participation of managers, supervisors and team leaders is essential. The participation of customers is highly desirable, if not essential, certainly in the Interactive and often in the Custom types of process.
- Do not rely excessively on kaizen events – they are only a small part of wider Lean implementation.
- Events should be co-ordinated through a wider Lean implementation program. Although non-bottleneck kaizens are acceptable from the point of view of motivation, the first priority should be on bottleneck or problem areas that will make an impact on cost, quality and delivery.
- All participants should have a clear understanding of how the particular event will contribute to the overall Lean vision and objectives.
- A good facilitator is essential.
- Early successes are contagious.
- Visual management (e.g. a 'war room' for maps) is needed.
- Recognition is vital.
- Involve a few 'outsiders' – people outside the area but not necessarily from outside the company.
- A standardised approach should be developed on a site.
- Write up the event on an A3 and display it on the wall for a standardised period of perhaps 18 months.
- Follow up is crucial. Loose ends must be closed off within a few weeks at most.

The Kaizen Event Process

Some weeks ahead of the event:

- Select the area – probably from mapping an end-to-end value stream or from an accumulation of problems. Certainly take the overall 'systems view' of the process, including the customer, to avoid working on a process that should not be there in the first place.

- In service events, give specific consideration to whether the system boundary or problem area should be extended to include customer systems.
- In all service cases it is important to see the process from the customer's perspective. This aspect must be covered before the event begins.
- Select an appropriate time for the event. This is more important in an office than a factory because variation is usually larger.
- The group needs to be warned about the event, and participants from the group sought.
- Measures: decide on relevant measures for the area, and take the measures. But be very careful that measures remain measures, and do not become targets.
- Team selection: one or more facilitators, front line managers from the area, the event owner, participants from the area, subject matter experts, people from the next most likely area for an event, outsiders. Around twelve is a good number – bigger for bigger areas, smaller for smaller areas.
- Give consideration to 'tagging' in office areas where there are longer cycle activity durations. Tagging could involve placing 'travellers' on documents, or it could be done electronically - requesting people to enter arrival times and departure times on the traveller. Of course, this needs to be explained to the group.
- Draw up an 'Event Charter'. This sets out
  - the focus or principle concern of the event;
  - the aims of the event – what it is hoped will be achieved;
  - current issues in the area to be addressed during the event
  - the event boundary;
  - demand data: how much work the office or area handles per day, and how this varies across the day, week, month;
  - the dates of the event and duration;
  - who the participants are to be – including the facilitator;
  - what extra rooms will be used;
  - catering arrangements;
  - health and safety considerations (if electrical points or heavy items may be moved)
  - any approvals that may be needed should be signed off;
  - the extent to which work will continue in the area (if at all) during the event. If not, what to do.
  - any training that may be required.

The event itself (typical)

- **Day 1**: introductions, aims and scope, background. Why the event is important, event methodology, basic Lean training including mapping, waste awareness, tools such as the fishbone diagram, and, if relevant, practice on observation timing.

- **Day 2**: go to the area and observe, map the routings, time durations, discuss the process with the people. Possibly with the customers in some types of service process. Many offices have longer cycle operations so it may not be possible to observe or time all activities, so tagging (see above) or sample events may be used. If possible observe several cycles. Begin to generate ideas.
- **Day 3**: generate ideas, discuss round the maps, formulate plans to implement. Start the implementation.
- **Day 4**: the main day for implementation. Try out and adjust. Discuss with office workers and other shifts. Begin to prepare flipcharts for the presentation on Day 5. Check or estimate the measures.
- **Day 5**: a final check and adjust. Document the new process. List follow-up items. Prepare an A3 summary sheet. Finish flipcharts for presentation. Present to area managers and senior directors. Agree next steps. Enjoy the free buffet.

After the event it is necessary to

- Close off any outstanding points. On the last day of the event the persons responsible for doing or coordinating these mopping-up mini-projects must be identified. The event champion or a line manager MUST follow these up. In at least one service organisation, kaizen events lost credibility due to the ever-increasing list of outstanding topics that were never closed down.
- Have a review session every (say) month for a period of (say) six months. These may be very short meetings. But they are there to look at the continuing performance of the area, and, very importantly, to record lessons learned. In other words they are 'after action reviews'.

Some lessons learned about kaizen events over recent years

- The workshop itself is the easy part. The harder and longer part is the preparation and follow-up. An approximate time split is 40% preparation, 30% workshop, and 30% follow-up.
- The participation of managers in events is essential. Without this they will be lukewarm or even critical. Management participation also helps to overcome the problem of seeking authorisation.
- The participation of the supervisor or team leader from the area is essential.
- Moreover, the supervisor should attend one or two events in other areas before it is the turn of his or her area. Think how you would feel if a team descended on your area for a week and produced a 40% productivity improvement. Not too good – you may be motivated to show that what has been done was not all that good in retrospect. Ideally, when it is the turn of the supervisor to have a kaizen event in his area, he will already be the most enthusiastic participant, having experienced it elsewhere.

- Kaizen events should be co-ordinated through a Lean Promotion Office (or similar) in relation to a wider Lean implementation programme, via value stream mapping.
- All participants should have a clear understanding how the particular event contributes to the overall Lean vision or objectives.
- A good facilitator is invaluable. The ability to spot waste and opportunity builds slowly. Take the opportunity to transfer some of these skills.
- Blitz events work better in supportive companies. See the quotation from Henry Ford above. Do not set expectations too high. Under-promise and over-deliver.
- Sustainability remains the big issue.

Finally, we have identified a number of good and not so good practices:

Good:

- Have a systems view of the context into which the study area fits.
- Evidence of senior management leadership and direction setting, staff access to management, and recognition of successes.
- Link the event to some benefit to the employees – such as space saving used for a coffee area, or improved furniture.
- Have a short follow up review session every month for a few months.
- Customer and stakeholder focus.
- Employee involvement.
- Training and development and use of the Investors in People Standard.
- High energy and participation from everyone involved.
- When management is engaged, roadblocks are removed quickly.
- When everyone involved in events is prepared to 'roll up their sleeves' – this has a strong impact on the people on the office floor.
- External help is invaluable in events until they become well established.
- Have events across the board at all stages end-to-end: customer facing, clerical, administrative, operations, distribution, maintenance.
- Awareness of Lean generates pull for training in some areas of the organisation.
- Learn from failures. Some events will fail – have a careful look back and seek answers.
- Measurement and feedback on the measures are important.

Cautions:

Although Kaizen Events can be very successful in delivering productivity gains in a local area, and for creating attitude change, a manager should be aware of the following:

- Does the kaizen event have the effect of shifting problems to another area? Many kaizens make great, and justified, claims relating to the area but in fact make things worse elsewhere. Keep in mind that it is the end-to-end performance that matters.

- Are the improvements real? In other words is the improvement merely 'common cause' variation, or is it significant 'special cause'? A good way to tell is to draw a run diagram of the relevant measure starting some time (months?) before the event, and ending some time after the event.
- Is the improvement merely the 'Hawthorne Effect'? In other words, the main change is as a result of the short term interest being taken in the area by managers rather than a fundamental process change? Such improvements are likely to disappear as soon as manager interest decreases.
- Is the improvement the result of a 'work harder' cycle rather than a 'work smarter cycle'? As explained by Repenning and Sterman, the 'work harder cycle' generates short term improvement but longer term decline (as a result of reducing improvement time), whereas the 'work smarter' cycle often means a short term decrease in performance (whilst learning occurs), but a longer term improvement.

Other cautions include....

- Target kaizen events on key business metrics, not just in areas willing to participate.
- Build on what has been learned and leverage to other areas without it necessitating another kaizen event.
- Develop internal competencies – don't depend on external consultants/trainers
- Ensure all actions chosen for completion during kaizen event are directly related to achieving the charter.

Not so good:

- lack of identification of critical success factors;
- lack of understanding of the concepts of quality and continuous improvement by some managers and employees;
- insufficient integration of continuous improvement activities;
- existence of a 'blame culture' when mistakes occur which may inhibit innovation;
- benefits not showing on financial radar, benefits not reaching the bottom line;
- poor follow through – failure to close out on actions;
- lack of visibility for non-participants – use visual displays/ storyboards on the floor during and after the event – keep everyone informed of progress;
- reliance on 'quick fixes' and fire fighting.

Further Reading

Nicola Bateman, *Sustainability: A Guide to Process Improvement*, Lean Enterprise Research Centre, Cardiff University and Industry Forum, 2001. *See LERC website.*
Sid Joynson and Andrew Forrester, *Sid's Heroes: 30% Improvement in Productivity in 2 Days*, BBC, London, 1996
Anthony C Laraia, Patricia Moody, and Robert Hall, *The Kaizen Blitz: Accelerating Breakthroughs in Productivity and Performance,* John Wiley and Sons, New York, 1999
Siobhan Geary, *Kaizen Blitz*, MSc dissertation, LERC, Cardiff, 2006
The best magazine/journal on 'kaizen blitz' is *Target: The Periodical of the Association for Manufacturing Excellence.* More recently the magazine has begun to include office and administration examples.

Acknowledgements

Thanks to Andy Brophy
Thanks also to Bjarne Olsen of SAS who really brought home the importance of involving the customer.

4.13 Idea Management

Using the Ideas of your people: 6 Steps

One of the potent but under-utilised concepts in service is to use the ideas of staff for improvement. 'Ideas are Free,' says Alan Robinson.

Here follow 6 steps

    1   Communicate the vision

It has been said that change is only possible when there is either a crisis or a clear vision. The ability to visualise and articulate the future state for an organisation is vital. Toyota has a phrase for this long-term vision – "True North". The vision or purpose should align and energise the entire workforce. It should connect with our emotions; we are driven by emotions not reason. Vision or purpose is the essence of what the organisation is delivering. This must be instilled into every level of the organisation and be utilised as a source of inspiration for improvement ideas. It becomes the magnet to set in motion the energy for congruent ideas. This clarity of purpose is not achieved overnight; hence we need to develop and filter ideas quickly (ideally self-filter) to support the vision.

It is no good having ideas about improving activities that should not take place at all – that are part of an inappropriate system design – unless the ideas are directed at removing such activities entirely. Hence the need for clear vision or purpose.
It is management's prime task to foster improvement. That means continually communicating the vision or direction, encouraging a questioning attitude, ensuring that movement towards the vision takes place, removing barriers, and insisting on testing assumptions, ideas, and hypotheses.

    2   Generate ideas – continually, not in batches like kaizen events

Idea activity needs to develop into an "everyday ideas" practice. Instil the mindset of the tortoise versus the rabbit. The rabbit makes progress in quick bursts but sleeps frequently along the race, so much in fact that he loses the race to the tortoise with his slow but persevering pace.

Regular kaizen events are positive, especially at early stages of Lean implementation, but should not have the effect of batching ideas whilst waiting for the next event.
Idea submission needs to be made easy. No complex forms or procedures. Make it visible. Perhaps use an idea white board or small cards that move through the stages of implementation. Get the idea out in the open, and develop the detail later. Often, it will not be good enough to sit back and wait for ideas. The flow of ideas may be meagre. So, ideas will often need to be focused on a theme – like improving customer

experience, reducing delay, cutting weight, improving safety, or finding new customers.

3   Filter good and inappropriate ideas fast, and give feedback

Clearly, the generation of ideas from everyone can give huge competitive advantage. This is necessary but not sufficient. Ideas need to be filtered – good from inappropriate. At the same time, bureaucracy must be avoided.

Filtration needs to be done in such a way that it does not discourage further ideas. Indeed, even inappropriate ideas should be viewed positively as evidence that people are thinking about improvement. Encouragement may lead to a string of valuable ideas later. An unsuitable idea also brings opportunity to develop the employee. Why did they not know that their idea would be unsuitable? And some inappropriate ideas may be the seed for a valuable idea, because they have at least uncovered an opportunity.

4   Implement good ideas, fast, and give recognition

The most powerful and effective motivator for future ideas is recognition and implementation.

Not implementing an idea fast is the same as rejecting an idea. Maybe worse – if insincerity is suspected. Show the progress of implementation on a board – perhaps using a Plan Do Study Act cycle.

Thought will need to be given as to how to implement low cost, high return ideas almost immediately with the minimum of fuss and delay – perhaps decentralised budgets for this purpose. Indeed, this point, and points 2 and 3, all suggest that idea management needs to be as decentralised as possible.

It is said that Toyota has a greater than 95% implementation rate for ideas as many of them are not implemented in their original form, but are enriched with the employee.

Recognition needs to be compatible with the culture of the organisation, but bear in mind the ample evidence against large individual monetary rewards. Most ideas originate with a person but are developed and implemented by a team. Recognition, always starting but not necessarily ending with a simple 'thank you', needs to reflect this.

5   Communicate and spread ideas to other potential benefactors

The fifth element is to communicate and spread good ideas around the organisation, to other areas where the idea may be applicable. Otherwise it is wasted potential. This is a huge challenge, with two sub-problems. First, to identify (or self-identify) the area where the idea may be useful. Second, overcoming the 'not invented here' syndrome. Hence, 'roll in' rather than "roll out"; self-discovery rather than imposition.

Thought will need to be given to spreading ideas, ranging from a measles chart showing the location of ideas to data base solutions.

6   Create a culture for all this to work well

And finally, a management style or culture that fosters, or better insists on, the first five happening. As is so often the case with Lean implementation, success depends on both top-down and bottom-up effort.

An example: say someone has the idea that to process a big batch of documents all together is a good idea. After all, it may save the waste of 'changeover' and reduce errors. Do we simply accept and implement the idea? Of course not! Easy for a person well versed in Lean to understand that this would be counterproductive. But not necessarily easy for the person making the idea accept. Worse, out-of-hand rejection, may "turn that person off", causing resentment, and possibly discouraging the person from making a real break-though idea next time around. The best way to prevent this is by "Socratic Engagement": don't just reject the idea out of hand (or worse, don't give any reaction – just forget it) but talk it through by asking questions. "What would a large batch do to the completion of other tasks?" "What will that do to total work in process?" "What happens if the whole batch is found to be incorrect?" This must be genuine talk-through, genuine dialog including listening, not questioning merely to disprove. In fact, there may be a situation where a large batch IS warranted!

For questioning to be effective there must be clear vision of the ideal state. Is the idea moving us towards that ideal? This is one of the most challenging areas for management – to communicate the vision. Note that this is explicitly not setting "stretch goals" or KPI's for next year! It is Toyota's True North, The HP Way, The Apple vision of a beautiful, friendly machine, South West's vision of low cost but fun.

If the vision is clearly understood by all, a filter device is not required. Ideas will self-filter. That is an ideal in itself, possibly approached by Toyota. But for many, a degree of filtering will be required.

Further reading

Andy Brophy and John Bicheno, *Innovative Lean*, PICSIE Books, 2010

Alan Robinson and Dean Schroeder, *Ideas are Free*, Berrett Koehler, 2006

4.14 The Kano Model

Dr Noriaki Kano is a Japanese quality expert who is best known for his excellent 'Kano model'. The Kano Model has emerged as one of the most useful and powerful aids to product and service design and improvement. It is included here because of its relevance to QFD, the design process and R&D.

The Kano model relates three factors, which Kano argues are present in every product or service, to their degree of implementation or level of implementation, as shown in the diagram. Kano's three factors are Basic (or 'must be'), Performance (or 'more is better'), and Delighter (or excitement). The degree of customer satisfaction ranges from 'dissatisfaction', through neutrality, to 'delight'.

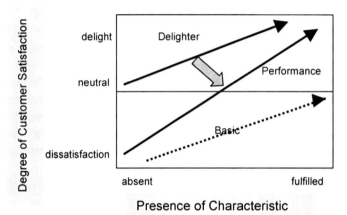

A Basic factor is something that a customer simply expects to be there. If it is not present the customer will be dissatisfied or disgusted, but if it is fully implemented or present it will merely result in a feeling of neutrality. Examples are clean sheets in a hotel, a station tuner on a radio, or windscreen washers on a car. Note that there may be degrees of implementation: sheets may be clean but blemished. Basic factors should not be taken for granted, or regarded as easy to satisfy; some may even be exceptionally difficult to identify. One example is course handouts, which a lecturer may regard as trivial but the audience may regard as a basic necessity. If you don't get the basics right, everything else may fail. To this extent it's like Maslow's Hierarchy of Needs: it's no good thinking about self-esteem needs unless survival needs are catered for. Market research is of limited value for Basics because they are simply expected. A service provider therefore needs to build up a list by accumulating past experience, by observation, and by organised feedback.

A Performance factor can cause dissatisfaction at one extreme, but if fully implemented it can result in 'delight'. This factor is also termed 'more is better' but it could also be 'faster is better' or 'easier is better'. Performance factors are usually in existence already, but they are neutral, causing neither 'dissatisfaction' nor 'delight'. It is not so much the fact that the Performance factor exists, but how it can be improved, which is important. The challenge is to identify it, and to change its performance.

Examples are speed of check-in at a hotel, ease of tuning on a radio, or fuel consumption. Performance factors represent a real opportunity to designers and to R&D staff. They may be identified through market research, but observation is also important, especially in identifying those that are causing dissatisfaction. Creativity or process redesign is often required to deliver the factor faster or more easily, and information support may play a role, as in the 'one minute' check-in at some top hotels. The 'cycle of service' (see separate section) is a useful starting point to identify Performance factors.

Finally, a Delighter is something that customers do not expect, but may increase delight. Examples are flowers and wine awaiting guest arrivals in some hotel rooms, or a radio tuner that retunes itself when moving out of range of a transmitter. Identifying true Delighters requires the study of early adopters. By definition, market research is of little use here, at least ahead of time: you cannot ask the customer, 'What don't you expect?' Once again, it is creativity, based on an appreciation of (latent) customer needs, which can provide the breakthrough.

We should also note that the Kano factors are not static. What may be a Delighter this year may migrate towards being a Basic in a few years time. And also, what may be a Delighter in one part of the world may be a Basic in another. Thus it is crucial to keep up to date with changing customer expectations. Benchmarking may be a way to go. From Kano we also learn that a reactive quality policy, reacting to complaints, or Dissatisfiers, will at best lead to neutrality, but proactive action is required to create 'delight'. As Schneider and Bowen state, 'If you dissatisfy customers by not meeting their expectations you can still recover', but 'If you dissatisfy customers by not meeting their basic needs you will lose them'. In a time when customer retention is increasingly important to profitability, the Kano concepts are therefore key.

The Kano Model works well with Quality Function Deployment. Basics should be satisfied, and Delighters can be explicitly traded off in the 'roof' of the QFD matrix. For example, fuel consumption may suggest a lighter car, but safety a stronger one - so the quest is to find material that is light, strong, and inexpensive.

Further Reading

John Bicheno and Phil Catherwood, *Six Sigma and The Quality Toolbox*, PICSIE Books, 2004
Readings in English are difficult to obtain, but an excellent article is Hofmeister, Walters, Gongos, 'Discovering Customer WOW's', *Annual Quality Congress*, ASQC, May 1996, pp. 759-770
Lou Cohen, *Quality Function Deployment*, Addison Wesley, Reading MA, 1995, pp. 36-41

4.15　Clues of Quality

In the two customer intensive segments of the service classification matrix, Interactive and Custom, it is the total customer experience that makes the difference between highly rated and indifferent service.

We have already learned about Jan Carlsson's concept of Moments of Truth, Cycle of Service, the RATER service dimensions, and the Kano model. Leonard Berry (building on the work of Carbone and Haeckel) has added to this already useful list with his concept of Clues of Quality. Clues of quality are anything that a customer experiences on his or journey through the Cycle of Service. These 'clues' may be what the customer sees, feels, hears, smells, touches, or generally senses. The word 'clues' is useful. A clue is a piece of evidence or something that gives an indication. Thus it is not necessarily definitive.

A point Berry makes is that today there are many services (like health care, financial services, consulting engineering) where the layman does not have the technical skills to judge the service. The customer therefore seeks 'clues'.

According to Berry, the process is taking place continually, and customers are constantly filtering and processing these clues in deciding on the quality of the service and whether they will stay, repeat buy, or communicate favourably. Perhaps this continual monitoring is what differentiates the concept from, moments of truth that are experienced at those particular moments when a customer comes into contact with the service provider.

Berry and his predecessors distinguish three types of Clues.

- **Functional clues** are related to the reliability dimension of RATER, but go further. They are clues that give an indication of the technical performance. These are the 'whats' of the service. They are the facts – did the service provider get it right from a fact point of view? It is the core of the service. Studies of the RATER dimensions have consistently shown reliability to be the most important aspect. But that is not enough....
- **Mechanic clues** relate to the tangible dimension of RATER but go further than the physical environment of things that can be seen and touched to include 'sights, smells, sounds, tastes, and textures'.
- **Humanic clues** relate to the assurance, empathy, and responsiveness but go further to include aspects like tone of voice, enthusiasm, and body language.

These last two are the 'hows' of the service. They relate to the emotions. How did the customer FEEL about the service?

Notice that a service provider can get it right from a fact point of view but not necessarily from an emotional point of view. Many have had the experience of a surly passport official who stamps you passport but does not make eye contact, say a friendly word, or even give an indication or clue that you are human. Likewise many will have had the experience of a friendly, happy secretary who is nevertheless rather incompetent. This leads to a 2 x 2 classification: What and How, against satisfactory and not. Only one of the four segments is likely to win and retain a customer.

The three types of clue are linked through expectations. And we know that expectations influence satisfaction. Whilst functional clues help customers decide on technical competence, 'mechanic' clues colour a customer's expectations. Many studies, including some in the field of 'behavioural economics' show that the physical environment has an effect on peoples' attitude and optimism as in the effect on sales of identical products in new and old stores, (music also plays a role here), or on student ratings of the same lecture given in different rooms. Hence the link between the two – they must match. Likewise humanic clues that Berry maintains give the opportunity to exceed expectations – the delighters as in the Kano model. So we end with the three-legged stool. Like the P's of the marketing mix, the types of clue need to be compatible. They should reinforce.

Mechanic clues are the prime concern of service design approaches. Refer to the sections on this important topic. Attention to detail is what is called for, often picked up by detailed observation by customers 'at the gemba'. The IDEO company favours not only detailed focused observation at the point of use rather than market surveys, but also prototype participation with customers.

Humanic clues should also not be left to chance. Berry gives a list of 'ideal physician behaviours' that doctors at Mayo clinic are coached on. In the TWI method (see separate section) one of the three skills that all supervisors should be taught is JR – job relations. A skill can be taught through practice. And TWI JR, for instance, teaches managers to treat people as individuals, to listen first –to get the whole story, not to jump to conclusions or to 'pass the buck'. Surely, these are ways to improve the humanic clues.

Further reading

Leonard Berry and Kent Seltman, *Management Lessons from Mayo Clinic*, McGraw Hill, 2008, Chapter 7
Leonard Berry and Lewis Carbone, 'Build Loyalty through Experience Management', *Quality Progress*, September 2007.

4.16 The RATER Dimensions and Service Gaps

Zeithaml, Parasuraman and Berry (or PZB as they are sometimes known) have developed over several years a well-researched and tested methodology for the 'dimensions' of service and the 'gaps' that exist between the service that customers expect and their perception of the service they have received.

The Dimensions

The PZB dimensions or determinants of service are known by the mnemonic RATER (easy to remember: how do you rate the service?).

R: Reliability: the ability to perform the service dependably and accurately. That is, doing what they say they will do, reliably and accurately. Understandably, surveys have found this to be the most important dimension. If your bank transactions are incorrect you don't care what the bank looks like or how friendly they are.
A: Assurance: the possession of the required knowledge, the skill to perform the service, and the ability to convey trust, confidence and security.
T: Tangibles: the physical appearance of the place, dress of the staff, stationery, signs, and equipment. The visual appeal of the facilities.
E: Empathy: the ability to understand the customer's needs and to provide an individual, sympathetic, caring, listening service.
R: Responsiveness: the willingness to help and respond quickly to individual requirements.

Together these are known as SERVQUAL, a registered phrase widely known in service. SERVQUAL is an instrument for measuring customer perceptions of service quality. The SERVQUAL instrument is available in PZB's book, *Delivering Service Quality*. It was developed from a large number of dimensions mentioned in customer interviews and reduced to five by statistical analysis. Of course, like many theories, the prime research was done in the USA and does not necessarily apply worldwide. For example, research by Mahesh at the University of Buckingham shows that Far East Airline passengers value respect above reliability.

The Gaps

Related to SERVQUAL is the very useful and widely known Gaps Model. Gap analysis helps to identify the causes of service quality shortfalls in each of the five RATER dimensions. The model is shown in the next figure.

According to PZB, customers build an expectation of the service to be received depending on four factors:

- word of mouth communication – the most powerful;
- personal needs;
- past experience;
- communications put out by the service provider, which create their own expectations.

Gap 1 results from the difference between what customers expect and what management perceives these expectations to be. This can occur, for example, as a result of management not undertaking sufficient research, or from communications failures between the front line staff who actually hear the customer's complaints and requirements, and management. It could be that management fails to 'Go to Gemba', in Lean speak.

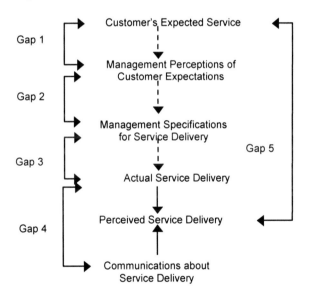

**The Gaps Model, adapted from
Zeithaml, Parasuraman and Berry
'Delivering Service Quality',
Free Press, 1990**

Gap 2 results from the difference between management perceptions of what customers expect and the specifications that management draws up, or fails to draw up, spelling out what service delivery actions are required. This can be the result of inadequate management commitment or interest, a perception that the staff already know what is required, a perception that it is impossible to convey the requirements, or a failure in the way in which the company sets its goals in relation to its customers.

This last point amounts to a failure in the Policy Deployment process, as described in a later section.

Gap 3 results from a mismatch between the service delivery specifications required by management and the actual service delivered by front line staff. There are many possible reasons for this gap. They include inappropriate training, poor teamwork, and inappropriate standards. A big reason, discussed several times in this book, is inappropriate targets or measures – for example inappropriate productivity targets in a call centre.

Gap 4 results from the difference between the actual service that is delivered and communications that are put out to customers about what to expect. Perhaps a misleading Service Level Agreement or a glossy brochure portraying an idyllic holiday resort. There is a common 'propensity to over-promise' which is distinct from a marketing puff that many would forgive. Better to under-promise and over-deliver, than the reverse.

Gap 5 is the overall gap resulting from all the other 'provider' gaps. This is the gap between the expected service and the perceived service experience. Notice the word 'perceived'. It means that service quality is relative, not absolute, and different customers may perceive the same service in different ways. It is the customer who has 'all the votes', not the service provider.

Of significance to Lean service mapping and process improvement is that Gap 1 more or less corresponds to Purpose, Gap 2 to process design, and Gap 3 to process implementation and execution. Gap 4 is not explicitly covered but is obviously important. PZB provide a survey instrument in their book, which enables the 'antecedents' of the various gaps to be identified. This is clearly a very useful addition to the improvement of any process.

Grönroos, in his usual thoughtful way, cautions about using measurement instruments that are based on comparisons between expectations and experiences:

- if expectations are measured after the experience, what is being measured is not really expectation;
- measuring expectations before the experience also has its problems because expectations may change during the experience.

Grönroos suggests seven criteria of good perceived service quality. These are

- professionalism and skills;
- reputation and credibility;

- Servicescape;
- attitudes and behaviour;
- accessibility and flexibility;
- reliability and trustworthiness;
- service recovery.

Professionalism is related to outcome, and reputation is related to image. The first two criteria may therefore prove unsatisfactory irrespective of the mechanical process. Servicescape is discussed under Interactive Mapping.

However, as Kano points out, the last four criteria are process-related and therefore of great relevance to this book.

Further Reading

Valerie Zeithaml, Mary Jo Bitner and Dayne Gremler, *Services Marketing*, 4th edition, McGraw Hill, Boston, 2006, Chapter 4
Valerie Zeithaml, A Parasuraman and Leonard Berry, *Delivering Quality Service*, Free Press, 1990
Christian Grönroos, *Service Management and Marketing*, 3rd edition, Wiley, 2007, Chapter 4

4.17 Loyalty and Retention

Customers need to be acquired and retained. Building loyalty is a key to both. But the lock for the key is good operations.

Loyalty and retention have become big issues in service and manufacturing, since the evidence has mounted that loyal customers buy more products and services over time and become ever more profitable. Witness the growth of loyalty cards during the 1990s. Loyal customers are less expensive to reach by advertising, are early adopters of new products and services, and tend to give an increasing share of their business to their preferred suppliers. Loyal customers are also the source of word-of-mouth advertising, which is highly effective, and free! However, the concepts are not without their critics. There is a need to distinguish between truly loyal customers and, for example, those who use the service because it is convenient or those who are locked in by contract.

For service operations it is necessary to understand that there are at least two categories of loyalty: to the brand, and to the service provider. These are inter-related. For example, a car dealership and maintenance centre may have customers who are loyal to the car brand or to the dealership or both. Research has shown that:

- the operations part of the service can destroy loyalty to the brand – as has frequently happened with car dealerships;
- where there is loyalty both to the service operation and to the brand there are powerful synergistic effects.

While brand loyalty is not the subject of this book, the building of loyalty through service operations is central. Lean service operations therefore play an important and synergistic role with marketing.

Assael, reproduced in Keiningham *et al*, has proposed a useful framework for thinking about loyalty. The Assael framework is redrawn and adapted below for comparison with the service mapping typology used in this book.

	Low Involvement	High Involvement
Active Decision Making	Limited customer decision making (Idealised?)	Intensive customer decision making (Custom?)
Passive Decision Making (acts historically)	Rote purchasing (Transactional?)	Brand loyalty (Interactive?)

Of course there is not supposed to be any one-on-one mapping between the mapping typology matrix and the matrix given above, but the parallels are clear.

The point is that high involvement customers begin with active decision making, and migrate towards the bottom right hand corner as successful purchases are made and the risk is seen to decline. There are interesting implications for service operations here: build up the positive experiences early on and then customers do less evaluation of other products and services as they become used to good service. But this does not mean that you can rely on such 'loyalty', because customers will still experiment with other service providers.

This can be compared with Stauss and Neuhaus, who suggest 'five quality levels of satisfaction'.

	Demanding Satisfied	Stable Satisfied	Resigned Satisfied	Stable Dissatisfied	Demanding Dissatisfied
Feeling	Optimism	Faith	Ignorance	Disappointment	Protest
Repurchase	Definitely	Probably	Maybe	Unlikely	No way

Measuring Loyalty

Reichheld, Sasser and others at Harvard originally established the principle of the lifetime value of a customer. The lifetime value can be estimated by multiplying the average spend per period by the estimated period of retention. Additional purchases and profits made from referrals can be added to this, and the savings made by not advertising to established customers can be subtracted.

By contrast, Reichheld suggests (1996) that a company may lose 50% of its customer base by not managing retention, and he therefore suggests that retention is as important a measure as profit or ROI.

Reichheld then proposed 'the ultimate question': 'How likely is it that you would recommend company x to a friend or colleague?' This 'ultimate question', Reichheld believes, captures both 'head' dimensions such as price, quality, ease of use and so on but also 'heart' dimensions or feel-good factors: the sense that the organisation understands, listens, and shares the customer's principles. The ultimate question is answered on a scale of 0 to 10, where answers from 0 to 6 are 'detractors', answers of 7 or 8 are 'passive', and answers of 9 or 10 are 'promoters'. Then the net promoter score (NPS) is the percentage of 'promoters' minus the percentage of 'detractors'. A positive score is the minimum acceptable. This is a good way of measuring the effectiveness of a service process.

Reichheld now believes that a lifetime value needs to distinguish between promoters and detractors – because promoters defect to other providers at lower rates, are less price-sensitive, increase their spend over time more rapidly, and are likely to use word-of-mouth promotion more widely.

TARP, a Boston based consultancy, has produced an often-quoted set of findings (Goodman). These are:

- problems decrease customer loyalty by 15% to 30%;
- most customers encountering problems do not complain to the company but many of them will tell their friends – hence the importance of actively soliciting complaints;
- quality of service can affect loyalty – perhaps a 50% gain in some industries: customers who are completely satisfied with the resolution of a problem exhibit no less loyalty and sometimes more; 'Mollified' complainants, by contrast, are only slightly more loyal than dissatisfied complainants;
- service can affect word-of-mouth behaviour – customers who are dissatisfied tell twice as many people about their experiences as do satisfied customers.

Reichheld identifies three categories of loyalty: customer, employee, and investor. Loyal employees are increasingly seen as being necessary for loyal customers. A prerequisite.

Zeithaml and Bitner suggest that there are four types of retention strategy:

1   **financial bonds**, for example, loyalty cards, pricing, and bundling;
2   **social bonds**, created by building personal relationships – these are more common in professional services;
3   **customisation bonds**, whereby the provider seeks to understand the detailed requirements of customers through anticipation and customer knowledge – for example books provided with customised covers;
4   **structural bonds**, where the service is designed specifically for the customer – for example by joint investment and in the book example by adapting the contents to specific company requirements.

These four levels may be seen as successive, with Level 2 building on Level 1 for example.

Reichheld (2001) also suggests that really to win loyal customers requires very senior managers to 'walk that talk'. He proposes six principles:

1   **preach what you practise**: the leader must articulate his views as well as practise them;
2   **win-win**: build loyalty by making sure that both the company and the customer win – it's no win if you take advantage;
3   **be picky**: choose the customers to work with, don't accept everyone just for short term gains;
4   **keep it simple**: decentralise and delegate real authority to make service decisions rapidly;
5   **reward the right results**: make sure that loyalty is rewarded, not short term gains;
6   **'listen hard, talk straight'**: 'Seek first to understand then to be understood': this is really a restatement of one of Stephen Covey's seven principles.

Is Loyalty worth pursuing for all Customers?

Apparently not. Some financial institutions now differentiate customers on a Pareto (ABC) basis. 'A' class customers are cultivated with great attention, but 'C' class are just not worth the effort. Worse, paying attention to 'terrorist' customers may divert attention from good prospects. Some institutions have actively tried to discourage some customers from running high transaction, low balance accounts. This may be sensible and pragmatic, but remember that some of the C class customers may eventually turn into A class. Dimensions other than current return are necessary.

The Opportunity Box concept may be useful here. See separate section.

The Myth of Loyalty?

How much of the theory on loyalty is a myth? Henry warns of six common flaws or myths about loyalty. Remember that retention is not the same as loyalty.

1. There may be many reasons for retention hiding under the heading of loyalty (i.e. geographically locked in, no alternative, switching costs, risk avoidance, other incentives such as frequent flyer schemes).
2. Profitability may be ascribed to loyalty when in fact superior business design drives both.
3. Managerial complacency. Customers aren't loyal they are just with the organisation for some temporary benefit until something better appears. But management believes them to be loyal.
4. Lifetime value is overstated. A realistic 'lifetime' may be only a few years, so be very conservative.
5. A competitor's apparently loyal customers discourage effort.

In hard times when cash is short, all of the theory about loyalty may go out of the window for all but the wealthy.

Keiningham *et al* give a list of an amazing 53 myths about loyalty grouped into six categories concerning, for instance, myths about customers, about loyalty programmes, about employees, and about goals and profitability.

Further Reading

John Goodman, Pat O'Brien and Eden Segal, 'Turning CFOs into Quality Champions', *Quality Progress*, March 2000, pp. 47-54
Timothy Keiningham *et al*, *Loyalty Myths*, Wiley, 2005
Frederick Reichheld, *The Loyalty Effect*, Harvard Business School Press, 1996
Frederick Reichheld and W Sasser, 'Zero Defections: Quality Comes to Services', *Harvard Business Review*, Sept-Oct 1990, pp. 105–111
Frederick Reichheld, 'Lead for Loyalty', *Harvard Business Review*, July-August 2001, pp. 76–84
Frederick Reichheld, *The Ultimate Question*, Harvard Business School Press, 2006
Christopher Lovelock and Lauren Wright, *Principles of Service Marketing and Management*, Prentice Hall, New York, 1999
Craig Douglas Henry, 'Is Customer Loyalty a Pernicious Myth?' *Business Horizons*, July-August 2000, pp. 13-16

Reference

W. Biemans, 'Satisfaction vs. Loyalty', Lecture Notes of University of Groningen, Holland, 2000

4.18   Mapping the Flow of Customer Feedback and Complaints

What happens when customers complain or give feedback? This can be as important as mapping the forward flows. The following steps are required:

- Is there a person who has responsibility for feedback and complaints (F&C)? If it is everyone's job, it will probably be nobody's. Appoint a person with F&C responsibility. This person is not responsible for taking the action – someone at the lowest and most immediate level must often take actions very quickly – but he does have the responsibility for making sure that the processes work.
- Identify the prime points at which customers complain or give feedback – typically front line staff, but also correspondence, internet, or telephone. Every Moment of Truth interaction is a potential point of feedback or complaint.
- Does every front line employee or person likely to encounter F&C have a standard procedure? Five immediate actions and two medium-term actions are generally required: apology, acknowledgement, thanks, resolution, and communication immediately, improvement and prevention in the medium term.
- What employee empowerment or authority is appropriate for short-term resolution? Levels of seriousness in particular should be considered.
- Is the path of communication clear, unambiguous, and immediate?
- Who is responsible for improvement and prevention?
- Where does the information accumulate?

The Opportunity Box and Transaction Box

The Opportunity Box is a conceptual tool to help with prioritisation of improvement activities, especially in relation to Interactive mapping. The intention is that it is applied at critical Moments of Truth – those that have high 'leverage'. The Opportunity Box idea can also be used in relation to loyalty considerations.

The basis is that there are different categories of customer, from favourably disposed to highly critical. How much effort should be put into converting customers into a more favourable category?

Here we will call the categories:

- **Apostles**: these customers are enthusiastic and loyal. They spread the 'good news' by word of mouth. They believe in the service provider. Their confidence is hard to shake. They often give helpful feedback because they have the welfare of the supplier at heart.

- **Hostages**: users of the service but with little loyalty. They only use the service because they have to. Perhaps they have a contract or they live near to the service provider – but when the contract changes or a new facility opens there is a good chance they will defect.
- **Apathetics**: couldn't care less. The service is regarded as satisfactory. They don't have great loyalty, but often are repeat customers through force of habit. They don't complain, nor do they praise. They just use the service.
- **Terrorists**: the habitual complainers. They actively use word of mouth to talk down the service. They may write letters to the company, the press, or to a blog. The worst kind are those who bring very little business to the service provider but cause big costs because of the time needed to deal with their incessant complaints.

There are several classifications available. See Johnston and Clark for many more categories. Keiningham *et al* propose three categories: desired customers, break-even customers, and costly customers.

Against this is the effort that is currently expended at the Moment of Truth – either minor, mid or major. 'Effort' could include changing the policies or procedures, reducing defects, making the service more convenient, or simply being friendlier.

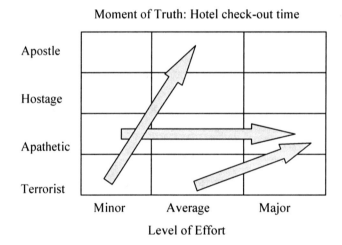

Moment of Truth: Hotel check-out time

The methodology is:

- Identify an apostle, hostage, apathetic or terrorist. The first and last types identify themselves, but market survey may be used.
- Ask that person for the stage in the service provision that they have found particularly good, particularly annoying, or, in the case of hostages and apathetics ask them simply to identify an important stage in their dealing with the service provider.
- Ask what needs to be done to improve that stage or Moment of Truth. What would it take at that stage to make the individual think differently about the service provider?

The Service Systems Toolbox

- Then assess what the present level of effort is and how much effort it would take to make the customer think differently.
- There are now two points in the opportunity box.

Putting extra effort into improving the apathetic is not going to pay off. Certainly a little extra effort into some 'terrorists' could pay big dividends. But putting in greater effort into the other group of 'terrorists' needs careful consideration. Perhaps it would be better to bribe them to leave.

Service Transaction Box: Four Elements of (almost) every Service Transaction

In service, it is the front line staff that has the greatest impact on customers and the greatest potential to delight or disgust. This happens many times every day.
Almost every service activity, but particularly front line, has four elements: arrive, wait, serve, depart – even if an element lasts for only a few seconds. These four elements warrant special attention at each activity because they may be important Moments of Truth, capable of ruining a complete value stream experience.
Hence the mapping symbol that acts as a reminder to check out each of the four elements.

Arrive
- What are the first impressions?
- What is the state of 5S?
- What led the customer to the transaction?
- How easy was it to access?
- How clear are the signs?
- Was the arrival noted or acknowledged?
- Is there a help line for non-satisfactory arrivals?
- Was the site open as advertised?
- --
- --

Wait
- How long is the perceived wait?
- How long is the actual wait?
- What was the expected wait and was this matched?
- Is the wait seen as fair?
- Is there information on the expected wait time?
- Are the servers seen to be busy or distracted or disinterested?
- Is an undue wait explained?
- Was the wait abandoned? (Why?)
- --
- --

Serve

- Were the opening words appropriate?
- Was the customer expected?
- Was service courteous?
- Did the server listen?
- Was the transaction dealt with correctly and accurately?
- Is the information correct?
- Were the customer's needs or expectations met?
- Was the customer greeted in a friendly manner?
- Was the customer greeted by name?
- Was the level of formality appropriate?
- Was the transaction dealt with efficiently?
- Was the server distracted during the transaction?
- Was the server dressed appropriately?
- Did the server give a sense of assurance?
- --
- --

Depart

- Was the transaction closed appropriately?
- Did the customer give feedback?
- Was the customer asked for feedback?
- Did the customer wish to give feedback?
- Could the customer give feedback?
- Did the customer depart with expectations met?
- --
- --

(This list was developed with the aid of MSc Lean Service students, 2007.)

4.19 Total Productive Administration, OEE, and OPE

In this section we consider how the principles of Total Productive Maintenance (TPM) can be applied in the office, in other service environments, and to the service worker rather than to the machine. But, as I warned in the Introduction, be very careful about simply adapting manufacturing tools to service.

TPM is a long-established area, very often closely integrated with Lean manufacturing. It aims, through anticipatory activities, to ensure that machines are available when needed. TPM has a number of 'pillars':

- **'autonomous maintenance'** – where operators take over considerable responsibility for routine maintenance and monitoring;
- **planned maintenance** – like taking your car in for routine service, thereby aiming to prolong life and reliability;
- **equipment improvement** – aiming to improve the operating characteristics such as quality capability, access, and problem detection (hence the expression 'a machine is at its worst when new');
- **early management of new equipment** – correct installation, training, procedures.

TPM recognises that the maintenance task goes well beyond the maintenance department, to involve all – hence 'total'.

A particular focus of TPM is Overall Equipment Effectiveness or OEE. OEE is the multiplication of
- Availability x
- Performance x
- Quality

These are related to the 'Six Big Losses'. Availability is subdivided into two forms of 'loss': breakdowns or equipment failure, and changeover and adjustment. Performance 'loss' is due to minor stoppages (usually defined as an unplanned stop of ten minutes or less), and reduced speed. Quality 'loss' is due to defects arising from process errors and from rework and scrap.

Thus an availability of 90%, a performance of 80%, and a quality rate of 95%, would equate to an OEE of $.9 \times .8 \times .95 = 68\%$

A point about OEE is that it highlights the area where attention is most needed. Having prioritised the areas for attention, root cause analysis can be applied to reduce or eliminate those losses.

Now use these principles with service professionals such as doctors, engineers, lawyers, and accountants. This is called Overall Professional Effectiveness (OPE).

These people also suffer losses, but often don't realise how much effective time is being lost and where it is being lost.

OPE Categories and the Six Big Service Losses

OPE Element	Six Big Service Losses	Examples
Availability	Failure and breakdown; in general time away from value adding activities	Internet not working; computer failure; major interruptions greater than 15 minutes
	Start-up losses and waiting; inter-task transfer time	Customers, patients, work instructions that don't turn up on time; waiting for colleagues; delayed start at beginning of day; stopping early at end of day; waiting for other people or information; waiting for machines; looking for misplaced documents or computer files
Performance	Interruptions	Any unplanned interruption during the day; non-work phone calls, colleague chit-chat, relaxation breaks, going for a coffee
	Skill losses; inefficient method or wrong person doing the task	Any work that could or should not be done at all, or that would be better done by others (less or more skilled)
Quality (and Failure Demand)	Process errors; dealing with complaints	Failure demand in general, Any form of rework; data entry errors
	Customer errors	Customer (both internal and external) errors causing rework or delays

Note that

- The categories are not 'faults' or 'people problems'. OPE should not be about blame. OPE (like OEE) should take the view that the vast majority of problems lie with the process, not with the person. It is only management that can fix the process. This is simply applied Deming philosophy.
- OPE is about recording and detecting problems in order that the situation can be improved.

- It is not about spying or checking up.
- The categories may not suit all service occupations. As with OEE, an OPE exercise must begin by defining suitable categories and gaining consensus.
- Trends are important rather than actual numbers.
- Follow up is required. OPE needs to be incorporated into a root cause improvement approach, possibly requiring fishbone analysis, process redesign, work redesign, and standards.
- As with OEE, the OPE is only recorded during the effective hours. Non-effective hours will therefore have to be agreed. Non-effective hours certainly include lunch and coffee breaks, but may also include, by agreement, group meeting times, training time, and a block of time for informal office networking etc.

OPE data is the basis for much further investigation.

Recording the Data

The recording of losses needs to be carefully thought out. Times need to be recorded across the day. To check, the sum of the time working plus the sum of the six categories of times should equal 100% of the working time. Note that working time is not break time, or meeting time. These times should be subtracted from the official length of the workday. Recording will certainly fail if it is seen as an imposition or worse, so a convenient and easy way must be found. Experience shows that recording will only work if a positive outcome is seen as the result, and people believe that so doing will improve both their own effectiveness and that of the organisation. Possibilities include:

- **voluntary self-recording**, activity by activity as work proceeds;
- **estimation**: at the end of every hour, or half day, or day the professional estimates the time spent on each category; one organisation uses timers that beep every hour as a reminder;
- **sampling and rotation**: everyone does not need to participate: a representative sample or done on rotation are possibilities;
- **tagging**: for paper intensive operations, add a traveller on which times are recorded; this requires further analysis or estimation;
- **observation**: get a secretary to record several people in the area, a nurse to record doctors and colleagues - and so on - all part-time activities, of course;
- some professionals, for example consulting engineers and solicitors already record their time usage for client billing purposes; only a small adjustment is needed to record OPE;
- **activity sampling**: this technique is discussed in another section of the book; it is also effective for OPE – with the agreement of those being sampled, of course.

Using OPE Data: Comparative Analysis

Three people with similar OPE figures may have very different causes of lost effectiveness. Consider three professionals, each working a net eight hours and with a planned time of fifteen minutes per client.

- A is delayed for two hours waiting for a client, she is interrupted for 63 minutes, and no-one needs to re-see her for clarification.
- B experiences no delays but has frequent interruptions totalling 2.5 hours and needs to re-see two clients.
- C is delayed for half an hour, has no interruptions, but needs to re-see one third of all clients.

	Availability	Performance	Quality	OPE
A	6/8=.75	297/360	1.00	62%
B	1.00	5.5/8	((5.5x4)-2)/22	62%
C	7.5/8=.937	1.00	.666	62%

So all three have approximately the same overall effectiveness, but the reasons are very different. This may then enable 'best of the best' analysis.

Best of the Best Analysis

'Best of the best' analysis is a useful initial technique in OPE that can be used wherever similar tasks are taking place – a sort of internal benchmarking. In the case just discussed the 'best of the best' is 100%. B is best on availability, C is best on performance, A is best on quality. Now, are there things that each person is doing which result in these high performance figures in their respective categories? What can they learn from one another? The power of this analysis is that the best methods are already in existence within the organisation – no consultants or process analyses are required. Just communicate the best practices, and embed them.

Five Whys, Six Serving Men, Fishbone Analysis, and Run Diagrams

Once you know the contribution of each OPE element to the overall OPE, you will be able to prioritise and focus attention on the critical losses. Conventional root cause analysis using the fishbone diagram (with the 'M's' of men/people, machine, method, measures, materials, mother nature/environment), together with asking 'Why?' several times over, may be a powerful way to identify possible countermeasures. This is also known as Concern, Cause, Countermeasure analysis. Gather the people from the area, draw out the standard fishbone and brainstorm possible causes. You can also use Kipling's 'Six Honest Serving Men': 'I knew six honest serving men, they taught me all I knew; their names are What and Why and When, and Where and How and Who'. This is also known (more boringly) as Five Ws and an H analysis.

- What is its purpose?
- Why is it necessary?
- When should it be done?
- Where should it be done?
- How should it be done?
- Who should do it?
-

You may find that a process map is unnecessary.

Another dimension is time. Here the run diagram comes into its own. The diagram is simply a graph showing the three elements of OPE against time – perhaps over a month. From experience, you know that availability, performance, and quality in service typically vary more over a month than they do in manufacturing. See the figure. Quality performance is stable but low. Availability seems to peak around the middle of the month. Performance drops off early in the month then recovers. Why is this? Look for the drivers that are influencing this behaviour.

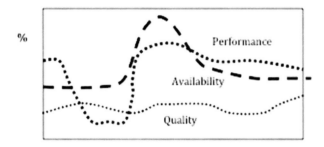

Extending OPE: Group and Value Stream

Peter Willmott, doyen of UK TPM consultants, recommends thinking about OEE on three levels, floor-to-floor, door-to-door, and value chain. Here we use the same concept, modified for Service.

Person OPE: this is OPE at the individual level, as discussed above.

Group OPE: this is the OPE of a group working on similar tasks. Don't average the results of individuals, but take the group as a whole. What is the group availability? The number up and running gives availability. Interruption time for the group can be estimated, as can the time spent working at an inappropriate skill level for the group as a whole. What is overall quality rate? Here snapshots may be more appropriate – like taking activity samples rather than recording the full times.

Value Stream OPE: this is the end-to-end performance of all sections and groups delivering the service or product. A good idea is to take value stream OPE from the customer's perspective. Availability refers to the system uptime or the percentage of time that clients can get the service they require. Performance refers to the percentage of the total remaining time (after availability losses) that the value stream is performing to the appropriate skill level. For example, the percentage of time that the doctors' group spends doctoring, researchers spend researching, engineers spend engineering. Quality measures how much time is lost due to interruptions and the overall wasted time or failure demand percentage for the group as a whole.

Extending OPE: The Full Service Delivery

In many service delivery systems there are typically three elements necessary to deliver full service: the person, the machine, and the system. These three elements apply, for example, in hospitals, banks, hotels, universities, airlines, and restaurants, as well as in logistics support services and maintenance.

In the example below we take a taxi service. The taxi driver needs to be skilled, the taxicab needs to be available, reliable and clean, and the cab company system needs to be able to direct the right cab to the right address at the right time. So each of these has OEE or OPE elements. The RATER dimensions have also been added. A possible measure of performance for each of the nine aspects is included, although the measures would have to be decided for each specific case.

Taxi Service	Availability	Performance	Quality
The Driver	Available when needed; fit for work; reliability; 'tangibles' (appearance) % time available; absenteeism record	Knows where to go – the best route; friendly?; assurance? ACTUAL TIME TAKEN AS AGAINST ESTIMATED TIME GIVEN BY GPS	Driving and traffic errors; knows how to talk to customers; can overcome customer problems; empathy; responsiveness Errors made per 100 trips; or customer satisfaction rating
The Taxi Cab (Convention-al OEE)	Available as needed; no breakdowns Cab availability	No adjustments needed; fit for the traffic conditions Rating on roadworthiness; mechanical state	Cab is clean; standard checks after each ride Rating on cab cleanliness and appearance

The Information System (may include computer system, GPS for driver, credit card machine, radio.)	Available as needed % uptime	Response time adequate Response time against standard	Good information given; no misdirection given to the cab driver. Number of errors (e.g. address, directions)

OPE and related concepts therefore provide a comprehensive framework for improvement.

Prevention and Monitoring in TPA

Peter Willmott uses a human health analogy for TPM: an apple for daily prevention activities ('an apple a day keeps the doctor away'); a thermometer for monitoring body temperature; and a needle for injecting vaccine to prevent disease over the longer term. These also can be adapted for TPA. Take the taxi service example again.

Taxi Service	'Apple'	'Thermometer'	'Needle'
The Driver	Keeping up with changes in the road network; keeping fit	Alertness, health check up, absenteeism	Advanced driving certificate? Taxi Drivers competence test
The Cab	Daily checks of cleanliness and roadworthiness	Inspection check on the condition of the cab – mechanical, appearance, comfort	Regular cab maintenance service, annual roadworthiness
The Information System	Housekeeping w.r.t. files, virus checks, checks that GPS etc. is working	System response time, uptime, accuracy of information held	Using the latest operating system, latest GPS maps

Note that the 'apple' and the 'thermometer' are related through what is termed 'Cleaning is Checking' in TPM. In other words when the cab is cleaned, perhaps once per day, various routine checks are also carried out.

The apple, thermometer and needle analogy used with person, machine and system has wide applicability in any field service operation, in warehousing and distribution, in services such as hotels and airline services, as well as in many office-based services.

The routines (activities and checks) are best developed by a representative team from the front and back offices. Beware of the front office and back office assumption; it is often a bad idea. The procedures need to be written up, and then ideally shown on a visual management board. For example, a magnetic board with counters that are placed each day when the activity is done, as well as a 'problems and issues' whiteboard where 'deviations' are noted, then responsibilities for their resolution. See the section on Communications Board.

Reference

Peter Willmott, 'Notes on TPM and Notes on TPA', MSc in Lean Operations, Cardiff Business School, 2007 to 2010

4.20 Inventory (and Information Inventory) in Service

In service there are two categories of inventory: information and physical. Both have been significantly affected by the internet, which has opened up whole new areas that can improve customer service and remove waste. Moreover, the economics of both types of inventory have changed significantly. Do not think only in terms of physical inventories – think instead of any work that can anticipate customer demand.

Anticipation and Service Inventory

There is a belief that service cannot be stored or inventoried. This is true for 'pure service' at the end of the product service spectrum. But remember that all administration, office, service work is best seen as lying somewhere along the product service spectrum. Customer-facing encounters cannot be stored, but some preparatory administration, documentation, procedures, and preparation can be done ahead of the encounter to smooth the customer flow and limit delays. So in administration and service, 'inventory' may not mean physical items but anticipatory information or activity.

There are precedents for this in traditional Lean, in at least four overlapping areas.

- **Changeover reduction** (Single Minute Exchange of Die or SMED) principles try to do as much preparation as possible before the actual changeover. This is not physical inventory but, like inventory, it makes prior preparation for the service delivery. See the separate section on this topic.
- **The Postponement Principle**, or variety as late as possible, attempts to keep options open as long as possible, thereby gaining efficiency from repetitiveness but also delivering unique customer packages. The classic example is in fact a service supply chain example – Benetton's 'Jerseys in Grey', where jerseys are manufactured but not dyed. Shops hold minimal inventory of each colour, but are linked by EPOS systems to allow jerseys to be dyed to order.
- **The 'variety funnel'** is a traditional Lean map that traces the stages at which variety expands. For example, a common car platform may expand into five body types, then into 25 engine-body types, hundreds of body-colour options, and millions of body-engine-interior combinations. The idea is to reduce unnecessary variety and also to squeeze the funnel so variety is retailed as late as possible. Similarly, the stages at which variety occurs in an administrative or service process can be mapped. In an insurance value stream the initial stages may be the same, but may then branch for different types of claim, or customer, or urgency. The question is how many channels are appropriate at each stage? Delaying the point at which the funnel expands helps to smooth the flow of work.
- **'Mass customisation'**, a phrase made popular by Joseph Pine, is where you try to get the advantages of volume (or 'mass') but one-at-a-time. An example is Dell's use of modularity in computer manufacture but also in service spares, enabling the

Dell model of direct build-to-order to operate. Other examples of mass customisation include variations of postponement discussed above: for instance, packaging and labelling as late as possible, and the increasing use of print-on-demand technology and make-your-own maps as offered by Ordnance Survey.

Other examples of anticipation inventory include the following.

- Anticipating a hotel or hospital check-in. Some hotels (like Ritz Carlton) prepare documentation in advance of arrivals from established visitors so that literally only one signature is required. Duplication of data entry is avoided. Moreover, this can be extended to include prior preparation of the guest room, for example type of bed and pillow, shampoo, and refreshments.
- Southwest Airlines has remained profitable through many innovations, one being to minimise turnaround times. This is the use of straightforward manufacturing changeover (SMED) principles.
- An unnoticed revolution is the provision of PowerPoint slides to course attendees, which reduces the need to take detailed notes. This in turn reduces time and improves quality. Today many students hear lectures on an iPod.
- The use of pre-prepared meals at restaurants, even up-market restaurants, is long-established. The issue is at what stage it is appropriate to hold the postponement buffer. Customer expectation of lead-time is the important variable, but others are taste and cost or risk.
- The 'Self' concept is also powerful. Allow customers to take over much of the task before the encounter in their own time at their convenience. Examples include pre-check-in at an airport computer terminal before proceeding to 'Fast Bag Drop' as at BA. BA also allows customers to print out their boarding pass at home. A European hotel chain allows at-home registration and automated key pick-up that minimises waiting and staff.
- Supermarkets can anticipate customer requirements more accurately by using loyalty cards, in order to be able to stock up the shelves at specific stores to cater for the specific local demand mix.
- Anticipating car service arrivals. The Portuguese car dealer Simao attempts to collect as much relevant information as possible over the phone before the customer arrives for the car service. This organisation was studied by Cardiff's Lean Enterprise Research Centre and reported in Womack and Jones' *Lean Solutions*. Simao ensures that not only are check-in delays minimised but also that the correct service parts are available as far as possible. This in turn helps to reduce physical inventories.
- Hospital theatre operations can adopt SMED principles by preparing as much as possible beforehand. The *Sunday Times* reported in 2006 on a UK hospital where operating theatres are run in pairs, the one being prepared while the other is dealing with a patient. Surgeons circulate between the two theatres with minimal delay.
- On some international trains, passports and documentation is checked en route. Why not on planes? Or even in the departure lounge?

Time reduction is the critical reason for anticipatory 'inventories', but quality is also likely to improve, through less rush, greater standardisation, and more automation. Time reduction and quality improvement in turn mean that cost is likely to fall.

Inventory Classifications

A standard way of classifying inventory is via ABC analysis. A items are expensive, B items intermediate, and C items low cost. This can be modified by importance. For instance, a low cost item in a hospital may nevertheless be life critical and therefore upgraded to A class. The same applies to difficult-to-procure items. A items need careful attention; C items you are not so concerned about – you may just decide to have sufficient so that you don't run out.

Another dimension is the frequency of use of the items. Use the 'Runners, Repeaters and Strangers' (RRS) classification. This book has a separate section on RSS when used in service mapping. Here a Runner item is used frequently, perhaps every day, whereas a Stranger is only used occasionally.

We now have a way of classifying service inventories as shown in the figure:

	A items	B items	C items
Runners	Worth specific design – tight kanban or pooling; kept on location	Kanban	Stock kept at location; kanban?
Repeaters	Small stock kept at location; others centrally; kanban	Keep centrally, loose kanban	Small stock kept at location; most kept centrally
Strangers	Kept centrally	VMI?	Centralised; VMI?

The table is just an example, but it illustrates some possibilities.

Kanban is a 'pull' replenishment system: when a container is emptied a card on the container is sent to signal replenishment. Tight kanban means that there is close control.

Decentralised means that replenishment decisions should be left with local areas. Wasteful bureaucracy probably offsets purchasing economies.

VMI is vendor-managed inventory: a supplier comes in regularly, sees what has been used, and tops up the quantity.

Colour Coding, the Square Root Function and other tricks for Service Inventory

Colour coding is simple and useful. Just paint the items that are supposed to be in the same location the same colour. Out-of-place items are immediately visible.

The Square Root function is a rule that says that with normal variation in demand, the amount of inventory needed centrally is the square root of the sum of the squares of the items that are needed if kept at decentralised locations. For example if 4 and 3 items are required to meet a certain service level at two locations, then the square root of 16+9 or 5 is needed at one location. Approximate. Think about this when considering how many ambulances, fire engines, policemen, emergency supplies, or distribution centre inventory are needed. However, against this must be set the decrease in response time. This may be an answer to the common practice in service and manufacturing of 'squirreling away' needed items – but of course trust is necessary. A systems approach!

Standardisation is (may be?) a great way to reduce inventory. Can all field service units, aeroplanes, wards be similarly equipped? Probably not, but what can be standardised? See the separate section on Standardisation.

RFID (radio frequency identification) is becoming more feasible – less expensive and more reliable – for A and perhaps B items. It can help to track the location of important items. Also for security. A high-tech solution that may signal a command and control mentality.

Information Inventory

Personal computers and the internet are allowing service providers to re-think the push-pull point, also known as the postponement or decision point. This is the point along the value chain downstream of which service provision must wait for customer pull. As you move towards the high interaction end of the spectrum, providers such as professional services have traditionally not been able to anticipate customer requirements, and so long lead times have been an inherent feature.

Anticipation information 'inventories' are now much easier. Consider the following.

- Automated check-in for an airline, either at the airport or, in the case of BA, by printing out your boarding pass at home. No queuing.
- Hotels that keep data on frequent visitors, including sometimes credit card details, and pre-print the registration card. Sign in and collect your key. No delays.
- Online travel booking that keeps customer details.
- Insurance companies that keep property details online before a customer has made the initial contact (according to Chopra and Lariviere).

- Law firms that anticipate applications for company registration or accounting firms that deal with tax completion. Segmenting the classes of applicant to smooth the delivery process does both of these.
- Online credit rating that can be carried out immediately while a loan application is being made.
- Decision support software, used by doctors and financial advisors, for example, to give quicker better service – or to be used directly by customers.
- iPod and PowerPoint downloads for lecture courses. This potentially changes the whole ethos of a university, and perhaps some schools.
- Print-on-demand technology for books.
- In general, standard letters and forms can be produced, but this carries the risk of inappropriateness, like standard menus from a call centre. Customers can pre-print and submit application forms.

All of these are possible because the cost of holding information inventory is very low, and has massive economies of scale – unlike physical inventories. Fast updating is also possible. Like some physical inventories, information inventory can become outdated. But in all these cases, the real opportunity is not cost reduction but convenience to the customer.

'Information inventory' can, of course, be an aid to improved flow and to reducing peak demands – both of which are important to Lean service.

A trade-off can be made between, on the one hand, opportunities for growth through improved customer experience and reduced cost – including reduced peaks and staffing – and on the other hand, the cost of setting up the systems.

The question as to where the push-pull point should be located is, as Chopra and Lariviere suggest, an important decision that applies to an ever-wider business audience.

So the fourth Lean principle, about the desirability of 'pull', is not quite the same for manufacturing as it is for service. In manufacturing it is almost always good to move the 'postponement' point as far downstream as possible. In service it is more complex and increasingly relevant.

Physical and Information Inventory Interface

The internet has also fundamentally changed physical inventories.

- As Christopher Anderson has pointed out in *The Long Tail*, the economics of some types of inventory, particularly downloadable types, has§ changed dramatically. In an audio store, CDs must compete for shelf space and cost money to hold. So an audio store can only afford to keep high-selling items. But on the internet, the cost of stocking an album is near zero. Even very low sellers generate profit. Hence the long tail, and less relevance to Pareto analysis. But more than this: the potential world of suppliers is also vastly increased. So, a visit to a record store in 2007 reveals that most audio CDs, except the top sellers, have gone. DVDs have replaced them. But will DVDs go the same way?

- To a lesser extent, the same applies to physical, (mainly) non-perishable items, distributed through warehouses rather than shops. Here the limitation is delivery: when will delivery companies learn that many people work during the day? Some companies are moving to overcome this – such as the use of dry-cleaner pick-up bins with an access key for out-of-hours collection. Could this be a trend that develops into each street having one cubic metre deposit boxes, accessed by pin codes that are given out by the deliverer?
- Loyalty cards, such as at Tesco UK, enable companies to track individual purchase decisions and preferences. As a result, Tesco tailors the blend of own brand 'value' items and 'finest' items to specific stores.

Physical Service Inventories

This book does not deal with physical inventory theory. This section comments on independent inventory demand, where there is no interdependency on an end item having a bill of materials (or 'recipe'). Independent demand inventory is, of course, a major concern for some service organisations such as shops and repair centres.

The inventory service level is related to cost in a non-linear way as shown in the figure. The figure also shows a typical current state. You can calculate the current state from routine aggregate inventory control theory, provided that you have reasonable knowledge of demand patterns for each stock-keeping unit (SKU).

Moving from the current state to any one of the alternative future states involves BOTH a decrease in cost AND an increase in service level. There are several alternatives, as shown: from retaining the current service level but reducing cost, to reducing cost but retaining the current service level, to improving both.

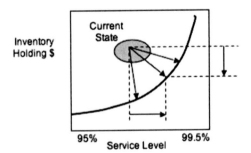

Service levels should be fixed for A (high value), B (medium value), and C (low value) items.

But what about forecasts? Conventional inventory demand control includes trend, seasonality, cycles, and random noise uncertainty levels. In service, a few more categories are necessary:

- **trend**: positive or negative;
- **seasonality**: yearly period or specific holidays;
- **new**: new product launch;
- **erratic**: up and down cycles caused by, for example, promotional activities;
- **lumpy**: caused by special but predictable events (e.g. sporting);
- **slow moving**: occasional demand;
- **dying;**
- **obsolete**: dead – no movement.

Each one of these needs separate consideration. In moving from the current state to an improved state, some categories (e.g. obsolete) may be cut, others (e.g. erratic) increased.

Dependent inventory demand (such as with a bill of materials) is usually found within manufacturing. But not exclusively. A 'bill of material' may be 'attached' to some service offerings:

- A cancer patient;
- A hotel guest, booked into bed and breakfast;
- An airline passenger.

In each case a standard list of requirements is made. There is uncertainty, of course, but as with manufacturing, the netting process (comparing what there is with what is needed) continuously makes corrections.

Distribution Inventory: A Lesson from Tesco

Tesco is the 'Toyota' of food retailers – although food is increasingly only a part of the offering at its supermarkets. Tesco has carried out the usual Pareto analysis of SKU usage, but it has gone further than most. Traditionally in grocery stores there has been a distinction between the ways in which fresh foods and ambient items are managed. But why? Tesco has adopted a method that they call 'Flowthrough'. This involves:

- **Little/no stock of fast moving, predictable lines**. Top usage items, perhaps the top 2% of SKUs that account for a much higher percentage of unit sales, are replenished several times per day by vehicles that go on a 'milkround' with mixed model loads. This gives enormous competitive advantage: inventories are kept low, allowing a greater range to be kept on shelves but also minimising stockholding costs.
- **Ordering slow moving lines on a 'pick by line' basis**. This is the pull system in operation. Instead of delivering low moving items in traditional larger quantities, Tesco has worked hard to reduce the economic order size.

This of course involves cooperation with suppliers as to packaging and also a re-think right along the distribution chain.
- **Matching product characteristics to the picking method**. Another break in traditional thinking is to push the actual pick point further upstream.

Tesco thinking on distribution was significantly influenced by a study, which showed that a very high proportion of distribution costs occurred in the final 50m of the journey to the shelf. This is where considerable unloading, moving, unwrapping, shelf stacking, arrangement and pricing occur. Much of this is necessary non-value added activity. So Tesco is moving to a 'one touch' method for higher volume items. Here the manufacturer pre-packs product directly onto trolleys, which are simply wheeled into their final place on the supermarket floor. No unpacking, double handling, shelf stacking. They look good, too.

The SKU Pareto is the vital tool that enables distribution decision-making. The SKU Pareto is simply cumulative demand against ranked products, enabling those few 'A' products that account for a high percentage of total demand to be identified. At the other end of the curve, the many 'C' products accounting for relatively small demand are also identified. This analysis can be done both by item number and by turnover along the cumulative demand axis. This is conventional, but Tesco takes it further.

Tesco thinks in terms of a cube with frequency along one axis (daily to weekly distribution), stocking point along the second axis (regionally to nationally), and distribution method along the third axis (flow to traditional stocking). Every SKU is found an appropriate location within this cube. There are sometimes other factors, such as temperature-sensitive or boxed products that require special distribution considerations. Typically, the highest moving A category ambient items are locally distributed with the highest volume SKUs flowed, intermediate moving B items are regionally distributed, and low moving C items are nationally distributed using pallets for higher volume and mini-loads for the lowest volume. Demand changes, of course, so the locations within the cube change too. An adaptive, learning system is thus required. So there is no one channel for all – a lesson that Coca Cola learned about its distribution channels to different types of customer many years ago.

Demand Amplification

Lean supply chain thinkers know the dangers of demand amplification: excessively large warehouses, inventory pipeline costs, and risk of obsolescence or past sell-by date. Tesco has worked hard to reduce the effects of amplification by:

- recognising the threat of amplification, and giving it management priority;
- reducing the number of levels in their supply chain;
- reducing the number of decision points (where another player in the chain decides on the quantity to order);
- encouraging the trend towards smaller, more frequent batch quantities.

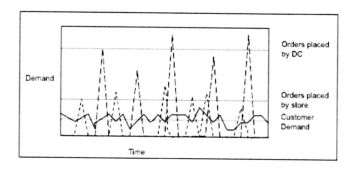

Further Reading

Sunil Chopra and Martin A. Lariviere, 'Managing Service Inventories to Improve Performance', *MIT Sloan Management Review*, Fall 2005, pp. 57-63

Chris Anderson, *The Long Tail*, Random House Business Books, 2006

Barry Evans, 'Obsessed with the Customer: The Success of Tesco's Lean Operations', *Proc. Innovations in Lean Thinking – Annual Conference*, Lean Enterprise Research Centre, July 2007.

Further details on the Cost – Service Level Trade Off curve may be obtained from Mobius Consulting, www.mobiusconsulting.co.uk

Conventional service inventory management is discussed in Richard Metters *et al*, *Successful Service Operations Management*, Thompson, 2003

4.21 Layout, Spaghetti Diagrams, Touches

The layout question is arguably the most pervasive problem in operations management. Every office, business and house makes layout decisions, however cursory. The first and over-riding point to make is that the layout should support the service concept. A layout analysis should follow the Level 1 systems analysis, and be part of the Level 2 analysis, in the case of Transactional, Interactive, and Custom process types.

Most offices are arranged in so-called functional layout: in other words, like functions (accounting, marketing, logistics, etc.) are grouped together. This layout type has the advantages of flexibility and of allowing members of a discipline to learn from and support one another. From a Lean perspective, however, functional layout usually has long lead times, inefficient movement, poor visibility, poor control (from an end-to-end perspective), and, worst of all, many handoffs, with many subsequent rework loops and defects. The value adding time is usually far less than the total lead time. Service cells could well be an answer. These are discussed below, but first some general points.

Spaghetti Diagrams and Service Layout Analysis

The Spaghetti Diagram is useful in any service or administrative system where there are face-to-face interactions between the customer and the provider, or where there is repetitive physical movement of people or documents. It is of no use where transactions are electronic. Spaghetti Diagrams are a useful supplement to many process maps, and fit in very well with the 'Servicescape' concept (see below). A Spaghetti Diagram could not be simpler: just draw a diagram of the physical layout and trace the movements of the customer, document or person. The following are useful:

PQRST and AEIOUX: Richard Muther in *Systematic Layout Planning* uses the easy to remember sequences PQRST (Product, Quantity, Routings, Support, Transport), and, for the relative importance of locating areas close to one another, AEIOUX (Absolutely necessary, Especially important, Important, Ordinary, Unimportant, and Undesirable).

PQ is the product/service quantity. Here draw a Pareto as follows:

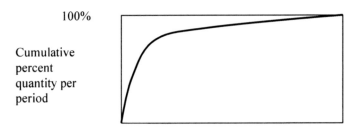

The steepness of the curve w (highest to lowest) sibilities – perhaps putting the highest-ranking services into a cell and the remaining in functional layout.

The following are more relevant in repetitive environments – it is much less relevant in custom environments.

R is routings: do all services follow the same route through the office? Draw the spaghetti. Look for dominant routes.

S is support: what support services are required? Internal or external? How should they best be accessed?

T is transport: the movement routes around the office, hospital, supermarket, etc. Is there a regular 'runner' route where post or medicines are distributed regularly, or do such movements simply take place as required? The Runner is a Lean manufacturing concept that has some use in repetitive service environments. This is a person who goes around a specific route at specific intervals – every two hours, twice a day, whatever. All document and material movement is via the Runner. On each route he picks up and drops off. Thus a regular drumbeat flow of work is established.

For functional layouts or areas only (not cells):

AEIOUX and the REL (or relationship diagram). Each area is set against each other. For example

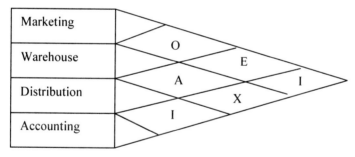

Then connect the area with lines: A: 4 lines; E: 3 Lines; I: 2 lines; O: 1 line; X: a wavy line.

For the current layout, the REL diagram is:

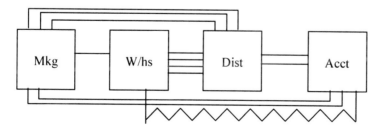

A better layout, seeking to minimise the number of multiple lines over long distances is:

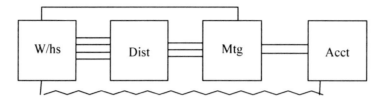

Cell Layout

Cell layout attempts to create the advantages of an efficient assembly line layout while retaining flexibility. The method is simply to line up the functions in process order and, ideally, flow work one at a time. This not only drastically cuts lead-time but also improves visibility and problem solving.

Consider the following case.

Process time is one minute per file at each stage.

Batches of ten are processed before moving.

> Time for first file to come out = 40 minutes
> Time for last file to come out = 40 minutes.

Now, if files can be moved one at a time:

> Time for first file to come out = 4 minutes
> Time for last file to come out = 14 minutes.

Example 1

A local authority's plans approval process involves the files moving through the following areas: Town Planning, Building Survey, City Health, Engineers, Water Authority, and Electricity Authority. Each is sited at a separate location. Applications are moved in batches. Overall lead-time is between three weeks and six months. Tracing files is difficult. Rework loops result in considerable delay.

So, reorganise into a cell that meets three times per week. Representatives from all the departments and authorities sit in one room, and progress the applications one at a time. Referrals back are dealt with immediately. Lead-time is reduced to between two days and one week!

There are, of course, organisational issues to be worked out.

Example 2
This is a story told by Hal Mather, at the Institute of Operations Management, UK. Six ships arrive together in a port with six cranes. A crane can unload $\frac{1}{6}$ of a ship per day.

Time in the port does not generate cash, so the quicker they can get to sea the better. If one crane is allocated per ship, all ships get out of port after six days. Average time in port is six days. Is there a better way?

All cranes work together on ship 1. It leaves after one day. Then all work on ship 2. It leaves after two days. And so on. Average time in port is (1+2+3+4+5+6)/6 = 3.5 days.

Moral: cell team working can be much more effective.

Split Tasks and Batches

A highly relevant point to both manufacturing and service cells, but particularly to service cells, is that jobs or tasks need to be broken down into the smallest feasible, sensible element. In Lean manufacturing the dangers of large batches and the advantages of small batches are well appreciated (see above). In service, a large batch is not necessarily a large number of similar jobs – think rather of a large batch as a long sequence of small tasks done by one person before being passed onto the next person. 'Batching' can cause major queues and delays. By contrast, 'levelling' the work means passing on smaller elements of the larger task so that the complete task can be worked on in parallel. This is particularly relevant where there are critical resources, for three reasons:

- the tasks may not all require the skills of the critical resource, thereby freeing up the most valuable constrained time;
- the critical resource is likely to be 'starved' of work less often;
- alternatively, the critical resource will be level-loaded, rather than work coming in waves.

Three Ways to Reorganise into Service Cells

All the following are much superior to functional layout, but they do have pros and cons.

1   The first is to allocate a <u>caseworker</u>, who works with a client through all stages. This is more personalised for the client, but there are training and expertise issues.
2   Clients are progressed through a cell, moving work one piece at a time between several workers. Workers can focus on areas of expertise. But client personalisation is lost.
3   Virtual cells. This makes use of workflow software that routes files between team members, and monitors any delays, but team members are not required to relocate physically.

Further Issues on Layout and Physical Movement

- **The cost of the last 50 metres**: Tesco has analysed where the costs lie in the distribution chain. Answer: lots of cost in the last 50m. Why? Because that is where there are many touches. Tesco aims to reduce the number of touches on the way to the final location on the supermarket floor. Today several SKU items are taken directly to the point of use on wheeled pallets.
- **Customers can participate**: at Sholdice hospital in Toronto, which specialises in hernia operations, patients who have had their operation show new patients around. This is good systems thinking. Those who have had their operation get fit quicker by walking around. New patients are reassured. Hospital staff can be used more effectively.
- **'Supermarkets'** is a service concept borrowed by manufacturing but in turn it has some utility in repetitive service. A 'supermarket' is a central location where common parts are stored and material handlers or 'runners' 'go shopping'. A service supermarket may contain files, food, or spares.
- **FIFO Lane**: instead of an in-basket that is often last in, first out, a first in, first out lane maintains the sequence of work. A good FIFO lane has a designated maximum length with visible warnings if it is exceeded. It is possible to use a 'lazy susan', which swings round when full.

Layout and Attention to Detail

Attention to detail in service environments can have a dramatic effect, but it is often not thought of, or given adequate attention. Why not do a mini 'kaizen event', taking just an hour or two to think through a good layout with the team?

Take four 'obvious' examples.

- **Layout of medication carts**: these are the equivalent of the changeover carts found in manufacturing. Include shadow boards. Think what items need to be included. Keep a record of how many times items are used, what items are needed but not included, and what are excluded. Consider what items should be on the top rack, for easy access, and what on the bottom. Is the trolley itself the right size, and does it have the required manoeuvrability?

- **Restaurant layout**: almost everyone is familiar with the batch and queue buffet process during mealtimes at conference venues. Why does it have to be that way? Consider a Lean or systems solution.
    - Distribute the cutlery at several locations to eliminate backtracking.
    - Have several mini-tables rather than one or two large tables that work at the rate of the slowest guest.
    - Separate the main foodstuffs within a course – say a carvery at one location, cold meats in another, vegetarian at another – all clearly signposted; and don't mix them in with others such as salads – this is to create what is called 'requisite variety' in systems language.
    - Use several smaller, separated bowls of a food, rather than one large bowl – distribute the possible bottlenecks.

- Have a kanban-like signalling system that guests can use to show that a replacement bowl is required.
- Mix dessert, salad and vegetables on the same table, so that queue batches don't 'float' according to course; have signs to explain this.
- Distribute most dishes directly to eating tables.
- Break up the queues by serving the first course directly at the eating tables.
- Continually review the most popular and least popular foods; keep a tally chart of usage.

- **Layout of the Registration Process**, at a conference or at the start of a university term. This is an aspect that sometimes gets attention. First: are there clear signs of where to go? Of course, delegate labels are prepared. But how are they laid out and grouped: alphabetically, by company/class or by interest group (to foster networking)? Again, have clear signs according to the grouping. What is the queue discipline: multiple queues or a single queue to several parallel servers? If several servers have to be visited, does everyone have to follow a strict sequence – and if not, can a checklist be provided on whom to visit? Should delegate packs be collected with the name badges or separately? How many servers are required, and can they move from queue to queue? Is some pre-registration or label printing possible, like online check-in at an airport? There is surely a 'one best way' for any registration...

- **Layout of stationery cupboards**: this is straightforward 5S – but are locations clearly labelled? Re-order points apparent? Frequently used items in the most convenient locations? And are these reviewed? Do you really need to have drawers and doors?

The Benihana Case is a famous Harvard Business School case study illustrating a systems approach to layout for a fast turn around, but fun, dining experience. Guests congregate in the bar where they are assembled into table-sized groups – but they also spend money while waiting. They move in a group to a U-shape hotplate table where the chef is already waiting in the middle. A group means that intimate, romantic but long conversations are minimised. Also there are minimal wasted vacant seats. Cooking takes place at the table so unproductive kitchen space is minimised. The chef bows and gives out the limited menus. The limited menu means efficient inventory control with reduced waste. The chef cuts meat while guests make up their selections – but the chef distributes small delicacies while selection is proceeding. Each waitress serves a limited number of tables. Cooking begins as soon as the selections are made. The chef puts on an entertaining knifework and cooking display. There are no delays while waiting for service. Dessert is offered and served almost immediately after the main course. It is ice cream. Why? Because it melts near the hotplate so the guests have to eat fast. After dessert and coffee, the chef bows and begins to clean the hotplate. Guests get the message. The show is over. They should be moving on. A fun experience with good food is had by all. In fact, the Benihana concept starts long before the meal, by understanding the customer and offering comfortable Western food (steak) in Oriental surroundings. What could be better than an Oriental evening but with your favourite food?

Servicescape

Zeithaml and Bitner believe that the 'Servicescape' affects service delivery by influencing both customers and employees. Their framework is useful. The 'inputs' are ambience (temperature, humidity, noise), layout (arrangement, relative locations, visibility, ease of movement) and artefacts (signs, furniture, etc.). These inputs produce responses in customers and employees: Cognitive (beliefs, impressions), Emotional (mood, attitude) and Physiological (comfort, convenience).

Further Reading

Richard Muther, *Systematic Layout Planning*, Richard Muther and Associates, New York
W Earl Sasser, *Benihana of Tokyo*, Harvard Business School Case No. 9-673-057
Valerie Zeithaml, Mary Jo Bitner and Dwayne Gremler, *Services Marketing*, 4th edition, McGraw Hill, 2006, Chapter 11 on Servicescape
Nancy Hyer and Urban Weemerlov, *Reorganizing the Factory*, Productivity Press, 2002, Section 5, Extending the Concept – Cells in the Office
Michel Baudin, *Lean Assembly*, Productivity Press, 2002. A manufacturing book but one that has many lessons for service.

4.22 Activity Sampling

Activity sampling is a long-established way to determine the relative time split between activities. It simply involves taking a number of random observations over a representative period of time and recording and categorising what is done at that particular moment of observation. Around 200 observations are required for reasonable validity. Formulas are available in work study/time and motion texts which give the number of observations required to obtain a given level of confidence, allowing for variation in the data. But these are seldom necessary. 200 is a good number, spread over a representative period in line with the chosen suitable period mentioned earlier.

Activity sampling is easy and powerful, but it has fallen into disrepute because of alienation between worker and management where it was seen as a means to spy or cut jobs. Today we hope that there is more trust. Activity sampling is best done by the area supervisor or by the workers themselves, in the full knowledge of what the data will be used for – to improve flow, service, and resource allocation with a guarantee of no job losses through an improvement activity. Activity sampling is efficient because it can be done part-time and it can observe several tasks at once.

A random observation needs to be random. One way to do this is simply to decide on the number of observations per hour, pull the appropriate number from a hat containing numbers one to sixty to determine the minute, and then make the observation exactly on the minute.

Classify the activities and record them against 'bar and gate'.

Activity sampling can be a most useful tool to quantify value adding time, the types of waste and necessary non-value added activities.

Begin by making a list of likely wastes, and then for (say) 200 random observations accumulate the type of activity (value added or waste type). You can often make multiple observations at almost the same random moment by observing several workers.

You may like to add notes to the observations - for example whether the office was busy or not.

Recording activity times can also be done in the same manner. Here, you would be interested in the distribution of times, not just the average time. Often the lowest repeatable time will be a good basis for capacity planning, although you will have to factor in breaks - say ten minutes in each hour.

4.23 Communications Board

In virtually all service situations, a Communications Board is a major device for improvement. It links directly with Lean philosophy, as it is a means of

- communicating purpose, and ensuring consistency;
- problem surfacing and resolution;
- waste reduction;
- teamworking.

The Communications Board becomes the focal point for communication, review and problem solving. Every morning there is a meeting around the Communications Board. Communication is two-way – from the group leader to the group and from the group to the group leader. A meeting should take less than fifteen minutes, and often less than ten.

The Communications Board may is an essential part of Visual Management and Leader Standard Work (LSW). See the section on LSW in Part 2.

Charts shown on the board may include:

- **The Policy or Strategy Deployment matrix**: this shows the aims, projects, measures and results for the area. It should also show how the area's activities relate to the wider organisational aims and projects.
- **Concern, Cause, Countermeasure (3C) chart**: any concerns should be raised and entered, and all outstanding concerns discussed at the daily meeting. Each stage of each concern should be dated. A standard methodology such as A3 could be used with the Communications Board showing the overall status. A3s relating to concerns could be displayed in an area next to the board.
- **Performance charts** linked to productivity measures such as throughput. It is important that these are a source of problem identification and NOT a means of blame or competition.
- **Ideas Board:** here ideas are made visible and are progressed through four stages using post-its. The stages are Proposed, Considered, Being Implemented, and Completed.
- **Quality chart:** tracking problem areas, complaints, and errors. Also a means for improvement not blame.
- **Management audits**: where different levels of management are expected to visit the area at appropriate frequencies – for instance CEO once per year, appropriate director quarterly, departmental managers monthly, section managers weekly, team leaders daily. Each turns over a magnetic counter from red to green when the visit is complete. The re-set dates (green to red) are stated. The set of activities that each is supposed to cover is kept on a clipboard next to the board.
- **Total Productive Maintenance/OPE** in the office charts - see the separate section on this topic.
- **Progress charts**: these are usually related to the stages of the regular work cycle.

- **A skills matrix** showing stages of development (learner, can do under instruction, can do working alone, instructor) against each skill category. These are often shown in a PDCA (Plan Do Check Act) or PDSA (Plan Do Study Act) format cycle with the quadrants coloured in as the skill level is attained. A skills matrix is not just a 'factory thing'; it has many uses in professional environments, from lecturer to engineer, to accountant.
- **A task allocation chart**: who is working on what projects.
- **A leave roster**.
- **General company notices**.

Each chart has a designated person responsible for chart maintenance and updating. This must be done by a designated time, before the daily meeting. But the Communications Board is to be used by the entire team.

Don't forget simple things like having a marker attached to a string and using a prominent location.

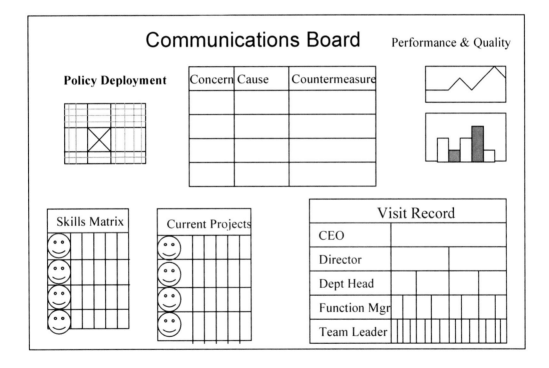

4.24 Changeover Reduction in Service

Changeover reduction was possibly the first Lean tool ever used by Toyota. This method was refined to allow quick die changeover time to take place between the pressing of automobile body panels. This enables small batches to be economic, thereby reducing inventory and helping Toyota move towards the ideal of 'one piece at a time' flow production.

Is this concept relevant in service? Absolutely!

For example:

- in design or consulting work, there are numerous administrative tasks to bring a new service, product launch, or product to fruition;
- many offices have deadlines, for example preparing for a conference;
- in a hospital operating theatres have changeovers between surgical operations and preparing beds between patients;
- airlines, and famously SouthWest make great efforts to minimise the idle time at a gate – an airline only makes money when flying its aircraft.

In all these examples there is a 'critical path'. This is not just the longest time for a sequence of activities but more importantly is the time spent by critical resources to get the task done. In the examples above the critical resources are, respectively, the engineer or artist, the busiest admin person for that activity, the operating theatre or surgeon or bed, and the aircraft.

The changeover methodology for manufacturing was made popular by Shigeo Shingo in his book SMED (Single Minute Exchange of Dies). The methodology involves separating 'internal' and 'external' activities.

The following are the steps for service. The team of people concerned with the task, working together as a team, best does these steps. Don't do this *for* someone, do it *with* that person.

1 Identify the critical resource for that particular activity. This is the value adding resource or activity. This resource may sometimes always be the critical resource (as in the aircraft) or it may change (as in the office or hospital).
2 List all the activities that are required to be done by or to the critical resource in order complete the work. 'The work' would for example be the design and administrative tasks done by the artist, or the necessary activities to be done to the bed or aircraft.
3 Designate each activity as 'internal' or 'external'. Internal activities can only be done by the critical person or to the operating theatre or aircraft *when it is not in use for its prime activity*. External activities do not necessarily need to be done by the critical resource person, or can be done before or after the physical

resource (operating theatre, bed, aircraft) while it is adding value (being used by a customer or passenger).

4 Separate internal and external activities.

5 Redesign the sequence of activities such that the critical resource time is minimised. As far as possible, unload the critical resources. Do as many of the external activities before or after the critical internal activities. Get other people to do the external activities where the critical resource is a person. See if it is possible to do external tasks in parallel with internal tasks, not sequentially.

6 Having now redesigned the sequence of activities and who is to do them, examine the internal activities along the new critical path. See if these activities can be more efficiently by, for example, using technology (computers?), rearranging the layout (5S?), or smoothing the workload on the critical resource. Can the critical person or resource be prepared beforehand while the person or thing is less busy or unoccupied.

As an example, a design office at a consulting engineer was able to reduce the end-to-end design briefing to completion process by several weeks. This was done not by 'crashing' the project with additional staff, but by 'going for flow'. Start-stop is very disruptive in intellectual activity, so hold-ups while waiting for information (for example soil tests for foundations) mean that some engineers have to be diverted to other projects. This involves more briefing. Time reduction was achieved by separating internal and external activities, working in parallel, and making sure that before actual critical design engineering activities were done the maximum possible preparation was complete. Although a technician may take longer than a professional engineer to do some activities, offloading such work onto a technician could reduce the critical resource path.

A famous example is SouthWest airlines gate turnaround time. The turnaround process was studied in detail to reduce the time. Of interest is the fact that job demarcation barriers have been removed so that all available staff, pilots, stewards, terminal crew, and ground crew, all play a role. The critical path lies along getting bags, passengers and fuel into the aircraft. Much prior preparation takes place before the aircraft arrives at the gate.

Finally, although not quite a changeover operation, consider a man or a woman making coffee for their partner in bed on a Sunday morning. The man puts water in the kettle, waits for it to boil, then makes the carafe of coffee. The woman puts water in the kettle, prepares the carafe, and then while the kettle boils, hangs out the washing and loads the dishwasher. Then, after pouring the water into the carafe, uses the surplus boiled water to clean up while the coffee draws.

4.25 Heijunka in the Office

Heijunka means 'level production'. Although it is established in repetitive manufacturing, it is virtually unknown in the office or in service. Essentially the Heijunka system divides the day into equal parcels of time, and divides up the work to fit into the parcels. In the classic Toyota system, a Heijunka card authorises a number of components to be made in each time parcel, called a pitch increment. A typical pitch increment may be fifteen minutes. In each pitch increment, the cell leader or the material handler is authorised to do exactly the work specified on the Heijunka card. Pitch increments are usually short – less than half an hour. So even if the same product is made all day, the day's work is divided into (say) 30 or more segments. Of course, each Heijunka card may authorise a different piece of work in each time parcel or pitch increment. In fact it is usual in a Heijunka schedule to use 'mix model' – that is, to alternate between products. ABCABCABC is preferred to AAABBBCCC because the work is more even, and if a fault is found with an A at least relatively few have been made.

Not all Heijunka systems use cards. Any system that paces the work can be regarded as a Heijunka system – for example an electronic overhead display may be effective. Note that a system that simply counts the number of completed jobs, as in many call centres, is not a Heijunka system. A count display in a call centre may have undesirable consequences like encouraging operators to rush calls to meet the target. In general, a Heijunka system is not suitable where work is triggered in real time. It can be very effective where work can be pre-planned a day or a week ahead.

The advantages are numerous, at least for repetitive operations.

- The work is spread out evenly across the day.
- Workers are assumed to work at a constant speed, neither too fast nor too slow.
- There is visibility of progress at any moment in the day – it is very clear how many time parcels a worker is behind. This allows extra work to be scheduled if necessary, and to give warnings to management and customers.
- The reasons for missing a parcel of work should be recorded – not for blame and punishment, but as a powerful way to surface problems and then to resolve them.
- In a factory, the flow of materials and components to the work area is even and steady throughout the day.

So how can the Heijunka concept be applied in administration and service?

To reiterate, it should be a powerful contender in any fairly repetitive process that can be pre-planned, where the task lengths can be reasonably estimated. Some examples.

In warehousing: order picking can be arranged into time slots, each requiring a number of picks. The picker begins and ends each order pick route at the Heijunka box.

In maintenance: a maintenance schedule – say for aircraft or machines – can be broken down by day and by hour within the day. This will probably require a pre-diagnostic phase. The cards are turned over when the work is complete. Note that a Heijunka system can be used for a time buffer to prevent work starting too early, thereby allowing adequate preparation to be completed. Once the work starts, there should be no delays, rather than starting and stopping.

In a hotel: room makeup can be scheduled using Heijunka. This has the advantage of pacing the work rather than rushing it and thereby introducing errors, and it also has the advantage of making the programme for the day visible.

Warehouse Level Loading Example

A warehouse generally knows the demand pattern. Maybe, morning 8-10am, 50%, late afternoon 3-5pm, (30%) high; otherwise 10-3 moderate (20%). A prediction can be made of tomorrow's orders. Then, morning pick cycles per hour required = demand x 50% / 2 hours. Morning pickers required = pick cycles required / takt time for a pick cycle.

Then, on a board, have a column for each picker. The rows are the pick cycles during the first two hours – one row per pick cycle. The cumulative times are shown. As the shift proceeds, each picker writes up the completion time of her pick cycle on the board. If there is a problem the picker writes up an appropriate error code. These error codes accumulate into Paretos. The focus for improvement work is then clear.

During the second period there will be another calculation, with another number of pickers. Excess pickers from the first period should be found other work – for example stacking shelves.

In pension fund administration: some pension fund administrators deal with numbers of new admissions, enquiries, and people going onto pension, each day. Although there is great variety between cases, the work can be paced over the day into segments.

In accounting: some accounting and finance offices have regular tasks that must be completed every day, every week, every month. Examples are expenses, billing, cash reconciliation, debtors.

In hospitals: a study has found that that the principle reason for waiting lists is temporary mismatches between demand and capacity due to variation. The variation in health service capacity far exceeds variation in demand. The study showed that this was principally due to the way that NHS work was organised. Variation between patients was much less important. So what should be the solution? Answer: Heijunka to smooth capacity!

Further Reading

Kate Silvester and Paul Whalley, 'Preventing the Deficit', *Healthcare Finance Journal*, July-August 2005.
Don Tapping and Tom Shuker, *Value Stream Management for the Lean Office*, Productivity, 2003
Drew Locher, *Lean Office and Service Simplified*, CRC Press, 2011

4.26   Strategy (Policy) Deployment

Strategy (formerly known as Policy) Deployment is just that: it is an effective way of deploying strategy – making sure that everyone is not only swimming in the same direction, but is fully committed and bought in to the steps that need to be taken. In essence Policy Deployment (or Hoshin Kanri) is about 'Nemawashi' (consensus building) and 'Ringi' (shared decision making).

Policy Deployment has become a well-accepted way of planning and communicating quality and productivity goals throughout a Lean organisation. Some Hoshin Kanri work (e.g. by Jackson, and by Hines) is very strongly strategy-related. Others accept that some other process makes strategies, and that policy deployment is about deployment. This section concentrates on deployment.

Here we will use 'Hoshin' and 'Policy Deployment' interchangeably. Strict Japanese-style Hoshin is hugely bureaucratic and form-intensive, so 'Policy Deployment' is a preferable phrase to distinguish it from the rather non-Lean 'Hoshin'.

Some writers and consultants include Strategy in Policy Deployment. Others do not. In any case it is the deployment process that should be central. To quote Pfeffer, 'What is extremely difficult to copy – and what therefore does provide competitive advantage – is the way a company implements and executes its strategy'. Anyone can talk about being the technology leader or providing outstanding customer service, but few organisations can actually make good that promise. That's why Wells Fargo CEO Richard Kovacevich once said he could leave the company's strategic plan on a plane and it wouldn't make any difference: 'Our success has nothing to do with planning. It has to do with execution'.

Hope and Fraser attack the wastefulness and dysfunctional behaviour that the traditional budget process engenders. The internal competitive behaviour that is frequently generated is the very antithesis of the cooperative systems approach advocated throughout this book. 'So long as the budget dominates business planning, a self-motivated workforce is a fantasy, however many cutting-edge techniques a company embraces.' So don't begin with the financial, and issue top-down command and control edicts. Instead, begin with the processes, which can create the aims and therefore bring about financial results. This is what Strategy Deployment enables you to do.

At the outset we should say that Strategy Deployment could be used in two ways. First (undesirable) is to use it in a 'command and control' way: top-down objective setting with little discussion, starting with the financial or other results in mind. This can and will encourage all the 'game playing' and pseudo-measurement practices that are so common in many command and control organisations. Second (much more preferable) is to use it in a systems way: understanding the needs of the system and then developing more detailed participative plans to meet the system requirements. Results come out of the process, not the other way around.

Strategy Deployment is in fact the PDCA cycle applied on an organisational level. Witcher and Butterworth talk about the FAIR model beginning with the Act stage: Focus (act), Alignment (plan), Integration (do), and Responsiveness (check).

Cowley and Domb provide a useful visual metaphor. This shows a road leading from the present position (the current state) to the destination (the vision or future state). The road is the plan or action plan. Along the road are scattered small rocks and large boulders that are obstacles or problems. SD is used to remove the boulders one at a time. Kaizen is used to remove the smaller rocks, although this is not what we are concerned with here. Also, there are boulders which are off the road and which should not be tackled. SD is about focusing on the 'vital few'. The vision must be shared, level by level. What not to do must be agreed. And alternatives must be developed. The road metaphor is even more useful when used with Maps – current and future state.

A 'Hoshin' is a word that is increasingly being heard in Western companies, to mean those few breakthroughs aims that have to be achieved to meet the overall plan. At the top level there may be only three to five Aims. But at lower levels, the Hoshins form a network or hierarchy of activities that lead to the top level Hoshins. They are developed by consultation. Hoshin objectives are customer focused, based on company wide information, and measurable.

Imagine a tree deployment process. At the top you have the broad aim: for example, to improve conference facilities at a hotel. This means that the hotel marketing, hotel facilities, hotel catering, hotel HR, and hotel operations all have roles to play. These departments need to cooperate on integrated projects: for example guest comfort, speaker requirements, and promotion. Then within each project there may be yet more detailed activities.

A good concept, with applications far beyond SD, is to use the Toyota concept of requiring all plans or projects to be written up as an A3. See separate section.

SD starts with the concept of homing in on the 'vital few'. Where there is little change in operating conditions, a company still needs to rely upon departmental management, and top management planning is not required. However, where there is significant change, top management must first understand the purpose of the system. Debate what the system requires. This involves strategic planning for future alignment (to identify the vital few strategic gaps), strategy management for change, and cross-functional management to manage horizontal business processes.

Departmental management should be relied upon for 'kaizen' (i.e. incremental) improvements, but breakthrough improvements, which often involve cross-functional activities and top level support, should be the focus for SD planning.

An important aspect is Learning. The future is uncertain, although the destination is clear. Treat every unexpected event as an opportunity to learn and to adapt.

There are various Learning loops. The projects that are thought necessary to achieve the aims are in fact hypotheses – they are not certain. So the correct spirit of Policy Deployment is one of experimentation. At the end of the year you need to look back and ask whether the hypotheses were correct, and what can be learned. Also, the Policy Deployment process itself needs to be specifically reviewed. This is very unlike the traditional planning/budgeting cycle, where every year new plans are made without ever looking back at past plans and the fifth year out always looks brilliant!

'Nemawashi' and Catchball

Once top management has identified the vital few strategic gaps, employees and teams at each level are required to develop plans as to how to close the gaps. The premise is that insights and ideas are not the preserve of management. Moreover, commitment is built by participation. This requires employees to have access to adequate up-to-date information, thus breaking down 'confidentiality' barriers found in many Western organisations. There must be a clear link, or cause-and-effect relationship, between the organisational aims, projects, delivery, and results. The employees themselves propose measures, including checkpoints. At each level, Deming's Plan, Do, Check, Act cycle operates. And there is also there is strong use of A3 methodology.

The main stages explained by Cowley and Domb, are: 'What do we need to do?', 'How should we do it?', and 'How are we doing?' The first stage is strongly linked with the strategy process, but benefits from feedback from later stages ('What did we learn from the last time?'). This stage also involves the identification of Hoshins and other actions that are delegated to 'Daily Management'. In the second stage the nemawashi and catchball process then deploys the Hoshins. 'Catchball' is a phrase from basketball that indicates throwing the ball among team members before scoring. There is both vertical and horizontal catchball. Another analogy is the knock-up in tennis where players hit the ball to each other, but without winners or losers. As deployment proceeds a group meeting takes place at each level. Ideas flow from all directions, and agreement is arrived at by consensus and negotiation, not authority. If a goal is really not feasible the upper tier is informed. The Japanese word for this system is 'Ringi'. Much use is made of affinity diagrams and post-it notes. The process can and should be tied in with the Future State and Action Plans developed under Value Stream Mapping.

SD uses the 'outcome, what, how, how much, and who' framework. A Policy Matrix is useful here. See the figure below. At board level, a visioning process covers the key questions of what is required from the system (the Purpose and the design), what is to be achieved (e.g. reductions in lead time), how is it to be done (e.g. by extending Lean manufacturing principles), and by how much (e.g. all areas on 5S by year end). Specific quality and productivity goals are established. Then, the 'who' are discussed. Normally there will be several managers responsible for achieving these objectives. Appropriate measures are also developed.

The SD plans are cascaded in a Tree Diagram form. This cascading process is also different from most traditional models. In traditional models, cascading plans come down from the top without consultation, and there is little vertical and even less horizontal alignment. In SD, the people who must implement the plan also design the plan. The means, not just the outcomes, must be specified. And there are specific and on-going checks to see that local plans add up to overall plans. The matrix is used to assure horizontal alignment.

As the plans are cascaded, projects at one level become the aims at the lower level. A final stage in the cycle is the Hoshin Review where achievements against plan are formally rolled up the organisation. This uses visual results where possible. Exceptions are noted and carried forward. Hewlett Packard does this very formally once per quarter, by 'flagging up' problem areas with yellow or red 'flags'. Intel uses a classification against each Hoshin, showing highlights, lowlights, issues, and plans. Again, root causes are identified. At Unipart in the UK, a policy deployment matrix like the one shown below can be seen in each work area. Staff are able to reconcile what they are doing with the wider organisation's aims.

So SD is in essence an expanded form of 'team briefing' but it requires written commitment, identification of goals, the setting of measures, and discussion at each level. In Western companies, top management sometimes spends much time on corporate vision but then fails to put in place a mechanism to translate the vision into deliverables and measures at each level in the organisation. Hoshin may go some way to explaining why in better Japanese companies the decision making process is slower, but implementation is much faster and smoother.

Correlation between Aims and Projects	What projects are needed to achieve the Aims?	Correlation between Projects and Deliverables
What are the Strategic Objectives?	Projects / Aims × Delivery / Results	What are the Project Deliverables?
Correlation between Results and Aims	What financial and other benefits are expected?	Correlation between Deliverables and Results

Further Reading

Y Akao, Hoshin Kanri, *Policy Deployment for Successful TQM*, Productivity Press, Portland, 1991

Michael Cowley and Ellen Domb, *Beyond Strategic Vision: Effective Corporate Action with Hoshin Planning*, Butterworth Heinemann, 1997

Pascal Dennis, *Getting the Right Things Done*, LEI, 2006

Thomas Jackson, *Hoshin Kanri for the Lean Enterprise*, Productivity Press, 2006

Jeremy Hope and Robin Fraser, 'Who Needs Budgets', *Harvard Business Review*, February 2003

Jeffrey Pfeffer, *What Were They Thinking?*, Harvard Business School Press, 2007, Chapter 25

Ellen Domb, *Hoshin Planning*, Material presented at Cardiff Business School seminar, 2005

Michele L Bechtell, *The Management Compass: Steering the Corporation Using Hoshin Planning*, AMA Management Briefing, New York, 1995

Index

The Service Systems Toolbox

Books and Games from PICSIE Books

The Buckingham Lean Game

An ideal game to learn about Lean Manufacturing. Unlike other Lean games this game includes several products, changeover, quality and right size machines. Can be adapted to multiple environments. Over 600 games have been sold.

The Buckingham Service Operations Game

Built around an actual situation, this game demonstrates several lean service concepts including service mapping, failure demand, 5S in service, and customer interactions. It has been used by several consultancies and universities. Danish and Swedish versions are available.

Fishbone Flow   John Bicheno   2006 A5 122 pages

This book is an extensive revision of the bestselling booklet 'Cause and Effect Lean'. Lean is explained in over 50 fishbone diagrams and supporting text. The framework used is a development of the powerful 'Thinkflow' model of Creating Flow, Maintaining Flow, and Organising for Flow that has won many accolades. From this high level concept, several levels of detail are developed, resulting at the lowest levels in specific guidance. A feature of the new book is the integration of three other world-class concepts of Six Sigma, TPM, and TRIZ.

Six Sigma and the Quality Toolbox Bicheno and Catherwood   152 pages

This book is a companion volume to **The Lean Toolbox** and this book but focuses specifically on Six Sigma methodology and a large range of tools for quality improvement and problem solving. The book also includes a section on the theories of the major quality gurus and a section on tools and concepts relevant to service operation – whether in a specific service company or as part of the product service bundle. The book has been reprinted by the Welsh Development Agency and is also widely used by consultants and prescribed by several universities. The down-to-earth, snappy style of former editions of the book has attracted wide non-solicited acclaim.

The Lean Toolbox 4th edition (2008) by Bicheno and Holweg is a more general book on Lean operations with a strong manufacturing slant. This book is a bestseller with sales of all editions together exceeding 100k copies. It has been adopted by universities and training organisations in UK and USA, and is prescribed by APICS (The American Production and Inventory Control Society). 290 pages.

Lightning Source UK Ltd.
Milton Keynes UK
UKOW030829280911

179383UK00001B/1/P